Selling
Online

Selling
Online

How to Become a Successful E-Commerce Merchant

Jim Carroll & Rick Broadhead

DEARBORN™
TRADE
A **Kaplan Professional** Company

This publication is designed to provide accurate and authoritative information in regard to the subject matter covered. It is sold with the understanding that the publisher is not engaged in rendering legal, accounting, or other professional service. If legal advice or other expert assistance is required, the services of a competent professional person should be sought. Prices for products or services quoted within the book were accurate as of time of publication. To verify price accuracy, please contact the product or service provider in question.

Acquisitions Editor: Mary B. Good
Senior Managing Editor: Jack Kiburz
Interior and Cover Design: FIZZZ Design Inc.
Back cover photos: Ray Boudreau (Jim Carroll),
Wolf Kutnahorsky (Rick Broadhead)

Published by Dearborn Trade, a Kaplan Professional Company

Printed in Canada

01 02 03 10 9 8 7 6 5 4 3 2 1

Library of Congress Cataloging-in-Publication Data
Carroll, Jim, 1959-
    Selling online : how to become a successful e-commerce merchant /
    Jim Carroll, Rick Broadhead.
       p.cm.
    Includes index.
    ISBN 0-7931-4517-1 (pbk.)
1. Electronic commerce. I. Broadhead, Rick. II. Title.

HF5548.32 .C363 2001
658.8'4—dc21

2001017089

Table of Contents

ACKNOWLEDGMENTS

This book was developed with the support and assistance of many people.

First and foremost, thank you to Robert Harris at CDG Books for championing this project and making it happen. In the editorial and production departments, thanks to Amy Black, Rebecca Conolly, and Susan Girvan for managing this project through an extremely tight publishing schedule. We're also extremely grateful to our copyeditor, Sarah Wight, for her meticulous work, and to Marnie McCann and Stella Partheniou at CDG Books for marketing and administrative support, respectively.

At Visa USA, thanks to Jim McCarthy for believing in this project and to Kim Ramirez and John Shaunessy for your valuable input during the book's development process. At Dearborn Publishing, we would like to thank Mary B. Good and Robin Nominelli for their support of this project.

Numerous organizations provided us with access to their Internet and e-commerce services so we could review them for inclusion in this book. We would like to thank Jay Cox, Barry Friedman, Mike Geis, Bob Georgius, and Brian Kovalesky at EarthLink; Amy Bowman at InterLand; Ian Harper, Jeff Meltzer, Mona Peloquin, and Jeff Williams at Verio; David Castella, Sean Jolie, and Anna Schwein at Mercantec; Rodney Bell, Kathy Blaney, Chuck Harris, Pollyanne Mapes and Bob Reichley at Paymentech; Chris Thompson at ValueWeb; Tom Evans and Maria Undgerman at AT&T; and Caryn Clough and Derek Finley at Miva Corporation.

We would also like to thank Mike Quinn and IBM Canada for e-commerce hosting; Osama Arafat at Q9 Networks for Web site hosting; Mark Jeftovic at EasyDNS for DNS services; Dara Schechter and Tibor Shanto at Dow Jones Interactive for access to the Dow Jones Interactive service; and Rob Sykes and the team at Clarity Inc. for helping us in various ways.

We would like to acknowledge the many Internet entrepreneurs who contributed their thoughts and opinions to Chapter 8. These individuals were extremely generous with their time and were kind enough to share their online experiences with us for this book. Thanks go to: Tane Chan of The Wok Shop, Bonnie Clewans of The Bead Gallery, Michelle Donahue-Arpas of Genius Babies!, Richard Flynn of Red Trumpet, Jason Friedman of J&R Music and Computer World, Kevin Gorman of WebCyclery, Chris Harrower of Choo Choo Barn, Bodega Bob Homme of The Submarine Store, Kim Michaux of One of a Kind Kid.com, Shell Miller of Picture Sticks, Ron Mis of Galeton Gloves, Christopher M. Mott of Mott's Miniatures, Diane Morgan of Morgan Mailboxes & More, Sherry Peterson of Main St. Toys, Ray Ritchey of Childbook.com, Sue Schwartz of YarnXpress.com, Rob Snell of ystore.com, Deb Steinberg of Nickers & Neighs, Rhonda Wells of Payless ShoeSource, and Doug Young of Noggintops.com.

Finally, the process of writing a book is always made easier by the unwavering support of our families. Rick would like to thank his parents as well as his sister Kristin and her husband Lionel. As always, Jim would like to thank Christa, Willie and Thomas for providing so many important distractions throughout the project, involving everything from massive ice structures to skating rinks, Lego projects and ongoing riddles. With respect to the latter, and in order to fulfill a promise, Jim would like to thank them all by asking a question: What is red, white, and black all over? An embarrassed Zebra.

ABOUT THE AUTHORS

Jim Carroll, FCA, is an internationally recognized expert on the "wired world" and the Internet, a popular media authority, keynote speaker and business consultant. He is author of the critically acclaimed book Surviving the Information Age, a motivational work that encourages people to cope with the future, as well as co-author of the popular book Lightbulbs to Yottabits: How to Profit by Understanding the Internet of the Future.

Mr. Carroll has rapidly emerged as one of North America's leading keynote speakers, providing motivating and challenging presentations for tens of thousands of people at annual conferences, meetings, corporate events, and seminars. Jim's views are also much sought after by the media. He has been featured and is quoted regularly and extensively in a wide variety of national print media, television and radio shows. He has conducted more than 2,000 interviews over the last five years on the topics of e-commerce, e-biz and the Internet.

Mr. Carroll is the host of several audio programs, including "e-Biz with Jim Carroll," a national radio show that focuses on the e-biz opportunity. He also writes on a regular basis for the media. His popular weekly e-biz / Digital Survivor column in the Globe and Mail Report on Business has gained a widespread international following for its perspectives on the impact of technology, the Internet and e-commerce. He writes for many other publications, with the result that he was named as one of "50 International Names to Know" by the Online Journalism Review, a widely respected international publication that examines the future of journalism in the Internet-age.

A Chartered Accountant by background, he has over twelve years of experience in the world's largest public accounting firm. He has a solid business and financial background in all major business, government and industry sectors. He was recently honored by the professional body which represents his profession by being named an FCA (Fellow of the Institute of Chartered Accountants), which is given to those who exhibit outstanding performance within their career.

Through his consulting firm, J. A. Carroll Consulting, he has provided professional services for over ten years to many Fortune 500 organizations. He excels at helping senior management map out a truly effective strategy for doing business in the new economy. His specialty is helping organizations gain strategic insight into the implications and opportunities of the wired economy at an executive level, and assisting organizations in articulating and achieving those strategic goals and visions.

You can reach Jim by e-mail at **jcarroll@jim-carroll.com** or via his Web site, **www.jim-carroll.com**.

Rick Broadhead, MBA, is renowned as one of North America's leading e-commerce experts, industry analysts, and professional speakers. He is the co-author of 29 books about the Internet, e-commerce, and e-business, including *Lightbulbs to Yottabits: How to Profit by Understanding the Internet of the Future.*

Specializing in helping organizations to capitalize on the latest Internet and e-commerce trends affecting their industries, Rick is a highly sought-after keynote speaker and consultant by industry and trade associations, small businesses, and Fortune 500 firms across North America. His clients include organizations as diverse as McDonald's, IBM, EMI Music, Arthur Andersen, the National Spa and Pool Institute, Freightliner Trucks, Travelodge Hotels, Microsoft, the Minnesota Office of Tourism, and Entel — one of the largest telecommunications companies in Chile.

Over the last six years, Rick has assisted executives and managers from hundreds of North American firms with their e-business strategies, including leading companies such as Kraft Foods, Ford Motor Company, Bayer, Sharp Electronics, Royal Doulton, Polaroid, Motorola, Volkswagen, Sears, Xerox, Nestle, AT&T, and Coca-Cola.

As an Internet industry veteran and bestselling Internet author, Rick Broadhead is regularly called on by both print and broadcast media for his analysis and commentary on events in the Internet and e-commerce industry. Over the last six years, he has conducted literally hundreds of interviews with radio stations, television networks, magazines, daily and community newspapers, and industry publications on topics ranging from the AOL/Time Warner merger to the wildly successful Harry Potter book series and its unprecedented impact on online retailing. In 1999, Rick partnered with United Media in New York, one of the largest newspaper syndicates and licensing companies in the United States, to create and launch "e-Trivia," a nationally syndicated newspaper feature about the Internet.

Rick can be reached by e-mail at **rickb@rickbroadhead.com** or on the World Wide Web at **www.rickbroadhead.com.**

CONTACT US

We are always interested in hearing from our readers. We welcome your comments, criticisms, and suggestions, and we will use your feedback to improve future editions of this book. We do try to respond to all e-mail sent to us.

Contacting the Authors Directly

We would love to hear from you! Here is how to contact us on the Internet:

To reach:	Send e-mail to:
Both authors simultaneously	authors@handbook.com
Jim Carroll	jcarroll@jim-carroll.com
Rick Broadhead	rickb@rickbroadhead.com

Our World Wide Web Sites

The World Wide Web site for all our books is www.handbook.com. There you will find information about our most recent publications as well as ordering information.

We also invite you to visit our individual Web sites as well, where you will find information about our consulting and speaking activities as well as other background information on the both of us:

Jim Carroll's Web Site:	www.jim-carroll.com
Rick Broadhead's Web Site:	www.rickbroadhead.com

Chapter 1

THINKING STRATEGICALLY AND REALISTICALLY ABOUT SELLING ONLINE

> *Selling on the Internet was supposed to be easy....Online retailing turned out to be just as hard as off-line, if not harder....*
>
> E-Commerce the Play; Act II: 10/22/2000 *The Washington Post*

This is a book about setting up a "store" on the Internet, a relatively narrow topic when you really think about it.

After all, selling products on the Internet is just one of many ways that you can use the Internet with your business. In addition to being a selling tool, the Internet can also be used for marketing, customer support, cost containment, recruitment, procurement, communications, and a variety of other functions. Indeed, there is hardly an activity in the business world that doesn't cross paths with the Internet.

But, undeniably, the most thrilling part of the Internet these days is e-commerce – using the Internet to sell products and services to a global audience that is growing by millions every year. It's not an understatement to suggest that the Internet and e-commerce will continue to be the most exciting technology of the twenty-first century.

But can you sell things online? The early experience of many dot-com startups would indicate perhaps not. After all, haven't we seen the collapse of many an online retailer in the year 2000, and isn't that a signal that the idea of selling online is doomed?

Not really – although nearly everyone now agrees that online shopping will represent only a small percentage of retail sales well into the future, the small percentages often obscure the market potential. Think about this: even if Internet sales reach only 5 percent of total retail sales in a couple of years, that's still billions and billions of dollars that will be spent online.

Lots of small businesses have expanded their markets and found new sources of revenue by using the Internet through the last several years: some of those businesses are profiled in Chapter 8, *101 Tips from Online Merchants in the United States*. Indeed, it is with the small business entrepreneur, not the high-profile, publicity-hungry, overly greedy dot-com startup, that we are seeing many of the more exciting online activities.

So while many early dot-com retailers might be struggling, the fact remains that there is opportunity to be had online – if you are realistic about what you hope to accomplish, about your expectations, and about the degree of work that you will have to put into your online efforts.

This book is about how you – as a merchant – can participate in this global economic revolution.

WHAT YOU NEED TO KNOW BEFORE YOU BEGIN

In this book, we'll help you understand the many different aspects of setting up a store on the Internet so that you can sell your products and services worldwide.

We'll discuss payment methods and security issues, review the most important components of an online store, help you market your online store and build brand loyalty, and bring you expert advice from companies that are already selling their products online.

But before you immerse yourself in the exciting world of e-commerce, you need to have a full appreciation of three important issues:

- You need to have realistic expectations.

- Setting up an online store is a detailed process that involves five stages: planning, preparation, development, execution, and refinement.

- Selling online should be just one part of your overall Internet strategy.

Another important point is that this book is primarily focused on how to create an effective online store aimed at consumers (often referred to as B2C, or business-to-consumer, e-commerce). It does not examine in depth the issues associated with B2B, or business-to-business, e-commerce.

Yet B2B is an extremely important type of e-commerce, and indeed, will far surpass the levels of spending to be seen with B2C e-commerce. That's why, later in this chapter, we examine some of the B2B issues that might also be part of your online strategy. Moreover, there is no doubt that B2B might affect your retail store strategy to a great degree as we discuss later in this chapter, "What about B2B?" Hence, while much of this book focuses on B2C commerce, many of the issues and strategies might be equally applicable to B2B commerce.

BE REALISTIC ABOUT THE INTERNET

What is the biggest problem on the Internet today?

Inexperienced people with overinflated expectations who create online stores with the belief that once they've done the work, the dollars will roll in.

We'd like to suggest that the most important thing you can do in your venture into the world of selling online is to take a serious look at your likelihood for success.

Before you begin thinking about setting up an online store, face some cold, hard facts about the reality of retail on the Internet.

The fact is, you might not succeed.

You might create an online store only to find that no one is aware of it. You might fail to sell anything online. You might be trying to sell a product that no one has an interest in purchasing. You might be destroyed by competition that is far more Internet-savvy, and that has far deeper pockets than you. You might not be able to keep your inventory up-to-date, or you might have problems in filling the orders you do receive.

e-Fact

North America has over 40% of the world's Internet users.

Source: Nua Internet Surveys (www.nua.ie)

The fact is, your online store might come nowhere close to meeting your expectations – with disastrous results.

The Drumbeat of Internet Hype

The biggest danger is that you might fall for the hype that often surrounds the Internet.

Get caught up in the hype, and you might fall into the trap of believing that all you have to do is establish an online store, then sit back and wait for the riches of this modern-day gold rush to fall into your lap.

Internet hype has surrounded us ever since the network first invaded the public consciousness, and even though the last few years have seen a bit of the shine come off of the Internet rose, the hype continues.

Consider the early days of electronic business – that is, around 1994 to 1996 – when mainstream media alerted people to the huge potential of the emerging Internet, likening it to a modern-day mother lode.

"The Internet is the gold rush of our times," read one headline. Other articles from the time followed in a similar vein: "The Internet explosion has been likened to a gold rush, with companies large and small racing to snag a piece of the action." Even Bill Gates got in on the act with an article entitled "The Internet Gold Rush Is On."

Much of this early hype resulted in a situation in which people believed it would be easy to get rich quickly by participating in the Internet. Consider this excerpt from an article titled "Gold Rush in Cyberspace" that ran in *U.S. News & World Report* in late 1995: "Businesses and entrepreneurs are rushing into cyberspace like forty-niners driven mad by gold fever. Just last week, the smell of money pervaded Boston's World Trade Center as 30,000 people representing multinationals, mom and pop shops, fortune hunters, saints and sinners spent four days wandering through Internet World's city-size landscape of exhibits, booths and marquees touting avenues to riches on the Net."

Such excessive overpromotion was largely responsible for the Internet stock runup that began in 1999 and continued through the first few months of 2000, until the dot-com stock price collapse of April 2000.

With the market collapse, the tune changed – online retail and dot-com startups were likely not the pots of gold at the end of the rainbow that had been promised by the Internet hype machine. A degree of reality entered the Internet world, as the public and investors woke up to the fact that online sales for many vendors were less than exciting.

The Hype Isn't Over

Yet even so, some of the hype about online shopping continues unabated. In addition, there continues to be an almost endless stream of stories about how easy it is to do business on the Internet and the magical benefits of conducting transactions online.

As a result, many businesses are being led down the garden path when it comes to online retailing. They think that achieving online success is simple: just establish an online store and watch the dollars flow in.

It's a major trap that you should avoid. Don't delude yourself into thinking online business is easy.

Don't fall for the hype.

If you plan on exploring the world of selling online, and business on the Internet in general, be realistic about what it takes and what is involved. Those who have implemented successful strategies know that it involves a lot of money, plenty of hard work, real commitment, and a strong will.

Even then, the returns might be a long time in coming.

Selling online isn't a game, it's a business.

Assess Your Likelihood of Success

With the massive and sensational hype that surrounds e-commerce and online shopping, there are many companies rushing to peddle their wares over the Internet. Yet many of these companies don't have sound business plans, nor have they done any market research.

Before you decide to pursue the concept of an online store as a business strategy, you should carefully assess the viability of your idea. For example, you may have a product or service that people don't want to buy over the Internet. While there are many success stories of ventures selling books, music, and travel services over the Internet, there are also many stories of Internet ventures that haven't gone quite so well.

Groceries? Lumber supplies? Lawn products? There are many who are skeptical about the likelihood that many people will buy such products online.

e-Fact

Convenience (73%), avoiding crowds (69%), and saving time (63%) are three of the top reasons why consumers do their holiday shopping online.

Source: Accenture
(www.accenture.com)

e-Fact

Worldwide e-commerce sales will reach $6.8 trillion by 2004.

Source: Forrester Research (www.forrester.com)

Survey several of your existing customers to see if they would consider buying your product or service electronically. This is an important bit of research to do – clearly, an online store will be useless if the demographic you are trying to reach isn't hooked up to the Internet, or isn't willing to shop there.

There's a lot that could go wrong. You may end up investing a lot of money in an online store, only to realize that very few of your customers are ready to buy this way. You could spend a lot of time building a sophisticated Web site, then discover months later that traffic to it is dismal. Or you may be seduced by the sophisticated Internet and e-business technology you use and fritter away many precious hours that should have been spent elsewhere.

There is a real danger in getting caught up in an online store, particularly if you are already in business. You might find that in your effort to move online, you've neglected your regular business activities, and that your business is suddenly in a rather precarious position.

That is why carefully assessing your plans is so important.

Why Do Online Retailers Fail?

- Business models that don't work

- Lack of profits

- Excessive spending on marketing

- Unrealistic expectations when it comes to online sales (companies failed to appreciate that consumers and businesses aren't going to change their shopping behavior overnight)

- Failing to appreciate how expensive it is to set up an online store (it is not a low-overhead business model as people once thought – consumers still expect customer service, for example)

- Intense competition

- Lack of focus on the issues that really matter: *profitability, gross margins, cash flow, quality of the business model,* etc.

- Not appreciating the fact that the Internet is just another channel

How do you avoid failure? Follow the advice that we provide in this chapter and throughout this book. In particular, Chapter 8 is required reading for every company that wants to sell on the Internet. Thanks to our panel of twenty online retailers, you'll learn about some of the biggest pitfalls of online retailing.

Cautious Optimism Is the Best Rule

Don't misinterpret our comments of concern and caution. Don't think for a minute that the Internet and e-commerce aren't worthwhile. Indeed, getting online now is important: you will gain valuable experience with e-commerce, and over the long term, the Internet will play a major role in the global economy.

Like many people, we are big believers in the potential of e-commerce. But we firmly believe that as you get involved, you must recognize what you are up against.

That's why in preparing your Internet strategy, you should carefully assess the weak points. Where can your strategy go wrong? What are its potential vulnerable spots? What can you do to protect yourself from anticipated problems in your strategy? Where should you be aggressive, and where should you be cautious?

The Internet is littered with the broken dreams of many entrepreneurs. In most cases, those who fell for the hoopla failed to approach e-commerce with a careful, well-thought-out strategy that clearly assessed the risks and examined the potential for success of doing business in the wired world.

This Is Serious Stuff

In the next chapter, we are going to take a look at how easy it is to create a store on the Internet.

The fact is, in some cases, you can be up and running in a little more than thirty minutes – at least, in terms of having a Web site that lists your products.

But the thing is, out in the real world, *no one sets up a retail store in thirty minutes.*

The Internet and e-commerce aren't a game – they are something real. If you plan on taking your business to the Internet, you've got to approach this as a serious, important business initiative. You've got to plan, strategize, prepare, implement, execute, and follow up with the highest degree of professionalism and attention. You've got to think about issues like customer service and product fulfillment.

Otherwise, you are condemning yourself to playing a game in which the likelihood of losing is extremely high.

Setting up an online store is a business, and you should never lose sight of that fact.

What Process Should You Follow?

As you go through the process of creating your online store, there are five main steps that you will go through. They are:

- Planning
- Preparation
- Development
- Execution
- Refinement

We discuss each of these steps below.

Step #1: Planning

Don't rush to create your online store. Instead, do your homework. Take the time to understand the opportunity that's before you, assess the risks, and figure out exactly what you hope to accomplish.

There are many questions that you need to ask yourself in the planning stage, many of which we cover below.

Twenty-three Questions to Ask Yourself about Selling Online

1. *What Are You Trying to Accomplish?* First and foremost, think about goals, goals, goals. Make sure that you clearly understand your goals, your mission, and your expectations before you set up your online store. What is it that you are trying to achieve? What are your objectives? What do you expect to accomplish a year or two from now? Put your

goals and dreams through a reality check and make sure they are realistic.

2. *Are You Prepared to Make the Commitment?* Setting up an online store involves not only a financial commitment but a time commitment as well. If you want to be successful, you'll have to sacrifice a lot of personal time to get your online business up and running. Even after launch, the business will still demand a lot of your time. Make sure that you're prepared to stay committed to your online business venture.

3. *Do You Have a Backup Plan?* In the event that your online business doesn't succeed, do you have a backup plan? Many people want to invest their life savings in an Internet venture, but they haven't thought about what they are going to do if their online business fails. Don't be foolish and throw all of your eggs into one basket. Don't assume that your online business will work. It may not. Think about what you're going to do if it doesn't succeed.

4. *Do You Have a Business Plan?* It's important that you put your plans down in writing so that you have a clear idea of where you are going and what you want to accomplish. A business plan is a written document that summarizes your business concept and your plans for your business. It includes an overview of the concept of your business, a market analysis, your sales and marketing strategy, financial projections, and an overview of how you intend to handle operational issues in your online store such as credit card security, customer support, shipping and fulfillment, and product returns.

In the event that you need a loan from a financial institution in order to set up your online store, a business plan will be essential.

A business plan is also crucial for a couple of other reasons. First, you're no doubt excited about the prospect of selling products on the Internet. But it's fair to suggest that perhaps you're too excited. Too many people rush on to the Internet with ideas that aren't sound. Preparing a business plan will force you to think about every aspect of your online business: to set goals, determine the resources you need, and identify obstacles and challenges you will face daily. A business plan can help you see the "big picture," which will allow you to make business decisions more clearly and confidently. Going through this exercise will give you an opportunity to organize your thoughts more effectively. It will also make it easier for you to identify flaws in your strategy. And since a business plan will force you to test the assumptions you have about your business, it can make the difference between a business that succeeds and one that fails!

5. What Is the Likelihood That Your Products Will Sell Online? Although we are strong believers that virtually any product can be sold over the Internet, not all products will sell well over the Internet. Don't go online blindly – make sure you fully understand the buying habits and preferences of your target market. Is there an adequate customer base on the Internet for you to sell to? What is the feasibility of your idea?

6. What Are the Online Sales Forecasts for the Types of Products You Plan to Sell? You should ensure that you take some time to understand whether the product you hope to sell online actually sells online. To do so, visit your local library or use online databases like Northern Light (www.nlsearch.com) or Electric Library (www.elibrary.com) to uncover articles and industry reports that project online sales in the industry that you want to enter. This will help you determine whether your idea is viable.

There are other useful resources that might help you assess your market, among them:

- NUA Internet Surveys (www.nua.ie/surveys/)
- eMarketer (www.emarketer.com)
- Shop.Org (www.shop.org)

You might also consider using online research from market research firms that specialize in the Internet industry, such as Jupiter Research (www.jup.com) and Forrester Research (www.forrester.com). But caution is warranted, given that such reports are costly and may be too expensive for a small business.

What Sells Online?

- The product appeals to the *technologically savvy*.

- The product is a *computer-related* item.

- The product appeals to a *broad segment of the Internet user base* (typically but by no means exclusively educated North American males under the age of forty).

- The product appeals to a *wide geographic audience*.

- The product is a *specialty item* that can be otherwise difficult to locate, particularly a *collectible* or item about which people are passionate.

- The product purchase is an *"informed purchase"* – it is typically purchased based on *information rather than hyperbole*.

- The product can be purchased over the Internet *less expensively* than otherwise.

Source: The Tenagra Corporation (www.tenagra.com)

7. *Are There Potential Sales Channel Conflicts That You Need to Be Concerned With?* If your company manufactures products, and you currently sell these products through retail outlets other than your own, you need to talk with your retail partners before you launch your online store. Why? Retail stores may be sensitive to the fact you are going to be bypassing them and selling your products directly to consumers and/or businesses on your Web site.

In fact, "sensitive" may be the wrong word to use. The retailers that carry your products may be downright angry if they learn that you're selling direct through the Internet, especially if you plan to undercut them on price. Of course, it's also possible that your retailers won't be upset by your plans. The only way to gauge their feelings is to let them know what you're doing and then see how they react.

Depending on your particular situation, losing the good relationships that you have with retailers may not be something you want to risk. Have a discussion with your retail partners and brief them on your online plans. Based on their reaction, you may decide not to proceed. If they express concern, see if you can arrive at some sort of a compromise. For example, price may be a key issue. If you agree not to discount your products on your own Web site, the retailers may be a lot less resistant. Alternatively, you could work out an arrangement whereby the retailers get free advertisements on your Web site.

One way that some organizations have dealt with channel conflict is to redirect any sales to their channel partners, rather than trying to sell direct. This has been particularly true in the airline industry. For example, many airlines will sell tickets directly to customers. But they have also built into their Web sites the capability for the customer to choose to have the ticket issued through their traditional travel agent, i.e., the channel partner of the airline. By building this capability in, the airlines are working hard to try to steer some business to their channel partners, and thus assuage their concerns. The same type of capability could be built into your own site if you are a manufacturer – redirect any actual sales so that they are fulfilled by your channel partners. Finally, you might decide not to sell all your products online, only some of them (this way, retailers get exclusivity on some products).

8. *What Are the Critical Success Factors for Internet-Based Sales in Your Industry?* Critical success factors are issues that can make the difference between the success and failure of your online store. Beyond basic critical success factors like customer service and return policies, which all online stores need to have, every industry has its own critical success factors that are crucial to online sales.

For example, some products are more information-intensive than others are. Selling books online is a lot different from selling cars. Customers who are shopping for a car will require a lot more information than customers who are shopping for books. If the products you are selling are high-involvement goods, and customers require a lot of information before making a purchase decision, you will need to take this into account when creating your online store.

e-Fact

Only 29% of Web sites meet consumer response time expectations.
Source: Jupiter Research (www.jup.com)

Also consider the issue of price. How critical is the price of your products going to be? Some industries are more price-sensitive than others.

Depending on your industry, shipping may be a critical success factor. For example, if you are selling chocolates, you will have to arrange for special shipping containers so that you can ship your chocolates to customers without melting. Failure to address that issue could spell the end of your online efforts.

You also need to think about the types of people you are targeting. For example, are you trying to convert your existing customers over to an electronic order process, or are you predominantly focusing on new customers? The latter might imply a heavier concentration on marketing as a key success factor for your store.

These are just a few examples of critical success factors that may affect your industry. There are many others. We suggest that you get out a piece of paper and list all of the critical success factors you can think of for the products you are intending to sell. Use this information as a basis for building your online business strategy.

9. *How Will Your Online Store Differ from Others on the Internet?* There are already tens of thousands of stores on the Internet. Have you thought about how you are going to differentiate your store from all the others? Product selection? Your product line? Price? Customer service and support? What unique value proposition are you going to offer your customers? Why should online shoppers shop at your online store instead of the others?

Your answers to these questions will be especially important if you intend to approach a financial institution for a loan or line of credit. Your likelihood of success will depend on how well you can differentiate your business from others in an already crowded online marketplace.

10. *Will You Be Focusing on a Niche Market?* Many people believe that one of the keys to success on the Internet is coming up with a business plan that targets a very specific market rather than a broad market. In other words, the more focused your product is, the better.

Rather than opening up an online bookstore that sells a variety of books, focus on a specific product category for books, such as travel books or hard-to-find books on some specialized topic. Needless to say, many of the major product categories are going to be dominated by big players with very deep pockets. That doesn't mean there isn't any room for new players, but you may have a much better chance of success if you specialize on a particular niche of a larger market category.

11. *Are You Prepared to Deal with Customer Support Issues?* Some organizations have discovered that once they put up an online store, they get flooded with customer support requests, and they're unprepared to deal with the volume of messages. Once you're in business, customers will begin inquiring about a wide range of issues, including shipping, returns and exchanges, order tracking, and of course, your products. Make sure that you anticipate your customer support requests in advance and that you're prepared to meet them. For guidance on putting together a customer support strategy, see the customer service section of Chapter 3, *Tips for Building an Effective Online Store*.

12. *Do You Have a Fulfillment Strategy?* Once you start getting orders, you must be prepared to package and ship products as quickly as possible. Not only that, but you need to be fully prepared to deal with returns and exchanges as well.

Fulfillment and return issues have actually been some of the biggest problems that online retailers have encountered so far. Learn from the mistakes that everyone else has made in the past and be determined to work hard to avoid these problems in your own online initiatives.

Make sure that you work through how an order will flow from your Web site through to the packaging and shipping processes. Needless to say, you can't afford to have a disorganized fulfillment system, otherwise you'll quickly find yourself in over your head. We recommend that you get out a piece of paper and create a flowchart of how an order will move through your store. This will help you to visualize your order logistics.

As you'll discover in Chapters 2 and 3, figuring out your shipping options can be an extremely complicated process. Make sure that you thoroughly investigate the shipping options available from the U.S. Postal Service and each of the major courier services.

13. *What Are Your Core Competencies?* Many organizations try to do everything themselves and end up overwhelmed. Even big retailers have made this mistake. Toys-R-Us, for example, tried to do its own fulfillment on the Internet until it realized fulfillment wasn't something it was good at.

Toys-R-Us knew how to purchase and merchandise toys, but it wasn't an expert in packaging and shipping orders placed on the Internet. After a disastrous Christmas season selling on the Internet and getting fined by the Federal Trade Commission for misleading customers about delivery dates, Toys-R-Us partnered with another company to handle its fulfillment. Don't be afraid to outsource.

As you read this book, you'll notice that running an online store requires skills in many different areas: customer service, Web site design, fulfillment, accounting, marketing, inventory management, etc. Identify those areas you're good at and those areas you're not good at. Don't try to do everything yourself. This is one of the most important lessons that a small business can learn.

14. *Are You Ready to Ensure That Your "Real World" and Online Store Initiatives Are in Tune with One Another?* If you already have a land-based retail store, it's important that you set up your online business so that your land-based store and your online store are in synch with each other from an accounting, inventory, and pricing perspective. You don't want to end up with two different accounting systems, two different inventory systems, etc. You also want to avoid situations where your online store tells customers that a product is in inventory when in fact the item is out of stock.

Your online store must also be in synch with your "real" store from a customer service perspective. Too many stores haven't integrated their online and offline operations nor trained their in-store staff to deal with questions about their Web site. There's also the case of people buying online and then wanting to return a product in person. The whole issue of channel integration is key for any business that wants to sell both online and through traditional retail channels. We discuss this in more depth in Chapter 3.

15. *Have You Analyzed the Competition?* A key part of building an online business is surveying the competitive landscape. Before you build your online store, make sure you spend

time visiting Web sites that will compete with yours. In particular, get answers to the following questions:

- Who are your competitors, both online and offline?
- Of all the competitors you've identified, which ones have the largest market share?
- What are your competitors doing to attract visitors to their online stores? Do they have affiliate programs (for an explanation of affiliate programs, see Chapter 6)? Are they advertising in industry publications or on radio or television? Do they have an e-mail newsletter for their customers?
- Are any of your competitors receiving either good or bad press coverage? Have they issued any press releases recently?
- Do they have any strategic partnerships with online or offline firms?
- How does each competitor compare in terms of product selection, price, customer service, appearance (i.e., Web design), and reputation?
- What special features and/or services are your competitors offering?
- What are the strengths and weaknesses of each of your competitors?
- Are any of your land-based competitors not yet selling online? If the answer is yes, can you ascertain if or when they are planning to launch their online stores?

Use all of this information to help you assess whether there is an opportunity in the market that is being missed by your competitors. For example, your analysis may reveal that there is a certain segment of the market that your competitors are not catering to. Alternatively, you may discover that customer service is severely lacking at your competitors' Web sites. These types of findings will help you build a strong business that builds on your competitors' weaknesses.

16. *What Is It Going to Cost to Sell Your Products Online?* Selling products on the Internet involves a variety of costs. They include:

- Internet access fees
- Merchant account fees
- Credit card transaction fees

- Web hosting fees
- Domain name registration fees
- Online marketing expenses (e.g., affiliate programs, advertising, etc.)
- Professional service fees (e.g., e-commerce consultants, Web designers)

We discuss many of these costs throughout the book. Selling products online may be more expensive than you think! Make sure that you itemize all of your potential costs and create a budget before you start to create an online store.

17. *How Much Revenue Do You Need to Generate Every Month in Order to Break Even?* Alternatively, figure out how many sales you need in a month (and the average dollar value of those sales) in order to break even.

Most small businesses ignore this important calculation in their planning. It's crucial that you figure out these numbers before you set up your online store. It requires that you take all your costs into account and figure out the gross margins you will earn on every sale (i.e., the difference between your selling price and what you paid for the product).

You may find that the final numbers are completely unattainable, which means that you will have to go back and reexamine your cost structure, your pricing, and perhaps your business models. Given the costs of Web hosting, domain names, real-time credit card processing, and your time, you may be surprised at how much revenue you have to bring in just to break even!

18. *Have You Taken the Time to Learn from Other Online Merchants?* One of the most valuable ways to learn about e-commerce and online retailing is to talk to people who are already selling online. Don't be afraid to pick up the phone and call people (even complete strangers!) who you know are selling their products on the Internet. You'll find that many people are more than willing to share their experiences with you. As a first step, we suggest that you consider subscribing to the I-Sales discussion list. I-Sales is an electronic mailing list dedicated to online sales issues. It's an excellent way to exchange information and gain

valuable insights into online selling, from people who are already doing it!

If you do sign up, be prepared for a lot of reading. Every day, you'll receive a "digest" of messages that have been posted to the list. If you can bear the high volume of messages, you'll find that the list is an excellent way to obtain lots of tips and online selling advice from other Internet users. You can subscribe to I-Sales discussion list by visiting the I-Sales Web site at www.audettemedia.com. There is no cost to join.

19. *Have You Identified Web Sites That You Like?* It is important that you do some "best practices" research. Scour the Web to find sites of companies in your industry or area of work, and study what they have done. Take a look at your competitors, and other online stores in similar lines of business. Determine what you like and don't like within a wide range of comparable Web sites. Consider adapting the best of what you see for your own online store.

As part of this process, you should also familiarize yourself with the elements of good and bad Web design. The Internet is littered with Web sites that just don't cut it. Many suffer from poor design that is guaranteed to chase customers away as soon as they arrive. That is why you should take some time to understand Web design concepts. In addition, when examining your competitors' Web sites, pay special attention to how their sites are designed. As we explain in Chapter 3, the design of your Web site will influence the perceptions that customers have about your business.

A good starting point for understanding basic Web site design principles is the Web Pages That Suck site (www.webpagesthatsuck.com). This site features both good and bad examples of Web site design and it does an excellent job of pointing out common design flaws.

Other excellent Web sites on good Web site design are ZDNet's E-business Best Practices site (accessible from www.zdnet.com/ecommerce) and goodexperience.com (www.goodexperience.com).

20. *How Are You Going to Find Your Customers?* This is a crucial question for any business that intends to sell online – where are your customers going to come from?

This is extremely important – after all, you can build a great store, but if your customers don't know it exists, then even the best Web design and product selection are rather useless. Hence, we address this question in more depth in Chapter 6, *Marketing Strategies for Your Online Store.*

Make sure you avoid what has come to be known as the "The McDonald's Complex":

"A majority of people who start a business, whether it be a brick and mortar store or an Internet business, assume that once they open, customers will flock in without any marketing or promotion. UNLESS YOU ARE McDONALD'S THIS WILL NOT HAPPEN."

Source: Pat Bishop, *The Daily Oklahoman*

21. *How Soon Can You Be Profitable?* You need to work out a timeframe for your expectations, and then determine if you can wait that long. Do you have the financing to see you through the inevitable early period in which you will likely be operating at a loss? How long can you go before things become desperate?

22. *Does Your Business Model Make Sense?* One of the reasons Internet businesses fail is because they have lousy business models – several years ago, the business model was the last thing that people looked at, but now this is one of the first things you should ask yourself about.

Ask yourself, "Are my expectations reasonable?" "Do my plans make sense?" "Are they overly optimistic?" It may be a good idea to hire a consultant or trusted advisor to review your plans and evaluate your projections and expectations to see if they are realistic and attainable.

Take the time to do a serious self-assessment – a reality check, as it were. And remember, you might be guilty of drinking your own wine. You might get so caught up in your plans that you don't realize that some of your assumptions are overoptimistic.

That's why you should test your plan with others – get independent reactions from friends, family, business acquaintances, or Internet professionals.

23. *What Features Do You Want in Your Online Store?* Part of the planning process involves listing the design elements and functional features that you want to have on your Web site. In Chapter 3, Tips for Building an Effective Online Store, we give you lots of advice in this area. You should also consult Chapters 6 and 7 to learn about some of the marketing and loyalty-building elements you can build into your online store. Identify some of the features and services that are important to you. Obviously, unless you have an unlimited amount of money to spend, you won't be able to do everything. However, you need to have some idea of what you want in order to move on to the next stage and get accurate price quotations from Web designers and online storefront services.

Step #2: Preparation

Once you've gone through the process that we outlined in the planning section above, you should be ready to map out your online store on paper.

Consider putting together a "site map," which is a representation of all of the sections you want to have on your Web site. The site map should be accompanied by a list of features that you want to have in your online store. Keep in mind that your site map doesn't have to be fixed in stone. If you decide to work with a Web designer, you may want to modify the layout of your Web site based on his or her suggestions.

Once you have your site map in hand, and you have a clear understanding of what you want your online store to look like, you're ready to get cost estimates from different storefront services, e-commerce developers/consultants, and/or Web design firms. The solution that you ultimately select will depend on how much money you are prepared to spend, whether you want to build the Web site yourself or have someone else do the work for you, and what types of features you want to build into your online store. In Chapter 2, you'll find an extensive discussion of the different options for creating your online store.

Step #3: Development

Once you've selected a company and/or service to help you build your online store, you're ready to move on to the development phase. Development involves actively building your online store using the software and professional services that you've chosen. As we discuss in Chapter 3, you'll also need to thoroughly test your online store before launch to make sure that it is functioning properly. Throughout this process, unless you're doing all the work yourself, you'll need to manage the activities of the companies you're working with.

Step #4: Execution

The execution phase occurs once your store is "live" on the Internet and ready to accept orders. After your store is up and running, you'll have to put in a lot of time and effort to ensure that it is working correctly.

Make sure you understand just how much time it will take to keep your store running – many people involved in online selling sit back and think the store will run itself, but that isn't true. You've got to keep prices up-to-date, shipping rates correct, stock levels properly indicated – there are all kinds of details that you will be following up on a regular basis.

Don't expect that your store will be a bed of roses once you have it up and running. The fact is, things will go wrong – and sometimes you might not even know about it.

Consider what happened to the online store belonging to one of the authors of this book. The system that processes credit card orders on his online store suddenly stopped working one day, preventing customers from placing orders on his Web site. Customers who tried to place orders were greeted with an error message and were unable to continue. Only when a customer notified the author a few days later did he become aware of the problem! Had the customer not informed him about the difficulties she had placing an order on the site, he wouldn't have known that the online store was malfunctioning. As a result, he could have lost a substantial amount of business without even realizing it!

e-Fact

By 2002, just five industries will make up half of all online business-to-consumer sales: computers and computer equipment, travel, brokerage, auction, and books and music.

Source: Giga Information Group (www.gigaweb.com)

The fact is, most customers who encounter a problem on an online store aren't going to take the time to contact the owner of the store. They'll just go shop somewhere else.

Hence, you've got to monitor your store constantly to ensure it is in proper working order. That includes continually examining every aspect of your store. In this case, the author would only have known that there was a problem with the credit card process if he had gone through and tried to order a book himself. Does that mean that he should regularly check this aspect of his store by doing an actual test order? Perhaps.

Of course, the execution phase involves more than just monitoring your online store for problems. Execution implies all the things that you need to be doing to ensure that your overall goal of selling online is functioning smoothly and properly.

Execution means ensuring that customer support requests are taken care of, that returns are promptly cleared and credited to customer accounts, and that any rejected credit card transactions are quickly followed up. You should also run focus groups on your Web site on an ongoing basis to make sure that it keeps pace with customer expectations.

The competitive analysis that you did in the planning stage should continue once your store is completed. Constantly monitor your online competitors to see what they are up to. You might want to experiment with a service called Mind-it (www.netmind.com), a free tracking service that will notify you when a competitor's Web page (or any Web page for that matter) has changed.

Step #5: Refinement

The Internet is constantly changing. New technologies are being developed, new competitors are entering the market, customer buying patterns are changing, and customers are getting more demanding with each passing day. If you want to stay competitive, you'll have to constantly tinker with your strategy and change the look and/or features of your online store in response to changing market conditions. The Internet will be unlike any other industry you've ever worked in. Business moves at lightning speed on the Web. Just keeping up is half the battle.

WHAT ABOUT B2B?

Of course, as you set up a store on the Internet, you're likely doing so as part of what the computer industry calls a B2C, or business-to-consumer, strategy.

Yet today B2B is all the rage, and folks are discounting B2C. We believe that they are wrong – as we noted at the beginning of the chapter, while early Internet retail sales estimates were far too optimistic, the fact remains that there are some very good markets emerging online.

But what about B2B? Should you worry about it?

That depends on who you are, what you do, and what is happening in your industry.

First, recognize that much of what we talk about in this book might be equally applicable to a B2B strategy. If you typically sell to other businesses, your online store might work very well in supporting your business activities with them. Credit card payments are likely to be less important, however, so make sure that you provide for payments on account and other forms of payment.

Second, you might find yourself being pressured to join up to a B2B Web site, or to what is known as a *vertical industry market*. These are large e-biz sites established by buyers or sellers of products in particular industries, built with the intention of driving all business purchases in that industry through the site. For example, the major auto companies have announced a large-scale B2B initiative, and have basically told their 27,000 suppliers that they must do business with them through that site. If you are in that industry, you will find yourself affected.

A third area in which B2B is taking off, often related to B2B sites, is e-procurement. The Internet is emerging as a tool by which companies streamline the way they conduct their purchasing process. General Electric Co., for example, has streamlined the procurement process for several divisions by moving to an Internet-based ordering system. It estimates that it has reduced labor costs by about 30 percent and material costs by up to 20 percent. (You can read about GE's experience at tpn.geis.com/tpn/resource_center/casestud.html.) It's a good example of e-procurement and typifies many of the initiatives that are occurring out there. You might find that some of your customers want you to get involved in their e-commerce procurement initiatives, rather than your own online site. They won't want to do business with you through *your* Web site – they want you to do business *their way*.

Finally, as you take a look at your market, you might find that it is easier for you to join up and establish your product catalog on a B2B Web site, rather than building your own store. In the world of B2B, we are seeing the emergence of many sophisticated sites that allow you, as a retailer or product manufacturer, to create, in effect, a "store" within the B2B site. By doing so, you might find that you can open up yourself to a far larger marketplace than if you create your own store.

Whatever the case may be, as you consider your retail plans, take some time to understand the B2B initiatives that are going on in your industry, or that might come to affect you, and determine how you might need to modify your activities accordingly.

Don't Forget Cost Savings Initiatives!

Last but not least – don't forget that e-commerce is not necessarily all about making money but also about saving money.

Too many businesses (note: it is not just entrepreneurs, but managers, CEOs, CFOs, etc.) have a one-track mind when it comes to the Internet and, in particular, e-commerce. They're constantly asking themselves, "How can I use the Internet to make money?" But in addition to thinking about how the Internet can generate revenue for your business, you should also ask yourself, "How can I use the Internet to save money?" For example, by sending an e-mail message, you can save the cost of a comparable long-distance telephone call, fax, or courier bill. Sending a document electronically rather than by courier means a potential cost savings of $12 or more! This can save you substantial sums of money.

A Web site is also an effective tool for containing costs, particularly when used for customer support or marketing purposes. Even though there is a cost (often significant) to set up a Web site and maintain it, you will save money over the long term every time an existing or prospective customer or client downloads information such as a brochure from your Web site. A Web site can save you courier or mailing charges, and over time, can help to reduce your printing costs.

Always keep in the back of your mind questions as to how you can use your online strategy tool in order to save money in the way you do business.

WHERE DO WE GO FROM HERE?

In the remaining eight chapters we will walk you through all of the steps involved in setting up an online store on the Internet.

In Chapter 2, *Options for Building an Online Store*, we describe some of the different methods that you can use to build an online store. They range from low-cost, do-it-yourself services to more expensive software solutions.

In Chapter 3, *Tips for Building an Effective Online Store*, we offer advice on how to deal with important issues such as pricing, customer privacy, shipping, return policies, checkout procedures, and customer service. We also review the important elements of Web site design.

In Chapter 4, *Merchant Accounts and Online Payment Processing*, we outline what's involved in getting a merchant account for your online store. We also describe the role of payment gateways and explain how you can process and authorize credit card transactions over the Internet.

In Chapter 5, *Online Security Issues and Credit Card Fraud*, we explain the security risks that you will be exposed to on the Internet and we provide an extensive checklist of questions to help you assess the security of your online store. You'll also learn how to protect yourself from credit card fraud.

In Chapter 6, *Marketing Strategies for Your Online Store*, we review a variety of different marketing vehicles for your online store, including permission marketing, affiliate programs, search engines and Web directories, and keyword-based advertising. We also discuss the importance of such issues as domain names and traditional advertising.

In Chapter 7, *Building Customer Loyalty in Your Online Store*, we outline how you can use strategies like site registration, contests, personalization, online communities, and opt-in e-mail to build customer loyalty and increase repeat sales.

In Chapter 8, *101 Tips from Online Merchants in the United States*, we've assembled a panel of twenty online merchants to talk about best practices and critical success factors for online retailing. This is a chapter you don't want to miss!

Finally, in Chapter 9, *Can You Do It?* we close with some of our thoughts about the future of online retailing.

Let's move on!

Chapter 2

OPTIONS FOR BUILDING AN ONLINE STORE

Putting a small business online is getting easier every day. No longer do businesses need to invest in expensive leased lines and run their own electronic commerce software. Instead companies all round the world are offering to take away the risk and pain that building an online store always seemed to entail.

"An Easier Way to Turn Clicks to Cash," *The Guardian*, 09/14/2000

One of the most challenging aspects of building an online store is figuring out how to go about it.

It can be a bewildering experience, given the wide range of different products and services that are available to you.

As you venture forth, you'll discover a wealth of marketing literature from e-commerce companies and others in the Internet industry, each of which promises the best possible method of building an online store. You will come across many different "storefront" software programs that purport to give you everything you need to create your store. Look further, and you will see many different descriptions of the "ideal" components of an online store.

You can quickly become confused about where to start. Worse, you might choose a certain direction, only to learn that you have made a serious mistake.

Given the many different approaches that you might take to building your store, it is important that you take some time to understand two areas clearly: the methods of building an online store, and the different features and capabilities that you might choose to build into your store. These are the two key topics that we address in this chapter.

APPRECIATING YOUR EXPERTISE – AND THE EXPERTISE OF OTHERS

As you will see in this chapter, there are many different ways to build an online store. These range from do-it-yourself software programs that hold your hand and walk you though a series of ready-made design templates, to complex software programs with a full range of features that can only be implemented by third-party organizations or individuals with a lot of technical expertise.

Which solution you select depends on a series of questions that you must ask yourself:

- How technically inclined are you?
- What is your budget?
- What types of products are you selling?
- How many products do you intend to carry?
- How quickly will you need to be able to expand your online store?
- Do you already have a retail store with its own financial and inventory systems that you want to integrate into your online store?
- What features and capabilities do you want your online store to have?
- Who are your competitors and what do their online stores look like? What features do their online stores have? Which features are desirable, and which are not?
- What elements do you want within your store to make it the best possible store? Do you even know what those elements might be?

As you will learn in this chapter, what might have seemed like a simple undertaking can all of a sudden become quite complex. You are now wrestling with two major issues:

1. Do you have enough experience with online stores to know what features you should be including in your own online store? When researching online storefront solutions, do you even know what features and options you should be looking for?

2. Do you have the technical and design expertise, and the time, to build your online store yourself?

Chances are the answer is no to these questions – indeed, that's probably why you bought this book. Let's put both of these issues into perspective.

Developing Your Expertise in Store Features and Elements

Regardless of how you go about creating your online store, you need to have some familiarity with the features and elements that make up a great online store. To help you develop your knowledge in this area, we will outline some of the common features and elements of storefront software programs later in this chapter. And in the next chapter, we'll examine a laundry list of different features that you may want to consider for your online store.

But before you read those sections, it is important that you take some time to develop your own opinions on what constitutes a great online store. You can do this by examining a variety of online stores, particularly those that involve your industry or marketplace, and by thinking about what works and what doesn't work.

Hence, we believe a good starting point for you is to visit as many online stores as you can. This will give you invaluable information as you develop plans for your own online store.

e-Fact

By 2005 consumers will spend 20 times more on the Internet when using a high-speed broadband connection than they do with traditional analog dial-up modems.
Source: Gartner Group
(www.gartner.com)

What do you want to accomplish through such research? Let's use an example: suppose you want to set up an online store to sell chocolates.

In order to figure out what features should be part of your online store, you should research your competitors to see what they have done online. In addition, look at as many online stores as you can – both large and small – in the confectionery industry. Broaden your review to gift shops and other types of online stores that are selling the same types of products that you intend to sell.

As you browse these online stores, keep track of the features and services that they offer. Put yourself in the shoes of a typical customer. Carefully examine the design and layout of each Web site that you visit. What features do you like? What features don't you like? Is there anything that impresses you? Examine the purchasing process in depth. You might actually go so far as to place a few orders in some of the online stores to see how the ordering process works and to see how the products are packaged and delivered.

Make careful notes about the strengths and weaknesses of each online store that you visit. This will be important information later when you begin determining which elements you would like for your own store.

This is critical research. Examining these stores gives you a good sense of what you should be doing, since you can see how well various approaches might work. It can also help you understand where your competitors are weak and how you might improve on these weaknesses.

Keep in mind that you don't have to limit your competitive analysis to U.S. companies. Because there are no borders on the Internet, customers can shop as easily at stores located in other countries as they can in the United States. Therefore, make sure you examine online stores in other countries as well.

Where can you find directories of online stores to look at? Most of the large search engines and Web directories maintain lists of online stores that you can browse. In addition, sites like BizRate.com (www.bizrate.com) and ePublicEye.com (www.epubliceye.com) that rate online stores for shoppers list hundreds of online stores. You should also visit the Yahoo! Web directory (www.yahoo.com) and browse through the Shopping and Services section (from the Yahoo! home page, click on "Business and Economy," then

"Shopping and Services"). Browse through the different product subcategories until you find the one that most closely resembles the type of business you're in. Keep in mind that most of the Web sites listed in the "Shopping and Services" section of the Yahoo! Web directory are simply commercial Web sites without any online ordering capability. But some of the Web sites listed in the "Shopping and Services" area *are* online stores, so it's a good place to start your preliminary research. Yahoo! does have a separate area on its Web site called Yahoo! Shopping (shopping.yahoo.com) that only lists online stores, but only certain online stores are listed there, so it's a good idea to visit the general Yahoo! directory as well.

When browsing through online store directories such as the ones we've listed below, you'll come across a wide range of online stores, some of them built by small businesses and others built by large businesses with million-dollar budgets. If you're a small business, you probably won't be able to afford an online store like Wal-Mart's (www.walmart.com) or RadioShack's (www.radioshack.com), but looking at these sites will give you a good idea of what's possible in an online store.

e-Fact

Unsolicited e-mail messages account for 10% of total e-mail volume in the United States.

Source: eMarketer
(www.emarketer.com)

Web Sites Where You Can Find Online Stores to Look At:

America Online Shopping	www.aol.com/shopping
BizRate.com	www.bizrate.com
ePublicEye.com	www.epubliceye.com
Excite Shopping	shopping.excite.com
Lycos Shopping	shop.lycos.com
Netscape Shopping	www.netscape.com/shopping
Yahoo! Shopping	shopping.yahoo.com

Learning about the Expertise of E-Commerce Developers and Consultants

Once you begin to look at different online stores on the Internet, you may be terrified by the complexity of some of the online stores you come across, from both a technical and a design point of view. Fortunately, however, many of the storefront solutions that we will discuss in this chapter require very little, if any, technical knowledge on the part of the merchant. This is particularly true of the template-based services, which allow you to create a small-scale store with little effort. In fact, the technology has become so easy to use that even someone who hasn't used a computer before can set up an online store without much difficulty.

However, depending on your situation, it may not be appropriate for you to build your online store yourself – you might want to concentrate on starting or running your business, and leave the technical and design issues to someone else. Not only that, but given that online-store-building is rapidly turning into a field that involves rather specialized expertise, you might quickly conclude that out-side assistance is required with all aspects of building your online store, including creating a business plan. This is where an e-commerce developer/consultant might come in handy.

We should explain that the term "e-commerce develop-er/consultant" has a wide variety of possible meanings. We've used it as an umbrella term to include any firm that may provide services to help you with the process of estab-lishing a site to sell products and services online.

E-commerce developers and consultants include graphic designers, strategic planners, database integrators, program-mers, Internet security consultants, and a variety of other professions. Depending on the scale and scope of your online store, and how technically competent you are, you may want to hire an e-commerce developer or consultant to help you with the entire process of setting up your online store or just parts of it. And depending on the tasks you need help with, you may find yourself needing to hire several different e-commerce consultants and development firms.

If you decide to go with one of the low-cost, do-it-yourself e-commerce storefront solutions that use templates, you might want professional help customizing the look of your site. As we point out later in the chapter, one of the disadvantages of using a do-it-yourself storefront program is that all the stores end up looking like they came out of a cookie-cutter.

Whether you need help building and designing your online store, marketing it, adding special features (e.g., a gift registry), implementing security solutions, integrating existing inventory and customer databases into your online store, setting up customer relationship tools such as live chat services or personalization software, or doing anything else, there are literally thousands of e-commerce developers and consultants across the United States that can assist you. Here are just some of the organizations that you could hire to help you with different aspects of your online store:

- *Internet service providers* (ISPs – companies that sell access to the Internet) ranging from national companies such as EarthLink/Mindspring (www.earthlink.com) and PSINet (www.psinet.com) to regionally focused organizations that operate only in a specific state or region. There are also hundreds of locally based or mom-and-pop ISPs across the United States that serve specific cities and towns. Many ISPs have established e-commerce divisions to help clients set up storefronts on the Internet. Some only offer packaged do-it-yourself e-commerce solutions and no consulting or design services (although they may have established partnerships or alliances with companies they can refer you to). Others may offer more comprehensive e-commerce services to small and/or large businesses. Check with the Internet service providers in your community to see what e-commerce services they offer.

- *Web hosting companies* such as Verio (www.verio.com), Interland (www.interland.com), and ValueWeb (www.valueweb.com) that specialize in hosting Web sites for clients. In addition to hosting standard business Web sites, most Web hosting companies also provide e-commerce hosting and/or design services, ranging from do-it-yourself solutions to custom storefront-building services. As with ISPs, there are thousands of Web hosting companies in the United States ranging from large players with tens of thousands of clients to smaller firms with much smaller customer bases. You can access a list of some of these companies at CNET's Web Services Directory (webservices.cnet.com).

- *Web consulting firms* that specialize in Web site creation, design, and strategy. In this category, there are both high-profile players like Organic (www.organic.com), the company that developed the Web sites for Payless ShoeSource (www.payless.com) and Tommy Hilfiger (www.tommyhilfiger.com), among others, and smaller or lower-profile organizations. Web consulting firms often offer marketing services ranging from online media planning to online marketing campaigns. Some firms in this category may offer assistance with other areas of e-commerce such as logistics, fulfillment, and customer service.

- *Graphic designers and Web design firms* ranging from one-person operations to larger graphic design firms with dozens or hundreds of people on staff. There are literally thousands of small and large firms across the United States that specialize in designing Web pages. There are also many graphic designers with full-time jobs who do freelance work on the side. If you need help with graphics, ask around in your community for referrals to Web site developers as well as graphic designers who do work on the Web.

- *Telecommunications firms* like AT&T (www.att.com), MCI Worldcom (www.mci.com), BellSouth (www.bellsouth.com), SBC Communications (Ameritech, Pacific Bell, Nevada Bell, and other firms – www.sbc.com), Sprint (www.sprint.com), and Verizon (www.verizon.com), all of which have e-commerce divisions with e-commerce offerings for small and large organizations.

- *High-tech companies* ranging from small local operations to large global operations such as IBM (www.ibm.com), Dell (www.dell.com), Oracle (www.oracle.com), and Hewlett Packard (www.hp.com).

- *Management consulting organizations*, ranging from small operations to worldwide organizations like the Boston Consulting Group (www.bcg.com), Accenture (www.accenture.com), Gartner Group (www.gartnergroup.com), and Ernst & Young (www.ey.com).

- *Traditional advertising agencies* such as Leo Burnett (www.leoburnett.com), DDB Worldwide (www.ddb.com), and Grey Worldwide (www.grey.com). Virtually all of the big advertising agencies have established interactive divisions to handle Internet and e-commerce projects for their clients.

- *Specialist e-commerce developers/consultants* that specialize in a particular area of e-commerce, such as personalization (see Chapter 7), online payment processing (see Chapter 4), security (see Chapter 5), or customer relationship management (see Chapter 3).

- *Independent Internet/e-commerce consultants.* In addition to the Web consulting firms we mentioned previously, there are lots of small mom-and-pop consultants across the United States who have general Internet/e-commerce expertise or who have developed specialized expertise with certain e-commerce programs or storefront solutions. If you're operating on a small budget and simply want some professional input, you may want to find someone in this category whom you can hire on a hourly basis to advise you on setting up an online store.

- *Financial institutions.* Keep in mind that there are also some financial insitutions that have aligned themselves with particular e-commerce developers, so it's always a good idea to check with them. For example, First National Bank of Omaha (www.fnbomaha.com) has aligned itself with Innuity, an e-commerce developer.

eCommerce

Overview Benefits Features   Price   Options   About The Vendor

FirstStorefronts
"Full Service"

Powered by:

INNUITY ™

helping business e-volve

Web Building Done For You
Are you looking for a quick and affordable way to launch an online, commerce-enabled web site that is **built just for you**? First of Omaha® has teamed up with *Innuity* to bring you FirstStorefronts, the most complete web solution available. FirstStorefronts, powered by Innuity, integrates web-building services, e-commerce transaction processing and promotions to connect Internet merchants with online buyers.

Back to Top

Benefits
Easy Set-up - A dedicated web designer leads you through the set-up process.

Increased Sales - Commerce-enabled web sites offer a new and potentially explosive revenue source in the non face-to-face market.

Fleet (www.fleet.com) also provides, on its Web site, a list of what it calls "authorized storebuilders" and "preferred Web site developers," thus providing you with some guidance on companies that you might use.

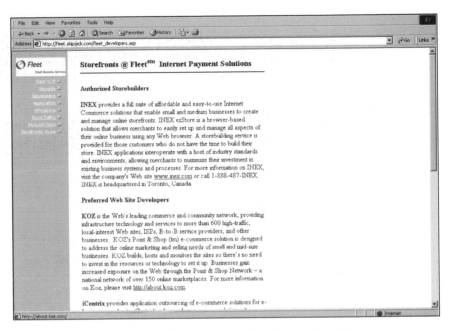

This list just barely scratches the surface! As you can see, regardless of your needs, there is probably an organization out there that can meet them. Take some time to identify your needs and learn how these different organizations can help you.

e-Fact

The number of wireless messages sent per month will reach 244 billion by December 2004.

Source: Cahners In-Stat Group (www.instat.com)

Clearly, given the extensive list of companies, if you decide to hire an outside firm to help you with any aspect of your online store, it is important that you carefully assess the skills and experience of the organization in whatever activity you're hiring them for. If possible, examine some of the work they have done for other clients. Ask for references. Talk to previous customers and ask the firm for examples of online stores or Web sites they have built or consulted for. If the company doesn't have a solid track record, and if you can't get any positive recommendations from previous or existing clients, you probably want to look elsewhere. It's important that you pick an organization that you're comfortable with.

How do you find e-commerce consultants and developers? In some cases, the Web site of the particular storefront solution you are looking at might lead you to certain authorized resellers or consultants. Better yet, browse the

Web for examples of small and large companies that are selling products online. If you see an online store that you like, call the company directly and find out who developed their online store and/or what consultants they worked with.

Another way to locate experts to assist you is to talk to people in your community who are active in the Internet and e-commerce industry, or talk to local high-tech associations. In addition, read the technology section of your local newspaper to see if there are any e-commerce companies advertising their services there. You could also check the Yellow Pages or phone your local Chamber of Commerce.

APPROACHES TO BUILDING AN ONLINE STORE

There are three options when it comes to building an online store:

1. Use an entry-level browser-based storefront creation service.

2. Use standalone shopping cart software.

3. Use advanced e-commerce software.

The rest of this chapter is devoted to exploring each of these options in more detail.

Before we discuss these methods though, let's put one other issue into perspective.

It is likely that you already have a Web site. If you do, and you create an online store using any of the methods above, it doesn't mean that you have to throw the rest of your Web site out. Instead, you can simply make a link from the pages within your regular Web site to your store. Of course, depending on the solution you choose, you might not have a consistent design between the rest of your site and your store.

If consistency in design is critical to you, then as you explore your options, make sure you determine how you can pursue the implementation of your store in such a way that it matches the "look and feel" and design of your existing site.

Option #1: Use Entry-Level Browser-Based Storefront Creation Services

Browser-Based Storefront Creation Services

Advantages

- Easy to use
- All tasks are handled from within your Web browser
- Your store can be updated from any Internet connection
- No need to install any software on your computer
- Fast setup
- Little or no technical knowledge required
- No need to find a Web hosting company (the store is hosted on the storefront service's own Web site)
- No need to develop a separate Web site
- Some of these services are free to use

Disadvantages

- Some services have limited flexibility in store design and layout
- Without additional programming or design work, your store may look similar to other stores created with the same product
- Customization may not be possible
- The user interface for some of these programs is awkward, slow, and/or clunky

Browser-based storefront creation services are the easiest services to use. They require very little technical knowledge and allow you to create your online store by filling out a series of templates or forms using your Web browser. Most of the popular browser-based packages have automated the setup of your merchant account and payment gateway, two of the most important components of your online store (see Chapter 4 for an explanation of these components). This means that it will be easy for you to accept credit cards on your Web site and process credit card transactions in real-time.

Browser-based storefront creation services are popular with small businesses because they don't require you to install or configure any software on your computer. Your entire online store can be created using your Web browser. Setting up an online store using one of these services is as easy as filling out a series of templates on the Web, selecting the layout you want for your online store, uploading (transferring) your company logos and product images from your computer to the service's Web servers, and answering a few questions. These services are typically very affordable for a small business. Pricing is usually on a monthly basis and ranges from free to several hundred dollars per month.

Because browser-based storefront creation services are quite easy to use, many businesses can use them to build their online stores without much outside assistance. However, depending on your situation, you might decide to hire an e-commerce developer/consultant to help you design your store or add additional features to it. At a minimum, you may want to engage the services of a graphic designer to help you design logos or other graphical elements for your site.

Browser-based services are designed for businesses that want a quick and easy way to get an online store up and running with minimal hassle. But this ease-of-use comes at a price. If you need an extremely powerful program with lots of flexibility in design and layout, you may be disappointed. Browser-based storefront creation programs usually aren't sophisticated enough for businesses that need powerful marketing and merchandising capabilities and want maximum control over the appearance of their online store. That's why it's important that you determine what you need in an online storefront solution before you select one to work with. You also need to think about how quickly you expect your online sales to grow and determine whether a browser-based program will be able to meet your needs as your business expands.

Where to Find Browser-Based Storefront Creation Services

A wide range of organizations offer browser-based storefront creation services.

First you could check with your existing financial institution. You might discover that they have partnered with a third-party e-commerce company, in order to provide their clients with an all-in-one solution.

For example, Bank of America (www.bankofamerica.com), has established eStores, an initiative to help you build your online store.

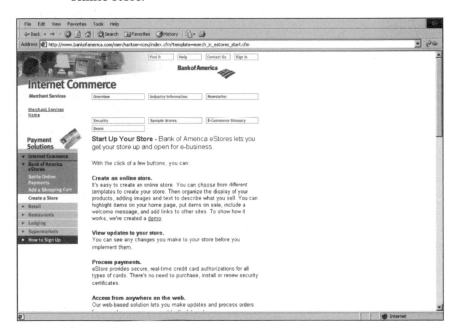

Wells Fargo has done something similar, with its eStore service:

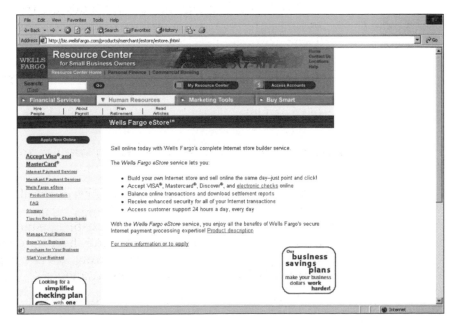

And Wachovia (www.wachovia.com) has established WMSesolutions.com in order to help their clients with e-commerce storefronts. You can use their "store wizard" in order to create an online store:

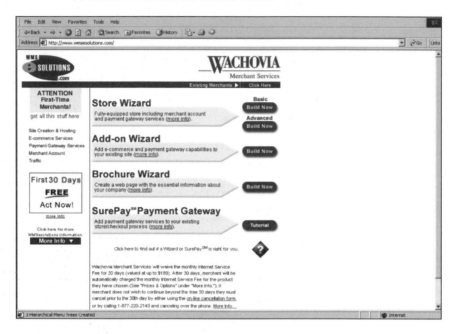

Other providers of browser-based storefront creation services include search engines and Web directories such as Yahoo! and Excite, telecommunications companies such as AT&T and Verizon, as well as hundreds of Internet service providers and Web hosting companies across the United States, including big companies like EarthLink, Verio, and Interland. As a starting point, check with some of the telecommunications companies, financial institutions, and ISPs that serve your community to see if they offer any e-commerce hosting services.

To help you with your research, we've listed examples of browser-based services in the table below. Some of these services are only available through resellers, meaning that you need to sign up with a participating Web hosting company or ISP in order to use the company's software. In most cases, you can visit the vendor's Web site and get a list of ISPs and Web hosting companies that sell the vendor's storefront software. The companies listed below charge a fee for their services. Later in the chapter, we'll look at some of the "free" browser-based storefront solutions.

Examples of Fee-Based Browser-Based Storefront Creation Services

AT&T Small Business Hosting Service	www.sbh.att.com
BizLand	www.bizland.com
FedEx eCommerce Builder	www.fedex.com
IBM HomePage Creator	www.ibm.com/hpc
iCommerce ShopZone (available only through resellers)	www.btsw.com
Interland ezAisle	www.interland.com
Mercantec SoftCart (available only through resellers)	www.mercantec.com
MerchandiZer (HipHip Software)	www.merchandizer.com
OpenMarket's ShopSite (available only through resellers)	www.shopsite.com
Prodigy Biz E-Commerce	www.prodigybiz.com
Yahoo! Store	store.yahoo.com

Virtually all browser-based storefront creation services will walk you through six basic steps:

- specifying the name and contact information for your online store;
- defining product categories and product information (product descriptions, prices, etc.);
- choosing the layout and design of your online store;
- specifying tax and shipping information;
- specifying which credit cards you want to accept; and
- setting up a merchant account and payment gateway (see Chapter 4).

The manner in which you complete these steps varies from service to service, but often you will be able to build your online store by using a friendly "wizard" interface that makes it easy to get your store up and running in a very short period of time.

For example, Interland (www.interland.com) provides a wizard interface for merchants who choose its ezAisle storefront service:

EarthLink (www.earthlink.com) has a similar wizard-based storefront creation service called TotalCommerce. Easy-to-follow screens like the one below guide merchants through every step of the setup process:

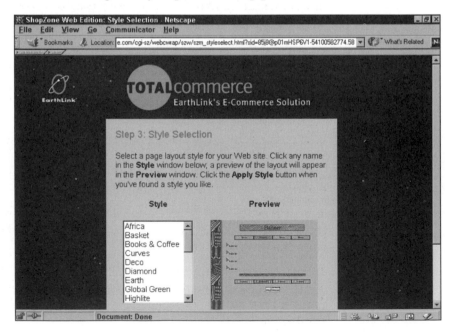

We want to emphasize that not all browser-based storefront services are alike. They vary widely in their capabilities and functionality.

Many ISPs and Web hosting companies offer several browser-based storefront creation services with varying degrees of sophistication. Some of them are designed for merchants who want a fully functional storefront in a matter of hours, while other packages are designed for merchants who need more features and customization.

The features and options that are available to you will vary depending on which browser-based service you're using. For example, at some point during the setup process, you'll be asked to choose a basic design and color combination for your online store. Some storefront services will give you a lot of control over the colors, while others will require you to choose from a selection of pre-designed color combinations. In addition, some browser-based storefront services have a very user-friendly interface while other services may be slow and awkward.

If you're interested in using a browser-based storefront service, don't sign up for the first one you come across. There are lots of different browser-based products for you to choose from, so it's important that you research your options carefully. In order to choose a browser-based storefront that best meets your needs, consider doing the following:

1. Compare the features of different browser-based services so that you fully understand the limitations and benefits of each service. In the last section of this chapter, we'll provide a checklist of some of the features that you should think about.

2. If possible, test-drive different storefront creation services. Some services offer trial periods so that you can test out the service at no charge (or you can get your money back at the end of the trial period if you aren't satisfied).

3. If possible, get an online demo of the product. Some services provide an online tutorial that shows you how the store-building software works.

4. Inspect the user interface carefully. How easy is it to add/delete/modify the products in your online store? Does the user interface look simple to use or does it appear cumbersome?

5. Create a checklist of the different features you are look-ing for in an online storefront and create a "short list" of storefront creation services that meet your requirements.

6. As part of your decision-making process, we highly recommend that you spend some time looking at online stores that were created using various browser-based storefront serv-ices. This will give you an idea of what the end product looks like. However, keep in mind that the appearance of a particular store may not reflect the full capabilities of the product that was used to create it. For each service you are considering, try to look at a wide variety of different storefronts created with it so that you see different ways that the service can be configured. Many browser-based storefront services have a "showcase" of sample stores that were created using their software on their respective Web sites. For example, on the Yahoo! Store site (shopping.yahoo.com/stores), you can look at hundreds of stores that were created using the Yahoo! Store software:

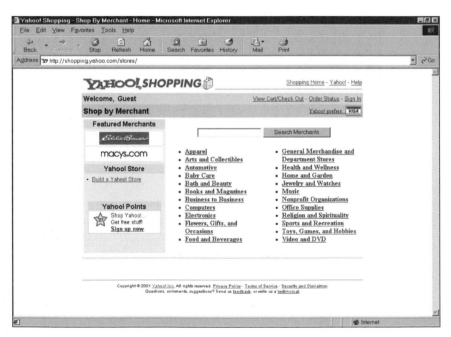

Building an Online Store – An Example

To show you how easy it is to create an online storefront using a browser-based service, we'll show you one of the browser-based storefront packages offered by Verio (www.verio.com), one of the largest Web hosting firms in the United States. Verio has a variety of storefront creation services that vary in cost depending on how many products you intend to sell and what types of options and features you require in your online store:

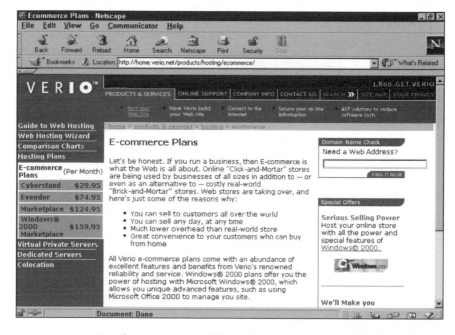

For the purposes of this demonstration, we'll select the MarketPlace account, which is designed for merchants who plan to sell more than one hundred products through their online store.

Verio's MarketPlace account uses a browser-based storefront creation program called SoftCart from Mercantec (www.mercantec.com). Mercantec doesn't sell its storefront software directly to consumers. To use the software, you have to purchase it through an authorized reseller such as Verio.

In the pages that follow, we'll walk you through the steps that you would typically follow if you were going to set up an online store using the SoftCart software. Keep in mind that the steps that we are about to show you are specific to the SoftCart software. If you're using another software package to create your online store, the user interface and options you see will be different, but the general process should be similar.

Once you've contacted Verio and signed up for the MarketPlace account, you'll be given a username and password and a Web address that you can connect to and begin the process of building your online store:

The next screen gives you two options:

To start building your online store, you can choose either the "StoreBuilder Wizard" or the "Store Manager." If you're a beginner, the StoreBuilder Wizard is the better program to use since it walks you through the process of creating your online store. The Store Manager allows you to do everything the StoreBuilder Wizard does and much more, but it doesn't guide you through the process. As you'll see later in this chapter, even if you decide to use the StoreBuilder Wizard, you'll eventually have to learn how to use the Store Manager, since this is the program that will allow you to see your online orders, generate reports, delete products from your online store, and perform other administrative functions.

For now, we'll show you how the StoreBuilder Wizard works. The first step is to input contact information for your online store. For this example, we'll pretend that we're creating an online store to sell scooters and scooter accessories. We'll call our online store "Scooter Junction":

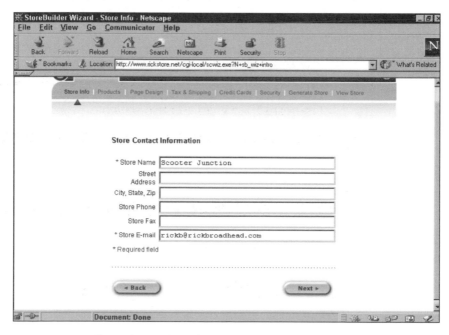

If you have already designed a logo for your online store, and you have it on your computer, you are given the opportunity to add the logo to the front page of your online store. You're also asked to provide a welcome message that customers will see when they access your online store:

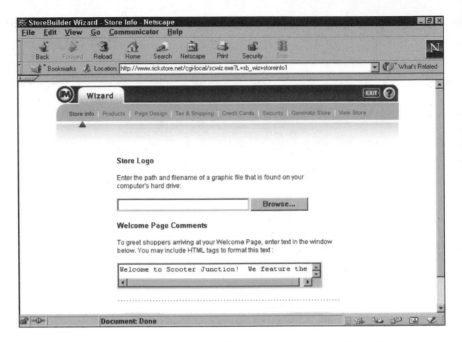

The next step is to build the catalog of products that you want to sell in your online store. For each product you need to provide basic information such as the product name, price, and product description. You can also provide an image of the product if you have one on your computer (this is highly recommended, since otherwise the customer can't see what the product looks like!):

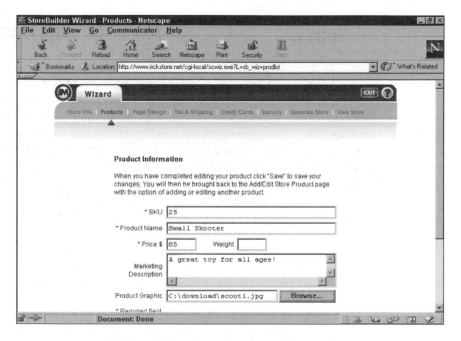

You'll need to repeat this process for every item you want to add to your online store.

Once you've created your catalog of products, you'll be asked to choose a design for the Web pages in your online store. You can choose from a variety of different layouts:

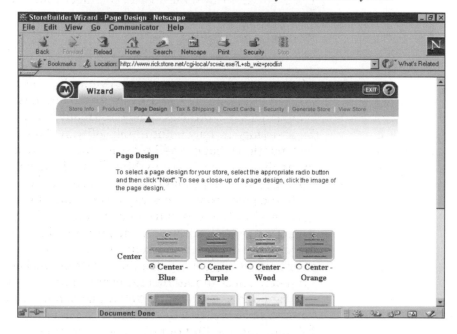

Once you've settled on a look for your online store, you'll be asked to specify your shipping and tax rates:

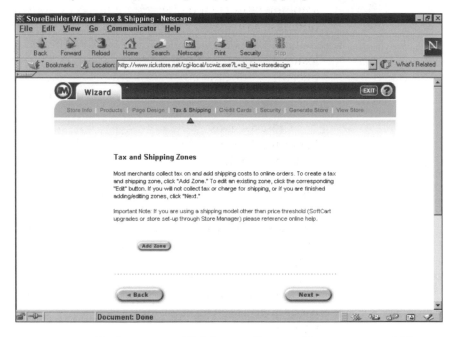

Under current U.S. law, online retailers are treated like catalog retailers. They are required to collect sales tax only from shoppers in those states where they have a physical presence such as an office or a warehouse. For most small businesses, that means you will have to collect sales tax only from shoppers in your own state. Therefore you will need to set up your online store so that it can distinguish between non-taxable and taxable orders. Most storefront programs will allow you to do this. If you are shipping to other countries, such as Canada, you will probably want to set up different shipping rates for each country as well. Keep in the mind that the tax laws governing Internet purchases could change. Make sure you contact your local or state taxation authority for the most up-to-date information.

Choosing the shipping rates can be one of the most complicated aspects of setting up an online store. If the shipping rates are too high, customers may not want to purchase a product from you. On the other hand, you want to make sure that you charge enough so that you are not losing money on your shipping expenses. To further complicate matters, the exact cost of shipping each item in your online store may vary depending on the weight and size of the item as well as the destination address.

There are many different ways to charge for shipping. For example, your shipping charges could be based on the total value of the items purchased, the total weight of the purchase, or the total number of items purchased. Alternatively, you could have a separate shipping charge for every item in your online store. Which method you choose depends on the types of products you are selling. For example, if your products are very consistent in terms of their weight and size, you are probably safe charging for shipping based on the quantity of products ordered by a customer or the value of the order. Charging by weight wouldn't be necessary if all of the products are approximately equal weights.

Although all of this may seem complicated, this is precisely the type of issue that you need to think about when setting up your online store. You need to make sure that the online storefront solution you select will support the type of shipping calculation that you want to use. SoftCart supports a variety of different methods for calculating shipping costs, as do most storefront creation programs.

Once you're through with the tax and shipping section, you can move on to the credit card section, where you need to select which credit cards you will accept in your online store:

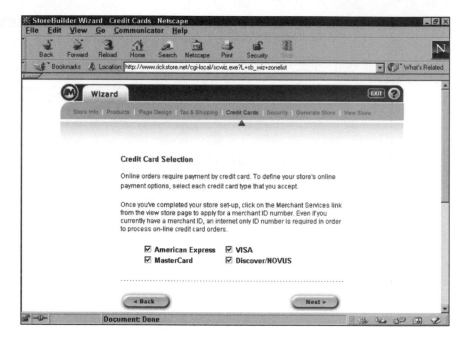

In order to allow credit card transactions in your online store, SoftCart requires you to install their encryption software on the computer that you will be using to download the orders that you receive in your online store. The encryption software will allow you to unscramble the orders when you download them to your computer so that you can view them. The process of installing the encryption software takes several minutes, and for brevity, we've omitted those steps here.

Once the encryption software has been set up on your computer, you're ready to click the "Finish" button and you're done!

You'll see a message on the screen informing you that your store has been officially published on the Internet:

When you press the "View Store" button, you'll be able to see your finished store on the Internet:

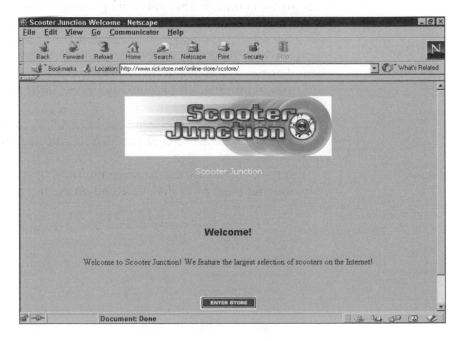

As you can see, what you end up with is a very simple-looking store. Customers who click on the "Enter Store" button will see the list of products that you entered during the setup process:

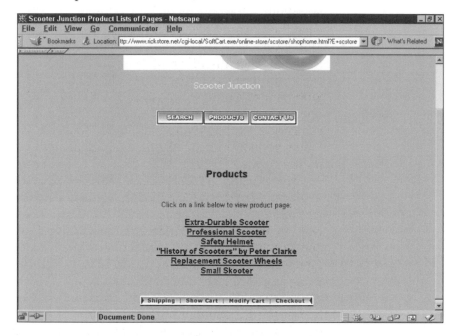

Clicking on a product reveals its price, a brief description, and a picture:

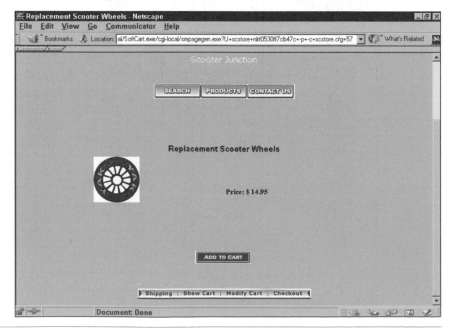

Customers can add an item to their shopping cart by clicking on the "Add to Cart" button. They can then proceed to check out of your online store.

For many merchants, the online store that the StoreBuilder Wizard creates is too simple. For example, what if you want a customized layout for your online store? Moreover, if you have lots of products, you'll probably want to divide them into different categories so that customers can easily navigate through your online store. SoftCart's StoreBuilder Wizard simply displays all your products in one big list – it doesn't allow you to organize products into categories. Another limitation of StoreBuilder Wizard is that it doesn't allow merchants to specify different sizes or colors for the products they are selling.

This is where SoftCart's Store Manager module comes in. As noted earlier in this section, if you want to incorporate more advanced features into your online store, you need to use the Store Manager program that is built into SoftCart. Many merchants build their store using the StoreBuilder Wizard and then add additional features later using Store Manager. Alternatively, if you don't want to be guided through the setup process step-by-step, you can bypass the StoreBuilder Wizard altogether and start building your store using Store Manager. The Store Manager screen looks like this:

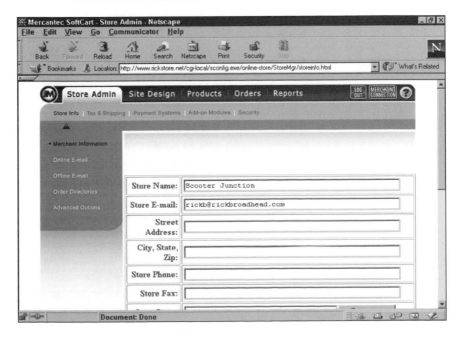

Along the top of the screen are the areas within Store Manager where you can change various aspects of your online store. Store Manager will allow you to:

- organize your products into different categories;
- add product attributes to each item in your online store so that customers choose from different colors, sizes, etc.;
- define discount prices;
- choose more sophisticated site designs;
- use another currency symbol (if you don't want to price your products in U.S. dollars);
- calculate shipping based on the weight of a product or the quantity of products ordered; and
- modify the acknowledgement message a customer receives once an order has been placed.

Store Manager also gives you access to a number of important functions that you can't access through StoreBuilder Wizard. For example, by selecting "Reports" from the top menu bar, you can access a variety of reports that show you how your online store is performing. The following report shows you how many orders each product in your online store has received:

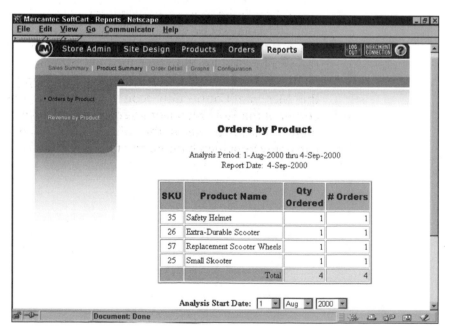

Perhaps most importantly, the Store Manager allows you to view detailed information about each order received in your online store:

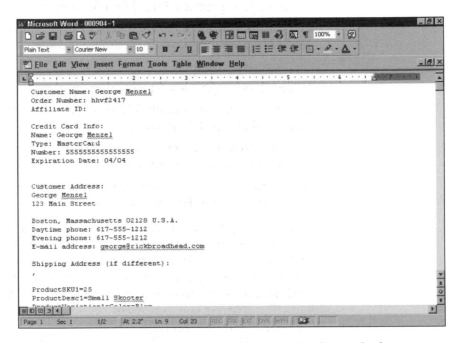

Although the process we've described over the last several pages may seem long and involved, it's actually quite quick. With SoftCart, you can have an online store up and running in a few hours or less. If you want to have real-time credit card processing on your online store, simply click on the "Merchant Connection" icon in the upper right-hand corner of the Store Manager screen. This will take you to the merchant services area of the SoftCart program, where you can apply for a merchant number:

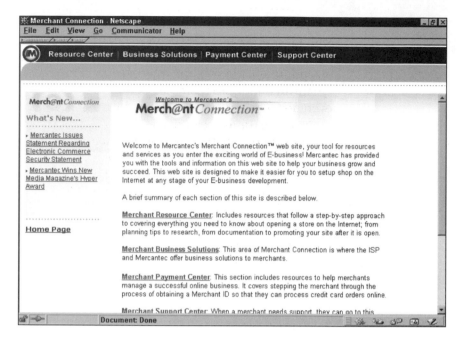

You would use this section to apply for an Internet merchant account so that you can accept and process credit card orders in real-time. With real-time credit card processing, each credit card order is processed while the customer waits. The process usually takes less than a minute and the customer is notified on the screen whether the order was approved or declined for some reason. Real-time credit card processing is quite a complex subject, so we've devoted an entire chapter to it (see Chapter 4, *Merchant Accounts and Online Payment Processing*).

A Word of Caution

Although browser-based storefront creation programs are supposed to make setting up an online store easy, you may find yourself getting frustrated. We tested many browser-based storefront programs for this book and were horrified by some of them. For example, some of these programs have a user interface that is slow and/or cumbersome to use. The help screens didn't work on one of the services we tried, and on another, technical support wasn't available late at night when we needed it most. Perhaps most importantly, the final product of your efforts may shock you.

Browser-based storefront solutions are notable for their simplicity and ease-of-use. However, when it comes to creating appealing site designs, they often leave merchants disappointed. Many of the browser-based programs will create an online store that may look amateurish to you, or even downright ugly. But that's to be expected since most of these programs are designed for entry-level users. You need to appreciate that there is a tradeoff when you use a browser-based storefront service. While you may get your online store up and running in a few hours or days, you certainly shouldn't expect the software to produce a magnificent-looking Web site design. For that, you're going to need to hire someone and be prepared to invest some additional money in your online store.

Fortunately, some browser-based programs give you a lot of control over the final design if you don't like the default designs that come with the software. SoftCart, for example, allows merchants to create their own custom SoftCart store templates. This means that you can hire a Web designer to design your online store to look the way you want. If you want to create a unique design for your online store and avoid the "cookie-cutter" appearance that many browser-based storefront packages create, make sure you select a browser-based service that gives you control over the final design and layout of your site.

Alternatively, if you want an online store that looks slick and cutting-edge, think about investing in a more expensive solution.

Free Browser-Based Storefront Creation Services

Most of the browser-based storefront creation services cost anywhere from $20 to several hundred dollars per month with extra fees for real-time credit card processing. However, if you're looking for a cheaper way to set up an online store, you may want to check out some of the free browser-based storefront creation services. We've listed some of the more popular ones in the table below.

Examples of Free Browser-Based Storefront Creation Services

BigStep.com	www.bigstep.com
eCongo	www.econgo.com
FreeMerchant	www.freemerchant.com
Excite Freetailer	www.freetailer.com
HyperMart	www.hypermart.com

Although these services usually don't charge for their basic storefront software, they do charge for real-time credit card processing, which is usually available for a monthly fee plus per-transaction costs. In addition, several of these services have many enhanced features, but you may have to pay for them.

As an example of what's possible, take a look at FreeMerchant (www.freemerchant.com), one of the most popular free storefront services.

The registration process for a free online store on the FreeMerchant Web site only takes a few minutes. Once you've signed up, you'll see the main menu, which looks like this:

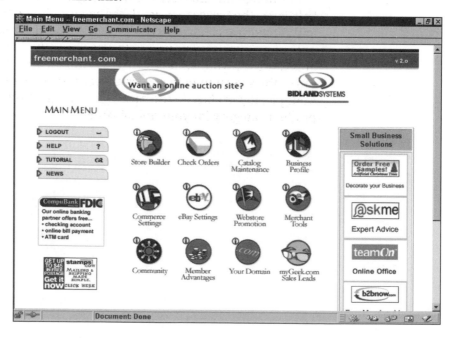

Simply click on "Store Builder" and you can begin building your online catalog of products:

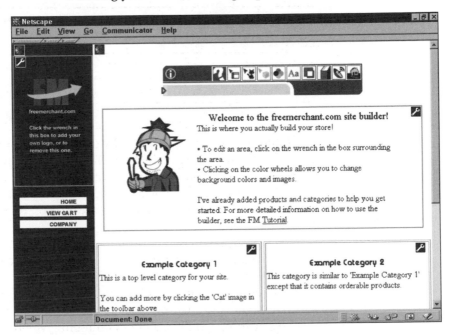

Although the interface is completely different from SoftCart's, the basic steps are the same. You define products and categories, create descriptions, prices, and attributes, upload pictures of your products, and select the layout and appearance of your store. You can use the menu bar at the top of the screen to help you set up your online store. For example, if you click on the cat symbol, you can set up a product category for your online store:

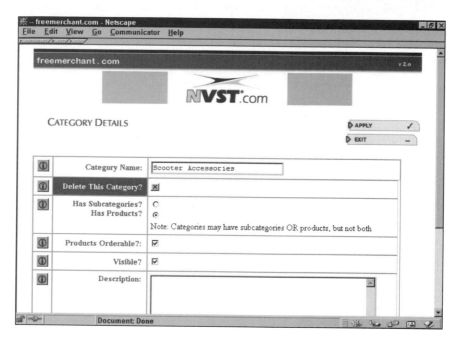

Like SoftCart, FreeMerchant allows you to specify shipping charges and tax settings for your online store. Simply select the states where you need to collect tax, and FreeMerchant will automatically calculate the tax on each order that you receive:

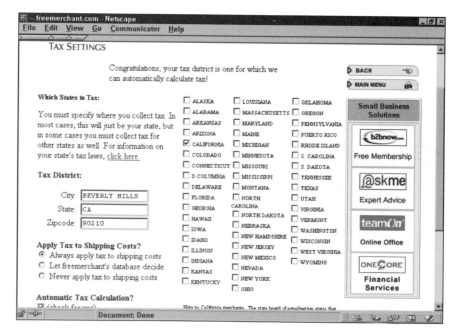

FreeMerchant has a number of other really useful features as well; some are free while others you may have to pay for. For example:

- *Inventory Manager.* You can use FreeMerchant's Inventory Manager to limit sales of your products to the exact quantity you have in stock. When you sell out of a particular item, customers will not be able to place any more orders for that product until you replenish the inventory. This prevents customers from placing orders for products that you have run out of.

- *Frequently Asked Questions Builder.* This tool allows you to easily build a list of frequently asked questions and answers.

- *Coupon Creator.* The Coupon Creator allows you to create electronic coupons that customers can redeem in your online store. You can include a coupon in your confirmation e-mail to customers (after they have made a purchase) as an incentive for them to visit your online store again!

- *Map Generator.* If you have a physical office or retail location, FreeMerchant can automatically generate a map and place it in your online store so that customers know how to find you.

- *Search Engine Submission.* FreeMerchant can help you submit your site to five major search engines.

- *Mailing List.* You can create an electronic mailing list for your customers so that you can notify them about product specials, end-of-season sales, or new additions to your online store. FreeMerchant will automatically prompt customers to sign up to your mailing list when they are checking out of your online store.

e-Fact

62% percent of online shoppers say that they saved time buying gifts online versus going to the store.

Source: Forrester Research (www.forrester.com)

Once you're finishing building your online store, simply click on the satellite icon in the menu at the top of the Store Builder screen, and your store will be placed on the Internet in approximately twenty-four hours. Our finished online store is pictured below. As you can see, the layout and design are very simple:

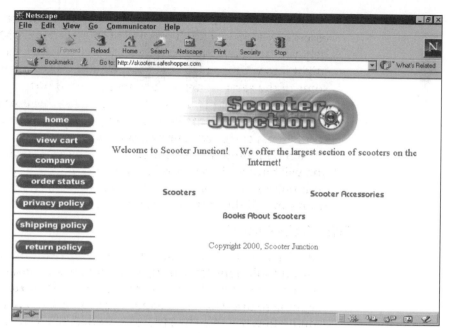

If you want to process credit card orders in real-time, FreeMerchant allows you to apply online for a merchant account from one of their partner organizations (see Chapter 4 for an overview of merchant accounts):

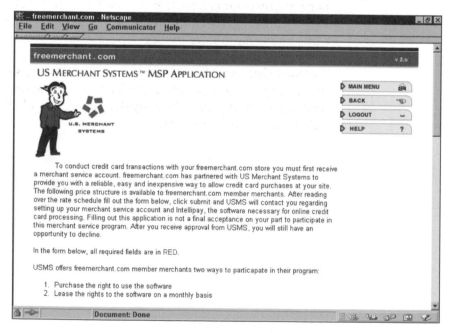

Because storefront services like FreeMerchant are essentially free, you might think that they can't possibly help you build a great online store. In reality, however, you might find yourself pleasantly surprised by how powerful some of the services are. In fact, tens of thousands of merchants in the United States are happily using these services as the foundation for their online stores. We recommend you try them out and draw your own conclusions.

Keep in mind that with most free storefront services, you will have limited control over the design and layout of your online store – one factor that sets these services apart from some of the more expensive storefront solutions.

What's the Catch?

FreeMerchant and other similar services are extremely powerful solutions for setting up an online store, especially when you consider the fact that the basic services don't cost anything to use. This leads aspiring online merchants to wonder how a service like FreeMerchant can afford to give its services away for free. The answer is quite simple. Free storefront services usually make their money by selling value-added services, licensing their technology to other organizations, and referring merchants to value-added partner organizations such as companies that supply online stores with merchant accounts so they can process credit cards online. Free storefront services may also generate revenue from advertising. For example, when using FreeMerchant, you'll notice advertisements on the site promoting a variety of online services for businesses. In the next screen, notice the ads along the top, left-hand, and right-hand sides of the screen:

Other free online storefront services operate in a similar manner. Some even go so far as to place ads from their sponsors on your online store, which may not be acceptable to you. BigStep.com actually places a "Powered by BigStep.com" advertising banner across the top of all of the sites that are created using its software. In this way, every site created using BigStep.com becomes an advertisement for the company. You can see the banner on the online store below, which was created by the BigStep.com program:

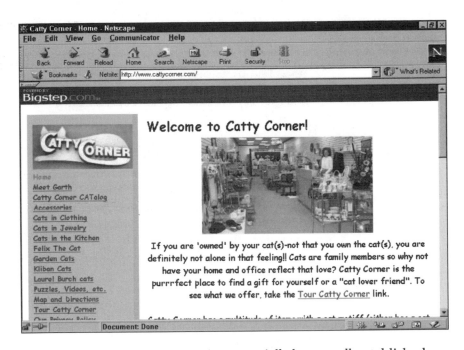

To some companies, especially large, well-established ones, having this type of advertising banner on their online store may seem tacky. It also shows customers that you are using a free Internet service to create your online store, which may not be the type of image that some companies want to project. But for other businesses, it's a small price to pay in order to a get a free online store! (In fact, over 150,000 businesses have set up their online stores using BigStep.com.) If this worries you, before using a free storefront service, find out if there's any requirement for you to display its brand name on your online store.

We'll be frank with you. Whether or not free online store services can survive with this type of business model is anyone's guess. It is very possible that services like FreeMerchant and BigStep.com could shut down or be acquired by other organizations if their business models prove unsuccessful. If this happens, your storefront could be shut down and you'll be left scrambling to set up your online store elsewhere. This is a risk that you need to consider when using a free storefront creation service.

What If You Already Have an Existing Web Site or Need More Design Flexibility?

Most browser-based storefront creation programs include tools that allow you to design a complete online store, including the main entry pages for your online store as well as the shopping cart pages. The shopping cart is the e-commerce software that allows customers to select and then purchase the products they are interested in. The shopping cart program keeps track of the items that a customer has selected until the customer is ready to check out. At this point, the software will collect shipping and billing information from the customer, automatically calculate the appropriate taxes and shipping charges, and allow the customer to choose a payment method, such as a check or credit card.

But what if you already have a Web site and you simply want to add online shopping capability to it? Many online merchants design their Web site using their own software (or with the assistance of a graphic designer) and then simply link their Web site to a catalog they create on a service like IBM HomePage Creator, FreeMerchant, or any other browser-based storefront service. This allows you to have control over the appearance of your Web site while taking advantage of the powerful shopping cart features found in the browser-based storefront solutions. It's one way to get around the design restrictions of so many browser-based storefront programs.

e-Fact

Kids and teenagers will spend $4.9 billion online in 2005.

Source: Jupiter Research (www.jup.com)

If you want to design your Web site yourself, there are a lot of Web site–building programs that you can purchase. Some of the most popular include Microsoft's FrontPage (www.microsoft.com/frontpage), Macromedia's Dreamweaver (www.dreamweaver.com), Allaire's HomeSite (www.homesite.com), and NetObjects' Fusion (www.netobjects.com).

If you're going to attempt to integrate a storefront program into an existing Web site, make sure that you have at least some control over the design of the shopping cart pages so that the overall look of your Web site can be kept as consistent as possible. Otherwise, your Web site will appear disjointed and piecemeal. If it turns out that you don't have much flexibility in choosing your own design, you may want to consider one of the standalone shopping cart programs that we discuss in the next section.

Option #2: Standalone Shopping Cart Software

Standalone Shopping Cart Software

Advantages

- Store owner has complete control over store layout and design
- Perfect for individuals/firms who already have an existing Web site
- Store is hosted on your Web servers (or those of your Web hosting company)
- Highly customizable

Disadvantages

- Requires software installation and setup
- Usually requires some technical knowledge and some familiarity with HTML
- Usually requires HTML programming and Web design work

If you want complete control over the layout and design of your online store, you may want to consider using one of the many standalone shopping cart programs that are available today. These programs allow you a lot more freedom with the design of your online store, since you aren't limited to the design templates that come with a browser-based storefront solution. Some can be purchased in retail stores or downloaded from a Web site via the Internet. Others are only available through resellers.

With shopping cart softwear, it's expected that you have your own Web site, whether you have built it on your own or have hired a graphic designer or Web developer to do it. Your Web site is then integrated with the shopping cart program.

There are usually two elements to standalone shopping cart software:

1. *Server software.* This software is run when someone is browsing through and shopping within your store.

2. *Design software.* This is the software that you use to design your store. You either run it through your Web browser by linking to the server software above, or by running a separate program in Windows that lets you design your store.

In some instances the server and design components are combined into one softwear package. In other cases they are separate modules.

Once you find a shopping cart program that you like you have three choices:

a) you can install it yourself on your own server. That might be tough to do, since you might not have the expertise

b) you try to convince your ISP or Web hosting company to install it. That might be tough to do, since they might not want to install it

or

c) you find an ISP/Web hosting company who has already installed that softwear (including the server and design elements).

We won't kid you – setting up a shopping cart program and integrating it into a Web site is not as easy as using one of the browser-based storefront solutions that we described earlier in the chapter, especially if you encounter a situation in which you have to install the server portion of the program.

It can be a lot easier if you select the shopping cart software you want to use, and then find the ISP/Web hosting company that has pre-installed that softwear.

For example, some ISPs have aligned themselves with particular shopping cart programs. In doing so, they have pre-installed the necessary server portions of the program on their computers, and if necessary, the design portion of the software.

For example, visit NetNation (www.netnation.com), a Web hosting company that provides e-commerce hosting services. You can choose a number of e-commerce hosting packages from them:

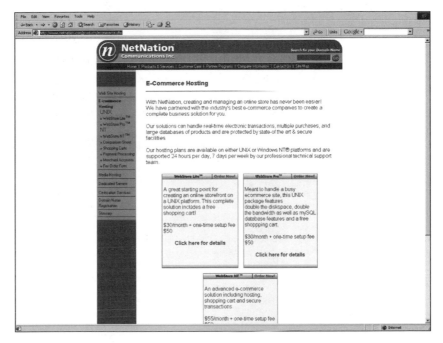

Take a look at the WebStore Lite option, and you'll notice that they use the Miva Merchant Shopping Cart software program. So what they have done is installed both the design part of the program (that you can use to design your store) and the server portion of the software (that is run when someone accesses your store):

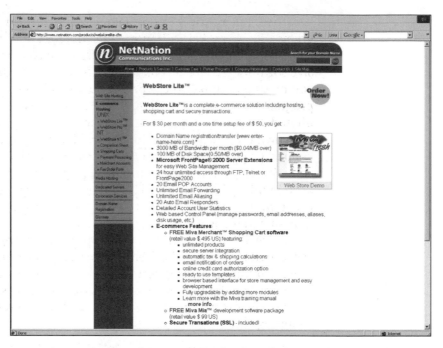

The best thing to do is check with the vendor of the shopping cart software you're interested in to see if there are any ISPs or Web hosting companies that have pre-installed it.

Otherwise, you will be in a situation in which you and your ISP (if they are willing) have to figure out how to install the shopping cart software you have chosen. For this installation, you may need to download the software via the Internet and be familiar with HTML. Even if you are familiar with HTML, you could still run into some problems while installing the software. For example, when one of the authors of this book was trying to install one of the popular shopping cart programs, he ran into some technical problems and had to get help from the company whose software he was using. Hence, one of the important considerations when choosing shopping cart software is the quality of technical support that you will receive. Fortunately, some of the companies that sell shopping cart software may actually be willing to install their software for you if you run into difficulty installing it yourself. Ask whether this type of service is available before you purchase the software so that you're not surprised later if the software vendor isn't able to help you.

There are a variety of standalone shopping cart programs on the market with numerous different features and price tags. They range from free programs to more expensive software costing several hundreds of dollars. Although you may be tempted to use one of the free shopping cart programs that are plentiful on the Internet, these programs often don't come with support, which means that you're on your own if you run into technical problems. However, we encourage you to try them out and draw your own conclusions. When evaluating different shopping cart programs, keep in mind that you get what you pay for. A shopping cart program that costs $10 will probably be a lot less powerful than one that costs $400.

We've listed some of the more popular shopping cart programs in the table below. A good site for finding other shopping cart programs is the Shopping Cart and E-Commerce Guide at www.onlineorders.net. This site contains an extensive list of both free and commercial shopping cart programs.

Examples of Standalone Shopping Cart Programs

Cart32	www.cart32.com
CartIt	www.cartit.com
EasyCart	www.easycart.com
PDG Shopping Cart	www.pdgsoft.com
QuikStore	www.quikstore.com
smc WebStore	www.smctechnologies.net

Using shopping cart software has two big downsides. First, as we have already mentioned, integrating a shopping cart program into your Web site can be a bit tricky if you don't have any technical knowledge. If you're not comfortable installing software and configuring computer code, you might run into some difficulty setting up the software. Second, a standalone shopping cart program isn't a complete storefront solution – it typically only provides the shopping cart. Unlike the browser-based storefront creation programs, a shopping cart program requires you to design a lot of the entry page items for your store, plus other sections within your site such as product support, technical support pages, marketing information, and other details.

In other words, most shopping cart programs won't help you build all the areas of your site – they are not an all-in-one solution. For example, some of the store elements that are automatically created for you with some of the browser-based storefront products, such as "Return Policy" and "Info" buttons, are not generated with most shopping cart programs.

Before choosing a shopping cart program, consider doing the following:

- Spend some time looking at online stores that use the shopping cart program you're considering. This will give you a feel for how the software works. Most shopping cart software vendors have links to sample online stores on their Web sites. Visit some of these stores and actually go through the process of placing items in your shopping cart so that you can see what the customer interface looks like. You might even want to go so far as to e-mail some of the companies that are using the software to find out what their experiences have been.

- Carefully review the installation instructions and the skills required to set up the software so that you know what you're in for. Some shopping carts only require knowledge of HTML (the language used to build Web pages) while others may require more advanced programming knowledge.

- Find out what type of technical support is available should you run into any problems. Is there a manual that comes with the software that will walk you through the setup process? How thorough is the technical/help documentation?

- Take time to review the list of features offered by the shopping cart software. Does it meet your needs? How do the features compare to other shopping cart programs on the market?

- See if a free trial of the software is available so that you can play around with the software before making a commitment.

- Find out whether the shopping cart program allows you to make changes through your Web browser. Or, do you have to make the changes on your computer using a separate software program, and then upload them to your Web hosting company's computer?

- Find out what payment gateways are supported so that you can accept credit card orders in real-time.

e-Fact

Slow-loading Web pages caused 21% of customers to abandon shopping carts before making a purchase.

Source: BizRate.com (www.bizrate.com)

Once the shopping cart software has been installed on the appropriate computer, you can begin configuring it with information about your products. With many shopping cart programs, such as PDG Shopping Cart, you can do this through your Web browser. Once the PDG Shopping Cart software is installed, the installation instructions will direct you to a special address on your Web site, where you'll be able to see the setup screen for the software:

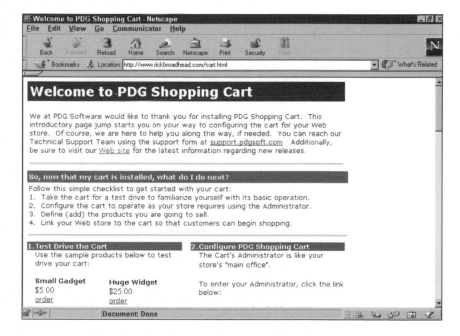

From here, you can access the Merchant Administration screen, where you can input information about your products, choose what shipping methods you want to support, specify the payment methods you want to accept, and control other aspects of your online store:

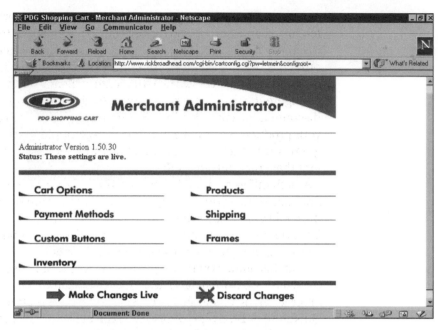

Clicking on any of the above options will allow you to set up and modify these aspects of your online store. For example, selecting "Products" will bring you to a screen where you can specify prices, descriptions, discount levels, attributes (e.g., color, size), and other details for each product:

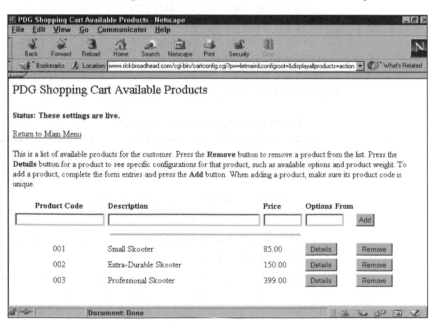

Shopping cart programs can have extremely powerful features. For example, PDG Shopping Cart allows you to track inventory levels, send e-mail notification messages once an order has been received by your online store, and specify quantity discount rules. The latter feature means that you can configure the shopping cart software to give the customer a discount if the customer buys a minimum quantity of one of your products. As noted earlier, because shopping cart programs vary widely in their capabilities and options, it's important that you think about the features that you want and research different shopping cart products before you make a final decision. If you've never set up an online store before, you probably don't know what features you want. That's why it's important to spend time on each shopping cart program's Web site, comparing features and pricing information.

At this point, you may be wondering, "Should I use a browser-based storefront package like SoftCart or FreeMerchant, or should I use a shopping cart program like QuikStore or PDG Shopping Cart?" The answer depends on your budget, your technical skills, and how much customization you require in your online store. If you are simply looking for a quick and easy way to start selling on the Internet with minimal hassle, you're probably better off going with one of the browser-based storefront programs. On the other hand, if you already have a Web site, and you're looking for a powerful, highly customizable shopping cart solution for your existing site, you can choose to purchase a standalone shopping cart program.

Option #3: Advanced E-commerce Software

Advanced E-commerce Software

Advantages

- Fully customizable

- Provides a complete storefront solution

- Most powerful e-commerce solution

- Often includes advanced features like Web site analysis and personalization

- Can often be tied into an organization's back-end systems

Disadvantages

- Need to install software
- May require programming expertise to set up and install
- May involve a long setup process
- Bigger investment required: $1,000–$1,000,000+

The last option for building an online store is an advanced store-building software package. The "advanced" category includes low-end, mid-range, and high-end e-commerce packages. In most cases, the software will be physically delivered to you, but you may be able to download some of the low-end packages off the Internet. Pricing starts at around $1,000 and goes higher than $1 million.

On the low end of the price spectrum, there are packages such as AbleCommerce that are suited for small businesses as well as large organizations. AbleCommerce costs around $1,000 and uses a browser-based interface so that merchants can set up an online store without the need for any programming knowledge.

In the middle range, there are solutions such as IBM's WebSphere Commerce Suite or Microsoft Commerce Server. To give you an idea of how powerful some of these programs are, IBM's WebSphere Commerce Suite comes on several CD-ROMs. Although these programs are capable of just about anything, they are tailored to large organizations with large budgets rather than small businesses. Although Microsoft's Commerce Server costs less than $10,000, the "pro" version of IBM's WebSphere Commerce Suite costs over $30,000. Clearly, such packages are overkill for most small businesses and mom-and-pop storefronts. They're more appropriate for businesses with high-volume online stores that want a fully customized look and a wide range of reporting, analysis, and promotional tools. In particular, mid-range solutions are usually notable for their personalization features, relationship marketing tools, and cross-marketing capabilities, which are usually not available in the entry-level packages discussed above. For example, both IBM WebSphere and Microsoft Commerce Server allow merchants to personalize the content of Web pages based on a customer's demographic information or purchase history.

At the high end of the spectrum are packages like Blue Martini Software's Customer Interaction System and BroadVision's Retail Commerce Suite. These programs are designed for organizations with complex e-commerce needs. For example, businesses may want to develop a highly personalized e-commerce experience for their customers, tie their e-commerce operations into call centers, or integrate their Web site with their warehouses or fulfillment operations. Blue Martini's software, for example, costs over $1 million and requires at least a couple of months to set up.

While a program like AbleCommerce won't require you to call in an army of Web developers, mid-range and high-end programs like WebSphere, Commerce Suite, and Customer Interaction Suite will almost certainly require you to use expert computer programmers to build your online store, given the extensive range of options and capabilities of the software.

One of the benefits of using an advanced storefront package is that you won't outgrow it as quickly as you might outgrow one of the entry-level solutions. If you start off with one of the entry-level packages and your online store becomes really successful, you may quickly find yourself needing to expand beyond the capabilities of the package you are using. Moving an e-commerce site over to an entirely new platform can be a lot of work. On the other hand, if you start off with a higher-end package that has lots of room to grow as your needs change, you can minimize disruptions to your online store down the road.

Examples of Advanced Storefront Solutions

AbleCommerce	www.ablecommerce.com
Blue Martini Software's Customer Interaction System	www.bluemartini.com
BroadVision's Retail Commerce Suite	www.broadvision.com
IBM WebSphere Commerce Suite	www.ibm.com/websphere
Intershop Communications' Enfinity	www.intershop.com
Microsoft Commerce Server	www.microsoft.com

WHAT TO LOOK FOR IN AN ONLINE STORE SOLUTION

Now that we've reviewed the three basic methods of setting up an online store, you need to start thinking about the features that you want to have in your online store so that you can identify the solution that best meets your needs.

One of the most important considerations when choosing a storefront solution is your future needs. As hard as it may be, try to anticipate your future needs now so that you don't have to continually change your storefront software. As you begin selling online, you may discover that your existing storefront product is inadequate.

That's to be expected as you grow your business and learn more about e-commerce. But it's quite a disruption to your business if you have to move your entire store over to a different software package to upgrade it. Imagine if you had to move your home every year or couple of years! Moving your online store can be quite a hassle and very time-consuming, especially if you have hundreds of products in your inventory. If you think you may expand your product line or make significant changes to the features in your online store in the immediate future, make sure you choose a storefront solution that can meet your needs as you grow.

Some online store owners have decided to custom-build their online storefront software (often using an e-commerce developer) rather than using any of the existing storefront packages that we have reviewed in this chapter. This can be an extremely costly approach and it isn't something that a small business would normally consider, but the advantage is that custom-built software doesn't have the limitations that canned software does. It's yet another option that you may want to think about if you can't find an existing storefront product that meets your needs.

In the pages that follow, we provide you with a checklist of some of the features you should be aware of as you research storefront solutions. The purpose of this list is to get you thinking about different storefront features. By no means are we suggesting that the storefront package you ultimately select should include every feature listed here. If you want one of the features below that is not included in a storefront package you are seriously considering, contact the company and find out whether the feature is going to be added to the product in the near future. It may turn out that the feature does exist after all and you just didn't realize it! If the feature doesn't exist, find out whether it will be possible for you to hire a developer or programmer to add the feature to your online store. If you're thinking of using a standalone shopping cart, some of the shopping cart software vendors may be willing to custom-program a feature for you if you're willing to pay for it. As we have noted several times in this chapter, many of the entry-level storefront packages limit the amount of customization that you can do. If there is a feature that you absolutely must have, and the storefront package you're considering doesn't have it, and you can't add it yourself, you should consider using a different storefront package.

Affiliate Program Support

Does the storefront software have built-in support for affiliate programs? As you will see in Chapter 7, many online stores use affiliate programs to increase the number of visitors to their stores. An affiliate program involves signing up Web sites to promote your online store. In return, you pay affiliates a flat fee or a percentage of the final sale if they successfully refer a customer to your store. In order to keep track of all of the referrals and commissions, you need to monitor who is referring visitors to your store. Some storefront software has features that make it easier to manage affiliate programs. If you think that you may be starting an affiliate program in the future, you may want to look for storefront solutions that provide this type of support.

Auction Capabilities

With more and more Web sites offering online auctions, you may want to investigate whether the storefront solution you are considering supports online auction capabilities. Alternatively, find out whether your storefront service is integrated with an auction site like eBay (www.ebay.com) so that you can easily publish your products to their Web site.

Back-End Integration

Can the store be integrated with your existing business systems? If you already have a retail business, you will probably want a storefront solution that can be integrated with

your existing accounting, inventory, payment, and fulfillment systems. Otherwise, your retail systems will be out of
step with your Internet systems and you could wind up
with some significant logistical and financial challenges as a
result.

Capacity

Can the software handle heavy volumes? Does the site that
will host your online store have a fast connection to the
Internet? If you expect your store to attract a lot of customers every day, make sure the software can support those
volumes. More importantly, make sure that your Web hosting company has a fast connection to the Internet. You will
quickly lose customers if your online store is sluggish and
slow to navigate.

Cookie Support

Does the software allow you to keep track of your customers using cookies? Does the software support "persist-
ent cookies"? These allow a customer to load up a shopping
cart, leave your online store, and come back at a later time
and pick up where he or she left off. Can the software track
your customers in other ways, using their IP addresses, for
example?

Customer Registration

Does the storefront solution include customer registration
capabilities and does it retain customer information once a
customer has left your online store? Many online stores
allow customers to register, which usually entitles them to
special features such as access to special promotions (see
Chapters 3 and 7 for more information on customer registration). Online registration also allows customers to store
billing and/or shipping information on the site so they
don't have to reenter this information every time they make
another purchase at your online store. Registration requires
that the customer provide his or her name, e-mail address,
and any other information the merchant requests. A registration feature is valuable because it allows a merchant to
build a profile of its customers and this information can be
used for marketing and promotional campaigns (provided
that the customer has consented to this use).

Customization

To what degree can you customize the overall design and layout of the store? Ask the following questions:

- Does the service or software allow you to customize the appearance, layout, and look of the store, or are your choices limited?

- Can you control fonts, colors, and background colors and images? If the service uses design templates, how many can you choose from?

- Can you customize the messages displayed throughout the store and at checkout?

- Can you upload your own HTML pages to your online store?

- Can you customize product and category pages?

- What restrictions exist on customization?

- Are other customization possibilities available?

Data Export Capabilities

Can you export your sales data into a database, spreadsheet, or accounting program? If you plan to use a spreadsheet program or an accounting package like Intuit's QuickBooks to keep track of your online sales, find out if you can export data from your online store into the software program you are using.

Data Import Capabilities/Spreadsheet Support

Can you import an existing spreadsheet or database file into your online store? What spreadsheet and database formats does the store software support? For example, suppose that your online store will carry one hundred different products and all of your product information is already in a database. Will you be able to import the database into your online store or will you have to manually enter in the product information item by item?

Database Support

Will the software allow you to build a database-driven store so that your product information is created on the fly from a database, or are you forced to use static HTML pages?

This would not be possible with most of the entry-level storefront packages, but may be possible with some of the standalone shopping cart programs. Database support would definitely be a standard feature of all the mid-to-high-range e-commerce solutions.

Domain Name Registration

Can your online store have its own domain name? Find out if the storefront service that you choose allows you to register a domain name for your online store (e.g., www. yourstorename.com). If so, what is the cost of registering the domain name and having it linked to your online store? Having a unique domain name for your online store gives it a more professional image and a simple address that customers can easily remember.

The whole issue of domain names can become quite complex. For example, if you can have your own domain name for your online store, why stop there? You might consider registering multiple domain names, all of which link to your store. That way, you've got multiple different addresses (i.e., based on product or trademark names) that lead customers to your store.

Then, you might even consider using, in addition to your ".com" domain, other extensions such as ".net" and ".org". In addition, keep in mind that over time, new types of domain names that are alternatives to ".com" domains, such as ".store," ".firm" and ".retail" might become available, and so you might want to register within these domain extensions as well.

Electronic Mailing List Support

Does the storefront software come with its own mailing list capability? Some software programs have built-in features that allow you to manage a database of customer e-mail addresses so you can regularly send out promotional e-mail messages to targeted groups. Keep in mind that many people consider such unsolicited e-mail to be junk mail, so be careful how you use this feature. Some storefront solutions may impose a limit on the length of the e-mail messages that you can send through the mailing list or on the number of customers that you can add to the mailing list. Make sure you are aware of any such restrictions. Also find out whether it is possible to set up mailings to selected customers based on their demographic profiles, previous purchases, or other criteria.

E-mail Acknowledgement to Customers

Find out if the storefront will allow you to send an e-mail acknowledgement to a customer once an order has been received by your online store. This type of e-mail acknowledgement system can be a very desirable feature since it assures customers that their orders have been received. It also can save you time and money, since it reduces the need for customers to contact you to find out the status of their orders. Therefore, check out the level of e-mail integration that is possible with the storefront solution that you choose. Also find out whether you can customize the content of the e-mail message that is sent to customers.

E-mail Address Forwarding

Determine whether you can set up the storefront solution so that it forwards order information to different e-mail addresses. For example, suppose you want one copy of each online order to go to the owner of the company, a second copy to go to the sales department, and a third copy to go to the fulfillment department. Will the software do this?

Fraud Protection

What type of fraud protection measures are available to you? Some storefront programs have built-in fraud protection services that may be available for free or for an additional charge. Fraud is a serious issue and one that we discuss in more depth in Chapter 5, *Online Security Issues and Credit Card Fraud.*

Help Files and Documentation

Does the software or service come with tutorials or online help files? Is the documentation comprehensive? Needless to say, make sure that any software or service you consider comes with adequate documentation and help files in the event that you need them.

Information Templates

Does the storefront solution give you templates so that you can easily create your own shipping policies, privacy policies, and return policies and automatically add them to your Web site? Are there templates for adding basic contact information and background information about your company?

Integration with an Existing Web Site

Can the storefront software be integrated with an existing Web site? If you already have an investment in a Web site that you don't want to have to overhaul or subject to significant changes, then you should look for a storefront solution that can be easily integrated into your existing Web site.

Integration with Shipping Companies

What shipping options does the software support? Can the customer choose between the United States Postal Service (USPS), United Parcel Service (UPS), and Federal Express (FedEx), or is only one or two of these options supported? Can you add your own courier companies? Also find out if the storefront software features any integration with the rate schedules of courier or shipping services. For example, some storefront products will automatically calculate the appropriate shipping cost for different carriers based on the weight of the products and the origin and destination of the shipment. Services like these will make it easier for you to calculate shipping costs for your customers.

International Orders

Are there any restrictions on accepting credit card orders from shoppers outside the United States?

Inventory Management

What inventory management features does the storefront software have? For example, find out whether the software will track inventory levels, so it in effect becomes an inventory management system. Will you and/or your customers be notified when you run out of stock of a particular item? If the stock of a product drops to zero, will the software automatically remove that item from the online store or inform customers (before they place an order) that the item is temporarily out of stock? Can you be notified if inventory runs low on any product in your online store?

Language and Currency Support

Will the storefront software support different currencies and different languages? If there is no built-in support for different languages and currencies, how difficult is it for you to add different currencies or languages to your online store, or is it even possible? For example, suppose you want to change all the menu buttons in your online store to another language – can you do this? This will be an important consideration if you intend to attract a lot of international business or if your online store will cater to a specific country or demographic group where English is not the predominant language.

Minimum Order Amount

Depending on the types of products you are selling, and their prices, you may wish to set a minimum order amount. Some storefront software programs will allow you to do this. Customers who don't meet the minimum amount will not be allowed to check out of your online store until they increase the total amount of their order. This can be an important feature if you are selling low-priced items and you want to ensure that you are generating a good profit margin on each order.

Multimedia Files

Does the storefront service allow you to add multimedia files to your online store? For example, are you able to include sound or video files or Shockwave animations? Can you upload files such as PowerPoint presentations or Adobe Acrobat documents?

Online Marketing Programs

Does the storefront solution you are considering offer any marketing programs to help you drive traffic to your online store? For example, does the company maintain an online shopping mall or directory of online stores that you can add your site to? Does it run any type of a banner exchange program so that you can trade advertisements with other online stores (for a discussion of banner ads, see Chapter 6, *Marketing Strategies for Your Online Store*)?

Order Encryption/Encrypted E-mail

What type of encryption software does the storefront software use to protect the transmission of online orders by the customer? Given concern that still exists in the United States and around the world regarding online credit card security, you will want to ensure that the storefront solution you are considering supports credit card encryption so that orders from your customers can be transmitted securely over the Internet. The most widely used type of encryption on the Internet is SSL (Secure Sockets Layer) encryption.

You should also check to see if the software supports e-mail encryption. When orders are e-mailed to you by the storefront software, you may want them to be encrypted so that they can't be read by a hacker while in transit. One of the most popular e-mail encryption tools is Pretty Good Privacy (PGP). Some storefront software packages support PGP-encrypted e-mail.

Order Method

What order methods does the storefront solution support? In addition to online ordering, you may also want to offer customers the capability to place their orders by telephone, fax, or mail. Not all customers are comfortable with sending their credit card data and personal information over the Internet, so it's generally a good idea to build in other options.

Order Notification

Will the storefront solution notify you by e-mail and/or fax when a new order is received, or do you have to log into the Web site to find out whether you have received any new orders? When comparing storefront solutions, find out what method the program uses to notify you when an order has been placed. In addition, consider how the order information is presented to you on the storefront software's Web site. For example, when you review orders on the Web site, are they easily accessible and presented in a user-friendly manner, or is it a cumbersome process to call up orders and examine them?

Order Tracking

Does the storefront software allow customers to check on the status of orders they have placed with you? This is a handy feature to have, since customers can log onto your Web site after they have placed an order to find out whether their order has been shipped and/or processed. Some, but not all, storefront solutions provide this feature.

Packing Slips and Invoices

Does the storefront solution automatically generate packing slips and invoices? Are invoices automatically delivered to customers by e-mail? What do the invoices look like? Can you customize the packing slips and invoices to your specifications? Find out if the software or service will automate this type of paperwork for you. If you are doing a lot of transactions, this can save you a significant amount of time.

Payment Methods

What payment methods does the storefront solution support? You might want to establish a variety of payment methods for your online store, including credit cards, purchase orders, checks, preestablished accounts, COD, and other options. Make sure that the solution you choose supports your requirements. Also find out whether you can create your own list of payment methods or whether you're restricted to what the software provides. Determine the credit cards you want to accept and make certain the storefront solution supports them. For example, not all storefront solutions will accept Discover, Diner's Club, and JCB.

Personalization Features and Customer Profiling

More and more storefront programs are implementing "one-to-one" marketing capabilities that enable a merchant to personalize product offers or Web pages for specific customers. While advanced personalization features are typically only found in the mid- or high-range storefront solutions, some entry-level packages do offer some personalization capability. Because personalization capabilities can help you cross-sell and upsell products to your customers, they are an important feature to think about when choosing a storefront solution. Investigate the following issues:

- Does the software come with cross-selling capabilities? Will the software allow you to cross-sell products to customers based on their initial selections? For example, some storefront products can be set up so that when a customer chooses a certain product, other similar products are recommended to the customer.

- Does the software make it possible for you to track a customer's shopping habits? As your customer base grows, you may want the ability to target your frequent customers with special offers based on their purchasing activity.

Pricing Structure

How will you be charged for your online store? Make sure that you understand the product's pricing structure and contract terms before making any commitments. Find out whether there is a minimum contract period for your online store or whether you can shut down the store at any time without financial penalty.

The charges you incur will depend on the type of storefront software that you are using. With most browser-based storefront services (with the exception of free services such as FreeMerchant and BigStep.com), you are usually charged a one-time setup fee and then a flat monthly fee, which increases with the number of products you are selling. The fee may also be based on how much disk space you use on their server and/or how much data transfer your online store generates (data transfer is a measure of how much information is being transferred from your Web site to the visitor's computer. In general, the more people visiting your site, the more data is being transferred).

Under certain circumstances, some browser-based solutions may take a percentage of sales in addition to a monthly fee. Yahoo! Store, for instance, invites merchants to list their stores in Yahoo's shopping mall, called Yahoo! Shopping. Depending on your sales volume, Yahoo! may take a small percentage of your mall-derived sales.

If you decide to purchase shopping cart software or a mid/high-range software program instead of a browser-based solution, you simply purchase the software and then you own it. However, you will need to pay a monthly fee to a Web hosting company or Internet service provider so that your online store can be placed on the Internet (unless you choose to run your own Web servers).

If you decide to process credit card transactions in real-time, you will also incur various credit card processing fees. These are more fully discussed in Chapter 4.

Product Restrictions

Some storefront creation vendors will not allow you to sell certain products through their service. For example, if you intend to sell adult/sex products, you may find it difficult to find a storefront service that will accept you. If you plan on selling a product or service that would be considered explicit or high-risk, make sure that you clearly understand any rules or restrictions that may be in place with the storefront service you are considering.

Quality of Appearance and Navigation

Does the software produce professional-looking online stores? What navigation aids are built into the software? On the Internet, the look of your online store is crucial. A professional-looking store that is easy to navigate builds credibility, user satisfaction, and sales, while a store that is visually weak and hard to navigate scares off customers. If you are using a browser-based solution, make sure that the end product looks professional. As recommended earlier, look at examples of stores that have been created using the storefront programs you are evaluating. This will help you to assess what your store will look like, and help you determine whether the end product is professional-looking or amateurish in appearance.

Real-Time Credit Card Processing

Will the storefront solution support real-time credit card processing so that your orders can be approved in real-time over the Internet? What fees does the storefront solution charge for this service, and how do these fees compare to the fees charged by other storefront solutions?

Another important factor is the payment gateway and the merchant account provider the storefront service is linked to. To accept credit cards in your online store, you will need a merchant account, and in order to process your credit card orders in real-time, you will need to use a payment gateway, We discuss payment gateways and merchant accounts in Chapter 4, *Merchant Accounts and Online Payment Processing*.

Some storefront solutions may restrict you to a specific payment gateway and/or merchant account provider, which will affect the credit card processing fees that you will have to pay. Make sure you fully understand what restrictions, if any, exist regarding payment gateways and merchant account providers. For example, can you use any merchant account provider or payment gateway or are you restricted to using companies that have alliances with the storefront service? What if you already have a merchant number – can you use it or do you have to apply for a new one? What fees does the storefront charge for setting you up with a merchant account and payment gateway, and are they competitive?

Sales and Marketing Reports

What type of sales information does the storefront software give you? How detailed is that information? In addition to tracking sales activity on your Web site, you will also want to be able to determine where your customers are coming from, what search engines they are using, and what keywords led them to your online store. Make sure that you select a storefront package that generates useful sales and marketing reports. As the volume of orders in your store increases, you will begin to depend on these reports to identify best-selling and worst-selling products and to determine other sales and marketing trends in your online store. Find out if the software will answer questions such as:

- What are the top-selling products on your Web site?
- What products in your online store are generating the most revenue? The least revenue?
- Which pages on your site are generating the most visits? The least visits?
- Where are your customers coming from?
- What is the average revenue per order?
- How many orders are you receiving per day?

Also investigate the following issues:

- Are the reports strictly numerical or can you get graphical reports as well?

- Can you view orders by date and customer name as well as by product?
- What other options exist to sort/filter your orders?
- How frequently are the reports updated? Once a week? Once a day? Several times a day? In real-time?

In order to get as much information as possible about how customers are using your Web site, you may need to supplement your storefront software's reporting capabilities with a Web site analysis tool such as WebTrends (www. webtrends.com), which will give you detailed reports that not only show where your visitors are coming from but what path they take through your Web site and where customers are abandoning your online store. Mid-to-high-range storefront solutions often come with extremely powerful reporting capabilities. However, if you use an entry-level package, such as a shopping cart or browser-based storefront solution, you may find that you need to purchase a separate Web site analysis tool in order to gain a complete picture of how customers are using your Web site. In fact, many of the shopping cart products don't have any reporting capabilities at all! Most of the browser-based storefront solutions do have reporting capabilities, but some focus strictly on sales data, and won't give you an overview of where your customers are coming from or how they are using your Web site. For more information about Web site analysis tools, see Chapter 6, *Marketing Strategies for Your Online Store*.

Sales and Promotions

Does the storefront solution allow you to implement sales and promotions? Merchandising products on the Internet isn't much different from merchandising them in the real world. From time to time, you will want to put certain items on sale or provide product discounts to your customers. Investigate such issues as:

- Does the storefront software make it easy for you to display new products prominently or highlight special promotions?
- Can customers redeem coupons on your online store?
- Does the software allow you to create and/or e-mail coupons to customers?
- How easy is it to put items on sale or reduce all the prices in your store by a certain percentage?

- Can you set up discounts that start and finish on certain dates/times?
- Does the software make it easy for you to implement quantity discounts (e.g., buy three, get one free)?

Scalability/Inventory Restrictions

Some storefront solutions have a maximum number of products or product categories that you can have in your online store. Other storefront products may have different monthly fee levels depending on how many products you intend to have in your online store. Some packages may not impose a limit on the number of products or product categories that you can carry, but instead will have recommended maximums so that your online store doesn't slow down to the point where it's sluggish for you to update and slow for customers to use. Think about how many products you intend to carry and how many different product categories you will need to define. Make sure you find a storefront solution that can support your needs. If you think you will need to expand the number of products or categories that you carry, make sure that the storefront solution you are considering will be able to accommodate your needs as you grow. For example, if you want to expand the number of products that your store carries from one hundred to one thousand after the first year, will you have to switch to another storefront program? Also find out if there is a limit on how many different attributes (e.g., color, size) you can assign to each product in your online store.

Search Capability

Does the storefront software allow you to build a searchable index of your product catalog or your entire online store? When customers enter your online store, they may want to search your online store by keyword rather than browsing page by page through your site. Find out whether the storefront solution includes a search engine and whether you can customize the search results.

Search Engine Submission

Will the product submit your online store to some or all of the major search engines and Web directories? Once your online store is created, you'll want to submit it to each of the major search engines and Internet directories (we discuss this issue in Chapter 6). Find out if the storefront service you are considering includes this capability, or whether you have to do it yourself.

Security Holes

When doing your research, we recommend you investigate whether the storefront solution you are considering has experienced any security problems or security breaches. You should also try to get a feel for how seriously the company takes security issues. You can often get this information by talking to previous or existing customers or by talking to people who have some expertise in the field of Internet security. One survey, by a company called Internet Security Systems (www.iss.net), found that eleven popular shopping cart software programs had security vulnerabilities. Even worse, one-third of the companies didn't take corrective action to fix the security holes when they were notified of the problems. One of the identified security vulnerabilities allowed a hacker to access an online store and modify the store's prices! Another problem involved a shopping cart program that had left a default password in place, making it easy for hackers to access credit card numbers.

A separate investigation by a United Kingdom–based company called Cerberus Information Security (www. cerberus-infosec.co.uk) found that a popular shopping cart program contained a secret password that could allow a hacker to gain access to customer credit card information and other confidential information. The password was put in place by the software developer to allow technical support staff to remotely access the software if they needed to. However, most of the online store owners using the shopping cart software were unaware that the password even existed! Of even greater concern was the fact that hackers could have easily found the secret password since it was easily identifiable in the computer code used to create the software. Thankfully, when this story broke, the company in question quickly fixed the software.

These two events alone underscore how important it is that you investigate the security record of any storefront solution you intend to use. You can read more about online security issues in Chapter 5, *Online Security Issues and Credit Card Fraud.*

Security Infrastructure

What type of measures has the storefront service taken to protect the orders your online store is receiving? Is the storefront service in compliance with the Visa "top ten" security rules that we list in Chapter 5? For example, are your customers' orders stored behind a firewall in an encrypted form so that they can't be accessed and read by a hacker? See Chapter 5 for a list of some of the questions you should ask any storefront service you are considering.

Shipping and Delivery Options

What shipping options are supported? Can you customize shipping charges any way you want or are you restricted in how you calculate shipping costs? This is one of the most important questions you can ask when choosing a storefront solution. As noted earlier in the chapter, this can be an extremely complex area – you will probably need the storefront software to support different shipping rates for different areas of the country and different parts of the world. In addition, you will probably need to charge different shipping rates depending upon the quantity and weight of the items that a customer has ordered.

Before choosing a storefront solution, find out what options are available to calculate shipping charges. For example, can you calculate shipping charges by weight, geographic location, price, and quantity ordered, or are you restricted to only one or a couple of these methods? Can you assign a separate shipping cost to each item in your online store? If there are significant limitations on how you calculate shipping costs, it might be very difficult for you to manage your shipping costs or present attractive shipping alternatives to customers. For example, one package we looked at didn't allow merchants to customize shipping rates by country. This is exactly the type of problem that you should watch out for if you intend to be doing a lot of international business.

Before you start shopping for storefront software, make sure you know how you intend to calculate shipping charges for your products. Once you've decided that, you can look for something that meets your requirements.

Shopping Cart

All storefront solutions include a shopping cart. As noted earlier in the chapter, this is the component of your store that allows customers to select the items they want to purchase. It's one of the most important aspects of your online store. Because the shopping cart is the last part of your store the customer sees before checking out, it is important that it be as comprehensive and user-friendly as possible.

Take some time to look at the different types of shopping carts that various online stores use, in order to get familiar with their features. Then, when comparing different storefront solutions, thoroughly investigate the shopping cart technology being used, and ask the following questions:

- What type of functionality does the shopping cart provide?
- What properties/attributes can items in the shopping cart have (e.g., size, weight, color, quantity)? Can you easily define your own attributes?
- Does the shopping cart always show the total value of the order, including taxes and shipping costs?
- How easy is it for customers to add items to and remove items from their shopping cart?
- How easy is it for customers to continue shopping once they've placed an item in their shopping cart?
- Is it easy for customers to change the quantity of items in their shopping cart? Is the total automatically recalculated?
- Can customers see a running summary of the items that are currently in their cart? Can they see this information while they are still shopping?

Shopping Mall

If you are using an entry-level browser-based storefront creation service, find out if the service operates an online mall that lists all of their merchants. If so, is there a cost to get listed in the mall? An online shopping mall can be a great way to attract customers to your online store. If the online storefront service doesn't operate an online shopping mall, does it do anything else to help its merchants find new customers and drive traffic to their Web sites?

Software Interface/Ease of Use

If you're not a computer whiz but you want to try to build your online store on your own, look for a storefront solution that is easy to use. Investigate the following issues:

- Are the software's features and commands well organized?
- Is the user interface intuitive?
- How easy is it to upload images to your online store?
- Is the interface easy to use or slow and clunky?
- How easy is it to add new products and categories? Can you add multiple products at once or do you have to add one product at a time?
- Does the software walk you through the process of setting up an online store or are you left to figure out the steps on your own?
- Does the software assume you have any technical knowledge?
- How useful are the help screens?
- How easy is it for you to make changes to your online store?

Taxation

Many state tax laws stipulate that you must collect sales tax for orders shipped to addresses in the state where your business is based. For this reason, make sure you choose a storefront solution that makes it easy for you to calculate taxes, when necessary, for the orders placed in your online store. Some storefront solutions maintain their own tax tables so you don't have to worry about charging the correct amount of sales tax. Depending on which state you operate out of, you may or may not be required to collect sales tax on the shipping cost as well as the cost of the product(s).

Just like shipping costs, taxation can be an extremely complex issue. Contact your state government and make sure you thoroughly understand what taxes you are responsible for collecting in your online store and under what circumstances you must collect them. Only then can you begin to shop for a suitable storefront package. Once you understand your tax obligations, make sure that the storefront package you select is capable of the level of customization that you require. Investigate the following issues when evaluating different storefront solutions:

- How easy is it to define different tax levels for different states?

- Is the tax automatically determined by the storefront software or do you have to manually input the appropriate tax rates?

- If the storefront software maintains its own tax tables, how frequently are they updated?

- Does the storefront software allow you to distinguish between taxable and non-taxable products?

- Can you apply tax to shipping costs?

e-Fact

In a survey of 64 U.S. cities, Washington, D.C. had the highest proportion of on online shoppers.
Source: Scarborough
Research
(www.scarborough.com)

Technical Support

What type of technical support is available? Is telephone support available or just e-mail support? Regardless of what storefront solution you select, make sure that quality technical support is available when you need it. If your online store stops working in the middle of the night, is there a twenty-four-hour technical support line that you can call for help, or are you on your own?

Thumbnail Images

A thumbnail image is a small version of a larger product image. Once you start working with your online store, you may want to create both large and small images of your products. For example, you may decide to use several thumbnail images on a single Web page so that customers can see the selection in a particular product category at a glance. They can then see a larger image of any product by clicking on it. Does the storefront software support thumbnail images? Does the software allow you to create and/or upload thumbnail images easily? Some storefront solutions may create thumbnail images for you, while others will require you to create the thumbnail images yourself and then upload them to your online store.

WYSIWYG (What You See Is What You Get) Editing

Does the software allow you to see what your online store will look like before you publish it on the Internet? This is an important feature because it allows you to see the effect of changes to your online store as you make them. Without WYSIWYG editing, you would have to publish your store on the Internet every time you made a change in order to see whether it had the desired effect.

IT'S NOT AN EASY DECISION

By this point, you should have a better understanding of the various methods you can use to build your online store and the range of features that are available. As you have no doubt discovered by now, there are a lot of issues that you need to consider.

The software solution you ultimately select doesn't have to include every feature or option that we've covered. Picking a good storefront solution usually involves making tradeoffs. You may be hard-pressed to find a storefront package that includes every feature you want in addition to ease-of-use and a high degree of customization. What you need to do is prioritize the features that are most important to you and pick the storefront package that suits your budget as well as your current and future needs.

Chapter 3

TIPS FOR BUILDING AN EFFECTIVE ONLINE STORE

90 percent of online shoppers consider good customer service to be critical when choosing a Web merchant.

Source: Forrester Research (www.forrester.com)

It has been said that it is just as easy to lose customers on the Web as it is to attract them. This means that setting up a store on the Internet involves far more than just creating an attractive Web site to sell your products.

It is all about exceeding expectations.

To understand why this is so, keep in mind what you are up against on the Internet. First, you are likely facing far more competition than you have ever had before. Not only that, but online shoppers are far less tolerant of mistakes, errors, and poor support than they might be in the "real world." These are two very important factors that you really need to appreciate.

Consider the competitive aspect of the Internet: regardless of what you sell, you will find yourself up against some stiff competition. The Internet is massively global, with the result that your competitors are no longer just the fellows down the street – you are now up against a variety of people and companies from around the world. This means that you will always be compared against the best, with the result that you will always have to strive to do better. This competitive nature of the Internet means that customers are unforgiving, always expecting the best deal and the best customer service.

The other important fact is that many customers on the Internet will expect the customer service you offer online to match or exceed that which you offer in the real world. Not only do consumers on the Internet feel empowered in a way that has not existed offline, but they actually have been empowered. They can almost instantly compare your prices and service with other organizations. They can quickly find out if previous customers have been satisfied with your company. And they can post their own complaints online if they are unsatisfied with your service or support. In short, the Internet has shifted the power in the buyer-seller relationship to the buyer. You cannot afford to slip up when it comes to your online store. Excellence in execution and delivery is a must. That is why one of the most important things you can do at this stage is understand some of the best practices in the execution and design of online stores.

In this chapter, we outline many of the important elements of a successful online store. We've conducted an exhaustive review of dozens of online stores and we've assembled a comprehensive checklist of all the components you need to think about. We use extensive examples to illustrate and support our recommendations.

The chapter reviews both the aesthetic and functional aspects of an online store. Many of the functional examples that we look at were developed by the merchants themselves or by e-commerce developers that they hired.

While some of the store functions that we recommend may be built into the products we discussed in Chapter 2, some of the features and capabilities that we discuss might require you to hire a programmer or Web designer in order to implement them within your online store.

We should also note that in our research, it was hard to find a single store that had all the functions that we discuss in this chapter. Indeed, we're not suggesting that you implement everything we suggest. To do so would be too expensive for many businesses and, of course, not every feature is appropriate for every industry. However, if we had to design the perfect online store, these are the elements and features that we would recommend.

Our discussion is organized into fifteen sections covering the following topics:

- Image and appearance
- Content

- Reliability
- Credibility, trust, and respect
- Product information
- Design and navigation
- Order information
- Shipping information
- Exchanges, returns, and warranties
- Pricing information
- Checkout procedures
- Customer service and support
- Channel integration
- Internationalization
- Online market research

Let's begin!

IMAGE AND APPEARANCE

Many of the online stores that rated highly during our research shared one important trait – they looked professional. They had a cutting-edge appearance, were obviously up-to-date, and used compelling design to lure us into the Web site.

The look of your store is vital when you're operating in an environment as competitive as the Internet. Customers will often make a decision about whether to enter an online store based on the look of its front page. On the Internet, image isn't everything, but it is an important component of an online retail strategy.

In the previous chapter, we pointed out that one of the limitations of using browser-based services to create a storefront design is they often don't give merchants much flexibility in design. If you have difficulty creating an eye-catching design yourself, you may want to invest in the services of a professional Web designer or e-commerce developer. Whether you use a browser-based service or high-end storefront

e-Fact

82% of surveyed small office/home office (SOHO) businesses and 61% of surveyed small businesses say the Internet has increased the need for them to improve customer service.

Source: Cahners In-Stat Group (www.instat.com)

software, consulting with a professional can give your online store a sharp appearance so it doesn't look passé or amateurish.

In effect, the front page of your online store is like the window display in a brick-and-mortar store. It is what lures the customer into the store. If the design of your online store is ineffective, it will likely stifle sales.

Let's look at two online small businesses that sell candles. Below are the home pages of Sugarcreek Candles (www.sugarcreekcandles.com) and Bjon's Candle Company (www.bjoncandles.com) as they appeared when we last visited them in late 2000:

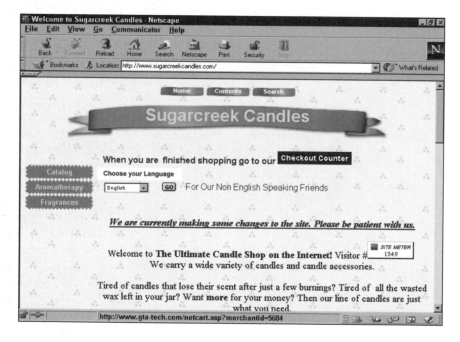

Which Web site is more effective at getting your attention? Clearly, the Bjon's Candle Web site is more appealing.

We're not suggesting that you spend tens of thousands of dollars designing your Web site. However, we want to point out the important role that design can play in making your online store successful. Stores that look exciting and are full of lots of activity will be more effective at getting people past the front page, just as interesting window displays lure people into retail stores. While this might not guarantee sales, it sure goes a long way toward turning browsers into buyers.

When WalMart (www.walmart.com) launched its new Web site in late 2000, the site's design created a lot of controversy. Here is what the home page looked like:

Many people said the new WalMart design had too much text and not enough graphics and product highlights. One analyst remarked, "They show you a map of the store, but they're not showing any products." As you can see from the previous screen, there's very little that draws you into the site. Compare WalMart's design to Target's Web site (www.target.com) at the time, which featured eye-catching graphics and product specials right on the home page.

In its defense, WalMart argued that it wanted to avoid fancy graphics and technology and focus on helping users to find products on the site, especially given the wide range of products that WalMart sells. Critics are in fact divided on whether WalMart's site is flashy enough to increase sales. Both sides make good points, although we tend to agree with those who find WalMart's site a little lackluster. It doesn't do much to engage you. This is extremely important because in order for a Web design to be effective, it must drive sales.

Web site design, user interfaces, and usability are complex issues that are far beyond the scope of this book, and the debate that raged around the WalMart site shows that there are no right answers. Ultimately, however, it's up to you to decide what balance you want to have between compelling graphics and ease of navigation.

That is why you might consider hiring someone who specializes in Web user interface issues if you need help designing an effective user interface for your Web site. If you already have a Web site, Web usability firms can help you test it and identify design problems that may be causing you to lose sales. There are several companies that specialize in this area. Two of the best known are the Nielsen Norman Group (www.nngroup.com) and Creative Good (www.creativegood.com). Companies such as IBM can also help you with usability testing. The services offered by Web usability firms are usually targeted at large businesses rather than small firms, so be aware that retaining this type of expertise may not be inexpensive.

If you are interested in learning more about effective Web site design and other usability issues related to the Web, Jakob Neilsen (www.useit.com) and Creative Good (www.creativegood.com) maintain two excellent resources. Both sites contain a wealth of information on how to design an effective and customer-friendly Web site for your customers. Goodexperience.com also has a free newsletter that you can sign up for.

CONTENT

If you want to maximize sales on your Web site, it is important to update the content on your Web site regularly and refresh the products featured on your front page.

Change the content on your home page just as often as you would change the window display in a retail store. Coordinate your products with the seasons or specific holidays as applicable. This keeps your Web site looking fresh, and lets customers know that your online store is very much alive and in business. For example, notice how CierraCandles (www.cierracandles.com) updated its Web site during the month of October, to remind customers that Halloween was rapidly approaching:

It doesn't take a lot of work to update your Web site with a little bit of current news, as in the example above. In fact, if the content on your Web site doesn't change from week to week, customers may begin to wonder whether your online store is still running.

Even simple modifications to your Web site like changing the color combinations on your home page or listing the current month, as Clinique (www.clinique.com) has done, can reinforce the fact that your Web site is being kept current:

There are other approaches to keeping your content fresh. The most popular technique is to spotlight different products on your home page each month. FTD (www.ftd.com) features different floral bouquets for each month/season:

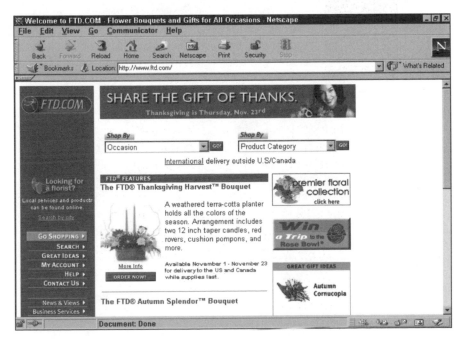

Similarly, Eddie Bauer (www.eddiebauer.com) regularly features images on its home page that correspond to the season and time of year:

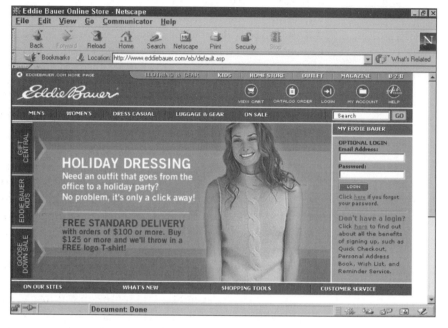

Some storefront software programs allow you to highlight and feature new additions to your store easily, so you can quickly and effectively give a high profile to new products.

Whatever you choose to do, it is important that the content on your home page be constantly changing.

RELIABILITY

When you operate a store on the Web, any downtime you experience can cripple your reputation – and your bottom line. By downtime, we mean any period of time that your store is unavailable to your customers due to technical or other problems that do not allow them to buy on your site, such as problems with the company that processes your online credit card transactions. If customers who come to your store to shop are turned away (i.e., they receive an error message that they are unable to access your store) because you are having technical problems, they may never come back.

As a classic example of what can happen, eBay (www.ebay.com), one of the largest auction sites on the Internet, experienced several computer crashes in 1999 that shut down parts of the site, angering tens of thousands of customers. Frustrated with ongoing technical problems, many once-loyal customers began taking their business elsewhere and auctioning their products on competing Web sites. As if that weren't enough punishment, eBay sustained financial losses of between $3 million and $5 million because of the business it lost during the shutdown. That figure is exceptionally high because of the high volume of business that eBay does on the Web, but there is an important lesson to be learned here.

Sometimes site availability problems aren't related to technical glitches but are caused by an overload of customers – due to the company not putting in place enough server capacity or enough Internet connectivity to support massive numbers of customers. This happened to Toys-R-Us during the 1999 Christmas holiday season. Many online shoppers couldn't get into the Toys-R-Us Web site because the site was so busy.

Once your business begins to depend on the Web, technical problems can be extremely costly. In particular, it is difficult to win back customers who have lost confidence in your business because of these problems.

Online merchants take this issue very seriously. When Amazon.com (www.amazon.com) experienced one of its first site crashes, the company offered customers a 10 percent discount off the purchase of books in an effort to repair the damage to its image and reputation.

It isn't just your store that could go down – it could be the company that processes the credit card transactions on your store. As you will see in Chapter 4, many organizations may be involved in such transactions, and problems with any one of them could cause problems within your store and prevent you from accepting credit card payments from your customers. One of the authors of this book once experienced a problem with his payment gateway that lasted an entire weekend; only when the payment gateway's staff returned to the office on Monday morning was his site fully operational once again.

How do you avoid these types of problems? When you are looking for a company to host your online store or process your credit card transactions, make sure you thoroughly investigate its reputation and track record. Find out what its policies are for support, whether support is reachable twenty-four hours a day, and what type of support is given outside normal business hours. (Some companies have scaled-back support in after business hours, which can make it difficult to get some of your problems resolved.)

Not only that, but ask for references. E-mail people who currently use the company's hosting services and ask for feedback. Ask the company directly about its technical record. Follow the same procedure if you're thinking of using a browser-based storefront service such as Yahoo! Store (www.yahoo.com) or FreeMerchant (www. freemerchant.com), or shopping cart software such as QuikStore (www.quikstore.com) or PDG Shopping Cart (www.pdgsoft.com).

How to Keep Your Web Site Up and Running

One way to make sure your online store doesn't go down without you knowing about it is to use a service like WatchDog (watchdog.mycomputer.com) that will constantly monitor your Web site and alert you via e-mail or text-based pager if it goes down for any reason. WatchDog costs between $299 and $999 a year, depending on how frequently you want it to check your Web site's availability. A service like this is certainly a good investment, since it can help you to identify technical problems with your Web site before you start to lose a lot of business!

If your online store does go down, more often than not the problem will be minor and you can get the site up and running quickly. But what happens if there is a serious computer problem and your online store provider loses all of your customer records and/or your entire online store due to a virus or other event? Hopefully this won't happen to you, but in case it does, make sure that you have your entire online store backed up and stored off-site so that you can recreate it if necessary.

Finally, make sure that your online store can accommodate spikes in traffic. Find out how many credit card transactions your online store is capable of processing simultaneously and determine how many online shoppers your Web site can accommodate at any one time. Proper

e-Fact

Surfers who visit a Web site's customer service area account for only 39% of online shoppers, but this group accounts for 50% of total consumer online spending.

Source: Cyber Dialogue (www.cyberdialogue.com)

planning will help you to avoid capacity problems and the lost business that usually results.

CREDIBILITY, TRUST, AND RESPECT

How important is credibility on the Internet? Extremely. Given the many horrible experiences that customers have had shopping on the Internet in recent years, with problems ranging from late deliveries to unanswered e-mail messages, online shoppers are most likely to do business with those companies that they know and trust. They will also avoid companies that have a notoriously poor record in customer service.

This underscores the importance of providing your customers with an online experience that will generate positive word of mouth. One of the biggest challenges for any online store is winning the trust of customers. This sense of trust will be based on five elements:

1. Assure your online customers that you are a real and credible business and that they will receive the products they have ordered.

2. Assure your customers that any private information they give you over the Internet will not be sold, misused, or inadvertently made available to anyone outside your organization.

3. Provide a safe shopping guarantee that customers can rely on.

4. Explain what you've done to protect your customers.

5. Take appropriate steps to protect your Web site from potential security breaches.

We discuss each of these issues in more depth below.

Establish Real-World Credibility

Building credibility with your customers is particularly important considering the number of Internet businesses that have gone bankrupt or shut down. That fact, coupled with the delivery problems that many online retailers have had, has left many consumers wary of shopping on the Internet. Many online retailers have had trouble getting products delivered to consumers on time, especially during busy periods such as Christmas. In fact, the Federal Trade Commission fined seven e-commerce firms a total of $1.5 million in 2000 for failing to deliver online orders to customers when promised, and for failing to notify customers that their deliveries would be late during the 1999 holiday season. Toys-R-Us, one of many companies that ran into delivery problems during the 1999 Christmas season, became known as "Toys-R-Late" when it was unable to deliver hundreds of products in time for Christmas. One of the lessons learned by online retailers that fateful year was never to promise your customers delivery dates that you won't be able to meet.

Consumers may also be wary, and legitimately so, of doing business with a Web site or company that they have no experience with. If you are a small business that doesn't have a recognized brand name, most customers will not be familiar with your company and its reputation, and may therefore be reluctant to do business with you on the Web. Compounding this problem is that, over the years, there have been many reports of fraud on the Internet involving Web sites that accepted payments and then never delivered the products that were ordered. News reports about such activities have many online shoppers on their guard. When they visit your Web site, they may be wondering whether it is a real, legitimate business. How do customers know your Web site won't vanish the following day, along with their payment?

We see four effective ways for you to build real-world credibility into your online store:

1. Provide background information.

2. Provide customer testimonials.

3. Apply to seal programs.

4. Use merchant rating programs.

Provide Background Information

First, include a section at your online store where customers can evaluate your company and its track record.

Regardless of the number of years that your company has been in business, provide customers with information about your real-world facilities and locations, your street address (not just a P.O. box!), your telephone number, and an overview of your management team. A toll-free number is a good idea as well. If the company has been in business for many years, highlight this fact on your Web site. If your company is a relatively new organization without a strong track record, this section can still make a big difference.

In addition, provide details as to your membership in local chambers of commerce or other business organizations. The more information you provide, the better. And it should be the type of information that customers can verify if they want to.

Many online stores create an "About Us" section on their Web site to communicate information about their organizations. This section usually provides information about the company, its management team, perhaps a message from the company president, press releases, and any other pertinent facts about the company that help to establish its real-world credibility.

Remember, on the Web, customers have no way of knowing whether your company is credible unless you tell them! We've come across many online stores that don't have any background information on the business at all. Leaving this type of information off your Web site could drive visitors away.

A good example of an "About Us" section is the one found at Silvergiftstore.com (www.silvergiftstore.com), an online retailer of silver products. Customers who click on the "About Us" button on the home page are given a detailed history of the company, including a picture of the company founder. The owners of this Web store clearly recognize the importance of giving a human context to their Internet presence:

> **e-Fact**
>
> *Delivery issues are the primary reason why customers contact online merchants.*
>
> Source: Jupiter Research (www.jup.com)

Another excellent example of an online store that builds real-world credibility is Main St. Toys (www.mainsttoys.com), a Lindsborg, Kansas, retail store that sells toys on the Internet. The site includes an overview of the store's philosophy, a picture of the family that owns the store, and even a picture of the store so that customers can see that it is a real organization:

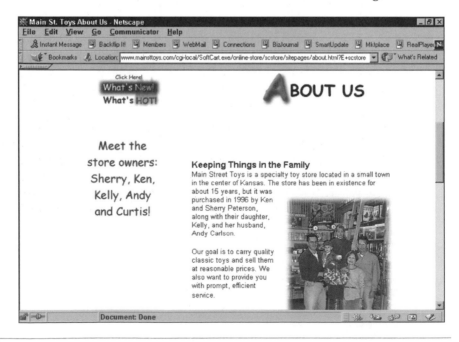

Background information such as this will definitely help put skeptical shoppers at ease!

Provide Customer Testimonials

You should also consider including testimonials or references from customers who have purchased products from you over the Internet and who have been happy with your service. Kimmys Kreations (www.kimmy.bigstep.com), an online store that sells handcrafted pet-related ornaments, uses this strategy very effectively on its Web site, which contains an impressive collection of testimonials from its customers:

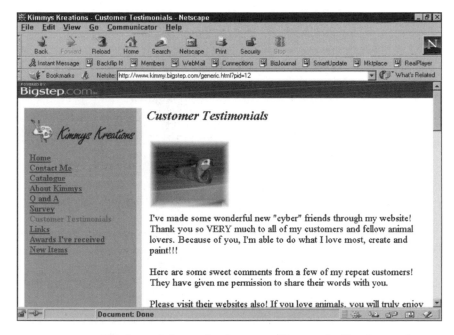

Testimonials are both compelling and effective and can help boost the confidence of any shoppers who may be hesitant to do business with you. We also found it impressive that the owner of Kimmys Creations says that she has gotten permission to share the customers' words. To us, that shows the company cares about the people it is dealing with.

Apply to Seal Programs

In addition to testimonials and including an "About Us" section on your site, consider applying to a seal program such as TRUSTe (www.truste.org) or BBB*OnLine* (www.bbbonline.com). TRUSTe, for example, is a program that oversees the privacy practices of Web sites. To join the TRUSTe program, a Web site owner must submit its privacy policy, complete a self-assessment questionnaire, and sign a license agreement stating that it has agreed to follow TRUSTe's privacy principles and comply with TRUSTe's oversight and consumer resolution process. TRUSTe charges an annual license fee which ranges from several hundred dollars to several thousand dollars depending on the organization's annual revenue.

e-Fact

40% of Internet users believe that they will do "almost all" of their shopping online within 10 years.

Source: AOL (www.aol.com)/ Roper Starch (www.roper.com) Cyberstudy

Once an organization is admitted into the TRUSTe program, it can display the TRUSTe logo on its Web site (shown at left), which lets customers know that it is operating in accordance with TRUSTe's privacy principles.

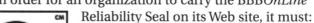

BBB*OnLine* is a different initiative run by the Council of Better Business Bureaus. It consists of two online seal programs, a Reliability Seal program, and a Privacy Seal program. Both seals are shown at left.

In order for an organization to carry the BBB*OnLine* Reliability Seal on its Web site, it must:

- be a member of the local Better Business Bureau;

- have been in business for at least one year;

- agree to abide by Better Business Bureau standards of truth in advertising;

- have a satisfactory complaint handling record with the Better Business Bureau; and

- commit to work with the Better Business Bureau to resolve consumer disputes that arise over goods or services promoted or advertised on its site.

In essence, the BBB*OnLine* Reliability Seal lets consumers know that the Web site carrying the seal has met Better Business Bureau's standards for reliable Web sites.

The Privacy Seal program, on the other hand, is designed to protect consumer privacy. To qualify for the BBB*OnLine* Privacy Seal, an organization must:

- post a privacy policy on its Web site telling consumers what personal information is being collected, how it will be used, and choices they have in terms of use;

- abide by its posted privacy policy;

- agree to a comprehensive independent verification of its privacy policy by BBB*OnLine*; and

- participate in BBB*OnLine*'s dispute resolution service.

Both seal programs involve a fee. The cost of the BBB*OnLine* Reliability Seal depends on the number of employees in the organization, whereas the cost of the BBB*OnLine* Privacy Seal varies according to the organization's annual sales. TRUSTe and BBB*OnLine* are just two of many seal programs operating on the Internet. Others include WebTrust, operated by the American Institute of Certified Public Accountants, and BetterWeb, operated by PricewaterhouseCoopers.

Seal Programs for Online Stores

BBB*OnLine*	www.bbbonline.com
BetterWeb (PricewaterhouseCoopers)	www.betterweb.com
TRUSTe	www.truste.org
CPA WebTrust	www.webtrust.org

Use Merchant Rating Programs

Another way to build trust with online shoppers is to join one of the merchant rating services that exist on the Web. These services rate customer satisfaction with online stores. They do this by asking customers to fill out a survey after they make a purchase from participating merchants who have agreed to let their customers be interviewed.

BizRate.com (www.bizrate.com) is the most popular rating service for online stores. Online shoppers can visit BizRate.com's Web site and review satisfaction ratings from thousands of online stores. The ratings measure customer satisfaction across ten dimensions of service ranging from product selection to customer support. Customers can look up ratings for individual merchants:

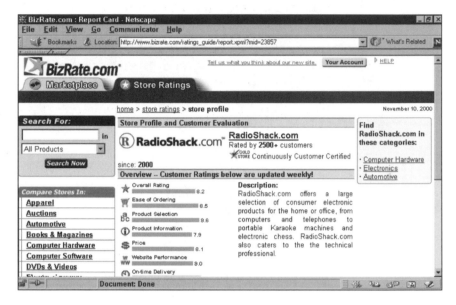

Or they can browse through product categories to find the online store that has received the best ratings from customers:

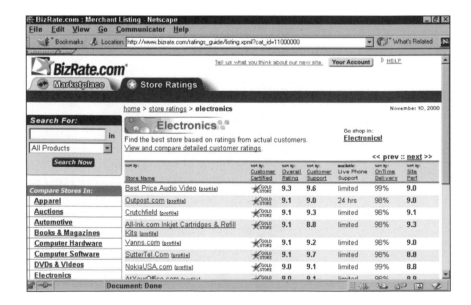

Online stores can sign up for BizRate.com's customer ratings service on the BizRate.com Web site. There is no cost to participate in the program. Participating merchants can display the BizRate.com logo on their home page, as Pacific Sunwear (www.pacsun.com) has done, to increase consumer confidence in their online stores:

Why would you want to use such a service? By giving prospective shoppers access to your customer ratings, you demonstrate your organization's commitment to superior customer service. After all, if you provide excellent customer service, you should have no fear of making your ratings publicly available through a service like BizRate.com. Naturally, ratings from customers who have already made purchases from you can be a very effective tool in winning credibility and trust from new shoppers who may not be familiar with your name or reputation.

While BizRate.com is by far the most popular rating service for online stores, a number of other similar rating services exist, including ePublicEye.com, a ratings service targeted at small and mid-sized online merchants, and WebWatchDog.

Merchant Rating Services for Online Stores

BizRate.com	www.bizrate.com
ePublicEye.com	www.epubliceye.com
WebWatchDog	www.webwatchdog.com

Limitations of Seal Programs and Ratings Services

The problem with seal programs and ratings services is that there's no guarantee that they will increase consumer confidence in your online store or increase the amount of business you get. Seal programs in particular have a number of limitations.

Hampering the success of seal programs is the fact that they're poorly understood by consumers or have credibility problems, a situation compounded by the many different seal programs vying for attention. Programs like BBB*OnLine* clearly have well-defined procedures for screening applicants, but many of the other seal programs on the Internet hand out seals much more liberally and may not have the financial resources or infrastructure to properly oversee compliance, rendering the programs essentially meaningless. One of the largest seal programs on the Internet, the TRUSTe program we described earlier, has come under attack for being too closely tied to its sponsors, which include big organizations such as Microsoft, Intel, and America Online. Hence, it's not surprising that many consumers have grown skeptical of seal programs and what they stand for.

The second problem is that seal programs don't guarantee a satisfactory online shopping experience. They let customers know that your online store has agreed to abide by the program's standards, but the seal itself doesn't guarantee that the customer's online shopping experience with your firm will be problem-free.

A third problem is that some vendors simply copy the logo and display it on their Web site without going through the seal program. This abuse devalues the benefit of participating in the program.

Lastly, don't overdo it. Rather than blanket your online store with seals, be selective about which seal programs you apply to, while keeping in mind that the financial return

> **e-Fact**
>
> *Brazil accounts for over half of all e-commerce revenues in Latin America.*
> Boston Consulting Group (www.bcg.com)/ Visa (www.visa.com)

from investing in these programs isn't something you can easily measure. Before applying to any seal program, make sure you understand how it works, what guidelines you have to adhere to, and whether a fee is involved.

Create a Privacy Policy

Many online shoppers are concerned about their privacy when they visit merchant Web sites.

In fact, for many consumers, privacy is a bigger concern on the Internet than security. For this reason, you should tell online shoppers how you intend to handle any personal information that you collect from them on your site. For example, if a customer fills out a survey on your Web site or buys something from you, how do you intend to use the information that customers give you?

If you plan on selling it or making it available to other third parties, think again. Once customers believe that their mailing address, telephone number, or any other information that they've given you might be sold to other organizations, they may be reluctant to do business with you. Misusing customer data in any way could be the kiss of death for your online store. You should also be careful about tracking what your customers do on your Web site. Several online retailers have been berated publicly for tracking customer activity on their Web sites without disclosing the practice to their customers. In fact, Toys-R-Us faced a class-action lawsuit in 2000 alleging that the company was violating its own privacy policy by allowing a marketing company to build personal profiles of its customers.

People are very concerned about privacy online – and rightly so.

Online shoppers are often worried that their personal information may be revealed or made accessible through a Web site, either on purpose or through error. There is also a great deal of concern that many companies collect private information online, often through the use of questionnaires, and then misuse it for various purposes, such as reselling it to other organizations.

To win the trust of online shoppers, you should prepare a privacy policy or customer information policy for your organization and

e-Fact

The number of domain names registered on the Internet passed the 30 million mark for the first time in September 2000.

Source: NetNames
(www.netnames.com)

post it on your Web site. The purpose of a privacy policy is to let customers know what types of information you collect from them, and advise them of how you intend to use that information. Your privacy policy should also tell customers what they need to do in order to delete their personal information from your records if they so desire.

When developing your own privacy policy, it helps to examine the privacy policies of other online stores. For example, the privacy policy posted on the Gap Web site (www.gap.com) says that the company does "not sell or rent the information" that customers provide to them but that the company does "share your information with third parties under certain circumstances":

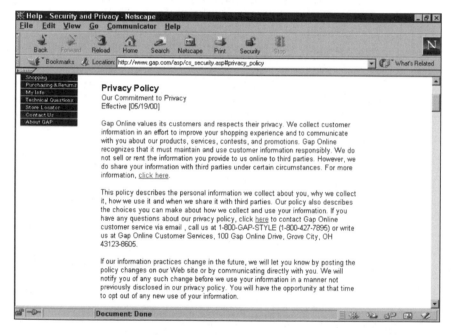

If you expect your Web site to attract children, it is a good idea to address this specifically both in your privacy policy as well as on any forms or surveys that you have on your Web site. Children's privacy on the Internet is a concern to many parents and many organizations make sure this issue is sufficiently covered in their privacy policy. For example, Gap's privacy policy states, "Consistent with the Children's Online Privacy Protection Act of 1998, we will never knowingly request personally identifiable information from anyone under the age of thirteen without prior verifiable parental consent. If we become aware that a subscriber is under the age of thirteen and has registered without prior verifiable parental consent, we will remove his or her personally identifiable registration information from our files."

For another good example of a privacy policy, visit the RadioShack Web site (www.radioshack.com):

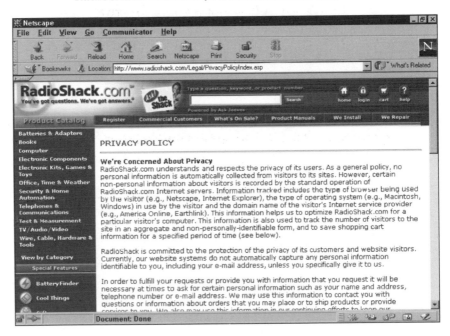

Like Gap, RadioShack explains in detail what information it collects from customers who visit the RadioShack.com site. RadioShack's privacy policy states, "We may, from time to time, need to place identification information or application programs on your computer to enable you to properly access, display or read our catalogue or other information or to permit information to follow you from page to page (in order to use a virtual shopping cart for example). This information may sometimes be called 'cookies.' Also, applications sometimes known as 'applets' might be downloaded to your computer to better display the information you requested from our website."

e-Fact

Nearly all consumers who use Web-based customer service say that 24-hour access is the top reason for doing so.

Source: Society of Consumer Affairs Professionals in Business (www.socap.org)

The approach you take in your own privacy policy is entirely up to you, and will depend on the types of products you sell and the types of information you plan to collect from your customers. Privacy policies aren't really optional anymore – they're an essential part of doing business online. If you need help creating a privacy policy for your Web site, try experimenting with Microsoft bCentral's Privacy Policy Wizard (privacy.bcentral.com):

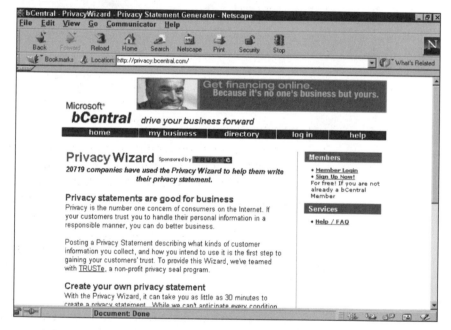

For additional help developing a privacy policy for your Web site, visit the TRUSTe Web site (www.truste.org), where you'll find a Model Privacy Statement that you can tailor to your own requirements:

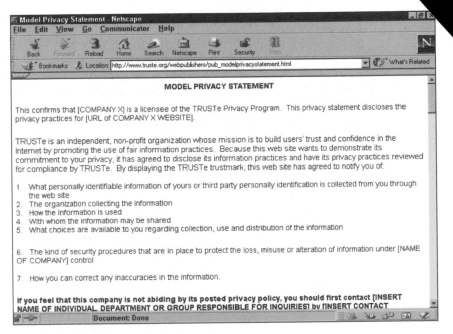

Create a Safe Shopping Guarantee

It is proven that fears about credit card security are hindering the growth of online shopping. According to one study, 53 percent of online consumers in the United States say that they are concerned that their financial or other sensitive information may be stolen as it is being transmitted to a Web site. Consumers in other countries have also expressed reservations about shopping on the Internet because they are concerned that their credit card numbers could possibly be stolen.

What most customers don't realize, however, is that under the Fair Credit Billing Act, it is unlawful for a bank in the United States to hold a customer liable for more than $50 of fraudulent charges on their credit cards. For example, if a thief stole a customer's credit card and used it to purchase $1,000 of merchandise, the customer would only be responsible for $50 of the $1,000 total. This fact alone should put your online shoppers at ease.

In fact, since all three major cards now have a zero-liability policy, this fact may be moot. Even so, the issue can remain a concern with many shoppers given that policies are continually evolving, so you want to do your best to reassure them. Hence, in the event that a bank does hold a customer responsible for any part of the $50 maximum liability, many online stores have adopted a policy stating that they will cover the liability as long as the unauthorized activity is clearly the fault of the merchant. This is called a "Safe Shopping Guarantee." It means that there is no financial risk for the customer to shop on your online store because in the event of fraud, if the customer is held liable for any part of the $50 maximum liability and the fraud is due to a security breach on your online store, you will pay it.

Many online stores have adopted Safe Shopping Guarantees to make customers feel more comfortable shopping online. At a minimum, point out to your customers that they are only liable for $50 of any fraudulent activity that occurs on their credit card, by law. For an example of such a policy, visit the online store of the Michigan Bulb Co. (www.michiganbulb.com), a company that sells garden products:

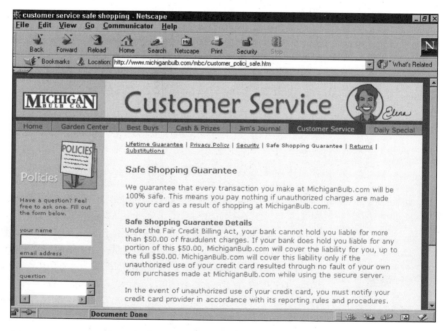

A similar policy is in place at the online store of the Great Lakes Popcorn Co. in Port Clinton, Ohio (www. greatlakespopcorn.com):

Safe shopping guarantees are fairly standard on the Internet, and you should strongly consider implementing a similar policy on your Web store.

Explain What You've Done to Protect Your Customers

In addition to a security guarantee, your Web site should provide an overview of the encryption method your Web site uses and explain the measures that you have taken to protect the transmission of credit card data. In short, tell your customers why it is safe to shop on your Web site. You don't need to get technical. The idea here is to explain, in layman's terms, how any personal or financial information that customers may send you over the Internet will be protected. You may also want to include information about what procedures you have adopted internally to prevent unauthorized employees from gaining access to confidential customer information.

For a good example of how you might approach a security information page on your Web site, take a look at the online store of Dickson Supply Co. (www.dicksonsupply. com). It features a page called "Some Features to Make You a More Comfortable Shopper" that describes what encryption is and how it is used to protect customer information:

We also suggest you have a look at the online store of Molecular Arts Corporation (www.molecular.com), a company that sells scientific and technical software on the Internet. Its Web site does an excellent job explaining to customers why they should feel safe ordering products from the company online:

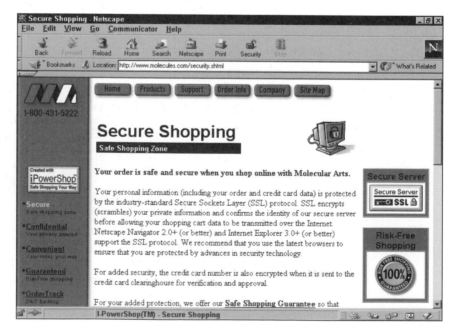

The company has also provided an extensive page of information to try to minimize customer fears about online credit card security:

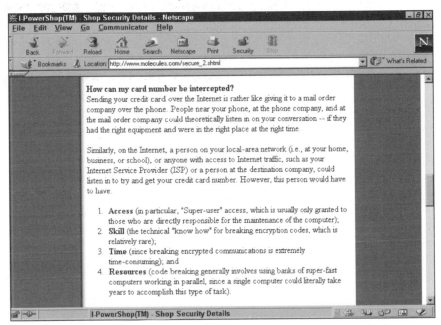

To emphasize how unlikely it is that a customer's credit card number would be stolen as it is being transmitted to the company's Web site, the company states, "Shopping over the Internet is as safe as shopping at a store in your neighborhood. We order products online all the time, both as a company and as individuals. When we use a credit card to buy something online, we feel at least as safe as we would using one in a store or restaurant. Put another way, you have a higher probability of being hit by lightning as you're crossing the street than having your credit card number intercepted from a secure Internet link." This is very true, which is why it's important to communicate this information to your online customers!

e-Fact

On Monday, December 11, 2000, online sales hit $222.4 million – an unprecedented high for a single day.
Source: BizRate.com
(www.bizrate.com)

Guard against Security Breaches

The final step in building credibility for your online store is ensuring that your Web site is not susceptible to the accidental release or disclosure of private information that you have collected from your customers. You need to make certain that your Web site has no security problems or weaknesses that might allow someone, whether unintentionally or illegally, to gain access to any of your customer data through the Internet.

If you were ever to have a security breach on your Web site, it could scare off potential customers and tarnish your organization's reputation.

If your online store is hosted by an Internet service provider or Web hosting service, find out what precautions it has taken to protect your store from any possible security problems. In Chapter 5, *Online Security Issues and Credit Card Fraud*, we provide a list of some of the security-related questions that you should ask the companies that will be supplying your online storefront software and hosting your online store on the Internet (as we discussed in Chapter 2, the same company may or may not provide both services, depending on what type of solution you use to set up your online store). As we explain in Chapter 5, many of the security problems that arise on the Internet are due to human error, negligence, or storefront software that has security weaknesses.

An organization can do itself incalculable damage by making private information accessible online, intentionally or not, or by misusing any private information that it collects. Hence, you must work hard to ensure that those who visit your Web site, and hence your store, believe that their private information is safe with you and that you respect the private nature of the relationship.

One way to check the quality of the security on your Web site is to hire security experts or "ethical hackers" who review your Web site for any unplugged holes or potential security problems. Security experts can be hired through companies such as IBM (www.ibm.com) or Ernst and Young (www.ey.com), but recognize that retaining such an expert is expensive.

The Most Common Complaints Voiced by Online Shoppers

- Gift was out-of-stock (62%)
- Product not delivered on time (40%)
- Delivery costs too high (38%)
- Connection/download problems (36%)
- No status report on purchase (i.e., customer did not receive an e-mail acknowledgement of their order) (28%)
- Selections were limited (27%)
- Web site difficult to navigate (26%)
- Not enough information (25%)
- Prices were not competitive (22%)
- Not enough gift ideas (16%)

Source: Accenture (formerly Andersen Consulting) survey of online shoppers after the 1999 holiday season (www.accenture.com)

PRODUCT INFORMATION

This section reviews some of the product-related issues you need to think about for your online store. We discuss the following eleven issues:

- Detailed product information
- Large images
- Real-time inventory information
- Brand names
- Holiday and special event hints
- Panoramic views
- Color accuracy
- Sizing information
- Online wish lists
- Favorite items lists
- Editorial integrity

Detailed Product Information

Don't stop at a simple one-line description of the products that you are selling.

Some of the most effective online stores we have seen are those that provide product descriptions that are both comprehensive and compelling. In other words, an effective product description should be persuasive as well as descriptive. Remember that you're trying to sell the product! Give the customer reasons to purchase it. If necessary, hire a copywriter with a flair for the English language to write short paragraph-length descriptions of each of your products for your Web site.

For an example of effective copywriting, browse some of the product descriptions on the Web site of Gardener's Supply Company (www.gardeners.com). You might think that there isn't a lot to be said about a garden hose, but take a look at the following description for an indoor/outdoor watering hose:

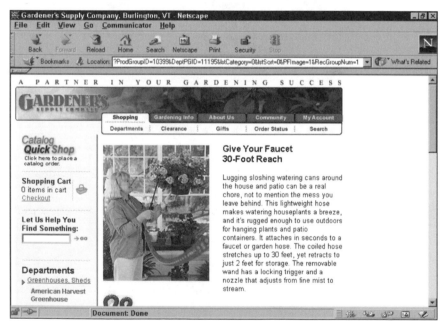

The copywriting is designed to make the customer say, "Yeah, I need that!"

Large Images

e-Fact

The top priority for online gift buyers is that the gift arrives on time.

Source: Forrester Research (www.forrester.com)

To minimize product returns and avoid disappointing your customers, give your customers the option to view enlarged pictures of the products you sell on your Web site. This will allow them to see product details and features that may not be visible in smaller images. For example, underneath product pictures on the JCPenney Web site (www.jcpenney.com) is a link that says, "click to view larger image":

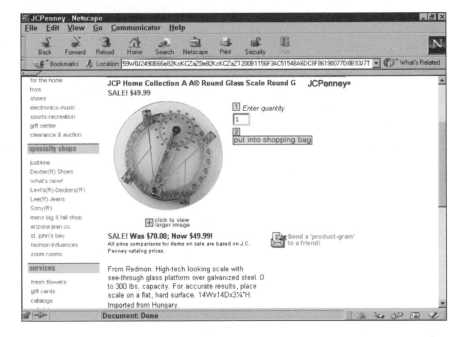

Customers who click on the link see a larger picture of the product:

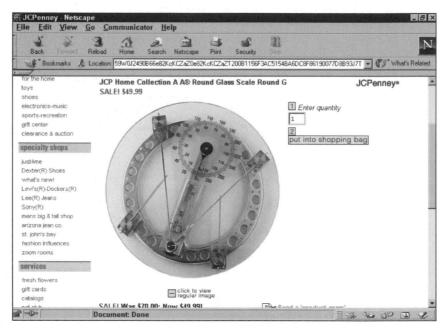

Rather than taking customers to a separate Web page to see the enlarged picture, consider opening a separate, smaller window onscreen. This technique is used by the Disney Store (www.disney.com). For example, the following page from the Disney Store shows a picture of a Mickey Mouse toaster:

Clicking on the "Zoom" button underneath the product picture makes a larger image pop up in a new window on the customer's screen. This is called a pop-up window:

Real-Time Inventory Information

There's nothing more disappointing than ordering a product on the Web and finding out afterwards that the product is on back order or out of stock. This happened to one of the authors of this book when he placed an order for a large-size T-shirt on an online store. A couple of days after placing the order and receiving an e-mailed acknowledgement, he was contacted by the online store and notified that there were no more large T-shirts in stock. He was also told that the online store would be out of stock of large T-shirts indefinitely. It was quite a frustrating, and disappointing, experience. Why accept an order for a product you know you don't have in stock? Unfortunately, many online stores don't provide their customers with real-time inventory information. This means that when an item sells out, the product continues to be displayed on the Web site as if it were still available.

> **e-Fact**
>
> *Online retailers will generate $36 billion in revenue from the sale of gifts in 2005.*
> Source: Forrester Research (www.forrester.com)

Give your customers peace of mind by letting them know right away if a product displayed on your Web site is out of stock or on back order. In Chapter 2, we explained that some online storefront solutions include inventory control features that will remove an item from your online store once you run out of stock. Other storefront packages will allow you to display an "out of stock" message when the supply of a product runs out. Take advantage of features like this – they will definitely save your customers a lot of grief.

For example, Gap's online store (www.gap.com) will actually notify a customer should a product not be available for immediate delivery:

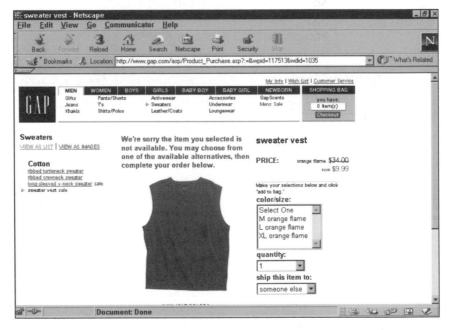

Talbots (www.talbots.com) does the same on its Web site:

If a product is in stock, you should display an "in stock" message beside or underneath the item so that customers know the product is available for immediate ordering and shipping. Office Depot uses this technique on its online store (www.officedepot.com). On the screen below, an "In stock" message appears near the price and unit information for the product:

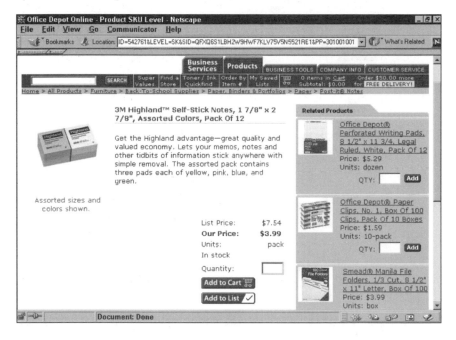

Brand Names

Depending on the type of business that you're in, carrying brand names that shoppers are familiar with may make them more likely to do business with you. Why? If you carry products and brand names that are relatively unknown, you may have a hard time building confidence in the products you sell.

If you carry well-known brand names that are backed by strong guarantees or warranties, communicate this information to your customers, as outdoor gear retailer REI (www.rei.com) has done:

This will help you build customer trust in your online store.

Holiday and Special Event Hints

If you sell products that make great gifts for Father's Day, Mother's Day, Valentine's Day, or any other holiday or special occasion, make sure you draw your customers' attention to these important dates as they approach. This can be accomplished with a simple graphic on your home page that mentions the special day.

For example, suppose it is two weeks before Father's Day. Shoppers on your Web site may not even be thinking about buying a Father's Day gift from your online store, but a quick reminder that the date is fast approaching may help to generate additional sales. Of course, you don't need to restrict yourself to popular holidays. For example, the online store for OfficeMax (www.officemax.com) placed a graphic on its front page that read, "Boss' Day is October 16th – Gift Ideas Under $30.00," as seen in the top right-hand corner of the following screen:

e-Fact

By 2003, 80-90% of firms in the United States will buy online.
Source: eMarketer
(www.emarketer.com)

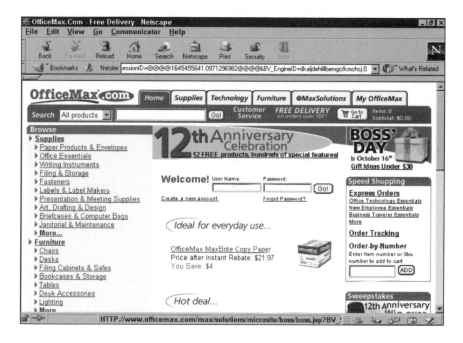

Customers who clicked on the graphic were shown a selection of gift ideas for their bosses:

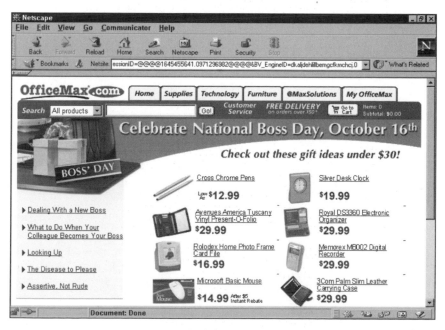

It's a great way to boost sales in your online store!

Panoramic Views

If you are selling products that can be difficult to visualize in a two-dimensional format, or if you're simply interested in making online shopping more exciting for your customers, you may want to consider allowing customers to view a 360-degree panoramic view of these products. The Sharper Image (www.sharperimage.com) is one of several online retailers using 3-D images on its Web site. Using technology from Viewpoint Corporation (www.viewpoint.com), The Sharper Image allows customers to rotate a product on the screen so that they can see how it looks from several angles, including the front, back, bottom, and top:

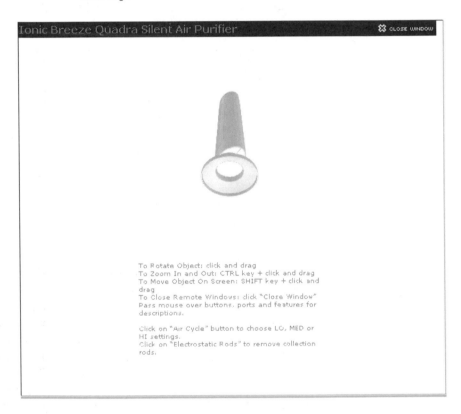

FAO Schwarz (www.fao.com) uses similar technology on its Web site, provided by a company called Pulse Entertainment (www.pulse3d.com). Customers can enter a virtual playroom and view different products at 360-degree angles:

Neiman Marcus (www.neimanmarcus.com) provides an even more advanced example of how 3-D technology can be used to enrich the online shopping experience. Neiman Marcus used technology from RichFX (www.richfx.com) to create a three-dimensional online boutique for shoe designer Manolo Blahnik. Using a mouse as well as "left" and "right" navigation buttons that are provided onscreen, customers use computer-generated video to browse the entire store, which is modeled after Blahnik's real store in Manhattan. Shoppers can click on a particular shoe to see a close-up view, just as they would in a real store. To simulate a real store, virtual sunlight or moonlight shines through the windows depending on what time of the day the site is accessed!

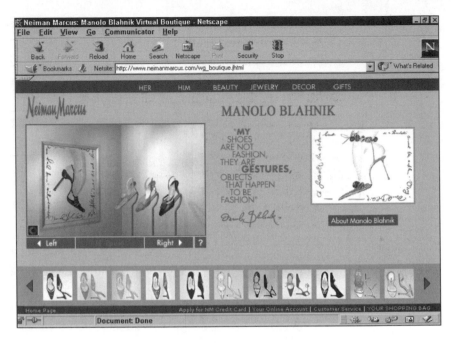

Some people think that 3-D technology is gimmicky and won't do anything to increase online sales. However, it certainly makes online shopping more fun and exciting. Moreover, as online shoppers increasingly use high-speed Internet connections, 3-D images will make the whole online shopping experience more user-friendly for your customers.

Color Accuracy

According to market research by Cyber Dialogue (www.cyberdialogue.com), 60 percent of Internet shoppers do not trust the colors they see on their computer monitors. As a result, some 30 percent of Internet shoppers surveyed had decided not to purchase a product on the Internet because they were concerned that the true color of the product was different from the color they saw onscreen.

This is an important finding if you are thinking of selling any product over the Internet (such as clothes, furniture, fabrics, automobiles, etc.) where color is a significant factor in the purchase decision. The problem is a technical one, caused by differences in how computer monitors, Web browsers, computer operating systems, and software programs display color. This means that pictures of products on your Web site will not look the same to all your customers. For example, a red sweater may appear orange to some of your customers, and varying shades of red to others.

Color problems such as these can lead to customer dissatisfaction. They can also cause a high rate of returns. The Cyber Dialogue study found that almost 15 percent of shoppers had returned items because the color of the actual product didn't match the color displayed on the Web.

What can an online retailer do? There are two U.S. companies, E-Color (www.ecolor.com) and Imation (www.verifi.net), working on solutions that online retailers can implement on their Web sites. In both cases, use of the technology is free for consumers, but retailers pay a fee based on the number of visitors to the retailer's Web site.

E-Color's solution, called True Internet Color, requires that consumers go through a one-time, two-minute online setup process, answering questions about how they see different colors on their computer monitor:

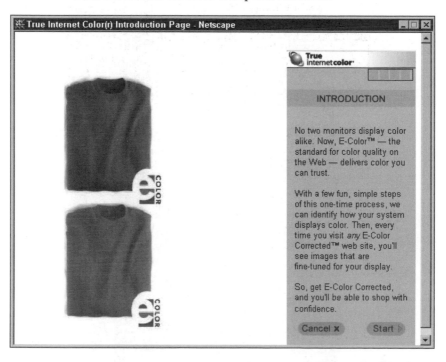

The result of the questionnaire is a profile, stored on the customer's computer, that gives E-Color information about how the customer's computer monitor displays different colors. The setup process can be completed either on the E-Color Web site or on the Web sites of participating merchants. Once the setup process is complete, consumers can visit any Web site that uses the E-Color technology without worrying about color distortions.

Merchants who want to use E-Color's technology need to modify the code on their Web pages, but no software needs to be installed. Whenever a customer accesses a page on a retailer's online store, E-Color accesses the color profile information from the customer's computer, and color-corrected images are delivered to the customer's computer screen along with the rest of the information from the retailer's Web site. The color-corrected images are kept on E-Color's Web site. Imation's Verifi works in a similar manner, although color-corrected images are stored on the merchant's computer servers, not on Verifi's.

Online retailers who are using the E-Color technology can display an E-Color/True Internet Color icon by the products they are selling. This lets customers know that the Web site has been optimized for True Internet Color technology.

Bloomingdale's (www.bloomingdales.com) was one of the first online retailers to implement True Internet Color technology in its online store. If you visit its Web site, you'll see the True Internet Color icon underneath the product photos:

What is the future for technology like E-Color or Verifi? Eventually, consumers won't need to go to a Web site to have their computers optimized for color. E-Color is developing partnerships with computer monitor manufacturers so that the E-Color setup tool can be bundled with their setup software. That way, when consumers are setting up their monitors for the first time, they will be able to set up and activate the E-Color technology.

Sizing Information

You may not have heard the term bracketing before, but it's an issue that a number of online retailers are dealing with. Bracketing is when an online shopper orders several different sizes of the same product with the intention of keeping only one size and returning the rest. This problem is normally associated with clothing purchases where customers aren't sure what size is appropriate. When purchasing from an online store, customers don't have the option of trying clothing on. So rather than running the risk that the garment will either be too large or too small, a customer will often order several different sizes of the same product. The customer will then keep the size that fits and return the rest to the retailer.

> **e-Fact**
>
> *Almost two-thirds of U.S. Internet users say that going online endangers their privacy.*
> Source: UCLA Center for Communication Policy (ccp.ucla.edu)

What's the problem, you ask? Imagine if hundreds of customers start to do this. It creates tremendous logistical problems for retailers who end up receiving large numbers of returned items. And since many online retailers pay the postage on returned items, handling large numbers of returns can be costly. If you are selling clothing or clothing accessories on your online store or planning to do so in the near future, one way to cut down on bracketing is to offer sizing information on your Web site so that customers can pick out the right sizes. Many online retailers do this, including Patagonia (www.patagonia.com), as shown in the following screen:

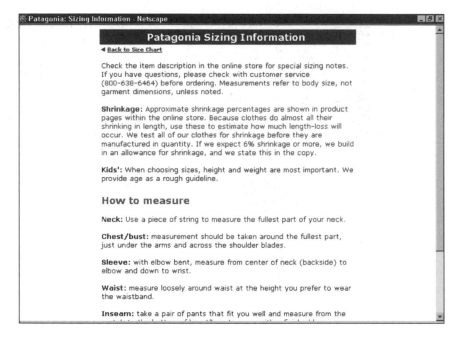

Keep in mind that offering this type of information on your Web site won't eliminate the bracketing problem entirely, but it can help you to cut down on product returns.

Online Wish Lists

e-Fact

Consumers are more satisfied making retail purchases online than they are shopping at traditional department and discount stores. Source: American Customer Satisfaction Index (www.bus.umich. edu/research/nqrc/ acsi.html)

An online wish list is like the modern version of a wedding registry, but online wish lists typically aren't used for weddings. An online wish list lets customers keep a permanent record of products they're interested in receiving as a gift, perhaps for a birthday, for Christmas, or for any other special occasion.

One Internet merchant that has implemented an online wish list is FAO Schwarz (www.fao.com). Once a customer has registered on the FAO Schwarz Web site, he or she can click on the "Add to Wish List" button beside any item in the online store (you can see the button in the lower right-hand corner of the page):

When a customer clicks on the wish list button, the item will be immediately added to the customer's wish list:

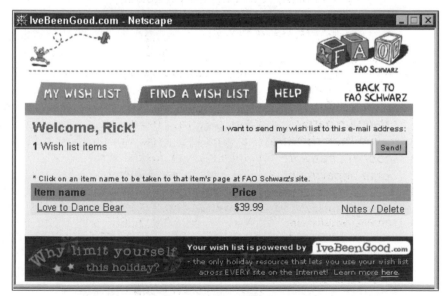

Friends and family members can access a person's wish list in two ways. First, the person who created the wish list can e-mail it to anyone by filling out the e-mail address box at the top of the wish list. Alternatively, anyone can visit the

FAO Schwarz Web site and search for a wish list by the person's last name, first name, or e-mail address:

If a matching name is found, the person will be able to buy products from the person's wish list by clicking on item names. As you can imagine, online wish lists can drive product sales on your Web site because they provide customers with a novel way to share gift ideas with each other.

Favorite Items Lists

Similar to a wish list, a "favorite items" list allows an online shopper to keep track of products he or she buys often, to avoid having to navigate through your online store every time he or she purchases the same items again. You can see this technology in action on the Staples Web site (www.staples.com). A customer can click on the "Add to Favorites" button that appears beside each product in Staples' online store, as seen near the bottom of the following screen:

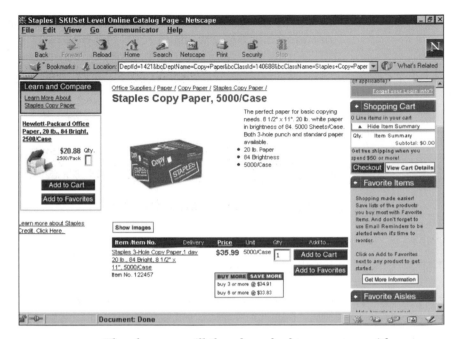

The shopper will then be asked to come up with a name for the list:

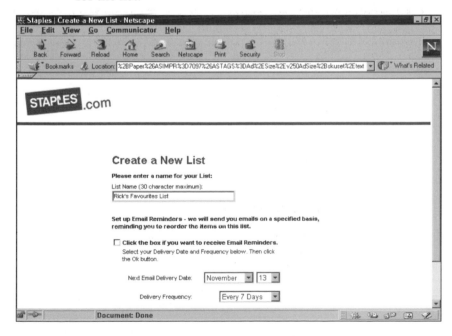

From that point forward, whenever the shopper returns to the Staples Web site, a link to his or her favorite items list will appear on the right-hand side of the screen:

At any time, the shopper can display all the items in a favorites list or add all the items to his or her shopping cart and check out right away. Shoppers can also create different favorites lists for different purposes (e.g., office, home, etc.). It's a great way to make online shopping easier for your customers!

Editorial Integrity

Online bookseller Amazon.com (www.amazon.com) came under fire a few years ago after it was alleged that the company was receiving payments of up to $10,000 from publishers in exchange for featuring their books prominently on the Amazon.com Web site.

Consumers were upset to learn that many of Amazon.com's recommended books were reportedly paid placements by publishers. While Amazon.com insisted that "only books selected by Amazon.com editors qualify for publisher-supported placement," customers became skeptical of Amazon.com's book recommendations. Were these books being praised because Amazon.com had received a fee from publishers, or did these books actually represent independent, unbiased recommendations from Amazon.com editors?

Under pressure from its customers and the media, Amazon.com announced that it would begin to identify which product placements were paid for by publishers.

The moral of the story is this: don't compromise the integrity and reputation of your business by doing anything that might be perceived by your customers as unethical. If your suppliers are paying you to feature certain products on your Web site, don't say that these products are recommendations from your staff.

DESIGN AND NAVIGATION

This section discusses some of the design issues to think about for your online store. We review the following nine issues:

- Easy navigation
- Different navigation schemes
- Search functionality
- Drop-down and pop-out menus
- Site maps
- Fast download times
- Browser compatibility
- Easy access to shopping cart contents
- Running totals

Easy Navigation

The design and layout of your store must be simple and straightforward, yet rich in features to satisfy the needs of the customer.

The best-designed stores provide customers with a navigation bar that follows the customer around the site. In other words, the navigation bar is always on the screen, regardless of where the customer is. This gives the customer one-click access to other areas of the online store, as well as any other areas of your Web site. The navigation bar also serves as a map, showing your customers where they are within the overall layout of your site so that they don't get lost.

A great example of this type of navigation scheme can be found on the Avon Web site (www.avon.com):

In the screen above, we're looking at the makeup section of the Avon online store. On the left-hand side of the screen, online shoppers see a menu that provides them with quick access to other areas of the Avon Web site. On the right-hand side of the screen, a second menu lets customers navigate through different parts of the makeup section. There is also a navigation bar at the top of the site that provides access to such important areas of the Web site as the Customer Service section. In addition, although you can't see it clearly here, the word "makeup" on the menu at the left appears in a slightly different color than the other words. This highlighting effect lets customers know where they are in the site.

We don't want to mislead you – designing an online store with this type of attractive, user-friendly interface takes considerable graphic design and Web programming skill. This is where outside expertise comes in, as discussed in the previous chapter. Depending on what type of software you use to set up your online store, your options for customizing the user interface may be quite limited. If the storefront software does give you the ability to customize the user interface and navigation buttons, you will need to be familiar with advanced HTML, the programming language of the Web, in order to create the type of attractive interface that we've shown you on the Avon site. If your knowledge of HTML and graphic design is limited, consider hiring a Web designer to help you develop customized navigation menus for your online store.

The consequences of poor site design can be severe. A study by Forrester Research (www.forrester.com) found that businesses with poorly designed Web pages can lose up to 40 percent of their repeat visitors. Needless to say, it pays to invest in a Web design that's easy for your customers to use.

Different Navigation Schemes

When designing your online store, think about the different ways that customers shop for the products you are offering. FTD's online store (www.ftd.com), for example, offers shoppers the option of shopping for flowers by occasion or by product category:

Shoppers simply need to click on the down arrow
beside either box to reveal a list of choices:

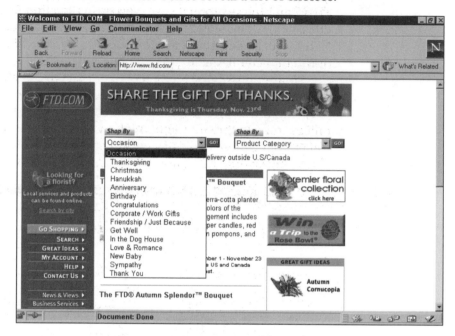

In order to maximize the user-friendliness of your store,
you should aim to provide customers with as many different
ways to find products as possible. For example, consider the
home page of FAO Schwarz (www.fao.com):

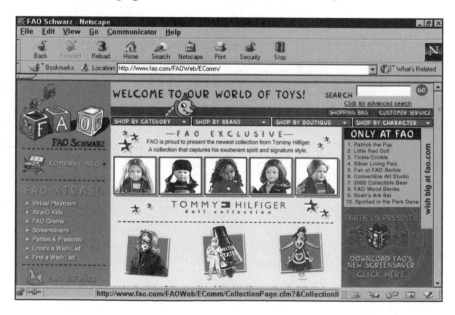

As you can see along the top of the screen, FAO Schwarz gives customers four different ways to find toy products. They can browse products by category (e.g., action figures, dolls, games), by brand name (e.g., Fisher-Price, Lego, Nintendo), by boutique (e.g., FAO Collectibles, FAO Games), or by character name (e.g., Pokemon, Winnie the Pooh).

Another possibility is to allow customers to search for products by price range. Illuminations (www. illuminations.com) has built this functionality into its online store. In the Gift Center section of its Web site, customers can choose to display gifts in any of four different price ranges (under $25, under $50, under $75, or over $75):

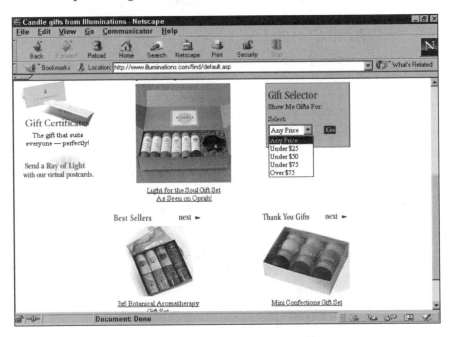

Sometimes it may make sense to give customers a complete listing, organized alphabetically or by category, of all of the products in your online store, as Pillsbury has done on its online store (www.doughboyshop.com):

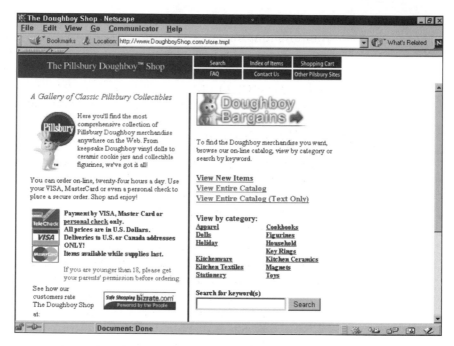

Customers who click on the "View Entire Catalog (Text Only)" link on the right-hand side of the Web site are able to quickly scroll through all of the items for sale in the online store:

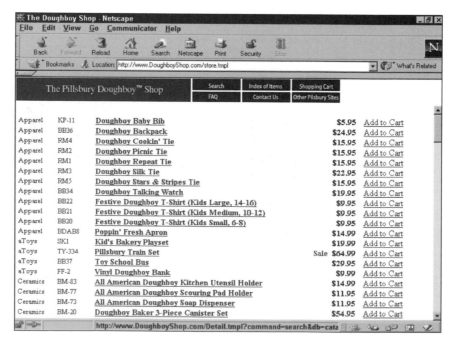

The navigation methods you choose to implement on your online store will depend on the types of products you sell. You may want to consider organizing a focus group of potential customers to try to understand how they would prefer to search for products on your Web site. Alternatively, get a group of friends together for a brainstorming session.

Search Functionality

Even if you give your customers dozens of different ways to browse your online store, there will always be some who want to search for products by keyword. There will also be cases when customers can't find what they are looking for using the menus you've provided.

It's always helpful if customers have the option of searching your entire store using the words or phrases they define. For example, the online store operated by Restoration Hardware (www.restorationhardware.com) provides a search box at the bottom of the home page.

Not only can customers search the entire online store by keyword, they can search specific product categories such as "Lighting" or "Home and Garden":

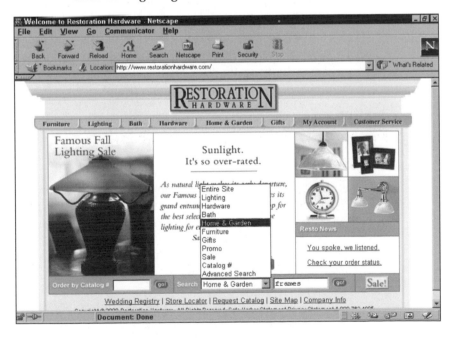

The results page displays matching products:

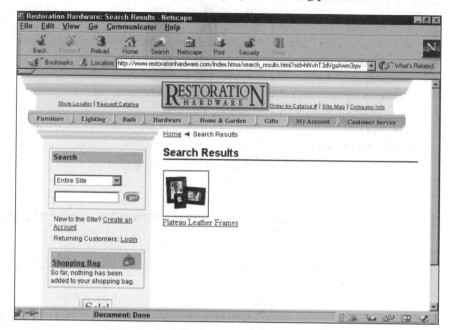

As you can see, search functions make finding products a snap, so your customers will really appreciate the convenience that such a feature offers. While some storefront software packages come with search capabilities, they may not be very powerful. If necessary, and if you can afford it, you can hire an e-commerce developer to add such search capabilities to your store, if your online store software will allow you to.

e-Fact

Fewer than one in five online retailers uses Web technologies such as Java, Flash, or chat functions to enhance the online shopping experience and close sales.
Source: Jupiter Research (www.jup.com)

Misspelled Searches

What happens when a customer decides to use a search engine on your Web site but then spells a product name or a person's name incorrectly? Will your search engine still direct your customer to the right product? Aware of this problem, some retailers have set up their search engine to catch misspellings. By doing this, you can eliminate the lost sales that might result when customers misspell the products they're looking for and therefore can't find them on your Web site.

e-Fact

Two-thirds of female online shoppers say they would not make a major purchase without first researching it on the Internet.

Source: International Data Corporation (www.idc.com)

Amazon.com (www.amazon.com) is a good example of a site that has implemented this type of capability effectively. For example, suppose a customer who is looking for a Barbra Streisand CD types the incorrect "striesand" into the search box.

Amazon.com has set up its search engine to recognize such misspellings. Even with her last name misspelled, Amazon.com recognizes that the customer is looking for music by Barbra Streisand and displays a list of available products:

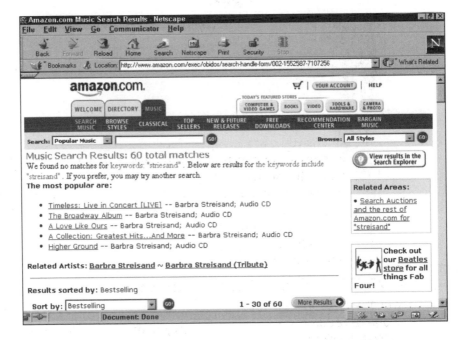

Adding this capability to your Web site isn't easy. A programmer must modify your search engine so that customers who misspell your product names are still directed to the proper Web pages on your site. Depending on the number of products you sell, this could be an expensive and time-consuming endeavor.

Drop-Down and Pop-Out Menus

One of the frustrations voiced by many online shoppers is the number of screens they often have to click through to get to the product they want. Drop-down or pop-out menus help shoppers on your Web site get to a desired area of your online store quickly. To see an effective pop-out menu, visit the JCPenney online store (www.jcpenney.com). Along the left-hand side of the Web site is a list of departments.

If you click on any of the product departments, such as "men's," a sub-menu pops out on the right:

Click on any of the items in the sub-menu, such as "business casual," and yet another sub-menu appears:

You can see an example of a drop-down menu on the
Eddie Bauer online store (www.eddiebauer.com). The concept is the same as a pop-out menu, but instead of the
menu popping out toward the right-hand side of the screen,
it drops down. Online shoppers only need to point their
mouse at any of the product categories along the top of
the site (e.g., "men's," "women's," "dress casual," etc.) and a
drop-down menu automatically appears with a list of
sub-categories that the customer can click on:

A slightly different implementation of a drop-down menu can be seen on the National Geographic Web site (www.nationalgeographic.com). Visitors to the site can click on the site index at the top of the page, which reveals a drop-down menu of different areas of the site:

As you can see, the benefit of having a drop-down or pop-out menu like this is that online shoppers can get to a specific area of your Web site in one quick step without having to navigate through a series of Web pages. Don't plan on putting together a menu like this on your own. You'll need to hire a Web programmer, and it's only doable if the online storefront solution you're using will allow this type of customization.

Site Maps

Another useful navigational tool is a *site map* – an index of all of the major sections and subsections of your site. Shoppers should be able to access the site map from anywhere on your online store.

A site map is an excellent resource in the event that customers get lost or can't find what they're looking for. For a good example of a site map, look at the Lands' End Web site (www.landsend.com). On the home page, click on the "Site Map" option. That will bring up a page that provides a handy list of all the areas on the site:

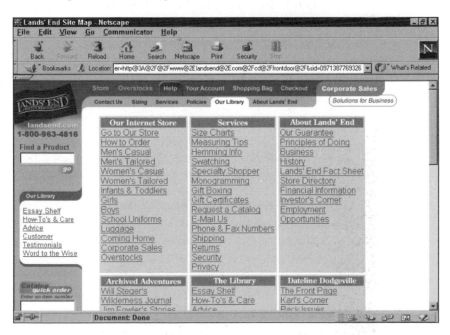

Fast Download Times

No matter how easy your site is to navigate, it will all be for naught if customers have to wait too long for your Web pages to load. Don't get carried away with a design that goes overboard in terms of layout and content. Specifically, don't fall prey to the temptation to overload your site with graphics, the latest and greatest programming feats, or other things that will bog it down and make it slow. We're not advising you to avoid graphics and animation on your home page, but make sure they don't adversely affect the performance of your Web site.

e-Fact

82% of online shoppers say that shipping costs are paramount to their purchase decisions.
Source: Forrester Research (www.forrester.com)

If your site is too slow, you'll most certainly lose sales and drive your customers away. A study by Zona Research (www.zonaresearch.com) found that U.S. retailers may lose as much as $4.35 billion a year because shoppers are frustrated by Web sites that operate too slowly. According to the study, over a third of Web users may give up trying to buy an item over the Internet if it takes too long for a Web page to download. Test your Web pages to see if they load quickly. If not, consider removing some of the graphics or using a commercial service such as GIF Wizard (www.gifwizard.com) that will compress your graphics so that they load faster:

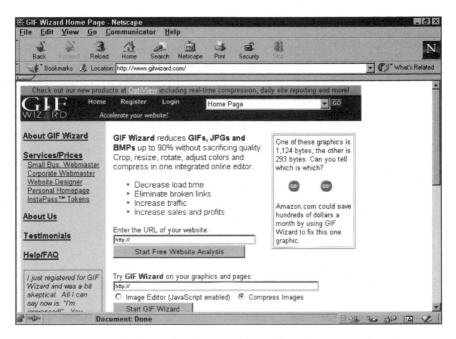

Another similar free tool is GIFbot by NetMechanic (www.netmechanic.com).

If your Web pages are slow, compressing your graphics may not be the only solution. Slow Web pages can also be due to poor Web site coding, the capacity of the server that is hosting your online store, the speed and congestion of the Internet connection used by your online store or Web hosting provider, the amount of content on your Web pages, or any combination of these problems. You need to take all these factors into account when you are trying to improve the performance of your online store. Depending on what type of storefront solution you are using, some of these issues may not be easy for you to control.

A good program for testing how fast your Web pages load is NetMechanic's HTML Toolbox, which can be found on the NetMechanic Web site (www.netmechanic.com):

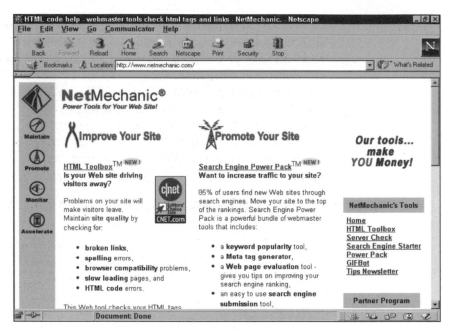

Although the program costs a nominal amount per year, you can try out the service for free and even test out the speed of your competitors' online stores! In the example below, we're asking for a report on Kmart's Web site:

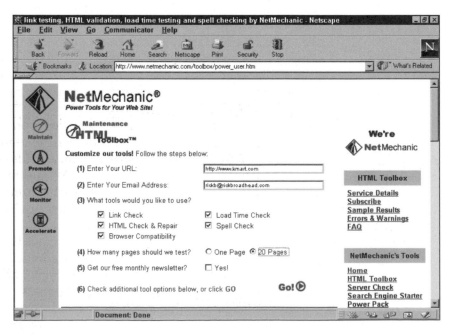

HTML Toolbox does more than just check the speed of a given Web site. It will also tell you if there are any broken links on your Web site, identify any potential problems in the computer code underlying your Web pages, check your spelling, and alert you to any browser compatibility problems, an issue we discuss in the next section. Once the site has been checked, an e-mail message will be sent to you containing a Web address where you can view the results of the test. For example, here is a report that shows how many seconds it took to load the front page of Kmart's Web site:

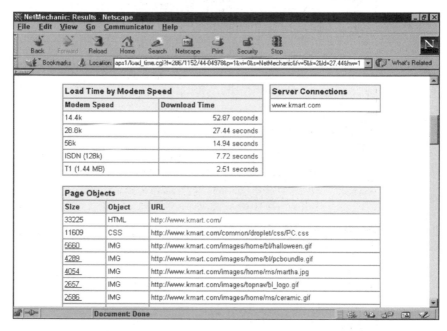

As you can see, it took fifty-three seconds for the site to load with a 14.4 kbps modem, just under twenty-eight seconds with a 28.8 kbps modem, and fifteen seconds with a 56 kbps modem. Try this test on your own online store before you launch it so that you can correct any problems before customers discover them!

Opinions differ on how fast your Web pages should ideally be. NetMechanic recommends that your Web pages should load in under twelve seconds on a 28.8 kbps modem, while other experts recommend that eight seconds is the maximum time it should take

e-Fact

58% of online purchasers believe that online prices are as high or higher than in retail stores.

Source: UCLA Center for Communication Policy (ccp.ucla.edu)

for any page to load, regardless of what modem speed your customer is using. Use your own judgement and have coworkers and friends give you their own opinions. Also check how fast your competitors' online stores load. If your Web site is a lot slower than your competitors, it's probably time for a tune-up!

Another excellent resource for download times is the Web site of Keynote Systems (www.keynote.com), a company that specializes in tracking and rating the performance of many popular Web sites. Every week, Keynote Systems measures the average response time to access and download the home pages of forty important consumer Web sites over standard telephone lines using a 56 kbps modem. The tests are conducted using computers located in eight major metropolitan areas in the United States. As a service to the public, the results are published on Keynote's Web site:

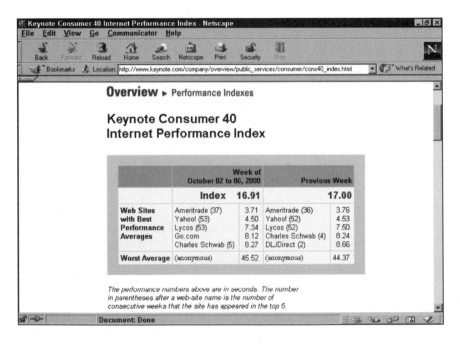

You can also apply for a free performance appraisal of your Web site:

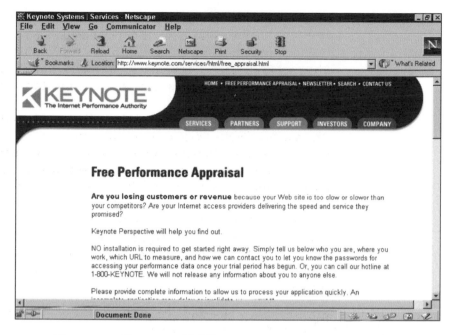

Browser Compatibility

Microsoft Internet Explorer and Netscape are the two most popular Web browsers on the Internet, and your customers will be using both of them. The problem is that each browser tends to display Web pages slightly differently. This means that when you design your online store, you should check how it looks using both programs. While a Web site may look perfect when viewed using Netscape, you may find misaligned columns or other problems when your site is viewed using Internet Explorer, or vice versa. These problems can usually be corrected by modifying the code on your Web pages. If this is beyond your capability, you may need to hire a Web developer to help you.

Easy Access to Shopping Cart Contents

One of the most crucial elements of any online store is the shopping cart. This is where customers can view the products that they've ordered, add and delete items, and see the total amount of their purchase. As we showed you in Chapter 2, shopping carts are included in all the major storefront solutions. Alternatively, you can purchase a standalone shopping cart program like QuikStore (www.quikstore.com) and integrate it into an existing Web site.

As customers browse through your store and order items, they often want to return to their shopping cart to review their order. Hence, it's important to design your store so that they have easy access to their shopping carts from any area of your site. Fortunately, most of the basic shopping cart programs and storefront software packages make it possible for customers to view the contents of their shopping carts from anywhere on the Web site by clicking on a button such as "View Cart" or "Show Order." As a general rule, customers should always only be one click away from their shopping carts regardless of where they are in your store.

A good example of this strategy can be seen on the Blockbuster Web site (www.blockbuster.com). As customers move around the Web site, the navigation bar at the top of the site never changes – and never moves. Notice the "View Shopping Cart" icon in the upper left-hand corner of the screen:

At any time, customers can click on this icon to view the current contents of their shopping cart:

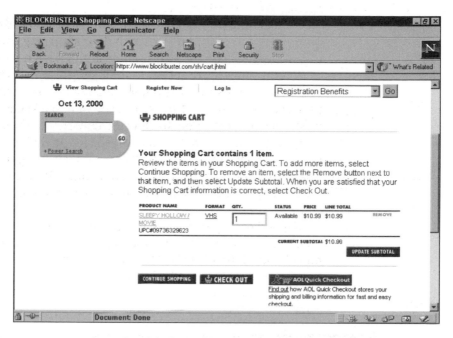

You should also make it easy for customers to continue shopping on your site once they've added an item to their shopping cart. In the example above, notice the button at the bottom of the shopping cart screen that says, "Continue Shopping." Blockbuster customers can click on this button if they want to return to the Web page they were previously on.

Unfortunately, many online stores don't do this, and it can be confusing for customers to figure out how to continue shopping. For example, when we visited the Tower Records online store (www.towerrecords.com) and added an item to our shopping cart, there was no button that invited us to continue shopping:

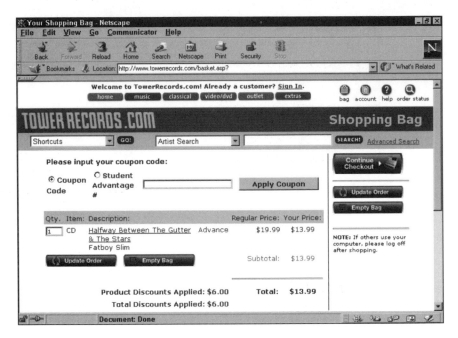

While it is true that shoppers can easily continue shopping by clicking on any of the navigation menus at the top of the Web site (e.g., "music," "classical," "video/DVD," etc.) it would be much better, and much less confusing, if shoppers were able to access a "Continue Shopping" button from within the shopping cart.

Furthermore, once several items were added to our shopping cart on the Tower Records site, there was no obvious way for us to remove a single item from the shopping cart. For example, in the following screen, there are three items in our shopping cart, but as you can see, there's no button that allows us to delete one of them:

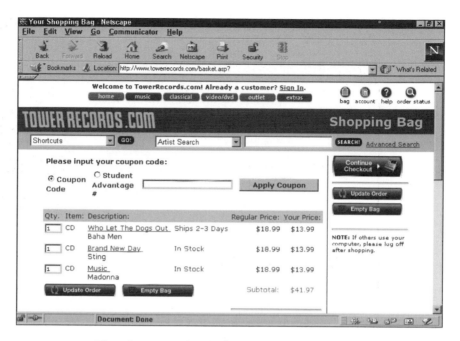

The closest option is "Empty Bag," but that removes *every* item from the shopping cart. We eventually figured out that if you change the quantity of an item to zero and then press "Update Order," the item will be removed from the shopping cart. But you can't assume that online shoppers are going to figure that out. When designing your online store, don't make it challenging for customers to modify the contents of their shopping carts.

As you are evaluating different storefront solutions, take time to review the features that are built into the shopping cart. Also make sure you understand how the shopping cart will be integrated into your store. Can customers access the shopping cart from anywhere in the store? Can they move back and forth easily between the shopping cart and the rest of your store? Can products be easily added to and deleted from the shopping cart? Make sure the solution you choose gives you the layout and features you desire, or find out if the software will allow you to customize the shopping cart to your specifications.

e-Fact

53% of online households have moved their furniture around to make the computer and the Internet more accessible.

Source: America Online (www.aol.com)

Running Totals

Online stores are beginning to realize that customers want to be able to see what's in their shopping baskets, or at the very least, a running total of their purchases, no matter where they are on the Web site. In other words, customers want to see a running total of their purchases on the screen *at all times*.

This feature allows customers to keep an eye on how much they're spending as items are added to their shopping cart. They don't have to return to their shopping cart to see this information, nor do they have to check out. The running total is always displayed on the screen.

One online retailer that has implemented this feature on its Web site is Restoration Hardware (www. restorationhardware.com). As customers navigate the online store and add items to their shopping cart, a current list of the selected items as well as the total amount of the purchase always appears along the left-hand side of the screen, as shown below:

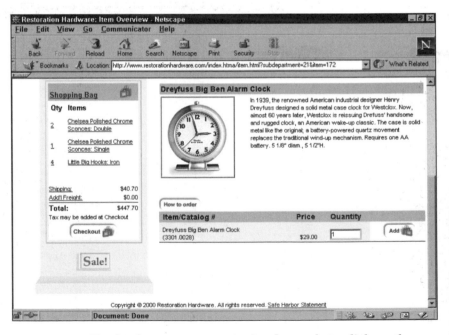

To check out, a customer simply needs to click on the "Checkout" button at the bottom of the shopping bag.

You'll find that your customers will appreciate having this information on the screen at all times because it avoids last-minute surprises at checkout. Unfortunately, this type of feature is not usually included in most of the entry-level storefront packages. If you like this idea, you'll probably have to hire someone to build this capability into your online store, provided that the online storefront package you are using allows customization.

ORDER INFORMATION

This section outlines some of the ordering-related issues that you need to think about for your online store. There are eight key issues:

- Step-by-step ordering instructions
- Ordering information
- Alternative shopping methods
- Instant payment services
- Order and shipping acknowledgements
- Online order tracking
- Order history
- Courier tracking

Step-by-Step Ordering Instructions

While it may seem obvious, don't assume that your customers already know how to order a product on your Web site. Consider providing a step-by-step guide that walks customers through the process of placing an online order.

A good example of this strategy is the "How to Order" page that Eddie Bauer (www.eddiebauer.com) has created for customers on its Web site:

Customers can refer to this information if they're unsure what steps to follow in order to place an online order. A section like this should be an essential part of any e-commerce Web site. For another example of a good "how-to" guide, visit the Avon Web site (www.avon.com), which provides step-by-step instructions on how to buy Avon products online:

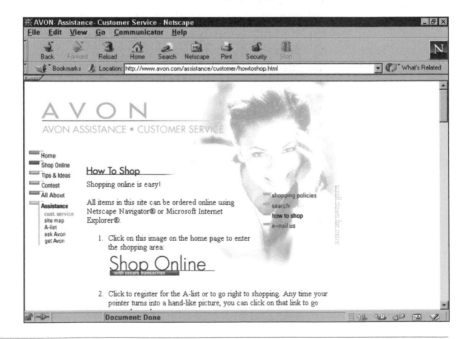

Ordering Information

Your customers will likely have lots of questions about ordering a product through your Web site. There are many issues to consider.

What forms of payment do you accept? Do you only accept credit cards or will you accept other forms of payment as well? Provide customers with information about the credit cards and forms of payment you accept.

How long does it usually take before an order will be shipped? Let customers know how long it usually takes for your organization to process the order once it's been received on your Web site. Most customers are under the impression that if they place an order on your Web site for overnight delivery, the order will definitely arrive the next day. Some organizations find it takes at least a day to process the order and get it ready for shipping. If you expect this to be the case, make sure customers are aware of this before they place their order. Otherwise, you may start receiving complaints from customers who didn't receive their orders when expected.

The Godiva Chocolates Web site (www.godiva.com), for example, contains this notice to shoppers: "All orders placed before 11:00 a.m. (EST) will be processed the same day. If your order is placed after 11:00 a.m. (EST), please allow 24 hours for processing." Amazon.com (www. amazon.com) also includes a cautionary note on its Web site, reminding customers that even if they select "next day air" delivery, they will not necessarily receive their products the next day:

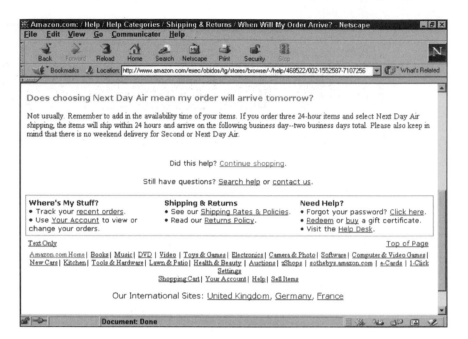

What order deadlines are in place for special days like Christmas, Father's Day, Mother's Day, etc.? If you sell the types of products that customers may be interested in purchasing as gifts for special days, post a list of order deadlines on your Web site so that customers know when they have to place their orders to receive the products on time. Godiva does this effectively on its online store (www.godiva.com):

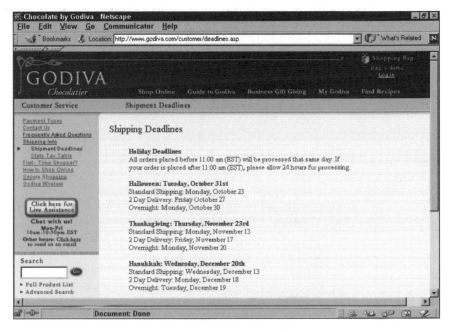

If you expect to be overwhelmed with orders, make sure the deadlines you post will give you enough time to get all of the orders shipped on time. Furthermore, make sure you take into account any deadlines imposed by the U.S. Postal Service and/or any courier companies you may be using.

e-Fact

Revenues generated by selling online customer service software will grow to $1.95 billion by 2004 — more than a 1,000% increase from 1999.

Source: Datamonitor (www.datamonitor.com)

When will my credit card be charged?
To allay concerns about fraud on the Internet, it's generally a good idea to tell customers when their credit cards will be billed. Although Visa and MasterCard rules require that you wait until the customer's order has been shipped, most of your customers won't be familiar with these rules. If you tell customers that you won't charge their credit cards until their orders have been shipped, this will help you to build credibility and trust in the marketplace and will make consumers more willing to do business with you.

What name will appear beside the charge on my credit card? If the company name you use with the credit card companies is different than the company name you use on the Web, note this on your Web site. It may also be possible to have your operating name and/or phone number added to your company name on the customer's credit card statement.

(Check with your financial institution or merchant account provider.) Otherwise, your customers will see a charge on their credit card statement from an organization they don't recognize. This happens quite frequently, because many organizations use parent companies or numbered companies for billing purposes but operate under an entirely different name on the Web. If a customer doesn't recognize a charge on his or her credit card statement, he or she will usually call up the bank and complain. This may lead to a charge-back, a situation that arises when a customer disputes an item that he or she has been billed for (for more information on chargebacks, see Chapter 4, *Merchant Accounts and Online Payment Processing*). Chargebacks are not only inconvenient, they can cost you both time and money, so it's important that you take as many precautions as you can to reduce the likelihood of chargebacks in your online store.

Do you accept orders from anywhere in the world? Finally, make sure you indicate whether you will accept international orders, and if so, from which countries. How about orders from the non-continental United States? For example, will you accept orders from Alaska, Puerto Rico, Hawaii, Micronesia, Palau, and other U.S. territories and dependencies? Will you ship to American military person-nel serving overseas? For example, will you deliver to Army Post Office (APO) and Fleet Post Office (FPO) destinations in different parts of the world? It is important that you care-fully spell out these policies on your Web site, including any additional shipping charges that may apply.

Other Questions Your Online Store Should Answer about Ordering

- Are there any countries you do not ship to?
- Do you offer any quantity discounts?
- Can I cancel my order at any time?

Alternative Shopping Methods

Many consumers remain terrified of sending their credit card numbers through the Internet. It is important that your online store respect these concerns, regardless of how valid they may be. Recognizing that many online shoppers aren't comfortable paying by credit card, many online retailers give customers the option of ordering by telephone, fax, or mail. For example, Kodak's online store (www.kodak.com) provides an order form that can be printed

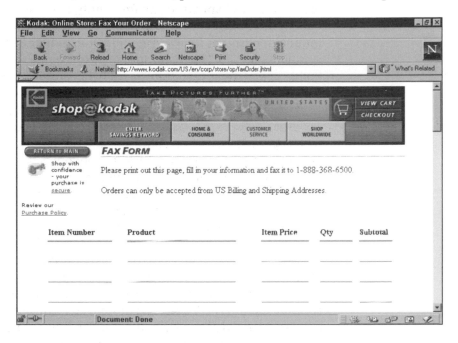

out, filled in, and faxed to the company:

Obviously, you should only accept orders by telephone if you have someone standing by to accept orders. It can be quite frustrating for a customer to call you on the telephone, only to have the telephone ring endlessly or an answering machine pick up the call.

If you decide to accept orders by telephone, fax, or mail, make sure this information is well publicized on your Web site, especially in the ordering and checkout sections, so that you don't lose customers who don't want to order online.

Instant Payment Services

While credit cards remain the most popular form of payment on the Internet, you may want to consider using an instant payment service such as PayPal (www.paypal.com) or Bank One's eMoneyMail (www.emoneymail.com) on your online store. These services have

e-Fact

More than 60% of online consumers say if they are dissatisfied with a company's e-commerce site, they are less likely to purchase from the company's traditional store.

Source: Boston Consulting Group (www.bcg.com)

traditionally been used on online auction sites but they are increasingly being used on e-commerce sites as well. Instant payment services are gaining popularity because they allow online shoppers to send money to merchants quickly and easily, even if they don't have a credit card number handy. The benefit for merchants is that they can accept credit card payments without a merchant account (for an explanation of merchant accounts, see Chapter 4, *Merchant Accounts and Online Payment Processing*).

Here is how PayPal works. Shoppers sign up for a PayPal account on the PayPal Web site by filling out an application form. They can deposit money into their account via personal check or electronic funds transfer. Whenever a shopper wants to send money to a merchant, he or she logs into the PayPal Web site and fills out a form, specifying whom the money should go to and how much. The amount is automatically charged to the shopper's credit card or deducted from his PayPal balance.

The merchant will receive an e-mail notification that a payment has been received. He or she can log into PayPal (or sign up for a new account if he or she doesn't already have one) and the money will immediately appear in the account balance. The funds can either be transferred to a bank account, sent in the form of a check, or left in the account for his or her own PayPal payments.

PayPal is free for consumers to use, but businesses pay a nominal fee to receive money via PayPal. As an alternative to receiving payments by e-mail, businesses can subscribe to PayPal's premium service and accept PayPal payments directly on their Web sites.

With millions of online shoppers in the United States using PayPal and similar services, we highly recommend you investigate these services as an alternate form of payment on your online store.

e-Fact

By 2002, 87% of consumers will use the Web to answer their questions, while only 13% will resort to using the telephone.

Source: Forrester Research (www.forrester.com)

Order and Shipping Acknowledgments

One frequently voiced complaint about ordering products on the Internet is the lack of communication from the merchant once the order has been placed.

Placing an order on the Web can sometimes feel like sending a credit card number into a black hole. Unless a customer hears back from the merchant, how does he or she know that the order was received? In this respect, ordering a product on the Internet is like sending an important fax to someone. If you don't hear back from the person you sent the fax to, you begin to wonder if it actually arrived.

As an Internet merchant, it's important to acknowledge every order by e-mail and stay in contact with the customer at various stages of the order and delivery process. For example, when customers order from FAO Schwarz (www.fao.com), they immediately receive an e-mail message like the one below confirming that their order has been received:

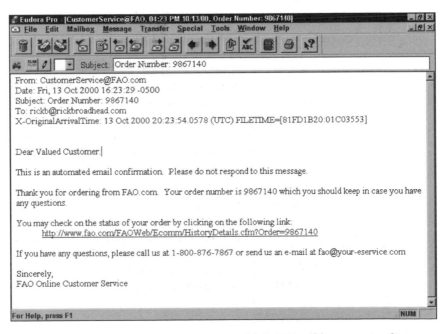

An even better strategy, which is used by many online stores, is a two-step acknowledgment procedure. First, the customer is contacted by e-mail when the order is received. This assures the customer that the order has been received successfully. A second e-mail message is sent when the product is being shipped. This lets the customer know the order has been processed and that it has been sent by whatever method the customer selected.

These confirmations are an important part of building a relationship of trust and credibility with your customers, and are almost considered *de rigueur* for online stores.

Not only do these types of confirmations help you provide excellent service to your customers, they also eliminate the need for customers to e-mail you with questions such as "Did you receive my order?" and "Has my order been shipped?" Many of the storefront solutions that we discussed in Chapter 2 allow you to send order and shipping acknowledgments to your customers.

Online Order Tracking

In addition to providing e-mail confirmations, consider enabling your customers to track the status of their orders on your Web site. For example, Nordstrom's online store (www.nordstrom.com) allows customers to find out whether an order has been received, packaged, or shipped:

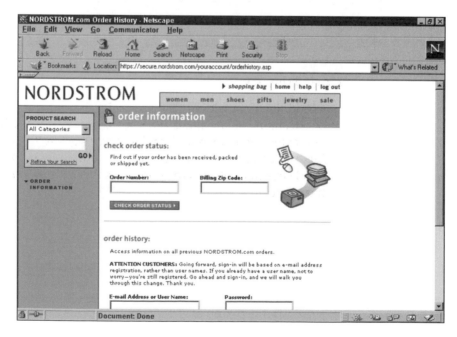

To access this information, a customer needs to enter
the order number that was included in the confirmation
e-mail message. Once the order number is provided,
Nordstrom displays the status of the order:

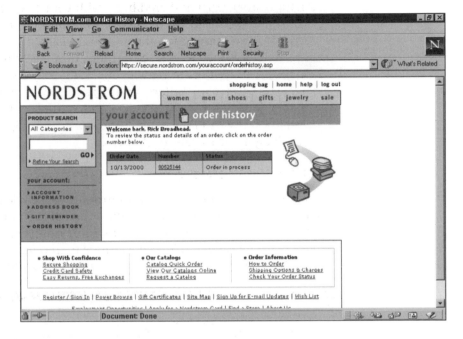

Order History

In addition to providing customers with the status of current
orders, many online stores allow customers to access a listing
of previous orders. Godiva's online store (www.godiva.com),
for example, has an "Order History" section on its Web site
that keeps track of all of the purchases that a customer
has made:

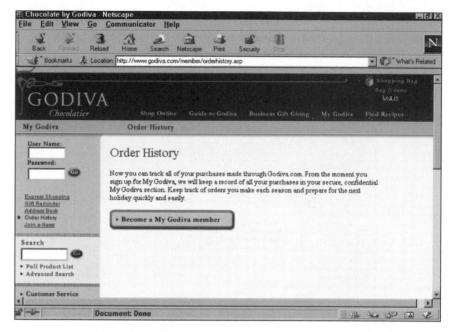

In order to limit who has access to this type of information, Godiva requires that customers register on the site and obtain a username and password.

This is the type of information that a registered Godiva customer would see when they access their order history:

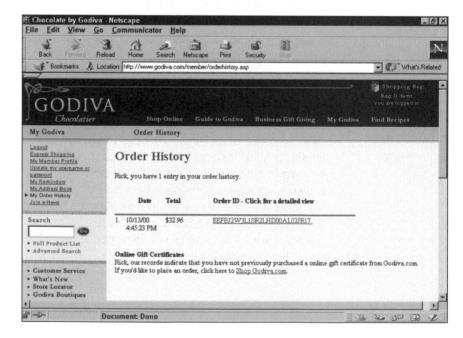

By clicking on the order ID code beside any item in the order history, a customer can obtain more detailed information on that particular order:

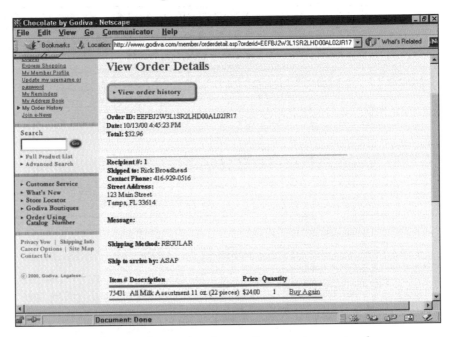

This service makes it easy for a customer to place a repeat order for a product ordered in the past. A customer who doesn't remember what he or she ordered can look up the information in the order history file. Although some products, like books, don't really lend themselves to repeat orders, gift products like flowers and chocolates do, and customers frequently forget what they ordered in the past. Order tracking also makes it easy for customers to look up details from past orders, such as a shipping address or the date an order was placed, without having to call or send an e-mail to your customer service department.

We should point out that implementing any type of registration system on your site, and linking it to an order tracking system, can be quite complicated. If this type of feature is important to you, make sure that the storefront software solution you select can support registration and order history/tracking.

Courier Tracking

Once an order has left your store or warehouse, it's in the hands of the postal service or courier company. As a service to your customers, consider giving them the ability to track their parcels on your Web site. For example, consider what REI has done on its online store (www.rei.com). When a customer places an order on REI.com, an e-mail acknowledgement is sent to the customer, along with an order number. Forty-eight hours after placing the order, the customer can access the order tracking page on the REI Web site and find out where the parcel is:

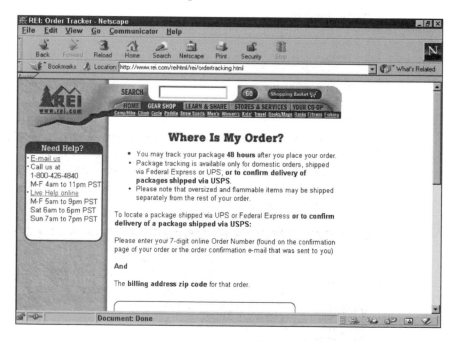

Some online merchants simply direct their customers to the Web sites of the courier companies for parcel tracking. For example, Amazon.com sends customers a confirmation e-mail message when their orders are being shipped. At the bottom of the e-mail message is a tracking number for the courier company that is handling the delivery. Amazon.com has a section on its Web site with links to the Web sites of various courier companies so that customers can track their own parcels:

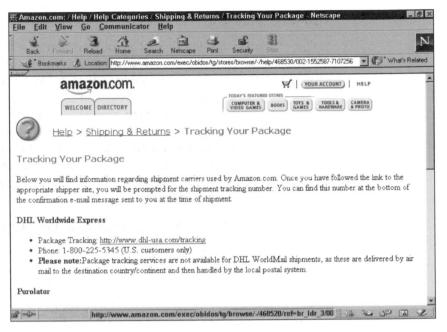

But why steer customers to another Web site when you can keep them on your own site? Consider integrating the courier company's parcel tracking system into your own site, as Avery (www.avery.com) has done on its Web site, as shown below:

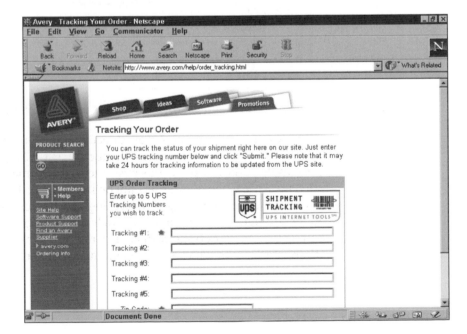

Contact the courier companies you work with for directions on how to do this. Placing the tracking forms directly on your Web site gives customers the convenience of tracking their shipments on your online store without going elsewhere to get the information.

SHIPPING INFORMATION

This section reviews shipping-related issues that you should think about for your online store. There are five issues:

- Comprehensive shipping policies
- Import duties and brokerage fees
- Handling fees
- "You're not too late" reminders
- Full disclosure of shipping prices

Before you read any further, we want to caution you to avoid the temptation of giving away free shipping. In their desperation to attract new customers, many online retailers have waived their shipping charges, hoping that this will encourage more customers to buy online. It's not uncommon to come across offers like this on the Internet:

e-Fact

More than any other reason, online purchasers return products simply because they are not what the consumer expected.
Source: PricewaterhouseCoopers (www.pwcglobal.com)

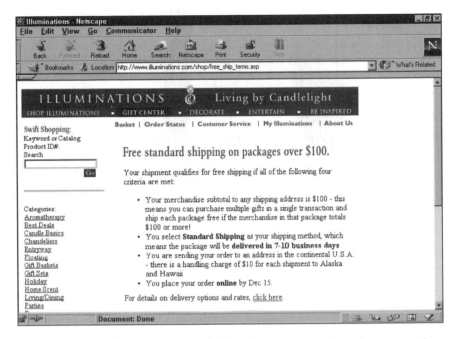

Indeed, the cost of shipping can sometimes be as much as the cost of the product being purchased, deterring many shoppers from buying online. However, before you offer your customers free shipping, make sure that you can afford it. Large online retailers can usually afford to subsidize the cost of free shipping more easily than smaller retailers can. But regardless of your size, giving away shipping can cut into your profit margins substantially, and you could wind up with some serious financial problems. If you're thinking of giving away or discounting the cost of shipping, make sure that your profit margins are high enough to support this practice.

Better yet, if you have one or more retail stores, and you're worried that customers won't purchase online because of the high cost of shipping, give customers the option of ordering online and picking up the product in person at one of your stores, a strategy we discuss later in the chapter. Another option is to build the cost of shipping into the price of your products and then offer free or low-price shipping, given that many buyers online have come to expect free online shipping. This could turn into a problem if you have a "real world" retail presence, though, since there would be a difference between your online prices and regular store prices.

Comprehensive Shipping Policies

Your online store should provide customers with a thorough description of shipping costs as well as the different shipping methods that you offer (e.g., regular service, overnight delivery, two-day delivery, etc.). To avoid disappointing your customers, make sure you explain the shipping times for each method. For example, if a customer chooses regular shipping, when is the earliest date the product would arrive?

Godiva's online store (www.godiva.com) is an excellent example of what you can do to help customers understand their shipping options. For each of the shipping methods offered, Godiva calculates how long it would take for the delivery to arrive if the product were shipped on the current date. This information is displayed to customers when they are making a purchase, so they can easily figure out which shipping method to use to get their order delivered when they want it:

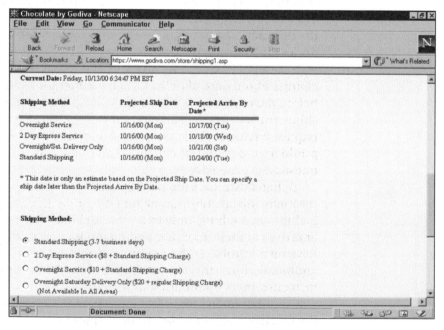

By providing information in this format, you reduce the chance of any misunderstandings about delivery dates.

If you expect most of the orders in your online store to be shipped to home addresses, you should remind your customers that if they've chosen to have their order delivered by a courier service, someone usually has to be home in order to receive it. Many online shoppers get frustrated because their orders are delivered during the day when no one is home. After several unsuccessful delivery attempts, the courier company may end up returning the parcel to the merchant. On your order form, you might want to recommend that customers use their place of work as their shipping address so that the courier company can deliver the order promptly.

You should also think about offering customers the option of purchasing insurance on shipments, especially if the products being shipped are valuable.

Some merchants have created a "shipping policy" on their Web site to cover all of these issues.

Import Duties and Brokerage Fees

If you plan to ship to customers in other countries, make sure that you fully investigate whether any import duties or brokerage fees are likely to be levied on your products by the destination country. Many countries charge import duties and/or other taxes on products arriving from a foreign country. Usually, the customer is notified of these charges at the time of delivery, and payment is required before the customer is allowed to receive the product. If the shipment is being delivered by courier, the driver may request payment of the duties and fees before releasing the product. Import duties can be substantial if the product in question is expensive.

When customers are buying from your online store, they may mistakenly assume that the price they are paying includes everything, only to be shocked later when a courier arrives at their door demanding more money. While you have no control over the amount of import duties levied by another country, this type of surprise may be enough to turn customers off ordering from your store again. This is why it is extremely important to prepare your customers for the fact that they may have to pay duties on the products they are ordering from you. A good example of this practice is the online store of Hickey's Music Center in Ithaca, New York (www.hickeys.com). Hickey's has a section on its Web site that informs customers about the possibility of import duties on products ordered from its online store:

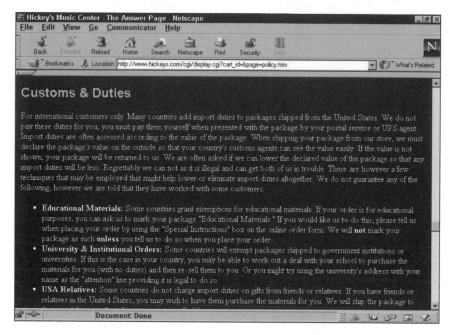

Customs & Duties

For international customers only. Many countries add import duties to packages shipped from the United States. We do not pay these duties for you, you must pay them yourself when presented with the package by your postal service or UPS agent. Import duties are often assessed according to the value of the package. When shipping your package from our store, we must declare the package's value on the outside so that your country's customs agents can see the value easily. If the value is not shown, your package will be returned to us. We are often asked if we can lower the declared value of the package so that any import duties will be less. Regrettably we can not as it is illegal and can get both of us in trouble. There are however a few techniques that may be employed that might help lower or eliminate import duties altogether. We do not guarantee any of the following, however we are told that they have worked with some customers.

- **Educational Materials:** Some countries grant exemptions for educational materials. If your order is for educational purposes, you can ask us to mark your package "Educational Materials." If you would like us to do this, please tell us when placing your order by using the "Special Instructions" box on the online order form. We will **not** mark your package as such **unless** you tell us to do so when you place your order.
- **University & Institutional Orders:** Some countries will exempt packages shipped to government institutions or universities. If this is the case in your country, you may be able to work out a deal with your school to purchase the materials for you (with no duties) and then re-sell them to you. Or you might try using the university's address with your name as the "attention" line providing it is legal to do so.
- **USA Relatives:** Some countries do not charge import duties on gifts from friends or relatives. If you have friends or relatives in the United States, you may wish to have them purchase the materials for you. We will ship the package to

Document: Done

If you anticipate a lot of sales to specific countries, you should take the time to try to determine, as closely as possible, the level of duties that will be charged on a purchase, and build this information into your store. There are many tax accountants who can assist you in this regard. Having said that, you should also ensure that customers understand that the ultimate amount of duty cannot be determined exactly up front, and that they are responsible for whatever duties are charged. This will help to avoid any misunderstandings.

Handling Fees

When figuring out the shipping rates for your online store, you may want to consider charging your customers an additional fee to cover your handling costs. Think about all the activities involved in preparing a product for shipping. You have to:

- purchase the packaging materials;
- enclose the appropriate paperwork (e.g., copy of the receipt);
- wrap and seal the package;

- complete and apply the appropriate labels and/or waybills;

- apply postage (if using the U.S. Postal Service); and

- take the shipments to your local post office or courier depot and/or call the courier company to pick up your deliveries, if necessary.

That's a lot of work, isn't it? There's labor involved, as well as the cost of the packaging materials (boxes, packing tape, etc.). Many organizations offset these costs by building them into a handling fee, which can be added to your shipping cost to form a "shipping and handling fee." Whether you want to do this depends on the types of products you are selling and what your competitors are doing.

"You're Not Too Late" Reminders

If you sell products that customers may want to give as gifts for Father's Day, Mother's Day, Christmas, and so on, it's a good idea to place "you're not too late" banners on your Web site right up until the last possible shipping day. These let customers know that they can still order products from your store in time for that special day. For example, shoppers who are on your site the week before Father's Day might assume that they can't get a gift from your store delivered in time. Depending on what shipping methods you offer, it may be possible for shoppers to place their orders on the Friday before Father's Day and still receive the shipment in time. But shoppers won't know this unless you tell them. Because many people leave their shopping until the last minute, keep reminding them right up until your last shipping day that they can still order products in time for the special day.

Remember that many online shoppers are distrustful of online stores and may not feel confident ordering from you just days before a special occasion. Why? Because they don't think that you can deliver the product on time. A simple statement on your Web site can boost confidence in your Web store and help you to close sales with last-minute shoppers that you would have otherwise missed.

Full Disclosure of Shipping Prices

Finally, when it comes to shipping, there should be no surprises.

Make sure that customers know exactly how much they will be charged before they place their order. Make your shipping fees highly conspicuous – don't bury them in a hard-to-find place on your Web site. To understand why this is important, think about how much people dislike car dealers. Many people who have bought a car complain that they encountered unknown or hidden sales charges at the last minute. Do the same thing on the Internet and you will foster the same sense of distrust.

Notice that on the front page of Godiva's Web site (in the bottom right-hand corner of the screen), there is a link to the shipping section so that customers have immediate access to it:

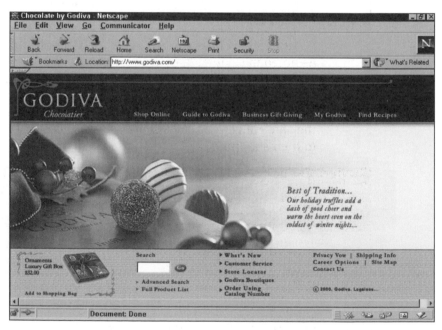

Many online retailers, such as Restoration Hardware (www.restorationhardware.com), have created comprehensive customer service sections on their Web sites that include information on shipping costs and policies:

It's up to you how you want to charge for shipping. As noted in Chapter 2, there are various ways to do this. Some online stores, such as Martha Stewart's (www.marthabymail.com), charge based on the dollar value of the purchase. This makes it easy for customers to see what they are going to be charged before they even add an item to their shopping cart:

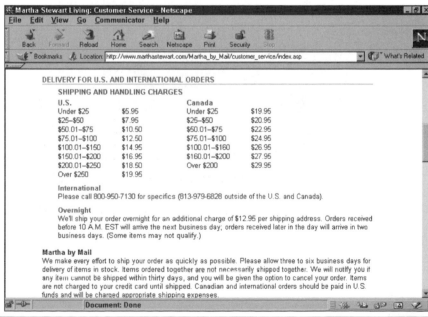

However, for many online stores, it's not possible to do this. Depending on the method you use to calculate shipping costs, you may not be able to give customers this type of comprehensive and accurate shipping information until they place an item in their shopping cart (at which time the shopping cart software will calculate the total shipping costs based on the criteria you've defined). This would be the case, for example, if you calculate your shipping costs based on the weight of the product or if you have different rates for every product in your online store. If so, simply tell your customers that shipping costs are calculated once they place an item in the shopping cart. Also let them know that they will have the option not to continue with the purchase at that point if they wish. Because international shipping rates vary depending on the destination country and product you are shipping, international shipping costs may need to be worked out on a case-by-case basis. In the previous screen, notice that Martha Stewart's online store asks international customers to call the company if they want information on shipping costs.

While it's best to tell customers what shipping is going to cost before they finalize their online order, some online storefront solutions will allow you to withhold this information until the order has been submitted to you. This will give you time to work out the shipping cost on your own without having to commit to a certain shipping cost on your Web site. Once you've determined what the shipping cost is going to be, you can e-mail the customer for approval. If the customer approves the shipping cost, you then proceed to ship the order. This method of calculating shipping costs is somewhat risky, however, because many customers may be leery about giving you their credit card number until they know how much they are going to be charged.

Regardless of how you calculate shipping costs, the point we're making is this: have a section on your Web site where you explain how shipping rates are calculated, even if you can't be too precise.

EXCHANGES, RETURNS, AND WARRANTIES

In this section, we discuss two important issues relating to exchanges and returns on your online store:

- Comprehensive exchange and return policies
- Satisfaction guarantees

Comprehensive Exchange and Return Policies

The lack of clear refund policies and cancellation terms on e-commerce sites is a common problem on the Web. Needless to say, an exchange and return policy is an integral part of an online store. Customers will want an assurance that if they are not satisfied with their purchase, they can return the product for a credit or exchange.

Hence, you should develop a clear, unambiguous policy regarding returns, exchanges, damaged products, and other problem purchases, and post it on your Web site.

Your Web site should also explain your cancellation policy. This policy should describe how customers can cancel their order, whether there is a time limit on cancellations, and whether a full refund will be issued (or whether there is a restocking charge), including shipping and/or other charges, in the event that the customer cancels the order.

In addition, customers might seek information with respect to any warranties or guarantees on the products you sell. You should add this type of information to your site as well.

Make it easy for customers to find your return, cancellation, and exchange policies; customers shouldn't have to search high and low for them. In fact, many customers will look for these types of policies before they even consider buying a product from you. If your return policy isn't displayed, you may lose the sale altogether.

Make sure you have a link to your return policy from the checkout area of your online store. A customer may decide to read your return policy at the last minute. If this information isn't immediately accessible and the customer has to leave the order page to go find it, you may lose the sale altogether. We like what Nordstrom has done on its online store (www.nordstrom.com). Through every stage of the checkout process, links are provided to the company's return and exchange policy, privacy policy, and security information (seen below in the bottom left-hand corner of the screen) so that customers can review this information at the last minute if they have any doubts or concerns:

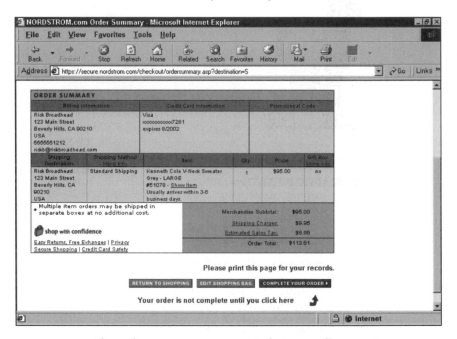

If you have one or more retail stores, allow customers to return merchandise purchased online to your physical stores. This type of return system has been difficult for some companies to implement, especially if customer service systems haven't been tied together across the company's online and offline operations. In that case a brick-and-mortar store might not have a record of a customer's online purchases from the same company. But online shoppers have made it very clear that they expect this type of integration, and online retailers are going out of their way to promote "no-hassle" return policies to consumers. For example, in the following screen, notice that the front page of Gap's online store (www.gap.com) draws attention to the company's "hassle-free returns" policy. Gap shoppers can return a product purchased on the Web to any Gap retail location:

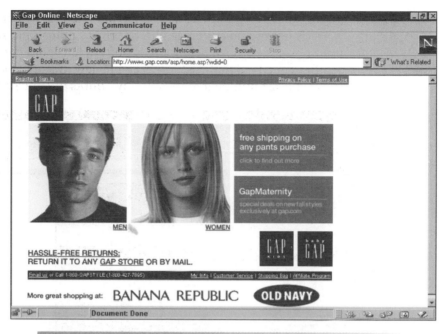

Items to Consider in Your Online Return, Exchange, and Cancellation Policies

- Under what conditions will you accept a return or exchange?
- How must items be returned (e.g., only by insured mail)?
- If you have one or more retail store locations, can purchases made on the Internet be returned in person to one of your retail stores?
- Where should the customer send returned items?
- What is your cancellation policy?
- Are shipping fees refundable?
- What happens if a customer receives a product in damaged condition?
- What must the customer include with the returned item? (A copy of the invoice? A description of the reason the item is being returned?)

Satisfaction Guarantees

To encourage customers to buy from your online store, consider establishing a satisfaction guarantee and publishing it on your Web site. For a good example, visit the online store of Dexter USA (www.dextershoe.com), which features a page called "Satisfaction Guarantee and Return Policy." Customers are told that they can return any product they are not 100 percent satisfied with within thirty days of purchase:

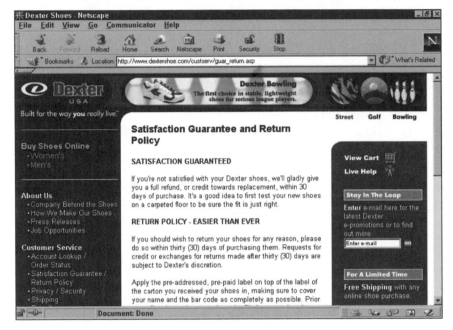

Isn't a satisfaction guarantee the same thing as a return policy? Not at all. Think about it. What has a greater impact on you – a section that says "Return Policy" or a section that says "Satisfaction Guarantee"? The guarantee should not replace your return policy, but complement it.

PRICING INFORMATION

In this section, we discuss two issues related to pricing products on your online store:

* Your pricing policy
* Currency conversion

Pricing Policy

Your Web site should clearly indicate what happens when there is a pricing error on your Web site or a discrepancy between an advertised price and a price on your Web site. There have been several high-profile cases of products accidentally listed on Web sites at several hundred dollars below the correct retail price. In some instances, retailers have chosen to honor the incorrect prices rather than upset their customers, sustaining losses of thousands of dollars as a result. Other companies affected by pricing glitches have canceled the orders they received only to endure the wrath of angry shoppers who felt they were misled. When a pricing glitch occurs on your Web site, you're really in a no-win situation. If you honor the incorrect prices, you lose money. If you don't honor them, you upset your customers. For example, in late July 2000, some lucky shoppers on Amazon.com's Web site encountered products that were inadvertently discounted by 50 percent or more off their regular prices. Once Amazon.com discovered the pricing glitch on its Web site, it refused to honor the incorrect prices and invited customers to resubmit their orders at the correct prices, resulting in several complaints to the Better Business Bureau.

To help you deal with these types of embarrassing situations, we recommend that you create a policy on pricing and typographical errors and publish it on your Web site. Pricing errors can happen very easily, due either to technical glitches or to old prices that were inadvertently not updated, so you should be prepared. For an example of a pricing policy, visit the Help section of Amazon.com's Web site and look at the "Pricing and Availability" page:

e-Fact

Abandoned shopping carts are costing online businesses $3.8 billion in lost sales.

Source: Shop.org
(www.shop.org)

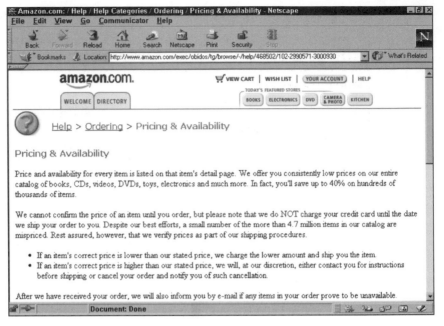

Currency Conversion

When setting up your online store, you need to think about whether you want to set prices in a currency other than U.S. dollars. The approach you take depends on the types of products you sell, where your competitors are located (do you have lots of competitors outside of the United States?), what your U.S. competitors are doing (do they accept foreign currencies?), and what your customers demand. For simplicity, and because the U.S. dollar is recognized around the world, most online stores in the United States only price their products in U.S. dollars.

To aid your international customers in converting a price on your Web site into their own currency, you may want to consider implementing a currency converter on your Web site. There are many free currency conversion tools available on the Internet, including the Universal Currency Converter (www.xe.net). For an example of its implementation, visit the Stained Glass Web-Mart (www.glassmart.com), an online retailer of stained glass tools and supplies. The site has integrated the Universal Currency Converter into one of its Web pages so that customers can convert U.S. prices into their own currency:

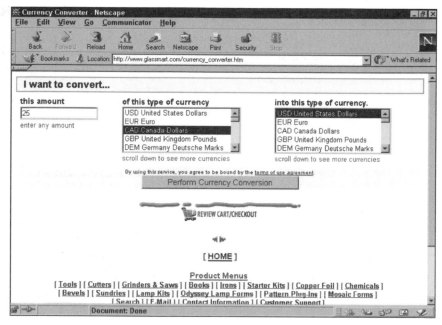

This doesn't allow customers to pay you in foreign currencies – it simply allows customers to type in a U.S. dollar amount and see what the equivalent amount would be in their own currency. If you use a tool like this on your Web site, make sure your customers understand that the results given by the calculator won't necessarily be the amount they are charged by their local credit card company. Many credit card companies charge high conversation rates that may not be equivalent to the rate used by the calculator. In addition, the currency converter doesn't take into account customs duties and other import fees that may be charged by local governments. Nevertheless, currency converters can give your international customers a good indication of what they will end up paying in their own currency on their credit card statement.

CHECKOUT PROCEDURES

This section reviews the three important elements that pertain to the checkout process of your online store:

- Express checkout services
- Address books
- Minimizing abandoned shopping carts

Express Checkout Services

Some Web merchants, in an effort to speed up the checkout process and make online shopping more convenient for their customers, have implemented express checkout services so that customers can store their shipping addresses, credit card data, and shipping preferences on the site. That way, they don't have to reenter this information each time they make a purchase. For example, customers simply need to register on the Eddie Bauer Web site (www.eddiebauer.com) once, and they never need to fill out their billing information again:

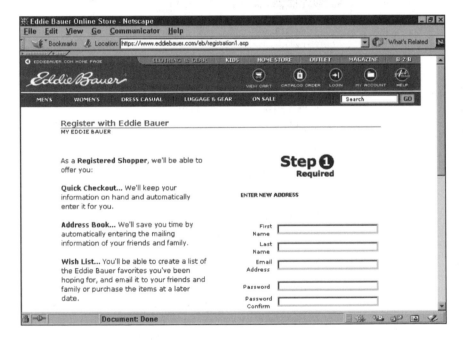

Address Books

If you use e-mail regularly, you're probably aware that most e-mail programs contain an address book, where you can store the names and e-mail addresses of the people you communicate with frequently, such as your friends, colleagues, and relatives. Whenever you want to send an e-mail message to someone in your address book, you just need to select the person's name from a list of names; the person's e-mail address is automatically added to your message without you having to remember it. A number of online stores provide a similar function on their Web sites.

The difference is that instead of storing the e-mail addresses of their friends and relatives, customers can store their postal addresses. This makes it easier for your customers to send gifts to their friends and family members without having to type in their full addresses every time they place an online order on the merchant's Web site. For example, on Nordstrom's online store (www.nordstrom.com), customers can store the addresses of people they frequently send gifts to:

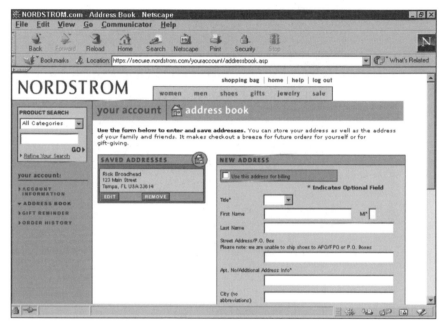

An online address book makes it easy for your customers to do business with you. Because this type of feature makes the checkout process faster and more convenient for your customers, it also can increase customer retention and customer loyalty.

e-Fact

In a survey of 12,000 online shoppers, 40% said they would use more than one route to customer service.

Source: Forrester Research (www.forrester.com)

Minimizing Abandoned Shopping Carts

Web store veterans will tell you that one of the most frustrating problems with an online store is that many visitors place items in their shopping carts, but never proceed to checkout. Instead, they simply abandon the cart and go elsewhere on the Internet.

Statistics bear this out. According to one study by Forrester Research (www.forrester.com), two-thirds of all Internet shopping baskets are abandoned before the order is completed. There are a number of reasons why a shopper may suddenly decide not to continue with an Internet purchase. Often, the reason is related to privacy or security concerns. A customer gets to the section of the Web site where a credit card number or other personal information is required, and suddenly gets cold feet. Perhaps the person is worried about personal information being misused or is afraid to send credit card information over the Internet. Sometimes customers bail out because they think the checkout process is going to take too long. Alternatively, they may have second thoughts about the credibility of the Internet merchant, not be satisfied with the return or exchange policy, or be scared away by shipping and handling charges that suddenly appear in the final stages of the transaction. Also, don't forget that online shopping is still a new phenomenon for many people. Lots of consumers experiment with online shopping even though they have no intention of actually going through with a transaction.

To help you minimize the number of abandoned purchase attempts that occur on your online store, we've put together the following seven suggestions:

1. Allow customers to register on your Web site so that their mailing address and credit card information is stored on your servers (provided you have implemented adequate security measures). This allows customers to make future purchases without having to key in all of their personal information each time.

2. Keep the checkout process simple and hassle-free. When a customer is ready to place an order, keep the number of questions to a minimum. Don't make the process overly complicated or time-consuming.

3. Number the steps in the checkout process so that customers know at each stage how many more steps they have to complete before they're done. Alternatively, display a graphic at each stage of the checkout process that illustrates how far along the customer is in the process and how many steps are left. An excellent example of this technique can be found at Eddie Bauer's online store (www.eddiebauer.com). Once a customer has decided to check out, a timeline along the top of the screen tracks the progress of the transaction and shows the customer how many steps are left to go through. A darkened bullet indicates the current step. In the following example, the customer is completing the second step of checking out and has two more steps to go:

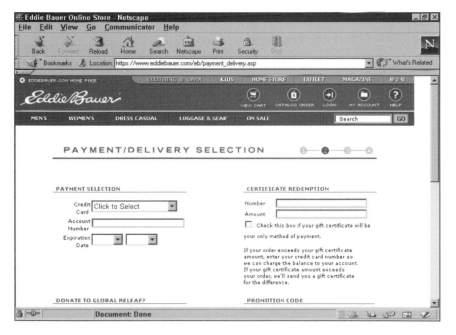

Needless to say, customers are less likely to get impatient and give up if you tell them they're near the end.

4. Display your security guarantee, privacy policy, and return and exchange policy throughout the entire checkout process in order to build confidence.

5. Fully disclose any and all shipping or handling charges before the customer keys in a credit card number.

6. Display a telephone number (or better yet, a toll-free number) that customers can call if they have any questions during checkout. Make sure that this toll-free number appears throughout the checkout process.

7. Don't force customers to download any special software programs or plug-ins in order to do business with you.

CUSTOMER SERVICE AND SUPPORT

It goes without saying that customer service has become the number-one priority for online retailers. In fact, online retailers have lost billions of dollars in sales in recent years because of shoddy customer service. If you want to build a successful online business, you have to take customer service very seriously. Although many large online retailers have invested millions of dollars to improve the quality of customer service they offer online, there are many things that you can do to improve customer service on your Web site without breaking the bank.

This section reviews the customer support issues you need to think about for your online store. There are nine important issues:

- Telephone support
- Contact information
- E-mail management
- FAQs (frequently asked questions)
- Online help and customer service centers
- Feedback and complaint mechanisms
- Reference materials
- Live sales assistance
- Prerecorded audio messages

Telephone Support

Many online shoppers will want to make human contact with you to verify that you are real, or to resolve a complaint if they are unable to get answers to their questions on your Web site. In the early days of e-commerce, it was mistakenly believed that selling online would actually reduce the amount of contact that customers would need with retailers. Online shoppers have proven that assumption wrong. Many online retailers have found themselves unable to meet the volume of incoming phone calls from online shoppers, especially during peak periods such as Christmas. Make sure that you have enough knowledgeable people on staff to handle telephone calls from customers who are shopping on your Web site and think about installing a toll-free number so that customers can call you without incurring long-distance charges. If you install a toll-free number, make sure that it works across North America (not just in the United States), so that customers in Canada can reach you. In addition, include a direct-dial number on your Web site so that customers in other parts of world can call you. We've come across many online stores where the only telephone number published is a toll-free number that only works from the United States. Needless to say, international customers won't be able to call you if you do this.

Contact Information

There is nothing more infuriating to an online shopper than not being able to find a telephone number, fax number, or mailing address on a store's Web site. In particular, one of the cardinal sins with an online store is not publishing a telephone number for your business. That is why you should make sure that your online store provides clear, unambiguous contact information. It should list, at a minimum, the full name of the business including its legal name (if different from the online name), telephone number, mailing address, and fax number. Make sure that your contact information is easily accessible from your Web site's home page – don't force customers to hunt for your telephone number and mailing address.

Consider posting information on how to contact particular departments or people for various issues, such as product support, shipment tracking, returns, etc.

A good example of this approach is the online store belonging to PETsMART (www.petsmart.com). PETsMART's "Contacting Us" section includes separate e-mail addresses for order questions, product suggestions, product questions, questions related to the Web site, and general customer service questions. The same page also includes the company's mailing address and toll-free telephone number.

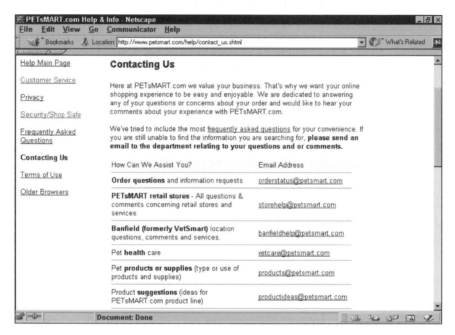

While setting up different e-mail addresses for different functions can be a good idea, too many choices can also be a source of confusion for customers. A study of customer service on the Internet by New York–based Jupiter Research (www.jup.com) uncovered one company that had eighteen different e-mail addresses for customer relations! Obviously, this situation is more frustrating than helpful for the customer.

There is no "right" solution for handling e-mail correspondence from customers. It depends on the size of your organization and the volume of e-mail you are receiving. If you're a small business with a small number of employees, you don't necessarily need multiple e-mail addresses. You can establish one e-mail address for all needs that a customer may have, and all customer correspondence will end up in the same mailbox. However, larger organizations that receive large volumes of e-mail are better off setting up separate e-mail addresses for different customer functions. This will make it easier to respond to messages in a timely fashion, since they can quickly be directed to the appropriate department in your organization.

E-mail Management

While it's important for customers to be able to contact you by telephone, many customers prefer to use e-mail. The problem with e-mail is that many online stores get overwhelmed with messages from customers and they can't reply in a timely manner. You should be able to respond to every e-mail message your site receives within a maximum of twenty-four hours. If you can't provide that level of service, you should consider hiring more people or investigate ways to automate the routing of your messages and the responses customers receive. For some customers, twenty-four hours is too long to wait, so many online retailers are trying to respond to e-mail messages within two or three hours. Recognizing how critical e-mail response times are, Lands' End (www.landsend.com) has actually installed software that measures the length of time it takes the company to respond to every e-mail message it receives from customers.

Once you publish your e-mail address on your Web site, it is essential that you respond to any customer questions promptly. You must never forget that on the Web, your competitors are only a mouse-click away. Online shoppers have little tolerance for businesses that don't provide prompt and courteous responses to their questions.

Because many organizations don't reply to customer e-mail messages quickly, online shoppers may be skeptical about contacting your store by e-mail. As a result, you could be losing sales and not even realize it. To encourage customers to communicate with your store by e-mail, we recommend that you establish an e-mail policy and display it on your Web site. An e-mail policy is simply a pledge to reply to customer questions within a certain time period. The point is to let customers know how long it will be before they receive a response from your online store. For example, Patagonia's online store (www.patagonia.com) contains the following message: "We read email from 8 a.m. to 4 p.m. PST every day except Sunday. In general, you can expect an answer the same day if you send the message in the morning; send it later and we can get back to you on the next business day."

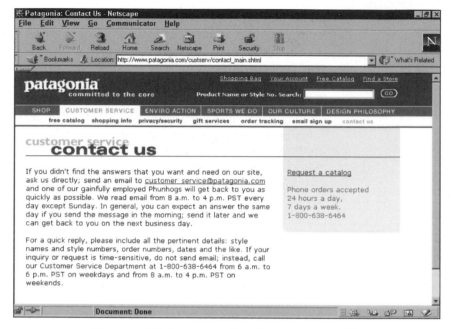

If you publish an e-mail policy on your online store, you'll find that customers will be more willing to contact you with their questions or concerns. However, make sure that you can honor whatever deadlines you establish. If you tell customers you'll respond to their e-mail messages within twenty-four hours and then take forty-eight hours to reply, you'll quickly lose their trust and confidence.

If you can't deal with the volume of e-mail messages you receive, post a message on your Web site to let your customers know that you can't guarantee a timely response. You're better off being honest with your customers than having them wait endlessly for a response to an e-mail message that you know you're never going to get to. However, you should give customers another way to get in touch with you.

Alternatively, if you find yourself dealing with a really large volume of e-mail messages, you may want to explore an e-mail management solution from a company such as Kana Communications (www.kana.com), eGain (www.egain.com) or Brightware (www.brightware.com). All of these companies sell e-mail management products to help online businesses deal with high volumes of e-mail. These products ensure that e-mail messages from your customers are intelligently, and automatically, forwarded to the right departments. In addition, e-mail management software often uses artificial intelligence technology that can interpret a customer's e-mail message automatically and reply with the appropriate canned response. Keep in mind that these types of applications can be expensive and hence may only be appropriate if you are receiving hundreds of messages a day from your customers. Many online retailers have found it necessary to resort to such software both to improve customer service and to reduce the number of phone calls they receive.

The other benefit of an e-mail management system is that it can automatically respond to customer queries even when your customer service department is closed and there are no employees available to answer e-mail messages personally.

Another option is to outsource your e-mail management and hire a company to answer your e-mail messages for you, either on an ongoing basis or only on an overflow or after-hours basis. PeopleSupport (www.peoplesupport.com) is one of many organizations that provide e-mail answering services.

FAQs (Frequently Asked Questions)

One way to cut down on the volume of e-mail messages from your customers is to create a FAQ document and post it on your Web site. This document contains answers to the most common questions your customers ask. Once this document has been created, create a link to it from the section of your Web site that lists your e-mail addresses and contact information, and encourage customers to read it before contacting you. You should also have a link to the FAQ page from your home page.

To see a good example of a FAQ page, visit the Web site of Walgreens (www.walgreens.com). The company has assembled a list of more than two dozen frequently asked questions and their answers:

> **e-Fact**
>
> *In 2005, consumers will spend more than U.S. $632 billion at brick-and-mortar stores as a result of research they've done online — more than three times the amount they will spend online!*
> Source: Jupiter Research (www.jup.com)

Online Help and Customer Service Centers

As customers are browsing your Web site, they may have questions about ordering, shipping, return policies, security/privacy polices, or other matters. In an effort to help online shoppers get answers to their questions quickly, many online retailers include a "help" or "customer service" button right at the top of their home page. Clicking on this button will lead customers to an online help center or online customer service center. For a good example of this strategy, visit PETsMART's online store (www.petsmart.com). Notice the "HELP" link at the top of the screen. This link always stays at the top of the screen regardless of which page of the site the customer is looking at.

Customers who click on the "HELP" link will be taken to the following screen, where they can get answers on everything from how to change their password to how to get in touch with the company:

Sears (www.sears.com) has a similar section on its Web site, called "Customer Service":

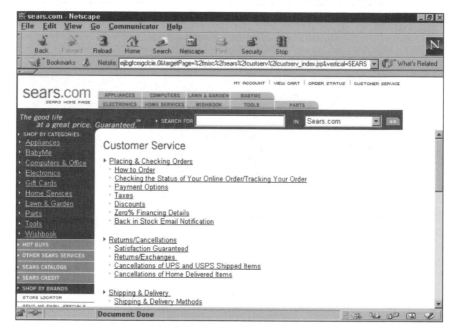

Make sure that you create a similar area on your Web site and provide a link to it from every page on your site.

Feedback and Complaint Mechanisms

We certainly hope that your customers won't need to contact you with a problem or complaint, but if they do, you should make it easy for them to get in touch with you. There are two types of problems that customers might have. First, they could have a technical problem with your Web site. For example, a customer may have difficulty using your site, or perhaps one of the links or forms is not working. Second, customers might have a complaint about an order they placed or a product they received from you. Because technical problems are distinct from product problems, you may want to establish two separate e-mail addresses, as Lands' End (www.landsend.com) has done on its Web site:

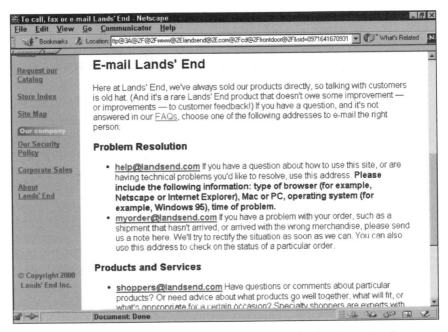

Under the heading "Problem Resolution," notice that Lands' End has one e-mail address for technical problems and a second one for problems with orders. There are also other e-mail addresses for general product inquiries and sales inquiries. Some people might argue that it's better to have one e-mail address for everything rather than confusing shoppers with multiple e-mail addresses, a potential problem that we raised earlier. It really depends on how big your business is and how many e-mail messages you're receiving from your customers.

Nevertheless, by creating a separate section on your Web site called "Problem Resolution," as Lands' End has done, you let your customers know that you're committed to resolving their problems quickly and efficiently. Of course, you don't have to use the heading "Problem Resolution." Pick any name you want – just make sure that customers know where to channel their complaints and concerns. You should ensure that you follow up on any complaints extremely quickly, given the unforgiving nature of the Internet that we discussed at the beginning of the chapter.

In addition to setting up an e-mail address for problem resolution purposes, make it easy for customers to offer feedback on your products, your service, or your Web site.

It goes without saying that customer feedback is extremely valuable to any merchant. As Lands' End says on its Web site, "it's a rare Lands' End product that doesn't owe some improvement – or improvements – to customer feedback!" So why not make it easy for customers to offer their suggestions and ideas to you? It's not hard to do – just set up a separate e-mail address for comments and suggestions.

If you don't intend to personally acknowledge every piece of feedback, make sure you say this on your Web site. Otherwise, customers may conclude that you don't care about their comments when they don't get a response. On the Lands' End site, the message beside the feedback e-mail address says: "If you have a suggestion or comment but don't need a response (other than to know we'll consider it carefully!) use this address." It can be extremely difficult to keep up with all the feedback you may receive from your customers, so there's nothing wrong with telling them that although you'll carefully consider every message you receive, you're not able to provide personal replies to every suggestion.

Reference Materials

Where possible, include information on your Web site that will assist your customers in making an educated purchase decision. An excellent example of this strategy is outdoor equipment/apparel retailer REI (www.rei.com). Its site is full of information to help customers make better purchase decisions:

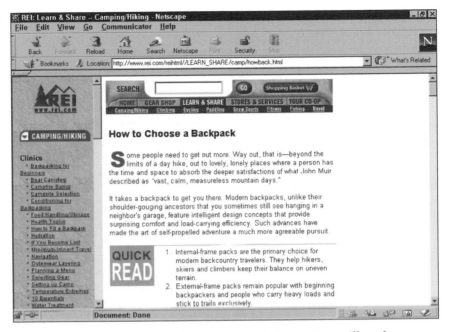

This type of helpful product information will make your customers more loyal to you and more inclined to use your online store. But perhaps more importantly, if you help customers choose the right products from your online store, it's less likely the customer will make the wrong choice and have to return the item. Product returns are costly – and frustrating – for both consumers and online merchants.

REI's Web site also contains a bulletin board where shoppers can ask each other for advice on topics related to the outdoors (e.g., hiking, climbing, cycling) and the products that REI.com sells:

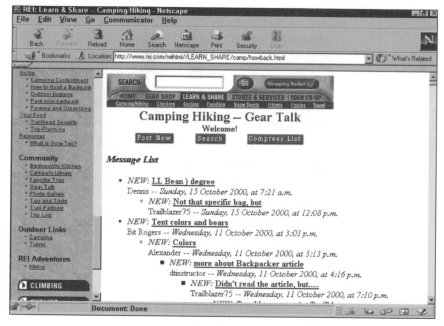

These are just two possible ways that you can support your customers and give them more confidence in the products they buy from you. You can also educate your customers by providing product tips, ask-an-expert features, product reviews, and informational articles.

Live Sales Assistance

Earlier in this chapter, we discussed the high incidence of consumers abandoning their purchases before completing an online transaction. In the box below, we've listed some of the main reasons why online shoppers fail to complete an online transaction.

Top Reasons Why Consumers Abandon Online Purchase Attempts

1. Too much information needed to be filled in (52%).

2. Customer did not want to enter credit card details (46%).

3. The Web site malfunctioned (42%).

4. Customer could not find product (40%).

5. Customer could not specify product (24%).

6. Customer was forced to call a customer service representative to get help with the transaction (16%).

7. Customer did not like the returns policy (16%).

Source: A.T. Kearney survey of experienced online shoppers in six countries, www.atkearney.com

Customers often back out of a purchase because of last-minute concerns or questions. For example, they may need help finding a product or they may have a simple question about the company's return policy. Consumers are often forced to call a customer service representative in order to resolve such problems, but according to the A.T. Kearney survey, 60 percent of online shoppers who are forced to call a company say that they find the process frustrating and would probably not go back to the Web site to resume their purchase.

Some online merchants are realizing that they can possibly curb this problem by giving customers a way to interact with a live person without having to pick up a telephone. FAO Schwarz (www.fao.com) is one of many online stores using this strategy. FAO Schwarz uses technology from a company called Face Time Communications (www.facetime.com) to offer its customers live access to its customer service representatives. Displayed in the customer service section of FAO Schwarz's Web site is an icon that reads "Live Help":

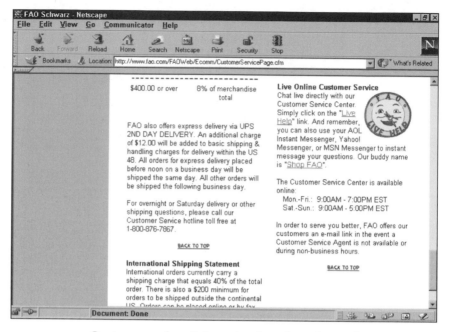

Customers who click on that icon have immediate access to a "live" customer service representative who can answer any questions they may have.

In the following pages, we'll show you how a typical dialogue between a Web shopper and a customer service agent would be established. After clicking on the "Live Help" icon in the customer service section, the customer will be asked to enter his or her name, e-mail address, and a question. In the screen below, Rick Broadhead, one of the authors of this book, is asking for a live chat session on the FAO Schwarz Web site:

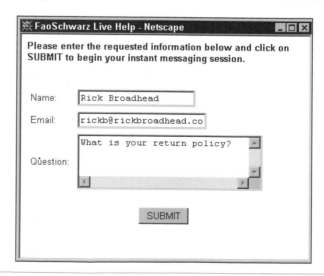

Once the question is submitted, Rick is told to wait for the next available customer service representative:

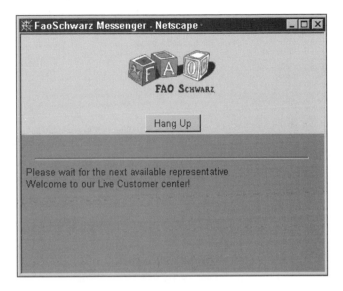

Once the connection has been established, the customer service representative's name (Michael, in this case) appears on the screen with the message, "How can I help you?":

At this point, Rick and the customer service agent can "chat" with each other by typing back and forth. To enter a question or a comment, you type a message in the white box and then press the "Send" button. Your question or comment will then appear in the bottom half of the screen. In the screen below, Rick is asking about FAO Schwarz's return policy (sometimes it can be helpful to repeat the question once you connect with a customer service representative):

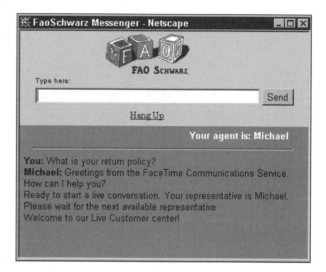

As you can see in the screen below, Michael immediately responds to Rick's question. Rick then responds with "Thank you!":

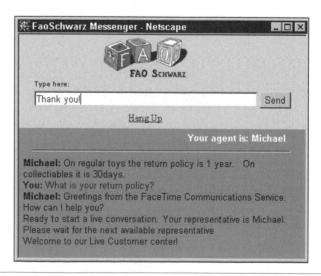

Michael then says "You're welcome." To end the chat session, Rick clicks on the "Hang Up" link (seen in the previous screen) and the session is terminated:

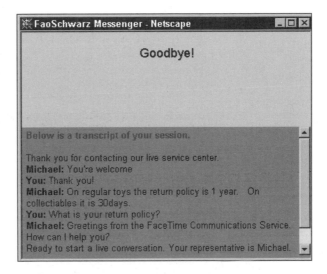

This technology adds a human touch to the often impersonal nature of online shopping. Not only does live-chat software improve customer satisfaction by giving your customers instant access to company representatives, it may also reduce the number of telephone calls and e-mail messages your company receives. Furthermore, many consumers only have one telephone line, which is occupied when they are accessing the Internet. Live chat technology allows the customer to ask a question without having to disconnect from the Internet to use the phone. This can help you to close more sales on your Web site because customers don't have to go through the time-consuming process of disconnecting from the Internet to use the telephone and then reconnecting to make their purchase once their question has been answered. In fact, as noted earlier, by the time a customer disconnects from the Internet and gets on the phone with you, he or she may decide not to bother going through with the purchase.

If you decide to offer a live chat service on your online store, you can control the hours that it is available. Some merchants chose to offer live chat around the clock while other merchants only offer the service on specific days of the week and during certain hours of the day. Customers who try to contact a customer service agent during off-hours will be asked to leave a message or will be redirected to an e-mail address.

If you plan on doing a substantial amount of business with overseas customers, you should consider offering live customer support twenty-four hours a day so that you can accommodate shoppers in other time zones. In addition, a lot of consumers in North America shop on the Web in the late evening and into the early hours in the morning, so providing live chat around the clock will help you service these customers as well.

The number of customer service representatives you need on hand will depend on how many live chat requests you start receiving. When a customer service representative isn't available, the customer will be told to wait until an agent becomes free. You obviously want to keep waiting times to a minimum, so you should be prepared to increase the number of customer service agents if waiting times become too long.

On the other hand, you may find that you don't get any substantial benefit from live chat services at all. Despite the obvious advantages of this type of online customer support, some companies are not convinced that the investment is worthwhile. One company executive we spoke to said she would rather her company spent the money on a better Web site so that customers don't need to ask questions. Indeed, there's no guarantee that live chat services will help you cut costs, increase sales, and increase customer loyalty. However, many companies are convinced that the technology is necessary to provide customers with top-notch customer service, something that is sorely lacking in many online stores.

If you do decide to implement live chat technology, make sure that you regularly review the transcripts of chats with customers to identify the types of questions that they are asking. You can then use this information to update the FAQ section on your Web site so that other shoppers with the same questions won't need to contact you via live chat or on the telephone. If you regularly update your FAQs in this manner, you'll be able to reduce your customer service costs.

To help research live chat solutions for your online store, we've listed some of the vendors of online customer service in the following table.

Vendors of Online Customer Service Software

Brightware	www.brightware.com
eGain Communications	www.egain.com
eShare Communications	www.eshare.com
eSupportNow	www.esupportnow.com
FaceTime Communications	www.facetime.com
HumanClick	www.humanclick.com
Kana Communications	www.kana.com
LiveAssistance	www.liveassistance.com
LivePerson	www.liveperson.com
ServiceSoft	www.servicesoft.com
WebLine	www.webline.com

Escorted Browsing

Many live chat programs support "escorted browsing," a feature that allows a customer service representative to guide an online shopper through the company's Web site. For example, LivePerson's software allows customer service representatives to "push" Web pages to a customer's Web browser. If an online shopper is lost and needs help finding a section on your Web site, the customer service representative can actually force the appropriate Web page to show up on the customer's computer screen.

LivePerson software can also be set up so that the customer service representative initiates the chat with the customer rather than the other way around. In the live chat session we showed you earlier, Rick initiated the chat request with FAO Schwarz. But what if FAO Schwarz were to initiate the chat request with Rick as soon as Rick entered the online store?

For example, when an online shopper enters your Web site, a box could pop up on the customer's screen with the message, "Can I help you find anything?" While this type of an intervention may scare customers (and heighten privacy fears), it can also impress customers when used in the right way. Think about how many times you've walked into a store and waited for someone to approach you and ask if you need any help. It's really no different on the Web. Personal service is something a lot of online shoppers would really appreciate.

Most live chat solutions, like LivePerson, don't require you to install any software on your own Web servers. In most cases, customers don't need to download or install any software or plugs-in either. They simply click on a button on your Web site and they can begin chatting with a customer service representative immediately!

The cost of live-agent software varies depending on the product. LivePerson, for example, has a one-time setup fee of $2,000 and each operator costs $350 per month. However, the cost per operator drops off as the number of operators increases. The cost also decreases if merchants choose to use some of the other online customer service tools that LivePerson offers.

Clearly, it's not an inexpensive investment, so you need to weigh the costs and benefits of using this type of a service on your Web site. If you're a small business on a tight budget, you may want to consider a live chat tool called HumanClick (www.humanclick.com). HumanClick is owned by LivePerson, but its basic service is available for free. You can download the HumanClick software from the company's Web site:

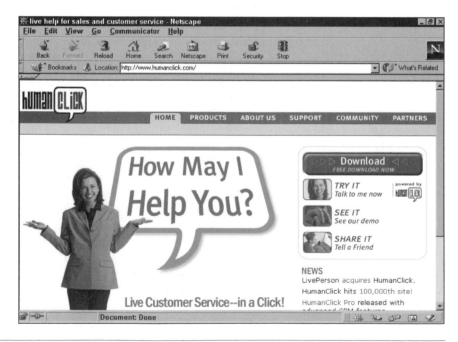

Once you've downloaded the free HumanClick software, you install it on your computer. The installation process is simple and takes only a few minutes. During the setup procedure, you will be required to install a few lines of computer code onto your Web site. This code will place a HumanClick icon on your Web site so that online shoppers can click on it if they want to chat with you. Obviously, this requires that you or someone in your firm be near that computer to respond to chat requests from customers. If you don't want to accept live chat requests or you plan on being away from your computer for an extended period of time, you can program the software to display a "Leave a Message" icon. This is what the online store pictured below has done. Notice the "Leave a Message" icon in the bottom right-hand corner of the screen:

Customers who click on this icon will see a pop-up screen where they can send you a message (which will be delivered to you by e-mail):

One of the best features of HumanClick is that you will be alerted by a "ding-dong" sound on your computer whenever a potential customer enters your Web site. Using the control panel in the HumanClick software, you will be able to see which Web site the customer came from, his or her host name (e.g., kodak.com), which Web pages on your site the customer has viewed, and more:

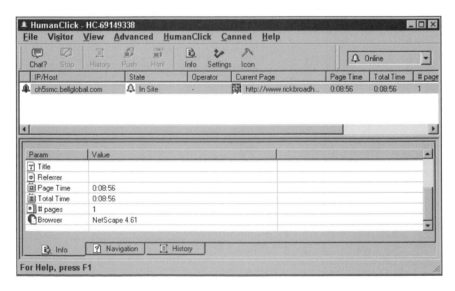

If you want to chat with the customer who is on your Web site, you simply click on the "Chat?" button at the top of the control panel. When you do that, an icon like the one below will suddenly pop up on the customer's computer screen.

If the customer accepts, you'll hear the sound of a ringing phone on your computer and a message indicating that the customer has started a chat session with you:

A chat window will pop up on the customer's computer screen like the following one:

And you will be able to chat with the customer using the HumanClick software:

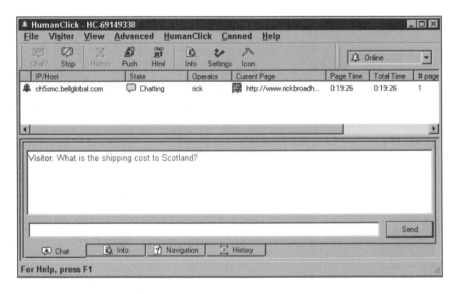

Although the basic version of HumanClick is free, a more advanced version, called HumanClick Pro, is available for download for an additional fee. HumanClick Pro allows you to do things such as:

- customize the HumanClick icons that are displayed on your Web site;
- customize the Chat and Leave a Message windows;

- display Web pages on your customer's Web browser;
- access chat transcripts from your Web site visitors
- prepare canned responses to frequently asked questions and send them to online shoppers.

HumanClick and even HumanClick Pro don't offer many of the advanced features that you will find in more expensive packages such as LivePerson. In fact, larger businesses may find that HumanClick is inadequate for their purposes. However, for small businesses that are serious about online customer service, HumanClick is an excellent starting package.

Voice Chat

While most online stores offering live sales assistance are doing so using text chat software, several merchants are offering voice chat as well so that customers can actually talk with a customer service representative. The call is actually carried over the customer's Internet connection and the customer doesn't need to have an extra phone line available. In order for this to work, the customer needs to have a microphone attached to his or her computer, as well as speakers and a sound card. Most new computers come with these features, although many customers may not have the microphone attached to their computer when they visit your online store, so they may not be able to communicate with you in this way.

The other problem with voice chat is that the sound quality isn't always reliable. Because the call is being routed over the Internet, it's not as dependable as a regular phone line. Nevertheless, the quality of Internet-based phone calls is constantly improving and more retailers are experimenting with the technology. For an example of a retailer using live voice chat, visit the J. Crew Web site (www.jcrew.com).

J. Crew uses a technology from a company called Estara (www.estara.com). In the "Contact Us" section of the Web site, customers are given the opportunity of chatting live with a customer service representative:

When a shopper clicks on the "click here" button, a connection is established with a J. Crew customer service representative:

Within a few seconds, a connection is in place and the customer can start talking with the J. Crew representative:

Although voice chat technology is still in its infancy, it's yet another way to offer excellent service to your customers.

Prerecorded Audio Messages

Many consumers find online shopping very impersonal. If you need help, you're sometimes forced to scroll through help screens and it's easy to get frustrated. You no doubt know the feeling your legs get when you've been walking around a shopping mall for countless hours. On the Internet, your legs don't get tired, but your eyes can get weary after looking at the computer screen for a long period of time. To make the online shopping experience friendlier, easier, and more personal, some online retailers have added friendly, prerecorded audio messages on their Web sites to put customers at ease and help them get answers to their questions. For example, customers on Macy's Web site can click on "Play Audio" to listen to help messages at various sections of the site (you can see the "Play Audio" message in the upper right-hand corner of the screen):

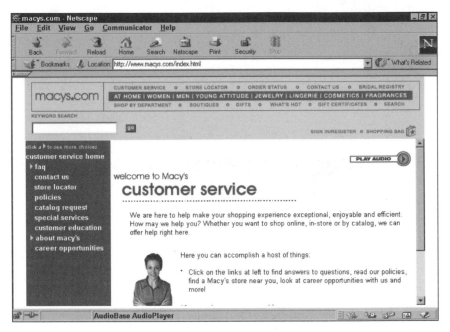

In order for customers to hear the recordings, they need to have a sound card and speakers on their computer. However, most new computers have this equipment.

Macy's audio technology was implemented by a company called AudioBase (www.audiobase.com). Working closely with Macy's, AudioBase wrote the script, hired someone to do the voiceovers, and taped the messages in a professional studio. It's yet another innovative way to improve the quality of customer service on your Web site!

CHANNEL INTEGRATION

You've no doubt heard the phrase, "The left hand doesn't know what the right hand is doing." Well, it seems to be true of a lot of organizations on the Web. The online part of the company doesn't interact well with the offline part of the company, resulting in poor service for customers. As companies try to integrate their online and offline channels, there are two important issues that need to be addressed:

- Customer relationship management (CRM)
- Multi-channel shopping

We discuss each of these below.

Customer Relationship Management

Although it is not a major issue for small businesses, one of the biggest challenges for large companies selling online is effective customer relationship management, also known as CRM. Although you will come across many different definitions of customer relationship management, we define CRM as the process of seamlessly integrating all the various points of customer contact into a single database. For example, a customer may walk into an organization's retail store and ask about an e-mail inquiry that was submitted several days earlier. Or a customer may call an organization on the telephone to follow up on a live chat session that the person had on the organization's Web site.

One of the authors of this book once called a hotel chain to try to cancel a hotel reservation he had made on the organization's Web site. The woman in the call center who took his call didn't have access to the Web reservations database, so she had to transfer him to another customer service agent who dealt with the Internet bookings. The problem? The hotel hadn't yet combined all its databases, so customers had to deal with different customer service representatives depending on whether their reservation was made online or over the phone. Obviously, this can confuse and aggravate customers, who don't want to experience delays when they contact an organization to resolve an issue. It's important to remember that your customers don't see your online and offline operations as separate entities. Regardless of whether they contact you by e-mail, phone, or live chat, they expect that the person at the other end will be able to help them.

This presents a big problem for a business: how to ensure that every employee has a record of all the interactions that a customer has had with the organization, regardless of what channel the customer used to contact the organization. In other words, an employee should be able to access a history file of all the customer's dealings with the organization, including e-mail correspondence, transcripts of chat sessions, order history, etc. The goal is to have a "360-degree view" of your customers. As you can imagine, pulling all of this information together into a single database that all employees can access is an extremely expensive and complex undertaking, often costing millions of dollars. But the benefit is greater customer loyalty and better customer service.

Not surprisingly, integrating customer service systems has become a top priority for online retailers. There are literally hundreds of companies that specialize in this area, including firms like Siebel Systems (www.siebel.com) and E.piphany (www.epiphany.com). In addition, most of the companies that specialize in live chat software and e-mail management software can also help you with CRM solutions.

Once you have synchronized all of your customer information databases so that customer service representatives can see a customer's complete purchase history across all of your divisions (e.g., phone, Web, catalog, retail stores), the marketing possibilities are enormous. For example, a customer service representative handling a live chat request or responding to an e-mail could cross-sell products based on the types of purchases the customer has made in the past. In addition, once all of your databases are combined, it will be possible to analyze customer purchase behavior and develop individualized marketing strategies and campaigns for each customer. Not only can this increase sales, it can improve customer service, since customers will be offered highly personalized product recommendations (for more information on the benefits of personalization technology, see Chapter 7, *Building Customer Loyalty in Your Online Store*).

If you are interested in learning more about the latest trends in the CRM industry, good sites to visit include RealMarket (www.realmarket.com) and CRMCommunity.com (www.crmcommunity.com).

Multi-channel Shopping

You may have come across the phrases "clicks and bricks" and "clicks and mortar." They refer to a strategy pursued by many organizations that have both an online store and a physical brick-and-mortar store.

In the early days of e-commerce, it was assumed that the Internet would cannibalize sales in traditional channels such as retail stores or catalogs. Many retailers were therefore hesitant to sell online, fearing that it would take away business from their catalogs and/or brick-and-mortar stores. That fear proved unfounded and retailers have since discovered that operating multiple channels can actually improve overall business. Now that retailers have concluded that consumers aren't going to stop shopping at brick-and-mortar stores, or catalogs for that matter, they're working on creating multi-channel businesses and, at the same time, creating closer links among their Web sites, retail stores, and catalog operations.

Once you begin to serve customers through several channels, you want to make sure that your channels are seamlessly integrated so that they reinforce one another. You also want to make sure that your online brand is consistent with your real-world brand. Customer relationship management technology is a big part of a clicks-and-bricks strategy, but there are other aspects as well. For example, your customers may want to:

- buy a product online but return it to one of your retail stores;
- research a product in one of your retail stores but then buy it online;
- research a product in your catalog but then buy it online;
- purchase a gift certificate in one of your retail stores but redeem it online;
- access your Web site from your retail stores; or
- order a product on your Web site and pick it up in person from one of your retail stores.

If you have one or more retail stores, think about ways in which you can offer greater synergy between your physical and online operations. Barnes and Noble, for example, has placed Internet kiosks in its retail locations so that customers can access the company's Web site to research products and order items that aren't in stock. Kmart, Sears, and other retailers have done the same.

Many online retailers that have catalogs have made it easy for customers to look up a product they saw in a catalog and then buy it online. For example, Illuminations (www.illuminations.com) has placed a box in the upper left-hand corner of its home page where customers can type in a catalog ID number:

In an effort to give customers more choice as to when and how they shop, many retailers are beginning to introduce what Sam's Club (www.samsclub.com) calls a "click-and-pull" strategy – allowing customers to place an order online but pick it up in person. The idea is to use your Web site to "pull" customers into your retail stores. This strategy also allows consumers to enjoy the convenience of shopping on the Web without having to worry about delivery times or shipping charges – two of the most frequently voiced complaints about shopping on the Internet. Customers of Office Depot's online store (www.officedepot.com), for example, are given the choice of picking up their online order or having it delivered to their home or office. If the pickup option is selected, the Web site will automatically find the closest retail location that has the customer's desired item(s) in stock:

Bloomingdale's provides an exciting glimpse at the future of clicks-and-bricks strategies, in a way that gives new meaning to the term "window shop." Via the Bloomingdale's Web site (www.bloomingdales.com), customers can actually browse the window displays from one of the company's retail stores and buy what's in them by clicking their mouse on the window:

One final word of advice in this section: the Web is simply another channel for customers to use. It doesn't replace retail stores or catalogs – it complements them. In fact, many retailers have discovered that customers who use more than one channel spend more than those customers that only buy through a single channel. Recognizing that customers are frequently using more than one channel to do business with online retailers, and spending more as a result, you may want to consider creating a catalog to complement your online store. If you operate in multiple channels, make sure you service your customers in a seamless, integrated way regardless of which channel they choose to use. The benefit of pursuing this type of tight integration between your online and offline channels is increased convenience and better service for your customers, and increased sales for you!

e-Fact

60% of Internet shoppers bookmark an average of seven shopping sites.
Source: Cyber Dialogue
(www.cyberdialogue.com)

INTERNATIONALIZATION

Although more than 85 percent of Internet users speak English as their first or second language, this will drop to less than 50 percent by 2002, according to a study by International Data Corporation (www.idc.com). For example, the number of Internet users in China is expected to exceed 120 million by 2004, giving China one of the biggest online populations in the entire world. Even within the United States, there are an estimated 32 million people that don't speak English, yet most Web sites don't have content in languages other than English. These figures have important implications for any U.S. online merchant that wants to sell its products to international markets – or simply to domestic Internet users who don't speak English.

In order to make your products and/or services more appealing to non-English-speaking Internet users, both domestically and abroad, you should consider translating your entire Web site, or parts of it, into other languages that help you to reach your target market. Consider Howard Johnson Hotels (www.hojo.com). In an effort to increase the business it does online with the Hispanic and Latin American population, the hotel chain hired a company called Global Language Solutions (www.globallanguages.com) to translate its Web site into Spanish:

If translating your entire Web site into one or more languages is beyond your financial means, consider offering just your ordering and shipping information in languages other than English. Amazon.com (www.amazon.com), for example, provides country-specific information on its ordering and shipping policies in a variety of languages, including Italian, German, Spanish, and Portuguese:

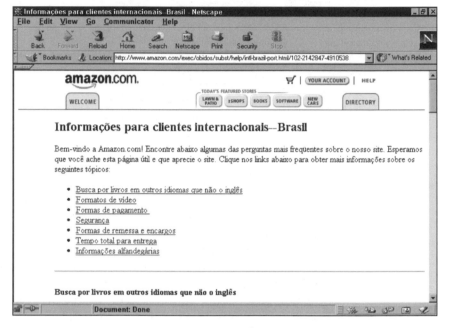

REI (www.rei.com) also offers order information in a variety of languages, including Spanish, German, and Dutch:

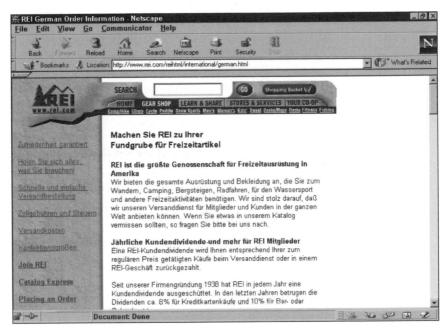

Before translating your site into multiple languages, think about the consequences. If you start to offer product information in languages other than English, customers will start to expect product support in those languages as well. In addition, customers will start to e-mail you in languages other than English. Then there's the issue of your invoices and other literature that you send with the products you ship – you'll have to translate that material as well. In other words, you are creating a whole new set of responsibilities for your online store once you translate sections of your Web site. Make sure that you are capable of coping with the consequences!

ONLINE MARKET RESEARCH

In this chapter, we've provided you with dozens of tips and techniques to help you maximize the effectiveness of your online store. But even more important than our advice is what your customers think.

You should thoroughly test your online store before you make it available to the public and you should also continue testing at regular intervals after the launch. Testing your store before it officially opens will help you to identify potential problems and work all the kinks out of your site before "real" customers start to use it. You can do this by having a group of your friends and colleagues test your site and identify problems, features they don't like, and features they'd like to see. Also ask them to give you feedback on the layout and overall design and appearance of your store. What improvements would they suggest you make?

In addition, have your friends place "test" orders on your Web site and get their feedback on the ordering process. Make note of glitches or unforeseen problems that crop up. You'll be amazed at how many useful ideas and suggestions this can generate. As noted earlier in the chapter, have people view your Web site using both Microsoft Explorer and Netscape Navigator. You will want to ensure that your Web site looks the same regardless of what Web browser the customer is using.

Also have your friends test your Web site using different modem speeds. For example, have one person order a product using a 28.8 kbps modem and then have someone try the same order using a 56.6 kbps modem. Although more and more consumers and businesses are using high-speed connections to the Internet such as cable modems and ADSL/DSL modems, you want to make sure that your Web site can be used by those consumers who are still using dial-up Internet connections.

It's especially important that you test your site after any major enhancements or redesigns. There are two reasons for this. First, you want to make sure that your site enhancements are working properly. Second, you want to make sure that your customers like the changes you've made. Unfortunately, it seems that few Web sites solicit feedback about their site redesigns. A study by Forrester Research (www.forrester.com) found that Fortune 1000 companies spend an average of $1.5 million to $2.1 million per year on site redesigns without knowing whether the redesign work makes their sites easier to use. Don't make this mistake with your online store – thoroughly test all changes to your Web site and solicit feedback from your customers regularly.

One way to measure customer response to your online store is to hire a professional online market research firm such as QuickTake (www.quicktake.com) to help you evaluate your Web site. Using QuickTake's survey creation wizard, you can build your own survey and ask your customers questions pertaining to your Web site design, product selection, pricing, customer service, or anything else you may be interested in. An online survey is also a great way to discover what customers think of your products, to learn how people are finding out about your online store, and to test the market potential of new product or service ideas you may be toying with.

A variety of question formats are supported, including multiple choice questions, open-ended questions and even rating scale questions that ask users to rate their feelings on a certain issue. For example, you could ask your customers to tell you how easy your Web site is to navigate on a scale from 1 to 5, with 5 being "very easy" and 1 being "very difficult." If you want to ask demographic questions relating to age, gender, marital status, income, etc., QuickTake has a library of preformatted questions that you can use so that you don't need to create them yourself.

QuickTake provides a variety of ways for you to deliver your survey. If you want to interview your own customers to find out what they think of your Web site, you could use the "site intercept" method. This means that visitors to your Web site will be randomly selected and asked to fill out the survey in a pop-up window that will appear on their screen. Alternatively, QuickTake will put your survey up on the Web and you can include a link to it in an e-mail newsletter if you have one. If you want to expand your survey beyond your own customer base and interview Internet users in general, QuickTake can help you target random users of the Internet. This is called an "Internet sample" survey and is appropriate when you want to get feedback on an idea or product concept. Pricing is based on the number of responses that you want to get, except in the case of an Internet sample survey where you are charged based on the target audience you choose and how many respondents you need. QuickTake surveys can be economical for a small business. For example, to survey a couple of hundred people on your Web site will only cost you a couple of hundred dollars. You can usually reduce the cost of a survey by reducing the number of people that you want to interview.

Creating a survey is easy. Once you've selected what type of survey you want to create (e.g., site intercept, embedded link, or Internet sample), how many respondents you want, and when you want your survey to start, QuickTake will help you create your questions and the answers you want respondents to choose from:

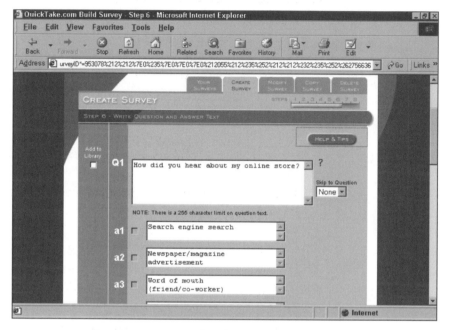

Once your survey has been completed, the results are tabulated in the form of a graphical report that can you view on the Web. If you don't want to wait for the final report, QuickTake allows you to monitor your results in real-time as they come in!

If you have the budget, consider using survey services such as this to test new ideas, and most importantly, to ensure that your Web site is meeting the expectations of your customers.

The Twenty Biggest Customer Service Mistakes You Can Make on the Web

1. Not publishing a toll-free number that works from both the United States and Canada.

2. Not publishing a direct-dial number on your Web site so that international visitors can contact you if the toll-free number doesn't work.

3. Not acknowledging a customer's order by e-mail.

4. Making it difficult for the customer to find the customer service section on your Web site.

5. Telling a customer a product is in stock when it isn't.

6. Failing to meet delivery dates posted on your Web site.

7. Not providing a list of frequently asked questions and their answers.

8. Not providing your staff with access to the information that a customer has entered on your Web site.

9. Unfriendly customer service on the telephone.

10. Ignoring customer e-mail messages.

11. Answering a customer's e-mail inquiry with a canned response that doesn't adequately address the question being asked.

12. Not being able to track a customer's order or e-mail inquiry.

13. Poor site design.

14. Not providing staff with access to all the interactions that a customer has had with your organization.

15. Failing to disclose return policies, cancellation terms, shipping costs, and warranty information.

16. Not updating your Web site frequently.

17. Subjecting your customers to frequent service interruptions and technical glitches.

18. Sending your customers unsolicited e-mail messages.

19. Selling your customers' data to another organization without permission.

20. Having a slow Web site.

Compiled by Rick Broadhead and Jim Carroll

MERCHANT ACCOUNTS AND ONLINE PAYMENT PROCESSING

Almost all goods and services bought on the Internet are paid for by old-fashioned credit- or charge-cards.

"The Personal Touch: Internet Payment Systems,"

The Economist, 08/05/2000

Because the most common method of online payment is the credit card, this chapter is devoted to dealing with credit card payments. There are two fundamental elements to accepting credit cards on the Internet:

- Merchant accounts
- Real-time credit card processing

In the pages that follow, we'll explain, in simple terms, what's involved in setting up your online store so that you can accept credit cards for purchases. We'll also show you what you need to do to process credit card transactions through your online store.

THE BASICS OF MERCHANT ACCOUNTS

In order to accept credit cards in your online store, you need to have a merchant account.

Most merchant accounts provide support for all the major card brands – Visa, MasterCard, and American Express – and some also provide support for other cards such as Discover and JCB, so in most cases, a single merchant account will allow you to accept credit card payments from customers regardless of which type of major credit card they are using.

What Is a Merchant Account?

If your business does not already accept credit cards offline, you might not know what a merchant account is.

A merchant account is not a bank account but rather a special account that you set up in order to accept credit cards as a form of payment. The merchant account is used to process credit card payments from your customers and then deposit them into your business checking account, minus any service and transaction fees (we discuss the fees associated with merchant accounts later in the chapter). Every month, you'll receive a statement from your bank or merchant account provider with a summary of all the transactions that were made in your online store.

Regardless of how an order is accepted – via a Web site, by fax, mail, or telephone – if it is a credit card order, you will need a merchant account.

Can You Sell on the Internet without a Merchant Account?

Absolutely! For example, you could have customers pay by check or money order and send you payment by mail. However, since credit cards are the most widely used form of payment on the Internet, we recommend that you accept credit cards in your online store. Most of your customers will want to pay by credit card, so you'll be losing out on a lot of business if you don't accept them.

What Merchant Accounts Do You Need?

Since most merchant accounts will allow you to accept all major credit cards, you'll probably only need one merchant account. At a minimum, make sure that the merchant account you obtain allows you to receive payments from Visa and MasterCard cardholders, since these are the most widely used credit cards on the Internet. You should also check to ensure that your merchant account can support payments from any other cards you wish to accept.

How Do You Get a Merchant Account?

There are two places you can go to obtain a merchant account:

- Acquirers ("acquiring financial institutions")
- Merchant account providers (also known as "independent sales organizations" or "ISOs") or their agents

Acquiring Financial Institutions

Your first option for obtaining a merchant account is to go to an organization known as an acquirer or acquiring financial institution. Many banks in the United States act as acquiring financial institutions and will be able to establish a merchant account for you.

If you decide to contact a bank for the purpose of obtaining a merchant account, make sure that the bank is aware that you plan on taking payment over the Internet in an online store. There are different types of merchant accounts and you will need to get a merchant account that allows you to accept credit card payments on the Internet. This is usually known as an "Internet merchant account." If you already accept credit cards in a retail store, you probably will not be able to use your existing merchant account in your online store. Most banks prefer that merchants establish a separate merchant account for use on the Internet.

Merchant Account Providers and Their Agents

Another option for getting a merchant account is to go through an organization known as a merchant account provider or independent sales organization (ISO). Merchant account providers are independent organizations that can sell merchant accounts to businesses on behalf of banks. Every merchant account provider is affiliated with one or more financial institutions that can process credit card transactions on your behalf.

e-Fact

More than half of U.S. Internet users have purchased online.

Source: UCLA Center for Communication Policy (ccp.ucla.edu)

In addition to individual ISOs, there are organizations that act as agents for ISOs. OneCore (www.onecore.com) is one such organization, acting as the agent for the merchant service provider Cardservice International. Whether you are dealing with an ISO directly or with one of their agents, the process for getting a merchant account is the same. For the remainder of the chapter wherever we refer to ISOs we mean ISOs or their agents.

E-mail Solicitations

We highly recommend that you avoid the temptation of getting your merchant account from any organization that sends you unsolicited e-mail messages like the one shown below:

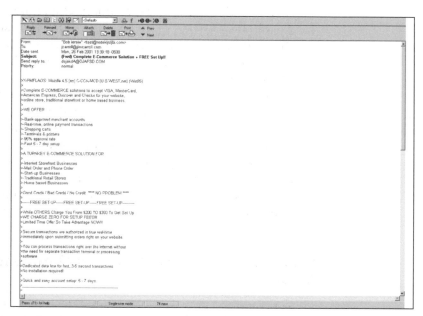

Unsolicited e-mail messages like this one are often scams.

What's the Difference between Acquiring Financial Institutions and Merchant Account Providers?

You may be wondering whether it's better to get your merchant account directly through a bank (acquiring financial institution) or through one of the hundreds of independent merchant account providers that exist in the United States that represent a bank. The answer depends on what you're looking for and what you're comfortable with.

Since banks operate in a highly regulated environment, some people argue they offer more stability and reliability than merchant account providers. Some people are simply not comfortable dealing with an unfamiliar company, such as a merchant account provider, for their credit card processing needs and prefer the familiar, structured environment of a bank instead. On the other hand, merchant account providers often have less stringent application requirements. Whereas some banks will insist that you provide articles of incorporation, recent financial statements, a business plan, and other documentation in order to get a merchant account, most merchant account providers won't ask for any of this information.

If you choose to set up your storefront using one of the browser-based storefront creation services that we discussed in Chapter 2, you may not have a choice as to where you obtain your merchant account. Many browser-based storefront creation services have partnered with a specific bank or merchant account provider and have integrated an online application directly into the setup process so that you don't have to contract for a merchant account on your own. In other words, when you are building your online store, you'll be given the opportunity to fill out an online application and apply for a merchant account immediately. Often, you can get approval in as little as forty-eight hours. In many cases, the storefront service requires that you obtain your merchant account from their partner organization. Even if you already have a merchant account, you may not be able to use it.

What Will You Have to Pay for a Merchant Account?

There are a variety of fees that you may have to pay in order to operate a merchant account. It is extremely important that you have a clear understanding of all these fees *before you sign a merchant account agreement.*

The different charges that you will commonly encounter include the following:

- Application/setup fees
- Discount rate
- Transaction fees
- Monthly fees

- Secure gateway fees
- Software fees
- Equipment rental fees
- Batch header fees
- Address verification fees
- Fraud screening fees
- Chargeback fees
- Holdback fees
- Escrow accounts

Each of these is discussed below.

Application/Setup Fees

You may be charged a fee for setting up the merchant account. Typically, this ranges from a nominal amount up to $400 or more, and can vary widely among different banks and merchant account providers. If your application for a merchant account is denied, the setup fee is usually not charged.

Discount Rate

The *discount rate* is a fixed percentage taken from every transaction you process in your online store. Typically, the discount rate ranges from 2 to 3 percent. For example, suppose you sell a product for $20.00 on your Web site. If the discount rate that applies to this particular sale is 2.5%, you would receive $19.50 on the sale and your bank or merchant account provider would keep $0.50 (2.5 percent of $20.00). On a $40.00 sale, the bank or merchant account provider would keep $1.00 (2.5 percent of $40.00) and you would receive $39.00.

You should be aware that discount rates vary among credit cards. For example, American Express usually has a different discount rate from MasterCard or Visa.

You should also be aware that the discount rate for an Internet merchant account is typically higher than the discount rate for a merchant with a retail store. This is because of the greater risk inherent in Internet transactions

e-Fact

Shopping is the most popular e-commerce activity online – ranking high above online banking, stock trading, and paying bills online.
Source: Yankee Group Survey of Online Households
(www.yankeegroup.com)

(for more information about the security risks of Internet transactions, see Chapter 5, *Online Security Issues and Credit Card Fraud*).

Transaction Fees

In addition to the discount rate, you may also have to pay a fixed transaction fee on every sale you process in your online store. The transaction fee is usually between $0.25 and $0.50 per sale, regardless of the amount of the sale. For example, suppose your transaction fee is $0.30. If you complete a sale for $25.00 on your online store, you owe your bank or merchant account provider $0.30. On a sale worth $40.00, the transaction fee is still $0.30.

Monthly Fees

Virtually all banks and merchant account providers will charge you one or more monthly fees on top of the discount rate and transaction fee. For example, you may be asked to pay a monthly statement fee (a fee for a monthly summary of the transactions that occurred on your online store), a monthly customer service fee, and/or a variety of other monthly charges. Sometimes the monthly fees are lumped together into one lump-sum payment every month and sometimes they are charged separately.

Many banks and merchant account providers charge a minimum monthly fee that will be instituted in the event that your discount rate fees and transaction fees fall below a certain level. For example, suppose your discount rate is 2.35%, your transaction fee is $0.30 per transaction, and there is a minimum monthly fee of $25.00. If you processed ten orders and $500.00 in sales in your first month, your transaction fees would total $3.00 (10 × $0.30) and you would also have to pay $11.75 based on a discount rate of 2.35% (2.35% × $500.00). This brings your total fees to $14.75. However, since your minimum monthly fee is $25.00, you would be required to pay an additional $10.25 ($25.00 – $14.75) to cover the $25.00 monthly minimum. In some cases, the minimum monthly fee is only levied on the discount rate fee. If this were the case in this example, you would have to pay $3.00 in transaction fees, $11.75 in discount rate fees, and an additional $13.25 ($25.00 – $11.75) to cover the monthly minimum of $25.00.

Secure Gateway Fees

Many banks and merchant account providers use an organization known as an Internet payment gateway to link into the credit card computer networks. The payment gateway is the service that connects to the credit card networks to obtain an authorization code from the customer's bank every time you receive a credit card order online. This lets you know that the customer's account is in good standing. The process of authorizing credit cards in this manner helps you guard against credit card fraud. It also prevents you from accepting credit cards from customers who are over their spending limit or whose accounts have been suspended for some reason. The payment gateway is also used to capture and settle credit card transactions, a process which we describe later in the chapter. You may be charged a monthly or per-transaction fee for the use of the gateway.

Software Fees

Some merchant account providers/independent sales organizations will include "Internet software fees" or "virtual terminal software fees" on their price lists. In some cases, you may be asked to "rent" this software on a monthly basis or purchase it outright. The cost for this software can sometimes run as high as $1,500. This software is essentially a Web site that will allow you to review your credit card transactions and manually process transactions if you need to. Some merchant account providers/independent sales organizations do not charge separately for virtual terminal software. Instead, it is included as part of your storefront package and it is not billed for separately. To compensate for this, merchant account providers/independent sales organizations that don't charge for virtual terminal software may charge higher merchant account fees. If you are planning on using a browser-based storefront creation service (see Chapter 2 for examples), consider getting your merchant account from the merchant account provider/independent sales organization that is aligned with the storefront service you are using. In most cases, if you do this, you will not be required to pay extra fees for the virtual terminal software. Needless to say, wherever you get your merchant account number, make sure that you understand all of the different fees that you will be responsible for. If you encounter a merchant account provider/independent sales organization that is charging a lot of money for virtual terminal software, you may want to shop around.

Equipment Rental Fees

A merchant account often includes a fee for the rental of a point-of-sale or swipe terminal. If you do not have a physical retail location and you are planning on processing all of your credit card orders online, *you do not need one of these devices.* Make sure that you don't end up paying for this service if you don't need it.

Batch Header Fees

With most storefront services, your credit card transactions will be batched at the end of each business day and sent to your financial institution or merchant account provider for processing through the payment gateway. Some merchant account providers/financial institutions charge a nominal batch header fee to cover the cost of this transaction.

Address Verification Fees

You may be charged a per-transaction fee to use the address verification service, which is used to prevent credit card fraud. It checks the cardholder's billing address against the billing address on file with the cardholder's bank to see if there is a match. You can learn more about address verification in Chapter 5, *Online Security Issues and Credit Card Fraud.*

Fraud Screening Fees

Some merchant account providers or financial institutions may provide a fraud-checking service that will allow you to screen your credit card orders for signs of fraud. There may be an extra charge for this service. For more information about online credit card fraud and the importance of fraud screening, see Chapter 5, *Online Security Issues and Credit Card Fraud.*

e-Fact

94% of Internet users want online privacy violators to be disciplined.
Source: Pew Internet and American Life Project (www.pewinternet.org)

Chargeback Fees

A chargeback is a request from the cardholder or the card issuer to reverse a purchase that was made on your online store. Chargebacks occur when a cardholder disputes a charge that has appeared on his or her credit card statement, perhaps because the person claims not to have received the goods or services ordered, because the goods or services were faulty or damaged, or, because the customer's credit card was used fraudulently. When a chargeback occurs, not only do you have to refund the amount of the original purchase, you may also have to pay a penalty, called a *chargeback fee*, to the organization that issued your merchant account. Chargebacks are an extremely important issue and one of the major risks of operating an online store. You can learn more about chargebacks and how to avoid them later in this chapter, as well as in Chapter 5, *Online Security Issues and Credit Card Fraud*.

Holdback Fees

To ensure it has the funds to cover any disputed charges, your acquiring financial institution or merchant account provider may withhold or *holdback* a percentage of your sales (e.g., for thirty days). To avoid being surprised, make sure you understand the holdback policy of your merchant account provider or acquiring financial institution before you apply for a merchant account.

Escrow Accounts

Banks and merchant account providers may also require an escrow account to be set up to ensure the merchant can cover any losses.

Are There Any Other Fees You Should Be Aware Of?

Yes! Be *extremely careful* when examining the fees that you will be charged for a merchant account. When comparing merchant account fees, make sure you take all of the fees into consideration. A merchant account provider that has a lower discount rate or transaction fee than another organization may compensate for these lower fees by imposing other charges and/or charging you higher monthly fees.

While a merchant account provider may have a lower discount fee than a bank, there may be other fees that may not be immediately apparent to you. For example, some merchant account providers may ask you to sign a contract for a minimum period of time that you can't break without a financial penalty. Make sure that you aren't being locked into a contract that you can't get out of.

Access to Funds

When a purchase is made on your Web site with a credit card, the funds owed to you from the purchase will eventually be deposited into your business checking account. Sometimes the discount rate fee and transaction fee are deducted from the amount of the purchase before the funds are deposited in your account. But in the majority of cases, the fees are deducted separately and appear as one or more charges on your monthly statement.

The length of time it takes for the funds to be deposited into your bank account will depend on the arrangement that you have with your bank or merchant account provider. In most cases, funds will be deposited into your account within several days.

Shop Around!

With thousands of acquiring financial institutions and hundreds of merchant account providers in the United States, it's generally a good idea to research your alternatives. The discount rates and various fees associated with merchant accounts will vary from one bank to the next and from one merchant account provider to another. In some cases, the rates and fees may be negotiable, depending on factors such as the types of products or services you are selling, your credit history, your expected sales volumes, and other criteria. This means that even if two businesses obtain merchant accounts from the *same* bank or the *same* merchant account provider, the transaction fees and discount rates each business pays could be completely different. For example, a business with an excellent credit history could have a lower discount rate and transaction fee than a business with a poor credit history.

The bottom line? Don't sign up with the first bank or merchant account provider you come across. Shop around and compare rates and fees. Ask a lot of questions, and don't fall prey to salespeople who will try to convince you (often with misleading information) that they offer the best solution for your business needs. Since each bank and merchant account provider evaluates risk differently, you should get quotes from several before making a decision.

e-Fact

Online music spending will reach $5.4 billion in 2005, accounting for almost 25 percent of total music spending.

Source: Jupiter Research (www.jup.com)

While one bank may regard you as a high risk and therefore quote you a high discount rate, another bank may look at your situation differently and offer you a lower fee structure.

Like most merchants, you'll naturally be price-sensitive and look for a bank or merchant account provider that can give you a good deal. But remember that price isn't everything. If you go with a merchant account provider that has rock-bottom prices, you may not get the level of technical or administrative support that you expect. It wouldn't hurt to ask the bank or merchant account provider for references. Alternatively, ask around in your community to see which firms have a good reputation for providing reliable merchant account services. You should also try to talk to people who are already selling online to get their advice on choosing a good bank or merchant account provider. We've heard horror stories from many online merchants who have had really bad experiences with particular merchant account providers.

Finally, before signing a merchant account contract with any bank or merchant account provider, read the terms and conditions of the contract carefully and make sure you fully understand all the fees that you will be responsible for. Don't forget to read the fine print!

APPLYING FOR A MERCHANT ACCOUNT

In order to apply for a merchant account in the United States, you must have a U.S. business address and a U.S. bank account. One item to consider when applying for a merchant card is to ensure that it is compatible with the storefront softwear you are intending to use.

Obviously, one of the best starting points when obtaining a merchant account is to inquire through your existing financial institution. You will have an established credit record with them, possibly one or more bank accounts, and in essence, perhaps enough of a history to make the process much smoother.

You will find that most financial institutions have established some very information rich Web sites that will help you further understand the merchant account application process, and some of the particulars related to merchant accounts for that particular financial institution.

Wells Fargo (www.wellsfargo.com), for example, provides extensive details on merchant accounts in its "Internet Payment Services FAQ."

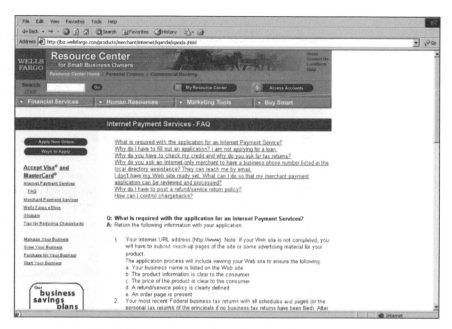

In addition to providing basic information about merchant accounts, you will find that an increasing number of financial institutions will allow you to apply for a merchant account online. For example, US Bank (www.usbank.com) allows you to do so directly through their Web site. First, they provide a summary of the information you will need to provide and an overview of the application process:

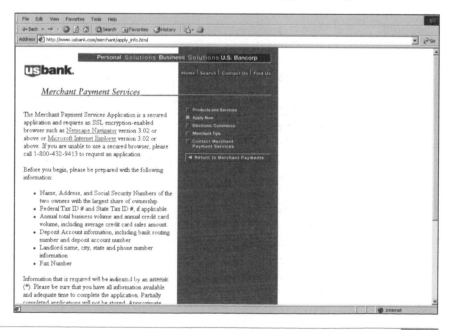

They then let you apply online through a secure section of their Web site.

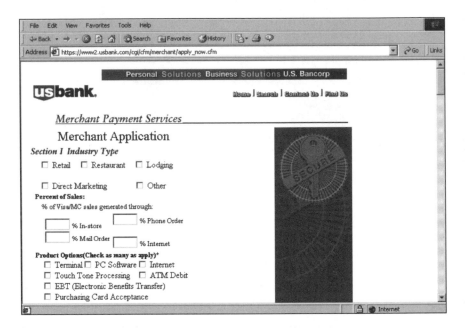

You can browse through these online application sites, in order to get a better sense of the type of financial information that you will have to provide. For example, the online application of the National Processing Company (www.npc.net) gives you a good sense of the information you may need to provide:

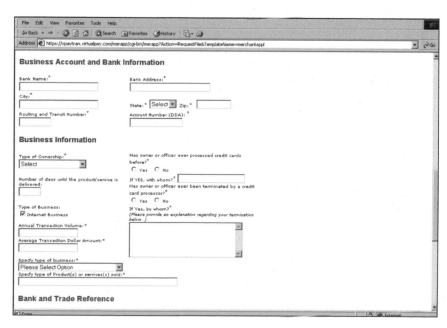

and in addition, detailed financial information about your company.

You will find that many browser-based storefront creation services have partnered with a financial institution or merchant account provider, and may include a merchant account application right on their Web site. This allows merchants to apply for a merchant account right away if they don't already have one. For example, if you are setting up an online store using the Yahoo! Store service (store.yahoo.com), you can fill out an online application to get a merchant account from Paymentech (www.paymentech.com), one of the largest merchant account providers in the United States.

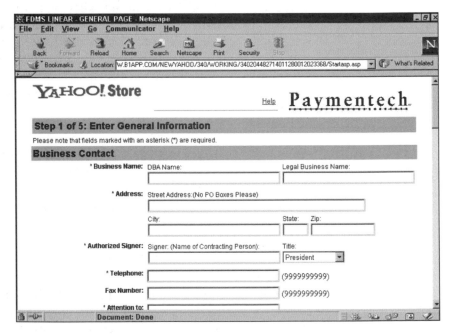

Similarly, online merchants who are using EarthLink's TotalCommerce storefront service (www.earthlink.com) can apply for a merchant account from Cardservice International (www.cardservice.com), another large merchant account provider in the United States:

If you are using standalone shopping cart software or one of the advanced e-commerce software packages, you will usually need to get your merchant account on your own. You can approach any bank or merchant account provider, but make sure that their system is compatible with the payment gateway(s) that the storefront software supports.

When applying for a merchant account, you could be asked for any of the following types of information:

- General contact information for your business – address, telephone numbers, legal name of business, Web site address

- Information about the business owners/partners/officers – names, titles, addresses, phone numbers, and social security numbers

- Information about your business – when it was established, where it is physically based, where you operate the business from (e.g., home office, retail storefront, warehouse, office, etc.), what types of products/services you sell, ownership structure (e.g., sole proprietorship, partnership, corporation, nonprofit, LLC, LLP, etc.), what state the business is incorporated in, your federal tax ID number (if incorporated), etc.

- Business/trade references

- Sales data about your business – existing or projected monthly and/or annual sales, sales by source (e.g., in-store, telephone/mail-order, Internet)

- Banking references – information about your business account, including the bank, your contact(s) at the bank, how long your account has been established, total dollar value of the account and average daily balance, and other pertinent information

- Bank routing information for your business checking account (you'll need your financial institution's ABA number, which is the first nine digits located at the bottom left corner of your check)

- Delivery process – how your products/services are delivered to customers, how long it takes before your products are shipped

- Description of your refund/exchange policies

- Marketing and advertising activities – how you promote your business

- Average "ticket" price for your online store (in other words, how much do you expect the average sale to be?)

- Names, addresses, and telephone numbers of previous credit card processors (if any)

In addition to supplying the above information online, you may also be asked to submit the following types of documentation by mail:

- Copies of your federal business tax returns or the personal tax returns of the owners/officers of the company if you haven't filed a business tax return for your company

- Your business plan

- Interim financial statements, balance sheets, and profit and loss statements

- Proof of business registration (if no business tax returns have been filed), such as articles of incorporation (for corporations), a partnership agreement (for partnerships), 501C letter from the IRS (for non-profit organizations), articles of organization and operating agreement (for limited liability companies), or fictitious business name statement/assumed name certificate (for a sole proprietorship)

- Voided check from your business checking account (if your business account does not have checking privileges, a letter from your bank confirming your business address will usually suffice)

In the absence of a business credit history, banks may instead look at your personal credit history and ask to see your business plan and financial statements for the next couple of years.

If tax returns, financial statements, and other "paper" documentation aren't required upfront, they may be requested after your application for merchant status has been reviewed. This could be the case, for example, if the financial institution or merchant account provider feels that it needs more information on your business before granting you merchant status.

If you are applying completely online, the application process is typically very quick and you will be notified within a few days whether your application has been accepted or declined. Usually this notification will come by e-mail.

e-Fact

40% of surveyed adults have changed their impression of brands based on online information.
Source: Cyber Dialogue (www.cyberdialogue.com)

For example, if you apply for a merchant account through Yahoo! Store, you will receive an acknowledgement of your application by e-mail within a few hours. It may look like this:

If your merchant account application is approved, in a few days you'll receive an approval message like this:

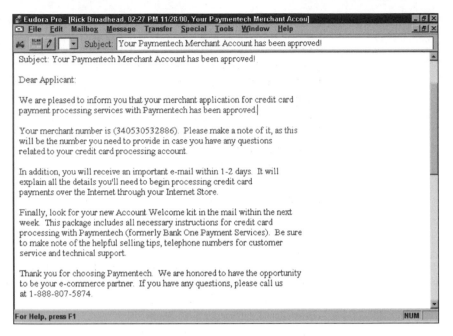

On the other hand, if your request for a merchant account is declined, you may receive a message like this:

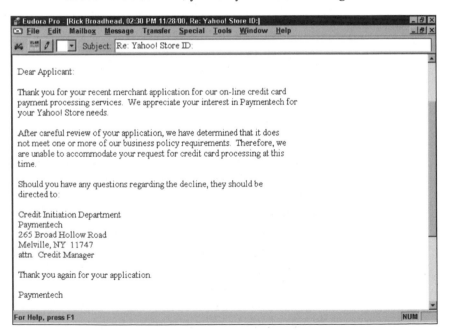

The exact messages you receive will depend on the financial institution or merchant account provider that you are dealing with.

Why Is the Application Process So Intensive?

The amount of information you have to supply in order to get a merchant account will vary depending on which bank or merchant account provider you are applying to. In some cases, the amount of documentation required may seem overwhelming. To understand why so much information is demanded of you, you have to appreciate the bank's or merchant account provider's position. When a bank/merchant account provider gives you a merchant account, it is essentially giving you an open line of credit. This is explained on one of the bank's Web sites: "A merchant credit card processing account is like an open-end line of credit. You send us your credit card transactions for processing, and we credit your business checking account, in most cases, within 24 hours. Those funds are available for you to use as you wish. But on the other end, the transaction is posted to the customer's credit card statement, which states that they have the right to dispute any charges posted. If they dispute a transaction, it can generate a chargeback that may come back to the bank and be debited against your business' account. This may take 120 business days or longer to reach your account. We want to make sure that you can handle any chargebacks. So a merchant account application is like applying for a business line of credit." (Source: Wells Fargo Internet Payment Services FAQ, biz.wellsfargo.com).

As noted above, chargeback occurs when a customer disputes a transaction that has appeared on his or her credit card statement. A customer may dispute a charge for a variety of reasons, including:

- *Merchandise not as described.* The cardholder states that the merchandise received from you was different from what was described on your Web site.

- *Defective merchandise.* The cardholder states the merchandise received was defective.

- *Credit not received.* The cardholder states that the merchandise ordered from you was returned and he or she hasn't been given a refund or credit yet.

- *Duplicate transaction.* The cardholder states that he or she was billed twice for the same purchase.

- *Non-receipt of merchandise.* The cardholder states that he or she never received the merchandise that was ordered.

Chargebacks also occur when a stolen credit card is used fraudulently to make an online purchase. We discuss online credit card fraud is more detail in the next chapter.

On the Internet, the risk of a chargeback is higher than in a physical retail storefront. When you accept a credit card order in your online store, there is no physical imprint of the customer's credit card. And you don't have the benefit of swiping the credit card into a point-of-sale terminal that has built-in features to identify unacceptable cards. The other problem with an online credit card order is that you don't get a written signature from the customer. As a result, it's much easier for customers to use a bogus credit card number or a credit card number that doesn't belong to them on the Internet than it is in a land-based retail store. It is also easy for customers to claim that they did not use their credit card on your online store, even when they did. This is called *friendly fraud*. In the absence of physical evidence, such as a signature or a physical card imprint, it is hard to prove a customer wrong.

As you'll learn in Chapter 5, merchants are usually responsible for any fraudulent credit card transactions that occur in their online stores. When a stolen credit card number is used on your online store to purchase merchandise, you are responsible for the amount of the purchase. Therefore, if a customer disputes a charge that has appeared on his or her credit card statement, your bank/merchant account provider will usually debit the amount of purchase from your bank account, in effect taking back the money that was put into your account shortly after the purchase was made. When reviewing your application for a merchant account, the bank/merchant account provider will look for evidence that you will be able to afford any chargebacks that occur.

Banks and merchant account providers also want to make sure that your business is credible, reliable, and reputable. They want to avoid situations when customers are calling in and complaining about defective merchandise or merchandise that was ordered and never delivered. Since there are many things that an online business can do to reduce the chance of chargebacks, a bank or merchant account provider may want to review your Web site to make sure you've taken the necessary steps to prevent chargebacks from occurring in your online business.

Here are some of the things that a bank/merchant account provider may look for on your Web site:

- Your business name or address is clearly listed.

- The product information is clear to the consumer.

- Product images are clear and large enough for the customer to see.

- The price of the product is clear to the consumer.

- A refund/exchange policy is clearly defined.

- A customer service phone number is displayed.

What If You Already Have a Merchant Account?

If you already accept credit card payments in a physical store, or by phone, fax, or mail, then you already have a merchant account. However, your existing merchant account may not allow you to accept credit card payments over the Internet. Policies vary from organization to organization, so check with your acquiring financial institution or merchant account provider – wherever you obtained your merchant account – for guidance. You may have to establish a separate merchant account for your Internet business.

Even if your existing merchant account can be used on the Internet, you may not be able to use it if it isn't compatible with the storefront service you are using or planning on using. If you plan on using one of the online storefront creation services that we discussed in Chapter 2, such as FreeMerchant or Yahoo! Store, you will need to contact the organization that supplied you with your merchant account to find out if your merchant account can be used with the payment gateway that the storefront service is using. If it is not compatible, you could look around for a different storefront service, or apply for another merchant account through the storefront service.

Regardless of what merchant account you already have, some online storefront services may require you to obtain another merchant account through their organization or through a partner organization in order to use their services.

For example, BigStep.com, one of the free storefront servic-es that we discussed in Chapter 2, has the following mes-sage on its Web site: "If you want to accept and process credit card transactions on your BigStep.com site, you'll need to apply for an online merchant number through our partner, Cardservice International (even if you already have another merchant number through Cardservice International)."

REAL-TIME CREDIT CARD PROCESSING

All online storefront solutions enable you to authorize and process credit card transactions in real time. Authorization ensures that online shoppers with valid credit cards can complete their purchases and shoppers with invalid cards are prevented from placing orders.

The result of the authorization process is either an approval code or a decline. A credit card purchase may be declined for a variety of reasons. For example:

- The credit card being used by the customer has been reported stolen.
- The spending limit for the card has been exceeded.
- The credit card has been canceled.
- The card number is invalid.
- An incorrect expiry date has been provided for the card.

With real-time credit card processing, you encourage customers to place their orders on your Web site using a credit card. A customer selects one or more products from your Web site, inputs his or her shipping information and credit card data, and then clicks a button to finalize the purchase. Information about the purchase is sent over a secure, proprietary connection (via the Internet) to the cardholder's bank. Within a few seconds, the authorization response is sent back to the merchant and the customer will be told onscreen whether the transaction was approved or declined.

The benefit of using real-time credit card processing is threefold. First and formost is the ability for your customer to place their orders immediately, rather than having to print out the order form and either mail, fax, or phone in

e-Fact

Office supplies, computer hardware, and computer software account for 54% of total online business-to-business spending by small businesses.

Source: Cyber Dialogue (www.cyberdialogue.com)

the order. We know of several online stores that have lost sales because the customer had to perform the additional steps of printing and faxing in their order. Secondly, the customer is told right away whether the transaction has gone through successfully. If the transaction is declined, the customer has a chance to use a different credit card number or fix the problem immediately without abandoning the purchase attempt.

The third advantage of online credit card processing is that it's faster and more efficient for you to process orders in this fashion. Although it is possible for you to manually authorize and process credit card orders (such as you would do if you received an order by e-mail, mail, phone, or fax), you would have to chase after customers if problems arose with the credit card information. With online processing, you can let the software do the work for you and catch problems before the orders go through!

In recognition of these advantages, most merchants on the Internet use real-time credit card processing. This brings us to the subject of Internet payment gateways.

INTERNET PAYMENT GATEWAYS

If you want to process your credit card orders in real-time, you will need to use an Internet payment gateway. The Internet payment gateway is the service that links your online store to a *payment processor*, sometimes referred to as a *payment network*. The payment processor links into the computer systems of the banks and credit card companies to process your credit card orders. A payment gateway is needed because many of the large payment processors do not have direct connections to the Internet.

The method by which an Internet payment is processed might seem quite confusing, but one of the most important things to keep in mind is that once again, financial Web sites and those of payment processors themselves often provide useful information to help demystify the topic.

For example, the Bank of America (www.bankofamerica.com), in its Internet commerce section, provides a useful flowchart that outlines how the payment process works:

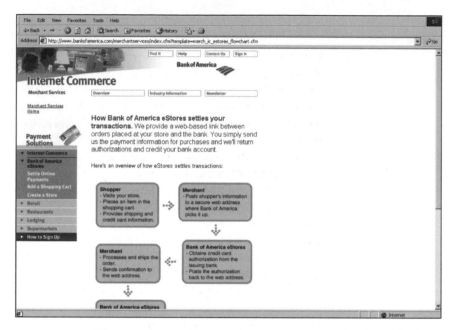

There are several large payment processors in the United States, including companies like Nova (www.novacorp.net), Paymentech (www.paymentech.com), Vital Processing Services (www.vitalps.com), and First Data Merchant Services (www.fdms.com).

We've listed some of the Internet's more prominent payment gateways in the table below.

Examples of Payment Gateways

Authorize.net	www.authorize.net
CyberCash	www.cybercash.com
CyberSource	www.cybersource.com
Intellipay	www.intellipay.com
LinkPoint International	www.linkpoint.com
SurePay	www.surepay.com
VeriSign (formerly Signio)	www.verisign.com

The Internet payment gateway serves two main functions – authorization and settlement.

Authorization

Once a customer has purchased an item in your online store, the payment gateway sends a request for *authorization* to the bank that issued the customer's credit card. As noted earlier in the chapter, authorization is the process whereby a customer's credit card account is checked to make sure it is in good standing.

If everything checks out, the bank will authorize the transaction and send a message back through the payment gateway to your online store, where the customer sees an onscreen message that the credit card transaction has been approved. As part of the authorization process, part of the customer's credit line is set aside for the purchase made in your online store. This ensures that the customer is kept within his or her allowable credit limit.

If the credit card number or expiry date is invalid, the card has been reported stolen, or the customer has exceeded his or her allowable spending limit, the transaction will be denied and the customer will be informed onscreen that the purchase did not go through.

In a traditional retail store, the store clerk would request authorization by swiping a credit card through a transaction terminal provided by a bank or merchant account provider. If the transaction was accepted, the store clerk would see an approval message on the transaction terminal. If the transaction were refused for some reason (e.g., the card had been reported stolen) the clerk would see a message on the terminal indicating that the transaction was declined.

However, with real-time credit card processing on the Internet, there is no transaction terminal for you to look at. When you log into your storefront to review your orders, you'll see whether a transaction has been approved or declined. If it's approved, you'll be able to see the authorization code. You may also receive this information by e-mail, depending on how you have the storefront set up to notify you of new orders.

e-Fact

76% of retailers are unable to track online shoppers across multiple channels.

Source: Jupiter Research
(www.jup.com)

Once you've received an authorization for a purchase, you can proceed to ship it, as long as you're satisfied that the order isn't fraudulent. As you'll discover in Chapter 5, an authorization from the credit card company does not guarantee that a credit card order is not fraudulent. See Chapter 5 for some of the warning signs of credit card fraud.

Settlement

Authorization only approves a customer's credit card purchase – it doesn't actually initiate the process of transferring the funds into your bank account. In order to get the money for the purchase, you need to submit a request through the payment gateway to "capture the funds" for each order that you have received. This is called *settlement*. Visa and MasterCard operating rules stipulate that you must not capture funds for an order before the product has been shipped. Therefore, you should only initiate settlement of a transaction once you have shipped the customer's order. If you settle an order before the order has been shipped, the customer may receive the credit card statement with your charge on it before receiving the product. If this happens, the customer may call up the bank to complain and initiate a chargeback (i.e., refuse to pay the charges). If this happens, not only will you not get paid for the purchase, the bank will charge you a penalty.

The exact procedure for settling and capturing funds depends on the storefront software you are using.

How Do You Find a Payment Gateway?

Which Internet payment gateway you choose will depend on how you intend to set up your Internet storefront.

In Chapter 2, we described a couple of different methods for establishing a storefront on the Internet. One way is to use a browser-based storefront creation service like Yahoo! Store or FreeMerchant. If you decide to use a browser-based storefront service, setting up your payment gateway shouldn't be too complicated, because most of these services have integrated the gateway setup directly into their storefront services. In these cases, configuring your online store to work with a payment gateway is as simple as answering a couple of questions or plugging some information into a Web page.

If you decide to use a financial institution as your store-front service provider, you will find that most financial institutions have aligned themselves with a particular payment gateway.

For example, Wachovia (www.wachovia.com), with its WMSesolutions storefront service, has aligned itself with the Surepay Payment Gateway service:

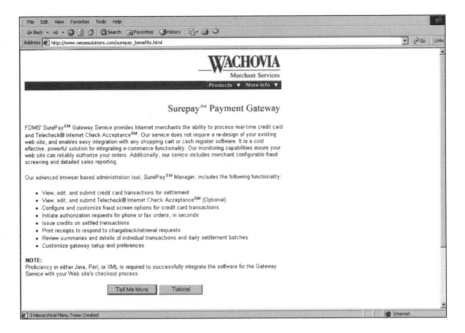

In order to use a specific payment gateway, you will need to obtain a user ID and/or password for that gateway. In most cases, these will be supplied by the organization that gives you your merchant account. As noted earlier, it's important that you get your merchant account from a bank or merchant account provider that can support one of the gateways that your storefront service uses.

To make things easy for you, most browser-based storefront creation services will recommend one or more merchant account providers or financial institutions that work with the payment gateways they use.

For example, the FreeMerchant storefront creation service (www.freemerchant.com) supports a number of different payment gateways, including Authorize.net and Intellipay. So that customers don't have to hunt around for a compatible merchant account provider on their own, FreeMerchant provides an online merchant account application from a company called OneCore.

OneCore, which is an agent for the merchant account provider Cardservice International, supports the Authorize.net and Intellipay gateways. When you receive your merchant account, you will also receive a login ID for Authorize.net or Intellipay, whichever you have chosen. Simply plug this information into the gateway settings page on FreeMerchant, and the payment gateway will be automatically configured:

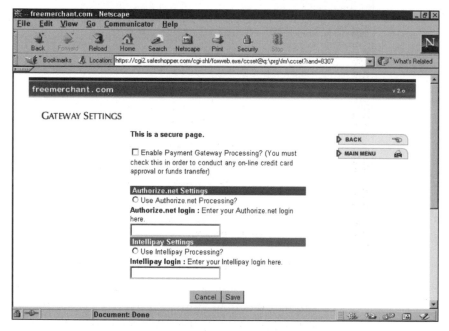

Unlike some browser-based storefront creation services, FreeMerchant allows merchants to shop around and get their merchant account from an organization other than OneCore. However, if you decide to get your merchant account elsewhere, you must make sure that it is compatible with one of the payment gateways that FreeMerchant is using (i.e., Authorize.net or Intellipay).

This leads us to an extremely important point. If the storefront service gives you a choice as to where you get your merchant account, it's generally a good idea to look around and get different price quotes. You may find that there are substantial price differences between different financial institutions and merchant account providers. If you are unsure about where to get a merchant account, try contacting the gateway services supported by the storefront service you are using and ask them to recommend a merchant account provider. Sometimes you'll find a list of affiliated merchant account providers on the payment gateway's Web site. For example, if you visit the Authorize.net Web site (www.authorize.net), you'll find a list of different merchant account providers that support the Authorize.net gateway:

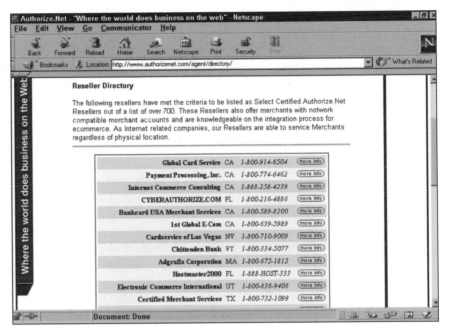

Similarly, CyberCash (www.cybercash.com), another popular payment gateway, has a list of organizations that can supply merchant accounts for use with the CyberCash gateway:

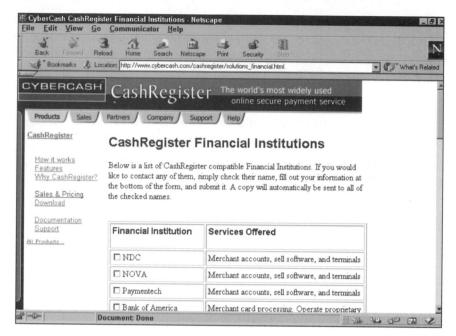

With some browser-based storefront services, you won't need to set up the payment gateway on your own. For example, Yahoo! Store has a built-in gateway that connects its merchants directly to First Data Merchant Services, a large payment processor. When you apply for a merchant account on Yahoo! Store, the payment gateway is automatically configured for you.

If you are using standalone shopping cart software or advanced e-commerce software, most of these programs come with built-in support for many of the leading payment gateways. For example, PDG Shopping Cart (www.pdg-soft.com) includes support for CyberCash and Authorize.net, among others. Because standalone shopping cart software isn't designed to be a complete storefront solution, the responsibility for getting a merchant account lies with you. Therefore, unlike browser-based storefront services, a link to a merchant account provider usually isn't included in the software. You'll need to shop around and find a merchant account provider or financial institution that supports one or more of the payment gateways used by the shopping cart software. Your merchant account provider or financial institution

e-Fact

The United States is the best country in the world for doing e-business, followed by Sweden, Finland, and Norway.

Source: Economist Intelligence Unit (www.eiu.com)

will assign you a user ID and password for the payment gateway, and you can plug the required information into the appropriate configuration screen in the PDG Shopping Cart software.

PDG Shopping Cart has different configuration screens for each of the payment gateways it supports. For example, if you're going to use CyberCash as your payment gateway, the configuration screen might look like this:

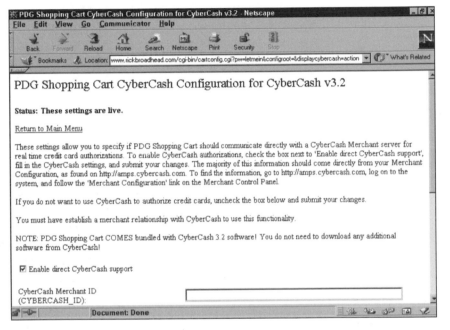

If you are building your own custom shopping cart or e-commerce store, most payment gateways can help you custom-program a connection from your online store to their Web servers. Obviously, this type of implementation requires a fair amount of technical expertise.

How Much Does a Payment Gateway Cost?

You will generally come across three payment gateway pricing models:

- The cost of the payment gateway is bundled into the monthly fee you pay to your hosting company or merchant account provider.

- The cost of the payment gateway is billed separately, usually in the form of a monthly lump sum secure gateway fee.

- You pay a per-transaction fee.

Most of the browser-based storefront services discussed in Chapter 2 charge either a monthly secure gateway fee or bundle the gateway fee into the other fees they charge you. It is just another item to consider when deciding which route to take.

Which Gateway Is the Right One?

At this point, you may be wondering whether it matters which payment gateway you choose. Some storefront solutions, like Yahoo! Store, don't give you a choice as to which payment gateway you use, while others do. For example, PDG Shopping Cart supports several different payment gateways, as does FreeMerchant. If you do have a choice, we recommend that you talk to the storefront solution you are using and ask which payment gateway they recommend. Find out if there are any important differences that you should know about. You should also contact several different merchant account providers and compare overall costs, including the cost of using each payment gateway. You may find that one payment gateway is cheaper than another. But don't make a decision based on price alone – make sure you fully understand what services and features the payment gateway is offering you and whether there is an advantage to using one payment gateway over another.

Offline Credit Card Transactions

Although we recommend that you process your orders online in real-time, some customers may still want to fax, e-mail, or phone in their orders. Generally merchants will authorize these transactions by phone, by using virtual terminal softwear provided by your bank or merchant account provider, or by using a physical card swipe terminal. One problem with this type of offline credit card processing is that the customer has already left your online store. If the credit card ends up getting declined, you then have to contact the customer to straighten out the problem. By the time you finally reach the customer, the person may no longer be interested in placing the order. If this happens, you lose an order that you would probably have secured if real-time credit card processing had been in place and the customer

e-Fact

By 2003, over 70% of small businesses will access the Internet.
Source: International Data Corporation (www.idc.com)

had been given the chance to fix the problem immediately. If you want to be able to process credit card transactions offline, check with your financial institution or merchant account provider for guidance.

TAKE YOUR TIME

We have tried to explain online payment processing in simple terms, but as you can see it is anything but simple. We can only suggest that you take your time to comparison shop, consider your options, and talk with people who are currently running their own online stores.

Chapter 5

ONLINE SECURITY ISSUES AND CREDIT CARD FRAUD

Fraudulent chargebacks are particularly painful for Internet retailers because they must usually reimburse the credit-card company that paid them the disputed charge, even though they have already shipped the merchandise. In the case of offline retail transactions, chargebacks are often absorbed by the credit-card issuer.

"Credit-Card Scams Bedevil E-Stores — With No Signatures to Prove Who Placed Orders, Sites Are Left Footing the Bills,"
The Wall Street Journal, 09/19/2000

In this chapter, we outline a five-step action plan to help your online store manage the security risks that exist on the Internet.

A Five-Step Action Plan for Securing Your Online Store

1. Learn about Internet security risks.

2. Assess your procedures.

3. Protect the security and integrity of your online transactions.

4. Let customers know your online store is safe.

5. Be vigilant!

First, be prepared to learn about Internet security risks. Regardless of your technical expertise, you must become personally involved in understanding the security risks that can affect your online store. This means that you need a good understanding of Internet security risks from a variety of different perspectives.

Second, assess whether you are satisfied with the security procedures and methods used by the services that build and host your online store. You need to make sure that the company that hosts your online store and the people you hire to build it have the technical experience and the know-how to secure your online store adequately, and that they are doing what they should to ensure it is secure.

Third, secure the transactions that flow through your online store. When customers place credit card orders on your online store, you must ensure that the transactions are secure so that credit card numbers cannot be accessed as they travel through the Internet. You also want to take steps to prevent bogus or stolen credit cards from being used on your Web site.

Fourth, battle perceptions. Once you are satisfied that you have proper security in place, you must assure your customers that any credit card orders they place on your online store are safe, and that any personal or confidential information they send to you is also safe.

Fifth, be vigilant about security. New security weaknesses and vulnerabilities are constantly being discovered on the Internet. You need to stay on top of these issues so that you can react to any potential security problems before they get out of hand. You can't afford to have a security slip-up of any type with your online store – it can be the kiss of death.

STEP #1: LEARN ABOUT SECURITY RISKS

The first thing you need to do is have a good appreciation of Internet security risks. At the most basic level, there are two concerns.

First, the Internet is a network that involves many, many computers – literally millions of them. The information that is stored on each computer is potentially accessible to someone else on the Internet unless specific precautions are undertaken to prevent such access. Over the last several years, there have

e-Fact

A majority of Americans (56%) are more concerned about loss of personal privacy on the Internet than about issues such as health care, taxes, or crime.

Source: Harris Poll Online (www.harrispollonline.com)

been many high-profile incidents of hackers breaking into the Web sites used by online retailers. In some cases, credit card numbers have been stolen. In others, credit card numbers have been held ransom.

The second risk is that information transmitted through the Internet from one computer to another is essentially "sent in the clear," meaning that it is not scrambled in any way, unless something has specifically been done to ensure it is scrambled.

How do problems come about?

With the first issue, in most cases problems arise because necessary precautions to prevent unauthorized access to host computers are not taken, with the result that the Web sites and online stores found on those computers are not properly secured. Many break-ins occur because of negligence or ignorance on the part of the people responsible for the system. Hackers are able to gain unauthorized access to a Web site because of errors in the computer code that make up the Web site or because a Web site has been incorrectly configured. In other words, human error is responsible for many of the security breaches that occur on the Internet.

The second problem is the result of programs called "sniffers" that hackers use to see the information that is traveling between computers on the Internet. A sniffer program could allow someone to steal credit card numbers as they are passed between customers and merchants on the Internet.

What do you need to do to protect your online store and the credit card numbers you receive from customers? First, make sure that your online store software and Web site are configured so as to minimize the risk of a break-in. Second, ensure that when customers send you their credit card information, it is transmitted securely over the Internet so that it can't be accessed by any unauthorized individuals.

Online Security Requires Your Involvement

It is actually *you* who should take responsibility for the two issues that we describe above.

This might come as a surprise to you; after all, isn't security the responsibility of the organizations that design and host your online store?

Not at all. The key to ensuring that your online store is secure is your personal involvement in security issues. Not only should you have a good understanding of the security risks, but you also need to make sure that all the appropriate precautions have been taken to protect your online store.

If you ignore security and don't become personally involved with these issues, you'll be relying on all kinds of other people to take care of your online security matters for you. They might or might not do so. It is more than likely that they'll do a good job, but the simple fact is that your lack of involvement increases the likelihood that they will focus less than 100 percent of their attention to important security issues.

We liken the situation to working with an accountant or financial advisor. The more involved you are in understanding what an accountant or financial advisor is doing with your money, the more prepared you'll be to ask questions, and the more likely it is that you'll catch mistakes. Dealing with security on the Internet isn't much different. While Internet security can be an incredibly complex topic, a minimum understanding of the issues will make you a much more effective online storekeeper. If you're aware of the issues, you'll know what questions to ask your online store provider, and you'll be more likely to catch mistakes or oversights.

We find it fascinating that so many store owners ignore fundamental security issues on the Internet, although they take those issues very seriously when it comes to their land-based stores. Imagine a real store located in a strip mall. Build it without any security or staff to watch what goes on, keep the front door unlocked, and the store will be tremendously insecure. Someone could walk up to the cash register and easily empty the till.

Does that happen in the real world? Not at all – most retail stores, large and small, implement a wide variety of security measures, ranging from security guards to sophisticated alarm systems. Indeed, the retail sector spends quite a bit on store security. Most organizations choose to spend wisely on experts to secure their stores, rather than leaving the front door open and the cash register unlocked. Furthermore, the owner or management of the store will take the time to learn about security issues, and gain an understanding of some of the fundamental risks that exist and how to minimize those risks.

Security Problems Are Often Due to Negligence, Ignorance, or Human Error

Experience has shown that most online security breaches come about because of negligence on the part of those responsible for the technology being used. It is only through your prodding and personal involvement that you can ensure that the people involved in building your online store will pay proper attention and give proper respect to security issues.

e-Fact

U.S. companies will spend more than $20 billion by 2004 to prevent their computer systems from being attacked.
Source: Forrester Research (www.forrester.com)

As an example of what we mean, consider what happened to Western Union in the fall of 2000. Hackers were able to break into the company's Web site and access the credit card numbers of over fifteen thousand customers who had used the Western Union Web site to transfer money. Why did the break-in occur? Western Union admitted that its Web site had been left unprotected while undergoing maintenance and that the incident was entirely due to "human error." The result was that confidential information on the Western Union site was easily accessible to hackers.

If you are using shopping cart software to build your online store (see Chapter 2, *Options for Building an Online Store*), you need to make sure that the software you are using has no known security weaknesses that haven't been adequately addressed. Many of these programs have been found to have security problems. For example, a survey of eleven popular shopping cart programs by Internet Security Systems (www.iss.net) in 2000 revealed that they all had security vulnerabilities. Even more shocking was the survey's finding that several of the software vendors did nothing to fix the problems.

What do both of these stories tell us? If the Internet remains insecure, it is often a result of the negligence or technical inexperience of the people who build and maintain Web sites and software for online stores. Some critics point a finger at software vendors who are in such a rush to get merchants online that they don't take the time to address security issues adequately. It is a sad fact, but often very true.

That's why it's important that you thoroughly check the reputation, competence, and track record of any company you are considering to host or build your online store.

Ask for references and/or look for examples of other online stores that are using the company's software. Contact those organizations and ask about their experiences. Find out if they have encountered any security problems that you should know about.

Security Problems Are Usually Due to Break-Ins

Many people think that the biggest security risk on the Internet occurs at the time of the sale – when a customer's credit card number is sent over the Internet to the merchant's computer. In the early years of the Internet, people were obsessed with the notion that hackers could grab credit card numbers while they traveled over the Internet. As a result, merchants focused their security efforts on protecting credit card data so that it could travel securely over the Internet without being intercepted, by ensuring that it wasn't sent in the clear, by encrypting it.

In reality, most security breaches happen after the sale is completed – when a customer's credit card number is sitting unprotected on the merchant's computer. That's what happened in the Western Union incident described earlier: the credit card numbers were stolen off of Western Union's computers, not as they traveled to the Western Union Web site.

Think about the mindset of someone who wants to steal a few credit card numbers by hacking into your store. There are two ways a hacker might go about it: the hard way and the easy way.

What is the hard way? The hacker might set out to monitor your Internet connection somehow, and hope that you aren't using encrypted transmissions that scramble any credit card numbers in transit between your customers and your store. Undertaking such a task probably involves a high level of expertise; it isn't beyond the reach of some hackers, but it does require specialized knowledge. All that effort might produce a credit card number or two.

The easy way? The hacker works at breaking into your Web site and store, and then browses around to see if there is a file that contains customer information, including credit card numbers. A successful hacker could net a file of several thousand credit card numbers this way.

Obviously, the second method produces "better" results. This means that protecting your Web site is as important – if not more important – than securing the transactions through your site.

Examples of Online Security Risks

There are many different types of security risks that could affect your online store. Here are just some of them.

Snooping Attacks

A snooping attack is what happens when someone "eavesdrops" on your Web site and attempts to capture customer data, such as credit card numbers, as it is transmitted by a customer to your online store. You can minimize your vulnerability to a snooping attack by encrypting the information so that it's scrambled, making it unintelligible to an eavesdropper. Although the risk of a snooper is slim, this is probably the one security issue that online shoppers are most terrified of.

The easiest and most popular way to scramble a customer's credit card number is to use a method of encryption called SSL (Secure Sockets Layer). Most online storefront products use SSL to ensure that customers can transmit their credit card data and other personal information to your Web site safely and securely. We discuss SSL in greater detail later in the chapter.

Web Site Break-Ins

A break-in occurs when someone forces their way into an online store or Web site in order to gain access to sensitive information, such as cardholder data, passwords, or billing records. This type of risk can be reduced by using firewalls and other sophisticated security measures to limit who can gain access to a Web site or a computer network. A discussion of these specific security technologies is outside the scope of this book, so you should raise this issue with the company that will host your online store.

Security Leaks

A security leak occurs when confidential information is visible on a Web site or online store when it shouldn't be. This usually happens because someone hasn't properly secured the Web site. In addition, security leaks can occur through unauthorized access by an internal party, or by someone at an Internet service provider.

Intentional Destruction of Data

Sometimes people break into Web sites with the sole intention of vandalizing the site in some manner. Usually the culprits alter the images or graphics on the Web and add their own in order to make a public statement of some kind. Even the Central Intelligence Agency has been a victim of this type of attack. If your store is not properly secured against unauthorized access, you could find yourself in a very embarrassing, and potentially costly, situation.

Accidental Loss of Data

You want to protect your online store in the event of a computer crash, power failure, flood, or other disaster at the location of your Internet service provider, storefront service provider, or Web hosting company. You could also lose data or even your entire online store through human error on the part of those responsible for managing your online store. For example, some commands on UNIX operating systems are so powerful that a single accidental command could wipe out everything. These risks are best avoided by restricting access to the computers on which your online store is located, as well as through regular and ongoing backups of your Web site and online store.

Denial-of-Service Attacks

There have been many high-profile cases of Web sites being shut down, or made inaccessible or intolerably slow, as the result of what is called a denial-of-service attack. This situation involves someone deliberately blocking access to your online store by bombarding the computer that hosts your online store with a stream of information requests. The information requests eventually overwhelm the computer, causing it to shut down. Such an attack exploits a problem within the operating system software or other software upon which a Web site or online store is based. The much-publicized attacks in 2000 that temporarily shut down several Web sites, including Yahoo!, Amazon.com, and eBay were denial-of-service attacks.

Your online store could be subject to a denial-of-service attack by a disgruntled customer, electronic joyrider, or, heaven forbid, a competitor. Denial-of-service attacks can occur because of known bugs in particular software programs, and thus are best avoided by ensuring that the software your online store uses, including the operating system and Web server, is kept up-to-date with the most recent versions.

Unauthorized Modification and Integrity Attacks

If someone can break into your online store, that person probably has the capability to change your prices or product information. This could have an embarrassing or indeed damaging effect on your business, particularly if customers make purchases in your online store based on the incorrect information.

Viruses

Viruses are malicious programs that can damage or delete data on your computer, modify files, steal passwords, and even transfer files from your computer to other computers on the Internet, often without your knowledge. An example is the famous Love Bug virus that paralyzed hundreds of thousands of computers around the world in 2000. The virus caused an estimated $15 billion worth of damage and forced thousands of organizations to shut down their e-mail systems. You can infect your computer with a virus by opening an e-mail or computer file that is already infected with the virus.

The best way to protect yourself against viruses is to install – and regularly update –virus protection software on your computer from companies such as McAfee (www.mcafee.com) and Symantec (www.symantec.com). Both companies provide extensive information on their Web sites to help you learn about viruses and guard against them. You should also ensure that all of the information on your computer is backed up in the event that a virus wipes out some or all of the files on your hard drive. Once you begin running your online store, think of all the important data that you will have on your computer systems – customer records, order history information, credit card numbers, product data, and more – it would be a disaster if you were to lose all of this information due to a virus.

Domain Name Hijacking

This occurs when someone transfers ownership of your domain name (e.g., nike.com) to another individual without your consent. When this happens, the hijacker is able to take control over your Web address so that when a customer types your Web site address into their browser, they are deliberately rerouted to another Web site, such as that of a competitor. This type of attack is more common than you may think. It happens when someone, by forging your identity or through other means, gains unauthorized access to the central registry database that stores the routing information for your domain name. Unlike the other types of security risks listed here, there is little that you can do to prevent this type of event from occurring. Security for Internet domain names rests with the various domain name registries that allocate domain names to individuals and businesses on the Internet. More information about the importance of domain names can be found in Chapter 6, *Marketing Strategies for Your Online Store.*

Cyber-Extortion

Cyber-extortion is what happens if a hacker or criminal breaks into your Web site and promises to destroy data, steal credit card numbers, launch a denial-of-service attack, or commit some other act unless a ransom is paid. This has happened to several firms with Web sites. In one case, an online retailer's Web site was broken into and customer records were accessed. The hacker threatened to publish thousands of customer credit card numbers unless $100,000 was paid. The company refused, and the hacker proceeded to post thousands of customer names, addresses, and credit card numbers on the Internet. This type of blackmail is an unfortunate reality of doing business on the Internet.

STEP #2: ASSESS YOUR PROCEDURES

In Chapter 2, we reviewed a number of different methods for creating an online store. You need to be confident in the security procedures and methods used by the companies you engage to host and/or build your online store. This section presents a checklist of questions to ask to help you undertake this assessment.

Keep in mind that you might find that your bank or merchant account provider requires you to demonstrate that you have addressed security to a reasonable degree, so these are not matters to take lightly. You might consider consulting a security expert who can assist you with these issues, both before and after the design of your store. Technology companies such as IBM (www.ibm.com) and consulting firms such as Ernst & Young (www.ey.com), as well as smaller, independent consultants, offer these types of services.

In addition, you might consider hiring an "ethical hacker," a company or individual who will test your Web site's security by attempting to break into your store. This can help identify potential weaknesses. These services can be obtained from consultants such as IBM and Ernst and Young as well. However, hiring a security consultant can be very expensive, so it's not usually the type of service that a small business or mom-and-pop online store would use.

Security Checklist for Storefront Hosting Services

1. Is the company security conscious?

2. Do they respond to your questions appropriately?

3. Do they keep up-to-date on security issues?

4. How is staff turnover handled?

5. How is access to the computers restricted?

6. Are unused services on the computers turned off?

7. Are there known risks with the storefront software?

8. Where is cardholder information stored?

9. What backup procedures are in place?

10. How are data transmitted?

Is the Company Security Conscious?

When you select a company to host or build your online store, assess whether the company pays proper attention to security issues. If you have any concerns, make sure they are addressed to your satisfaction.

At a minimum, determine what security procedures and technologies the company has in place to guard against security breaches and the types of problems that we described earlier. Don't simply assume that the company has excellent security – ask about it. And don't assume that the company knows what it's doing, as even the experts can get it wrong.

Do They Respond to Your Questions Appropriately?

A good e-commerce company will take the time to help you understand the security issues that affect your online store. If you find that the company dismisses your questions or has an arrogant attitude, then you will probably want to consider using another company. If an e-commerce company does not respond to your concerns appropriately, it is probably also far too willing to dismiss security issues in general. Don't be embarrassed by your lack of expertise about security. A good e-commerce company will recognize that you are trying to educate yourself and will respond in a professional manner.

Do They Keep Up-to-Date on Security Issues?

New security problems are constantly arising. What is the company doing to keep current on these issues? You want to deal with an organization that takes security seriously by keeping up to date.

How Is Staff Turnover Handled?

What security policies are implemented when an employee leaves the organization? What procedures ensure that former employees don't have access to passwords and critical files?

How Is Access to the Computers Restricted?

Find out where the company's computer facilities are located, including the computer(s) that will be used to run and store data from your online store. What steps has the company taken to protect unauthorized physical access? Are the facilities in a secure building? What about online access – who has access to the administrative and other special accounts involved with your online store? Are passwords to these accounts changed regularly?

Are Unused Services on the Computers Turned Off?

Security problems often arise because the Web server (the software that runs a Web site) hasn't been set to screen out certain types of Internet communications. Any methods of gaining access to the Web server not required for electronic commerce should be either removed or disabled. This will prevent a hacker or other unauthorized individual from gaining access to your Web site through a back door.

Are There Known Risks with the Storefront Software?

Ask the company if there are any known risks or security problems with the storefront software you have chosen. If there are, find out how those problems are being addressed. Obviously, if there are known security problems with a company's storefront software, they may not be willing to disclose this information to you for fear of losing your business. That is why it is important to ask for references and interview other people that are using the company's software. This will help you to uncover any security issues that the company may not have revealed to you.

Where Is Cardholder Information Stored?

Ensure that any customer information your store collects (e.g., credit card information, billing records, telephone numbers, mailing addresses) is securely stored on computers that can't be accessed from the Internet. For maximum protection, it is essential that customer information and credit card numbers are stored in an encrypted (scrambled) manner behind a firewall. This will make it difficult for a hacker or other unauthorized individual to get access to the data.

What Backup Procedures Are in Place?

Find out how often backups are performed on your online store. Daily? Weekly? Monthly? As soon as a customer order is placed? Are the backup copies stored in a safe, secure, locked location? Are the backups backed up in case the original copies are accidentally destroyed? If you plan to keep customer credit card information in a database linked to your online store, what is the procedure for destroying old copies of that database? It's crucial that the company has a backup of your online store in case there is a computer crash, natural disaster, or act of vandalism that causes you to lose all or some of the computer files belonging to your online store. The general recommendation is: the more frequent the backup the better!

How Are Data Transmitted?

Finally, make sure that the storefront software you are using will automatically encrypt customers' credit card information and other personal data when an order has been placed. This will prevent unauthorized individuals from intercepting and reading the information as it travels over the Internet to your online store. You should choose an online storefront solution that supports 128-bit encryption using SSL (Secure Sockets Layer) technology. This is the most popular form of encryption in use on the Internet and it will adequately protect customer data from being accessed while in transit.

Is All This Really Necessary?

Since it's unlikely that you're an expert on Internet security issues, your natural inclination will be to trust the company that you're dealing with. After all, how are you supposed to know whether an e-commerce company has taken all the appropriate security measures? Even if you ask all of the questions that we've listed above, you have no way to tell whether the company is being perfectly honest with their responses unless you're well versed in technical issues or have access to its facilities. Moreover, it may be difficult for you to contact a person who has enough knowledge to answer all of these questions.

To a great degree, you have to place your faith in the hosting company and software that you have chosen. However, any hosting company or storefront hosting firm that takes Internet security seriously should have basic information about its security infrastructure on its Web site and be happy to answer your questions by e-mail or on the telephone. Many companies are obviously not going to publish sensitive information about their security procedures on their Web sites, so you will probably need to have a conversation with someone in order to get detailed security information. Understandably, however, many companies are reluctant to reveal their security policies – even to a potential customer – in order to protect the integrity of their systems. While a company may not want to reveal publicly how it deals with certain security issues, at the very minimum you should be able to learn how your customers' credit card data will be handled, both in terms of transmission and storage, and what a company's backup policies are.

The bottom line is that you should never take Internet security for granted. Try to get a gut feel for how various e-commerce companies deal with Internet security. For example, a company that forwards you a two-page description of the security measures it has taken to protect your online store will likely give you more confidence than one that answers "trust us" to your questions. Finally, check with your bank or merchant account provider as many of these organizations are developing lists of approved hosts, gateways, ISP's, etc., that have met their security qualifications.

Consequences of Inadequate Data Security

What will happen to online merchants who fail to implement proper Internet security measures? Most importantly, they expose themselves and their customers to tremendous risks by not adequately protecting credit card data and other sensitive customer information such as names, addresses, and telephone numbers. If hackers are able to gain access to a merchant's credit card data, some or all of the merchant's customers could become victims of online fraud.

Think of the public relations damage that would result if word got out that your customer database had been broken into by hackers. Fearing that their credit card numbers wouldn't be safe, customers might stay away from your online store in droves, resulting in a sharp drop in business. The negative media attention that often ensues from a hacker attack could haunt a merchant for years, not to mention the devastating impact on the merchant's reputation.

Consider what happened to Western Union following the hacker attack described earlier in this chapter. The story was immediately picked up by the news media and reported widely. The negative publicity from this event harmed Western Union's reputation and credibility, making many customers think twice about using the company's Web site.

e-Fact

In 2000, only 25% of businesses that suffered serious computer security breaches reported them.

Source: Computer Security Institute (www.gocsi.com)

Inadequate security on your Web site could also result in the revocation of your merchant accounts (see Chapter 4 for discussion of merchant accounts). As noted in Chapter 4, every time a fraudulent transaction occurs on your Web site, you'll probably receive a chargeback for the purchase once the real cardholder discovers the fraudulent activity. If you start to receive a lot of chargebacks due to online fraud, Visa, MasterCard, and American Express reserve the right to revoke your merchant status so that you can't accept credit cards anymore. Obviously, this could be devastating to your business. More serious might be the fact that you, the merchant, can't fund the charge-back. That is a more likely risk to legitimate merchants who have a security lapse.

But those aren't the only consequences that merchants may face. Credit card companies such as Visa are stepping up their enforcement of Internet security and creating mandatory security rules for merchants and their service providers. Merchants and their service providers who fail to comply could face stiff fines, be subject to a cap on the dollar amount of sales they can process through their online stores, or lose their merchant status altogether. To avoid these penalties, check with your merchant account provider or acquiring financial institution (see Chapter 4 for an explanation of these organizations) to obtain the most current security rules for each of the credit cards you accept on the Internet.

Visa USA, for example, has created a Cardholder Information Security Program that includes minimum security requirements that must be followed by any organization (that means you, the organization that hosts your Web site, or any other service providers that might be involved with your store) that processes, stores, or has access to credit card data from Internet transactions. The program consists of a "Top Ten" list of logical requirements for protecting Visa cardholder information:

Visa's Top Ten List for Protecting Credit Card Information on the Internet

1. Install and maintain a working network firewall to protect data accessible from the Internet.

2. Keep security patches up-to-date.

3. Encrypt stored data.

4. Encrypt data sent across open networks.

5. Use and regularly update anti-virus software.

6. Restrict access to data by business "need-to-know."

7. Assign a unique ID to each person with computer access to data.

8. Don't use vendor-supplied defaults for system passwords and other security parameters.

9. Track access to data by unique ID.

10. Regularly test security systems and processes.

An additional two requirements address administrative and physical security issues:

11. Maintain a policy that addresses information security for employees and contractors.

12. Restrict physical access to cardholder information.

These rules have been developed for all organizations that work with Internet transactions. As you probably notice, a lot of these rules are simply common sense.

Some of these rules, however, may not apply in all situations, or to small businesses that don't run their own Internet servers. For example, if you don't have a computer with a full-time, dedicated connection to the Internet, a firewall is not a necessity. However, if you have customer information (e.g., names, addresses, telephone numbers) or credit card information stored on any of your computers, and those computers are linked to, or accessible from, the Internet in some way, you should have a firewall installed. We suggest that you check with the acquiring financial institution or the independent sales organization (ISO) that gave you your merchant number for guidance on your particular situation.

If you are operating your own Internet server(s), you will need to address these issues yourself. If you are paying someone else to host your online store on the Internet, or if you are using one of the storefront creation services such as Yahoo! Store or FreeMerchant that we discussed in Chapter 2, you should ensure that the company that will be hosting your online store is following these rules. At a minimum, e-mail or telephone the company you are using or thinking of using for your storefront and ask what security precautions it has taken to safeguard cardholder data. You can compare the response to the list above. If certain items are missing, ask about them. Don't be shy about pressing a company for answers about online security. It's your right to know, and any company that is serious about e-commerce will respect your questions. After all, if something goes wrong and a hacker is somehow able to access your customers' credit card information, it is you that will bear the brunt of the fallout, not the hosting company you are working with!

For the latest information on Visa's Cardholder Information Security Program, visit Visa's Merchant Resource Center Web site, which links off Visa's main site (www.visa.com). There, you can download a guide to Visa's security program. The guide contains an explanation of each of the top ten rules as well as examples of how merchants/service providers have addressed these requirements. To help you judge your current security situation, the Merchant Resource Center includes a self-assessment questionnaire that can be printed out.

The way that Visa verifies your compliance with these rules will depend on your size and how many transactions you typically store or process. For example, a small mom-and-pop merchant may only be required to complete an online self-assessment checklist. Larger merchants and service providers that process hundreds or thousands of transactions a day may be required to submit to onsite reviews, intrusion-detection testing, and ongoing monitoring of their firewalls.

If you're not sure whether your Web site and computers are adequately protected, hire an Internet security expert to assess your situation for you. It's better to be safe than sorry!

STEP #3: PROTECT THE INTEGRITY AND SECURITY OF YOUR ONLINE TRANSACTIONS

In addition to keeping your online store safe from break-ins, natural disasters, vandalism, and breaches of confidentiality, you need to protect the integrity and security of the order process itself. When a customer places an order on your Web site, you need to have security in place so that a customer's order information, including credit card details, can't be stolen or tampered with as it is transmitted over the Internet. This is an encryption issue. You also want to take steps to prevent stolen or bogus credit cards from being used on your Web site, i.e., fraudulent purchases.

> **e-Fact**
>
> *83% of online merchants say that fraud is a problem on their Web sites.*
>
> Source: CyberSource (www.cybersource.com)

These two issues are among the most technically complex subjects that you will have to deal with when you set up your online store.

Encryption

To secure the transmission of customer data, most online merchants use SSL (Secure Sockets Layer). SSL is supported by all Web browsers and is in widespread use on the Internet today. SSL encrypts credit card information as it travels from the customer's computer to the merchant's Web site. This minimizes the chance that the credit card information will be stolen while it passes over the Internet. However, despite the widespread use of SSL, consumers remain apprehensive about using their credit cards on the Internet. This has led some payment card companies to launch single-use credit card numbers that expire immediately after they are used.

American Express (www.americanexpress.com), for example, is using a service called "Private Payments" that involves the use of disposable credit card numbers. American Express cardholders can register for the free service on the American Express Web site. Once a cardholder is registered, he or she can download software that can issue a unique disposable credit card number whenever the cardholder wants to make an online purchase. The disposable number can be used at any online store that accepts American Express cards. Each unique number is only valid for a single purchase on the Internet and expires as soon as the purchase is completed. The merchant gets paid for the sale because each disposable credit card number is linked to the customer's real American Express account.

There are two primary benefits to these single-use credit cards from a security point of view. First, since the disposable number is only good for a single purchase, the number is useless to anyone who intercepts it during an online purchase. Second, even if someone were to break into the merchant's Web site and steal the number, it couldn't be used since the number would have already expired. Thus, even when SSL is used, the use of a disposable credit card number gives the consumer even greater protection.

Fraudulent Purchases

Fraudulent purchases derive from two risks. The first is the risk that someone tries to buy a product with a card that has been reported stolen, is invalid, canceled, or over its spending limit. These are authorization issues. Second, there is the risk that someone tries to use a valid credit card that hasn't been reported stolen but that doesn't belong to them. This is an authentication issue. Before we discuss these issues, let's first look at who is responsible for fraudulent transactions.

The Merchant *Is Responsible for Fraudulent Credit Card Transactions*

e-Fact

Information security professionals are more concerned about viruses than they are about computer break-ins.
Source: Information Security Magazine
(www.infosecuritymag.com)

You may be wondering who is responsible if you unknowingly accept an online order with a stolen credit card and then ship the merchandise to the address that was provided with the order. The answer is that *you* are on the hook for any fraudulent transactions that take place on your online store. This is so important we want to repeat it again. *You are usually forced to eat the loss for any fraudulent transactions that occur on your online store.*

Here's what would happen if an order was placed on your Web site using a stolen credit card. Let's assume that you process the order and ship the merchandise. Several days or weeks later, the real owner of the credit card receives a credit card statement and notices the transaction that took place on your online store. Since the real credit card owner won't recognize the transaction, the person will probably dispute the purchase. Because credit card statements are usually only mailed out to customers once a month, a customer may not receive a statement and file a complaint until several weeks after the order was made on your online store. By that time, it's quite likely that your bank or merchant account provider will have already deposited the money from this order into your bank account (as discussed in Chapter 4, money from online orders is usually deposited into your bank account within several days of the order taking place). Upon being notified of the customer dispute, your bank or merchant account provider will issue a chargeback and, in effect, will *take back* the money it gave you for the order, leaving you with nothing, even though you have already shipped the merchandise.

Herein lies an important lesson: *when online fraud occurs, it is the merchant, not the bank, that is ultimately responsible.* It's rather ironic. Throughout this chapter, we've been talking about consumers' fears of using their credit cards on the Internet. *But it's the merchants who bear the greater risk.* And to make matters worse, online merchants don't usually learn that an order has been disputed until many weeks after the order was placed. By this time, the merchandise is usually long gone, having been shipped weeks earlier by the merchant.

Consider the following advisory that Yahoo! Store (store.yahoo.com/vw/fraud.html) gives its merchants: "You often read in the press that consumers are worried about ordering online. In reality, it is not the consumers who have to worry, but the merchants. If you're a consumer, the chance of your credit card number being intercepted as it travels over the Internet is microscopically small. But if you are a merchant, the chance of getting orders with stolen credit card numbers is significant."

When a cardholder disputes a charge made at an online store, the merchant has no physical proof that the cardholder legitimately made the purchase, since the merchant does not see the physical credit card or a customer signature. So when cardholders complain that they never made an online purchase that has showed up on their credit card statement, the bank often sides with the customers, and the merchant in most cases is forced to eat the loss.

Recognizing that the system usually works in favor of the customer, some consumers buy goods on the Internet with their own credit cards and then deny ever making the purchases once they receive their credit card statements. This is called *friendly fraud*. Friendly fraud, however, accounts for a very small percentage of online fraud. Many organizations have aggressive programs in place to combat this type of fraud.

Let's now look at the two issues of authorization and authentication.

Authorization

Online stores can authorize their credit card transactions manually using a transaction terminal or in real-time using any of the payment gateways that we discussed in the explanation of authorization processes in Chapter 4. If the credit card has been canceled, reported stolen, or isn't in good standing, the purchase will be declined by the financial institution that issued the credit card. This is essentially the same process that occurs in a retail store when a customer makes a purchase.

What Does a Credit Card Authorization Really Mean?

Even if you receive an authorization from the credit card company for an online purchase, it is not a guarantee that the credit card is legitimate or that the person placing the order is the rightful owner of the card. *Contrary to popular belief, an authorization is also not a guarantee that you'll get paid for the order.* In fact, the credit card may be stolen and the owner may not know about it or have reported it yet. If a credit card hasn't been reported stolen, the credit card company has no way of knowing that there is a problem. So when the stolen credit card number is used on the Internet to make a purchase, the credit card company will authorize the transaction as long as the cardholder hasn't exceeded the allowable credit limit.

> **e-Fact**
>
> *Three out of four online consumers rate credit card data sent via the Web as their preferred method of payment.*
>
> Source: Zona Research
> (www.zonaresearch.com)

Authentication

One of the biggest challenges confronting merchants and credit card companies is authentication. How do you ensure that the person using a credit card is in fact the owner of that card number? As we explain below, one of the problems that merchants face on the Internet is that they can't see the customer's physical credit card nor can they get a physical signature from the cardholder.

Card Present vs. Card Not Present Transactions

When a customer makes a purchase in a retail store, the store clerk is supposed to compare the signature on the back of the credit card to the signature made by the purchaser. If the signatures don't match, it may be a sign that the purchaser is not the owner of the credit card. A purchase in a retail store is referred to as a *card present transaction* because a physical credit card is presented to the merchant by the customer. Merchants who follow the guidelines issued by credit card companies for card present transactions (including authorizing the transaction using the transaction terminal and checking for matching signatures) are guaranteed payment for the amount of the purchase, less any merchant fees, such as the ones we discussed in Chapter 4.

With an online transaction, the shopper enters a credit card number on the merchant's Web site and confirms the order. Because a physical credit card cannot be presented during an online transaction, online credit card orders are referred to as *card not present transactions*. And since neither the customer's signature nor any other form of identification has typically been required for online transactions, it has not been possible for the merchant to verify the identity of the cardholder.

It is important to note that card not present transaction status is not new – long before the Internet was around, it applied to mail order and telephone orders (the term *MOTO transaction* is also often used). So don't think that the credit card companies are out to treat you differently because of the Internet – they are simply applying their existing rules to card not present transactions.

Since neither a physical credit card nor a cardholder's signature is used in an online transaction, online credit card orders expose the merchant to fraud.

Assessing Your Risk and Comfort Level

In any online store, there is a good chance that someone with a stolen or bogus credit card number is going to try to place an order. It's important to understand that any online merchant can be affected by fraud, not just those merchants selling high-priced items like jewelry, electronics, or computer equipment. So even if you're selling a low-priced item like hand-painted earrings, you're not immune to online fraud. *It can happen to anyone!*

That being said, there are several things you can do to authenticate the identity of a credit card holder. It is your responsibility as a merchant to screen all of your orders before shipping them. In the next sections, we will help you understand many of the manual methods of authentication you might undertake in order to reduce your risk of loss. We will also talk about some of the computerized methods of authentication, such as address verification and fraud screening software.

Obviously, many of these procedures will cost you extra time and effort, and potentially, extra money. Therefore, you have to carefully determine how far you are willing to go in analyzing transactions for potential fraud, as well as the amount of effort that you are willing to make to verify the identity of the individual behind a credit card transaction that might cause you concern.

Clearly, if you are selling low-cost items with a very low margin, you might determine that you simply want to reject any orders that don't pass muster. If you are selling high-priced items with a big margin, you might be willing to undertake additional steps on a suspicious sale to determine if the risk is worth it.

Bottom line: what you do depends on what you are selling, and the effort that you are willing to apply.

Manual Methods of Authentication

Here are some manual methods of authentication to help you avoid credit card fraud on the Internet.

- Ask for both home and work numbers on your order form and then call to verify the order, particularly if you are dealing with high-value items. Out-of-service telephone numbers are an obvious sign that an order is probably fraudulent. *If you don't hear back from the customer, don't ship the order.*

- Check both the billing and shipping addresses on your orders to make sure they are legitimate. You might be suspicious if the billing address you have been given differs from the shipping address even though it is common for billing and shipping addresses to be different. Someone using a stolen credit card number will not want to have the order shipped to the cardholder's billing address, so another address will be given to you for shipping purposes. Be aware, however, that a billing address that differs from a shipping address is not always a sign of credit card fraud. A cardholder may be ordering a product on behalf of another person or shipping the order to a work address, another residence, or to a friend or relative's home.

- Be wary of orders that are placed using free e-mail address services such as Hotmail. This can be an indication that the person placing the order doesn't want to be found, or makes it difficult to verify the legitimacy of the identity used.

- Check to see if the e-mail address being used by the purchaser is located near the billing address provided by the cardholder. For example, if you receive an order from an e-mail address in Israel, and the billing address is located in the United States, this is a good indication that the order may be fraudulent. It's not always easy to determine in what part of the world an e-mail address is located, but sometimes you can deduce this information by looking at the domain name or using a bit of detective work. Some online storefront software packages might also provide the IP or Internet address of the purchaser, and you might be able to use this to verify their location. Later in this chapter we talk about some of the fraud screening technology that can help you deal with this.

- Be suspicious if the order you receive is unusual, such as an order for several high-ticket items, large quantities of product, or an assortment of products that typically wouldn't be ordered together. Rush delivery on a large-volume or large-value order may be another sign of fraud.

- Be careful when shipping to certain countries, such as Romania, Colombia, Belarus, Russia, and Macedonia. Because a high proportion of fraud originates from these countries, you may want to have a policy that you don't ship to those countries unless you receive payment in advance. Remember that you're not obligated to ship to every country in the world. When you develop a shipping policy for your online store (see Chapter 3, *Tips for Building an Effective Online Store*), carefully consider this issue.

While we don't recommend that you not ship outside of North America, you should carefully consider requesting payment in advance from some of the high-risk countries.

As a general rule, never ship an order that you're not fully comfortable with. Use all of the avenues available to you to verify the legitimacy of an order if you think it may be suspect, including financial institutions and telephone and address directories.

Don't rely on e-mail as a means of verifying an order. An e-mail message from someone confirming that they've placed an order on your Web site means nothing. How do you know that the e-mail message actually comes from the owner of the credit card used in the purchase? E-mail addresses and e-mail headers can be easily forged or altered to trick the recipient into thinking the message is coming from a particular person.

Remember that there are dozens of free e-mail services on the Internet. Anyone can create an e-mail account to resemble a person's name. That account could then be used with a credit card order so that the order seems legitimate.

Below are the most common signs of credit card fraud, according to the people who run Yahoo! Store (store.yahoo.com), one of the storefront services that we discussed in Chapter 2. Study this list and be on the lookout for any purchases in your online store that seem suspect.

> ### e-Fact
>
> *Companies conducting e-commerce are twice as likely to have their Web servers attacked by hackers.*
>
> Source: Information Security Magazine (www.infosecuritymag.com)

Warning Signs of Fraud

We've listed some of the warning signs of fraud below. The most important is the country of origin. Orders from some countries, particularly Romania, Macedonia, and Belarus, are nearly 100 percent fraud.

Unless you have a lot of experience with international orders, we recommend that you never ship to these countries, even if you get a valid authorization from the credit card company. (If you read the fine print of your merchant agreement, you will usually find that an authorization doesn't guarantee you'll get paid.)

Fraud is less of a problem with orders from North America, Western Europe, or Japan. But it is still a possibility. Here are the general warning signs of a fraudulent order:

1. Suspect shipping address. Most fraudulent orders come from Romania, Macedonia, Belarus, Pakistan, Russia, Lithuania, Egypt, Nigeria, Colombia, Malaysia, and Indonesia.

2. Untraceable e-mail address. In fraud orders, the customer's e-mail address is often at one of the free e-mail services, like Hotmail or Usa.net, which are comparatively untraceable.

3. Expensive items. Be wary of big orders, especially for brand-name items.

4. Multiple items. It is a bad sign, for example, if someone orders three watches or three Walkmen at once.

5. Express shipping. Most fraudulent orders specify overnight or one-day shipping.

6. Shipping address differs from billing address. If you are selling valuable items, it can be a good policy only to ship to the billing address of the card.

7. Suspicious billing address. If the billing address is 123 Main St., New York, the order is probably fraud. You can use Yahoo! Maps to see if the address really exists.

8. New site. Newly opened sites are more often targeted, perhaps in the belief that the merchants will be inexperienced.

9. Leave at door. If someone placing a very valuable order says just to leave it at the door, it could be a sign that a crook is using some unwitting person's house as a drop-off point. (Solution: require a signature.)

As a general rule, you should never ship a valuable order unless it checks out. And be aware that, for international orders, getting a valid authorization is no guarantee that the order is legitimate.

Source: Yahoo! Store (store.yahoo.com)

Computerized Methods of Authentication — Address Verification

In addition to manually screening your online orders for warning signs of fraud, we highly recommend that you use an address verification service. This service is offered by most banks and independent sales organizations and is usually bundled into the cost of obtaining a merchant account.

An address verification service checks to see whether the billing address and zip code provided at the time of the transaction match the cardholder's actual address and zip code on file with the issuing bank. When you accept orders on the Internet, you will be required to ask shoppers for both a billing address and a shipping address. If someone has stolen a credit card or the owner of the credit card has unknowingly lost the card, the person in possession of the card may attempt to use it fraudulently to purchase something in an online store. *Experience has shown that most perpetrators of fraud do not know the billing address of the cardholder whose account they are using.* As a result, they will usually make up a fictitious address, use a real address that belongs to someone else, or make the billing address the same as the shipping address.

This is where address verification comes in. When an online order is placed, the address verification service takes the zip code and the numerical part of the street address (excluding suite or apartment numbers) from the billing address and compares it to the information on file with the cardholder's issuing bank.

The result of the comparison is usually delivered to the merchant in the form of an alphabetic response code. The code will tell you whether there was an exact match, a partial match, or no match on the information or if the card issuer is in a foreign country.

The primary benefit of an address verification service is that it can help you to undertake an extra review of the information provided with an order to determine if you feel comfortable fulfilling the order. When you review the orders in your online store, you'll be able to see the address verification code that each order received. What you do at this point will depend on how much risk you are willing to accept, keeping in mind that as an Internet merchant, you are financially responsible for any fraudulent transactions that occur in your online store. Internet merchants are responsible for coming up with their own guidelines for handling address verification service codes.

What you decide to do may be different from what another Internet merchant does. There is no rule that says you can't process an order that receives only a partial address verification match. Ultimately, you need to decide how much risk you are willing to accept and whether you can afford to be financially liable for a transaction that turns out to be fraudulent. If after reviewing the address verification information, you decide that the risk is too high, you can contact the customer and try and sort out the discrepancy or you can simply refuse to fill the order unless payment is received in advance.

It is important to understand that a perfectly legitimate order may receive an address verification service code indicating that some or all of the cardholder's information doesn't match. For example, suppose a cardholder has moved but the cardholder's issuing bank hasn't updated its database with the new information. If this were the case, the billing address used by the customer on your Web site will differ from the information the customer's bank has on file, resulting in an unfavorable code from the address verification service. Similarly, if a customer mistypes his or her address or zip code on your Web site, you'll receive an address verification code indicating a full or partial mismatch. An unfavorable code can also result when the customer inputs a five-digit zip code but the bank has a nine-digit zip code on file or vice versa.

Since there are numerous reasons why valid orders may end up with bad address verification codes, you need to come up with your own policy for dealing with them. If you get into the habit of rejecting all the orders that don't have a favorable code, you could be turning away a lot of legitimate business. On the other hand, ignoring unfavorable codes from your address verification service could cost you a lot of money in the form of chargebacks if some or all of the orders do turn out to be fraudulent. Because an unfavorable address verification code may be a sign of fraud, the safest route is to try to independently verify (to your satisfaction) that the order is legitimate.

e-Fact

In 2000, female shoppers who believed it was safe to use a credit card online spent $830 on their online orders, compared to $459 for those women doubting transaction security.

Source: Cyber Dialogue
(www.cyberdialogue.com)

The best way to do this is to contact the person who is being billed for the order and, without accusing him or her of fraud, confirm the order placed on your online store. If the person confirms the order, try to determine why the billing addresses don't match (e.g., did the person move recently?). The problem, however, is that you have no way of knowing whether the person you are talking to is actually the owner of the card. The thief, for example, could give you his or her phone number on the order form and pretend to be the cardholder when you call.

Suggestions for Verifying the Legitimacy of Online Credit Card Orders

If an online order you receive seems suspicious, or you get an unfavorable address verification code, most merchants resort to directory assistance or online telephone directories such as Switchboard (www.switchboard.com) or InfoSpace (www.infospace.com) to verify the street addresses (both billing and shipping) and telephone numbers of individuals. You could also use one of the many "reverse lookup" services on the Internet (such as AT&T's AnyWho service at www.anywho.com), which will give you a name and telephone number for a given street address. You might even use an online mapping site such as MapQuest (www.mapquest.com) to verify that the addresses provided are legitimate.

However, keep in mind that only customers with listed phone numbers will appear in online or offline telephone directories. Also, if the customer has moved, the telephone directory may still list the customer's old address information, so you shouldn't assume that an order is fraudulent just because you couldn't verify the order information using a directory.

If the information you've been given does match the information in the phone directory, at least you'll know that the phone number belongs to, for example, John Smith, when you call the number to verify the order. If you call up John Smith and he denies placing the order, you'll know right away that the order is fraudulent. On the other hand, if John Smith confirms placing the order on your Web site, you still have no way of knowing that John Smith is actually the owner of the credit card that was used on your Web site. Although it is very unlikely that a thief would use his own address and phone number on a Web site when committing credit card fraud, anything is possible. To verify his identity, get John Smith to give you the address that the bank has on file so that you can run the address verification check again. If he is indeed the owner of the credit card, he should have no problem giving you another address that will match the one the bank has on file. This should result in a favorable address verification code.

While an address verification service can help you cut back on fraudulent credit card orders, it isn't perfect. When using the service, keep the following limitations in mind:

- Even if the card's billing address as provided on the Web site matches the real cardholder's real address and you get a favorable code from the address verification service, it doesn't mean that the card isn't stolen. The thief may know the cardholder's correct address! A favorable address verification code is not a guarantee that the order isn't fraudulent.

- An address verification service can't handle addresses outside of the United States, at least as of early 2001, although this will likely change. When someone in another country places an order on your Web site, you will receive an address verification code that indicates that the cardholder is out of the country. As we pointed out earlier, international orders can be risky because many of them are fraudulent. For this reason, and taking into account other factors such as the volume or orders you receive and the average amount of those orders, you may want to verify international orders over the phone in the same way you would verify domestic orders. Where possible, use online or paper telephone directories to make sure that the name, telephone number, and street address of the cardholder match what you've been given.

As you can imagine, tracking down an international cardholder can be difficult or next to impossible, especially if you're dealing with a foreign language that isn't familiar to you. Foreign telephone directories may be hard to find, and you may end up making a lot of expensive international telephone calls. Depending on the value of the purchase in question and your risk tolerance, there are a number of options available to you if you can't independently verify the order:

- you can fill the order and take the chance that you'll get a chargeback;
- you can refuse to fill the order;
- you can contact the person placing the order and ask for payment in advance; or
- you can adopt a "no foreign orders" policy as some merchants have done and simply not accept any orders from outside the United States.

Consider a Pop-up Screen for Address Verification Service Failures

Because an unfavorable response from an address verification service may be due to a typing error or a change in the cardholder's billing address (i.e., the cardholder may have moved recently), you may want to consider prompting customers with a pop-up menu whenever the billing address cannot be matched. For example, you could set up your Web site so that if the address verification service's response is a mismatch or only a partial match, a pop-up window appears on the screen, notifying the customer that the billing address isn't recognized. This would give the customer a chance to correct and resubmit information. If the billing address still doesn't match the one stored at the issuing bank after one or two more tries by the customer, the customer would be locked out. This type of solution gives customers the chance to correct errors, relieving merchants from the time-consuming process of sorting through unfavorable address verification responses and contacting customers to verify orders.

Pop-up address verification screens are not readily available with most storefront hosting packages, nor can they be easily implemented by a small business without outside assistance. It would require custom programming, which might be expensive if you're a small business and you don't already have computer programmers in your organization. Moreover, some storefront services may not permit you to install this type of a system. However, for larger organizations with bigger budgets and ready access to programmers, an address verification pop-up window is an excellent way to reduce the number of unfavorable verification codes your storefront would otherwise receive. And by reducing unfavorable address verification codes, you cut back on the amount of time that your employees have to spend personally contacting customers to sort out billing address discrepancies!

Authorization vs. Address Verification

It is important that you not confuse authorization with address verification. They are completely different procedures. The authorization process checks the card number to see if it's valid, checks the customer's credit limit, and verifies that the credit card hasn't been reported stolen. As explained earlier, authorization doesn't guarantee that the credit card isn't stolen. In contrast, an address verification service only confirms that the billing address provided on the merchant's Web site matches the cardholder data on file at the issuing bank. It is fully possible, therefore, for a credit card purchase to be authorized and receive an unfavorable address verification code at the same time. When a person places a credit card order on a Web site, an authorization request and address verification request are usually sent together over the Internet to the cardholder's issuing bank. The merchant will receive a response that contains *both* the service's code and an authorization number. If the address verification code is unfavorable (i.e., a mismatch or only a partial match), it will not result in the transaction being declined. The address verification code does not influence the authorization process in any way.

Computerized Methods of Authentication — Fraud Detection Software

There are several fraud-screening services on the market that can help online merchants reduce the number of fraudulent transactions they process. Many of the services use neural network technology that can analyze patterns in data and distinguish between a legitimate online order and one that is potentially fraudulent. Fraud detection software takes many different factors into account when determining whether an order may be fraudulent. For example, among other things, it will usually look at the IP address (a unique number assigned to every computer network connected to the Internet) of the purchaser and determine whether that address is located near the billing address provided by the customer. If the IP address is in Cairo and the billing address is listed as Rhode Island, the transaction will likely be flagged as potentially fraudulent.

Merchants will receive a "score" for each online order they receive that will indicate the likelihood that the order is fraudulent. Based on this information, a merchant can decide whether or not to accept the online order. The cost of fraud-screening technology varies depending on the supplier, but it is usually priced on a fee-per-transaction or flat-fee-per-month basis. Examples of fraud-screening services include eFalcon (www.efalcon.com) from HNC Software (www.hnc.com) and Internet Fraud Screen from CyberSource (www.cybersource.com).

The benefits of using fraud-screening programs are numerous. Most importantly, by flagging potentially fraudulent transactions for you, these programs can help to reduce the costly losses that stem from online fraud. In addition, by using fraud-screening technology in your online store, you are providing a valuable service to your customers, and consumers everywhere. Why? You are helping to stop credit card thieves in their tracks. This will help you to develop goodwill with both your current and future customers.

In addition to considering the use of fraud-screening services in your online store, ask the company that is processing your credit card transactions what measures it has taken to minimize the occurrence of fraud. Some credit card processors maintain a "negative database" of credit card numbers and/or e-mail addresses that have been used to commit fraud in the past so they can automatically identify those purchases as fraudulent.

How to Implement Fraud Detection Software in Your Online Store

If you are planning on using one of the entry-level storefront creation services described in Chapter 2, fraud-screening software may already be built into the service or it may be available from one of the payment gateways supported by the service. Check with the storefront service you are thinking of using to see if any type of fraud screening service is available. If you are planning on using shopping cart software, you should investigate the different payment gateways supported by the software to see if any of them offer fraud protection. You may want to make fraud protection one of the features you look for when comparing different storefront solutions.

If you are building your own online store using more advanced e-commerce software, you can approach companies such as HNC Software and CyberSource directly and integrate their fraud-screening software directly into your Web site.

Computerized Methods of Authentication — Payer Authentication

As we noted earlier in the chapter, credit card transactions on the Internet are known as card not present transactions, because a physical credit card isn't presented to the merchant. This exposes online merchants to fraud because a physical signature can't be obtained from the person making the purchase.

As you've seen, current ways of protecting merchants against online fraud, such as credit card authorizations and address verification services, have many weaknesses. For example, authorizations are sometimes given for stolen credit card numbers and unfavorable address verification codes are often reported for perfectly legitimate credit card orders.

In 1996, Visa and MasterCard announced a new technology called SET that promised to combat online fraud. SET features a built-in mechanism to verify the identity of the person making the purchase. In other words, SET can tell if the person using the credit card is actually the owner of that card. Because of SET's ability to authenticate credit card purchases on the Internet, which by definition SSL can't do, it was seen to fulfill a different purpose than SSL. Unfortunately SET never really took off in the United States because of its cost and complexity. Not only was SET difficult and cumbersome to use, it was expensive to implement. Today, SSL remains the primary means of securing online credit transactions. Virtually all online merchants use SSL to encrypt credit card information and also customer data as it travels from the customer's computer to the merchant's computer over the Internet. In addition, however, SSL doesn't do anything to protect merchants and consumers from online fraud. SSL merely encrypts the information sent between a customer and an online store.

In 2000, Visa announced an online service called payer authentication service or VPAS (Visa Payer Authentication Service) under the name "Verified by Visa." Verified by Visa is a method of confirming that the person using a credit card during an online transaction is in fact the owner of that credit card. The major advantage of Verified by Visa is that it's less complicated to implement – and much easier to understand — and it responds to requests by merchants for solutions to prevent fraud on the Internet.

For example, cardholders won't require any special software or devices in order to use Verified by Visa. All that is required from the cardholder is a simple multi-step enrollment process that can be completed on a special Web site hosted by their card issuing bank. Cardholders will be directed to the appropriate site by the bank that issued their credit card. The registration process only takes a couple of minutes to complete and it's completely voluntary for consumers. Bank participation in the Verified by Visa system is also voluntary. However, in order for a cardholder to participate in Verified by Visa, the cardholder's issuing bank must be also be participating.

Merchants can register for Verified by Visa by contacting their acquiring bank or merchant account provider/independent sales organization (ISO). Once enrolled, they will receive a "plug-in" software program specific to the computing platform and e-commerce server they are using. In some cases, the Verified by Visa software may already be integrated into the e-commerce software that the merchant is using, in the same way that merchant account applications and payment gateways are prepackaged with many of the e-commerce storefront solutions that were discussed in Chapter 2.

For more information about Verified by Visa, contact your acquiring financial institution or the ISO that gave you your merchant number.

How Cardholders Register for Verified by Visa

Here is how the system is designed to work:

1. Visa cardholders register for Verified by Visa by going to a designated "enrollment site" for the bank that issued their credit card.

2. Once at the site, the cardholder will be prompted for account information as well as information known only to the cardholder. This information can vary by bank.

3. At this point, you may be asking yourself, "What happens if a thief steals a customer's credit card and tries to register with Verified by Visa?" To prevent someone other than the

real cardholder from successfully registering with Verified by Visa, the cardholder will be asked for one or more pieces of "out-of-wallet" information in order to verify that the person is the legitimate owner of the credit card being r egistered. Out-of-wallet information is data that only the cardholder would likely know, such as the cardholder's maiden name or previous address. The number and type of out-of-wallet questions that a cardholder could be asked will vary depending on the cardholder's issuing bank. The questions would largely depend on the amount of information that the issuing bank has on file about the cardholder.

In some cases, instead of using its own file of information about a cardholder, a bank may rely on a third-party authentication service such as a credit bureau for the questions and answers during the cardholder verification process. For example, the cardholder could be asked questions such as "Who is your home mortgage with?" or "What is the make and model of your car?" This is the type of information that a credit bureau may have on file. It's important to understand that Verified by Visa is not checking the cardholder's credit history nor does the Verified by Visa system affect the consumer's credit rating in any way. When a bank contacts a credit bureau as part of Verified by Visa, it is strictly for the purpose of verifying the cardholder's identity.

The cardholder will also be asked to create a "Personal Assurance Message." This phrase will be displayed on merchants' Web sites when the cardholder is making a purchase. It lets the cardholder know that the site is really dealing with Verified by Visa and not an imposter. The Personal Assurance Message can be any phrase the cardholder wishes.

4. Next, the cardholder will be asked to enter a password that will be used to authenticate the cardholder when an online purchase is made. The cardholder will also be prompted for a "hint and response pair." The hint and response are used to confirm the cardholder's identity in the event the cardholder forgets the Verified by Visa password. The hint is a question that the cardholder will know the answer to, and the response is the correct response to that question. The cardholder is free to come up with any question as long as it's not a question that someone else would know the answer to. For example, a cardholder might want to use a question like "What street did you grow up on?" or "What is your mother's birthday?"

5. Once the password has been registered, the cardholder is formally enrolled in Verified by Visa and the cardholder's password is securely stored on the issuing bank's computer network.

How Verified by Visa Works During an Online Transaction

Verified by Visa is simple to use. In fact, most of the activity takes place behind the scenes and is completely transparent to the cardholder. Here is an overview of the process.

1. A cardholder shops online in the usual way, adding items to a shopping cart, proceeding to the merchant's checkout page, and completing the merchant's checkout forms, by providing payment information and the shipping and billing address.

2. When the online shopper presses the "submit" or "complete order" button to complete the purchase, a request is sent over the Internet to the cardholder's issuing bank to find out whether the cardholder is participating in Verified by Visa.

3. If the cardholder's issuing bank reports back to the merchant that the cardholder is participating in Verified by Visa, the customer will see a bank-branded pop-up window appear on the screen. The window will attempt to verify the identity of the customer by asking for the password that was supplied during the registration procedure.

If the cardholder's issuing bank reports back to the merchant that the cardholder is not participating in Verified by Visa, the transaction would proceed as it normally would and a request for authorization will be sent to the cardholder's issuing bank. The merchant would receive an approval or decline message in return and the customer would be notified onscreen if the order was processed successfully. At this point, the transaction is completed.

4. As noted in Step #3, if the cardholder is participating in Verified by Visa, a window will appear on the cardholder's screen and he will be prompted to enter his or her password. Once the cardholder has entered the password, the system checks to see if the password is correct.

5. If the password is verified, a receipt containing a "digital signature" along with an authentication response is delivered electronically to the merchant. Think of a digital signature as an electronic method of notarizing a document. The digital signature is important because it lets the merchant know that the authentication response hasn't been generated fraudulently. When the digital signature is returned to the merchant, it's automatically verified to make sure that it did come from the cardholder's acquiring bank or from Visa. Once this happens, the cardholder is considered "authenticated," meaning that his or her identity has been confirmed.

If the password is not correct, the customer is given three tries to enter the password correctly. Upon the third invalid entry, the cardholder is provided with his or her hint and asked to provide its response. The cardholder is given one chance to correctly enter the response. If the response is incorrect, the transaction will either terminate or continue depending on how the merchant has set up the Verified by Visa software. The Verified by Visa software gives the merchant complete control over what happens when the authentication process fails. If the transaction is halted, a failure message would be displayed to the customer. At this point, the customer might be advised to contact his or her issuing bank for further instructions.

6. Once the cardholder has been authenticated, or if the merchant has allowed an unauthenticated cardholder to continue a transaction, an authorization request is transparently sent to the cardholder's issuing bank. Included in the authorization request is the result of the authentication process. If the cardholder's account is in good standing, the transaction will be approved, and an authorization message will be delivered back to the merchant from the cardholder's issuing bank.

7. If the credit card transaction is approved, the cardholder will see a message on the screen indicating the transaction has gone through successfully and the merchant will be able to retrieve the order from his or her storefront software.

Remember that the entire seven-step process described above takes place in just a couple of seconds. Most of the steps are completely transparent to the customer, except the password pop-up window, any authorization or authentication failure messages that may appear, and the final confirmation or "thank-you" message if the transaction is approved.

What to Do in the Event of a Failed Authentication

Even though it is possible for you to let a transaction continue immediately following an authentication failure, it's not recommended. An authentication failure is a good indication of fraud, because it means that the customer didn't provide his or her correct Verified by Visa password. This would suggest that someone other than the legitimate cardholder is trying to make an online purchase. Of course, it's entirely possible that the customer has simply forgotten the password. But remember that Verified by Visa has a built-in system that will give the cardholder a chance to respond to a hint question if he or she forgets the password. Because it's quite unlikely that a cardholder would forget not only his or her password but also the answer to his or her hint question, it's highly inadvisable to let a transaction proceed if the authentication process didn't succeed.

If the authentication fails and you decide to go ahead with an authorization request anyway, it is possible to end up with a transaction that has a failed authentication and an approval from the authorization process. How could this happen? Remember that the authorization process checks only three things:

- Is the credit card number valid?
- Is the person over his or her credit limit?
- Has the card been reported stolen?

If the card hasn't been reported stolen and the account is otherwise in good standing, the authorization request would be approved. Authorization does nothing to stop someone from using a credit card that hasn't been reported stolen. This is why the process of authenticating an online credit card purchase is so important. It gives merchants a more effective means of stopping criminals from using stolen credit cards on the Internet.

How Big Is Online Fraud?

One of the most hotly debated issues surrounding online fraud is how big the problem is. Some reports have suggested that fraud can be as high as 40 percent of online sales. Other studies have indicated that online fraud is a much smaller problem than most people think. So which is it? Part of the reason for the discrepancy is that merchants experience different fraud rates depending on the products they are selling. For example, merchants selling adult entertainment services or digital goods, such as downloadable music, generally experience higher fraud rates than merchants in other product categories. Second, the amount of fraud a merchant experiences will depend on the precautions a merchant is taking. Merchants that carefully scrutinize every order looking for the warning signs of fraud as listed above will unquestionably experience lower rates of fraud than merchants who don't take similar measures. Third, many online merchants don't report fraud for fear of scaring away their customers or ruining their reputations. As a result, it is hard to know the exact amount of credit card fraud that occurs on the Internet.

> **e-Fact**
>
> *Nearly two-thirds of Internet users are concerned that online shopping sites store their credit card information online for future use.*
>
> Source: PricewaterhouseCoopers (www.pwcglobal.com)

Where Do Stolen Credit Card Numbers Come From?

Thieves can get valid credit card numbers from a variety of places, most of which don't require that the thief have access to a physical credit card. They may break into a merchant's Web site on the Internet to get numbers, as happened to Western Union. Alternatively, the thief may have "inside" access to credit card records at a store or business where you've previously made a purchase. Fraud is often committed by people who work inside an organization and have authorized access to customer credit card files. It is also possible that your credit card number came into the hands of a thief via one of the credit card number generators that exist on the Internet. These are programs or Web sites that randomly generate credit card numbers that seem to be valid

> **e-Fact**
>
> *81% of online retailers believe that sales would increase if online shoppers were not as concerned about fraud.*
>
> Source: CyberSource (www.cybersource.com)

but that might not have been issued. And of course, a thief could get your credit card the old-fashioned way – by stealing it from your home, wallet, or some other location where it may have been left unprotected.

Track Occurrences of Fraud

One of the most effective means of combating fraud is to keep good records. Keep an accurate list of all your chargebacks and the reasons for them. If you don't keep good records, fraud may be significantly cutting into your profits without you realizing it! By carefully documenting all of your chargebacks, you'll always know how much of a problem fraud is in your online store and you'll be able to identify weaknesses in your fraud prevention techniques before they escalate. As we explained in Chapter 4, a chargeback can occur for a variety of reasons, such as defective merchandise, not just in cases of fraud.

Knowing why chargebacks are occurring in your online store can help you to pinpoint problems and take corrective action. You need to determine whether the chargebacks are due to fraud or some other problem. For example, if your record-keeping reveals that fraud is responsible for 80 percent of your chargebacks and 10 percent of your sales, you know that you have a problem with fraud. Further investigation may reveal that 75 percent of your fraud occurs with international orders. With this information in hand, you may decide to revise your policies for accepting foreign orders.

On the other hand, your investigations may reveal that most of your chargebacks are due not to fraud but to some other reason. For example, you may find that 80 percent of your chargebacks are due to unhappy customers who complained that the merchandise they received from you wasn't as described or pictured on your Web site. If this were the case, you would need to check the product descriptions and/or pictures on your Web site to ensure that they accurately describe the merchandise you are selling.

Obviously, you can't make the right decisions if you don't know why chargebacks are occurring and to what extent fraud is affecting your sales, which is why meticulous record-keeping is so important. At a minimum, you should always know how big fraud is as a percentage of your gross sales.

As part of your record-keeping, make sure you keep details of each fraudulent transaction that occurs in your online store, including the name that was used, shipping address, billing address, e-mail address, telephone numbers, and credit card number. This is called a *fraud avoidance file*. Keeping a fraud avoidance file will allow you to identify patterns in the data so that you can protect yourself from future occurrences of fraud. For example, you may notice that several of your fraudulent transactions have the same shipping address. You could then flag that address and be on the lookout for any other orders that come through with the same shipping address. Depending on what payment gateway software you are using, you may be able to set up your online store to automatically reject any orders with that shipping address. Some of the payment gateway software in use on the Web today allows merchants to screen out orders that match specific card numbers, names, e-mail addresses, or billing/shipping addresses.

STEP #4: LET CUSTOMERS KNOW YOUR ONLINE STORE IS SAFE

Once you've addressed the issues that we've discussed in Steps 1 to 3, you need to reassure your customers that your online store is secure.

It's difficult. The inherent insecurity of the Internet has led to problems with online stores and the concept of online shopping since the earliest days of the World Wide Web.

e-Fact

98% of U.S. Internet users who have never purchased anything online say that they are concerned about credit card security.
Source: UCLA Center for Communication Policy (ccp.ucla.edu)

After all, when the Web was born – around 1994 or 1995 – many early pioneers set up what could be considered today to be primitive online stores. These stores usually consisted of Web pages that detailed products for sale, all of which pointed to a simple form that people could fill out to undertake a purchase. When the form was completed, it would be e-mailed to the owner of the store, or would be printed automatically. At this point, the credit card number used in the transaction would be authorized using traditional telephone or terminal authorization methods.

Such methods of conducting a credit card transaction were insecure, because the information was sent "in the clear" through the Internet. This meant that the credit card information, whether transmitted via the Web or e-mail, was never encrypted in such a way that made it inaccessible. In those early days, media reports soon began to emerge that it was not safe to use credit cards on the Internet. This was true, given the basic design of the Internet.

From the earliest days of the Internet, seeds were planted in the minds of many people that the Internet was fraught with risk. The result was a great deal of consumer misapprehension and distrust. These concerns linger to this day. Despite the development of technologies like SSL, which are virtually impenetrable, many online shoppers are still reluctant to use their credit cards on the Internet.

Battling the Internet Security Myth

When you are selling products on the Internet, it is important that you do two things:

1. remind customers that their online transactions are secure; and

2. show them what you have done to protect their credit card information.

Remind Customers That Their Online Transactions Are Secure

First, assure customers that credit card transactions on the Internet in general, and more specifically on your online store, are secure. Let's put it this way: it's estimated that it would take someone a trillion years to break the strongest encryption forms (SSL uses 128-bit encryption), which are in use on many online stores today. That's how hard the technology is to penetrate. But even if an online store doesn't use SSL, the chance that someone could obtain credit card numbers transmitted over the Internet is very remote. Every day, tens of thousands of credit card transactions take place on the Internet. In the last several years, there have been few, if any, reports of credit card information being stolen as it passed from one computer to another. Consumers are at more risk giving their credit card number to a waiter in a restaurant than they are giving their credit card number to an online merchant.

Therefore, the perception that credit card transactions on the Internet are inherently dangerous has little merit. Nevertheless, to be absolutely sure that no one steals the credit card numbers that customers give you over the Internet, and to make your customers feel comfortable, use SSL encryption or some other form of encryption transmission.

Show Customers What You've Done to Protect Their Credit Card Information

Next, demonstrate to your customers that you've gone to great lengths to ensure that credit card transactions on your Web site are secure. To gain their confidence, we recommend that you follow the advice about building online credibility that we provided in Chapter 3, *Tips for Building an Effective Online Store*.

e-Fact

Fraud is 12 times higher on the Internet than in the physical world.

Source: Gartner Group (www.gartnergroup.com)

To recap, first describe how an online transaction works on your Web site. Walk customers through the process so that they can see the security measures that you've taken. In addition, tell them what technology you're using to protect them.

For example, are you using SSL? Are firewalls in place to protect confidential data? Do you encrypt credit card numbers on your computers? Consider implementing a security guarantee or safe shopping guarantee on your Web site. As discussed in Chapter 3, a security or safe shopping guarantee is a promise by your organization that credit card transactions on your Web site will be safe. Under United States law, consumers are only responsible for a maximum of $50 in the event their credit cards are used fraudulently. It's common practice in a safe shopping guarantee to pay the $50 liability for the customer as long as the fraud was caused by a security problem on your Web site. However, the $50 consumer liability is essentially a moot point now that Visa, MasterCard, and American Express all have a zero liability policy for their credit card holders. This means that customers are *never responsible* for unauthorized transactions on their credit cards. It's a good idea to promote these policies on your Web site so that customers know they have nothing to fear when shopping online.

STEP #5: BE VIGILANT!

Finally, good online store security means constant vigilance.

Find out what your Internet service provider or Web hosting company does to monitor newly emerging Internet security issues, or in the case of your own systems, what your information technology staff does. If you are using a storefront software package or shopping cart software, visit the vendor's Web site frequently and subscribe to any mailing lists offered to keep abreast of product enhancements and security issues. You should also get into the habit of visiting the Web sites of anti-virus software vendors regularly so that you can learn about new viruses before they strike. Most importantly, keep an ear to the ground for new Internet security threats that might affect your online store. As a step in this direction, you may want to consider obtaining a free membership in the Worldwide E-Commerce Fraud Prevention Network (www.merchantfraudsquad.com). Established by American Express, Amazon.com, and a variety of other e-commerce companies, the organization's goal is to help online merchants of all sizes fight e-commerce fraud.

Merchants who join the Network receive a number of benefits, including free advice to help combat online fraud and a directory of companies that specialize in anti-fraud technology. A membership registration form is available on the Network's Web site.

Finally, you need to recognize that online security is an issue that will never go away.

Online storefront services, Internet service providers, credit card companies, financial institutions, security software companies, and online store owners are constantly introducing new technologies into the marketplace that can help merchants protect the security and integrity of their online transactions. Because the online security technology marketplace is changing so rapidly, it is important that you keep an eye out for new products or services that can help you protect both yourself and your customers from security threats and credit card fraud. In particular, monitor your competitors to see what products they are implementing.

> **e-Fact**
>
> *Virus attacks are the most common type of computer attack.*
> Source: Computer Security Institute (www.gocsi.com)

REVIEWING YOUR FIVE-STEP ACTION PLAN

We've covered a lot of ground in this chapter. Here, in summary, are the five key steps for securing your online store:

1. Develop a basic understanding of Internet security issues so that you can be a more effective advocate of good security on your online store. You don't need to become an Internet security expert – just educate yourself so that you can protect your business and look out for the best interests of your customers. Also, make sure that you comply with the requirements of your bank or merchant account provider.

2. Assess whether the company that builds your online store (if you've hired one) as well as the company that hosts it are taking appropriate security precautions. This will also give you a gut feeling for how serious they are about online security issues. As part of this interview process, find out what security measures, both physical and computer-related, they have implemented to protect your Web site from being accessed by hackers, vandals, and other unauthorized individuals.

3. Remember that there are two fundamental credit card transaction issues that you need to address. First, make sure that you encrypt credit card transactions on your online store. Currently, the best technology for doing this is SSL. Second, protect yourself against fraudulent purchases. Because an authorization from the credit card company doesn't guarantee that a credit card isn't stolen, use the fraud checklist we provided earlier in the chapter to monitor your credit card orders for signs of fraud. Never ship an order that you think may be suspect. Use an address verification service and make sure that you follow up on any orders that receive an unfavorable code from the service. For additional protection against fraud, keep good records and consider using one of the fraud-screening services that we discussed earlier in the chapter.

4. Include a section on your Web site to let customers know that you don't take security issues lightly. Describe what steps you've taken to protect their credit card data and other personal information. As we suggested earlier, a security guarantee would be a good idea.

5. Finally, keep your eyes and ears open for any new security holes or problems that might affect your online store. In addition, keep abreast of new technologies that can help you better protect your online store from vandals. Don't ever let your guard down.

Chapter 6

MARKETING STRATEGIES FOR YOUR ONLINE STORE

...the typical offline company spends three to five times more on customer retention than its online competitors. Smart e-business managers must now redirect their efforts towards identifying and retaining profitable customers.

"Real Battle Is for the Web Revisited Mckinsey & Company" 10/20/2000

Business Review Weekly 63

Nineteen Ways to Promote Your Online Store

1. Know your audience
2. Your brand name
3. Offline marketing
4. Your retail store
5. Gift certificates
6. Cross-selling
7. Product referral services
8. Affiliate programs
9. Syndicated e-commerce
10. Electronic greeting cards

11. Permission marketing
12. Search engines and Web directories
13. Search engine optimization
14. Online shopping directories
15. Online advertising and sponsorship
16. Banner exchange networks
17. Keyword-based advertising
18. Bidding on search terms
19. Links from other Web sites

Marketing your online store involves more than just registering your Web site with a couple of search engines and waiting for the world to beat a path to your door.

As the number of shoppers on the Internet has grown, so too has the number of Web sites and land-based businesses clamoring for a piece of the multi-trillion-dollar e-commerce pie. As many Internet companies have discovered, even with a multi-million-dollar marketing campaign, it's difficult to get the attention of Internet users – even for just a split second. After all, Internet users are bombarded with so many advertisements every day and see so many Web sites, it's hard for any one firm to stand out.

One of the most difficult jobs you'll have as an e-commerce merchant is figuring out what blend of offline and online marketing techniques to use to promote your Web site. If you're a small business, that challenge is even greater on a tight budget. The right marketing mix depends on many factors, including the types of products you are selling, the types of people you are trying to target, and, of course, your budget.

In this chapter, we'll review a variety of different techniques for raising the profile of your online store and attracting shoppers to your Web site. Marketing your Web site is not an easy task, nor is it a short one – you'll need to work hard and work continuously to make sure that your online store doesn't get lost among the estimated *two billion* pages of information on the Web.

Know Your Audience!

The key to successful marketing is very simple: know your audience. Before you spend any time or money on marketing, you need to know who your target market is. What types of customers are most likely to buy the types of products you are selling? For example, males or females? What age bracket? What income bracket? Are you trying to reach people with certain interests or skills? Once you know the profile of your typical customer, you need to find ways of reaching customers with that demographic profile. This may involve online advertising, offline advertising, or a combination of the two. But don't even begin to think about spending money on marketing until you've spent time thinking about *who* you are trying to reach. You may even need to do some market research to uncover this information. We can't emphasize this step enough. Your marketing efforts won't be successful unless you are spending your marketing dollars in the right places.

Your Brand Name

One of the most important marketing assets that you have is the name of your online store. Give it careful consideration. You should pick a name that's easy to remember yet distinct from other similar names on the Internet. Closely related to the issue of picking a name is choosing a suitable domain name. The domain name is the part of your Web site address that appears after "www." For example, the domain name for Office Depot is officedepot.com and the domain name for Eddie Bauer is eddiebauer.com. Therefore, Office Depot's Web site is at www.officedepot.com and Eddie Bauer's Web site can be found at www.eddiebauer.com.

To avoid confusing your customers, you will want to have a domain name that is as close as possible to your organization's name. This will also make it easier for customers to find your Web site. For example, customers looking for Eddie Bauer's Web site would probably start by typing "www.eddiebauer.com" into their Web browsers. In addition to being close to your business name, your chosen domain name should be short, easy for your customers to remember, and intuitive.

Finally, keep in mind that you don't have to have "www." in your Web address. Some organizations have chosen to drop it entirely, e.g., CBS promotes itself simply as CBS.com.

In addition, you can, with the help of the technical folks who support your site, sometimes use words or characters in front of your actual domain name, and get an extra "identity hook" that might be unique enough to draw attention to your site.

Perhaps the best example of this is the Web site Beer.com, which gained some attention during the 2000 Olympics. It ran an ad that used the address mmm.beer.com – indeed, during the commercial, the graphic showed the "www" flipping over to become "mmm," as the announcer mimicked the "mmmm," or "tastes good" sound. There was a huge increase in traffic to the site.

Domain Name Suffixes

Most online stores in the United States have a domain name that ends in .com, where the .com indicates that you are a "commercial" enterprise. Not-for-profit organizations usually have a domain name that ends in .org, which stands for "organization." If your organization is for-profit, you should not register a .org domain name. Another domain name extension you will come across is .net, which is used by many online stores on the Internet. Although .net addresses were originally intended for organizations that provided network-related (i.e., technical) services on the Internet, .net addresses have been used by organizations of all types in recent years.

Although .com, .net, and .org are the suffixes most commonly found on domain names, a number of new suffixes are being introduced to accommodate the growth in the number of Web sites on the Internet. Any accredited domain name registrar can give you a list of the different suffixes that you can register your domain name under.

If you are setting up your company for the first time, you may want to find a suitable domain name first, and then decide on the name for your company and online store based on the domain name you have selected. Why? Domain names are a scarce commodity. Suppose you decide you want to set up an online store to sell scooters. You decide to call your business "Scooter Shop" and you decide to incorporate your business. After the business is incorporated, you start to build your Web site and you decide to register the domain name scootershop.com.

A good site that you can use to see if a domain name is available is Register.com (www.register.com). Register.com is one of many organizations on the Internet that is accredited to allocate domain names to organizations and individuals on the Internet. Once you are at the Register.com site, simply type the domain name you are looking for into the box on the screen and select the domain name suffix you are interested in:

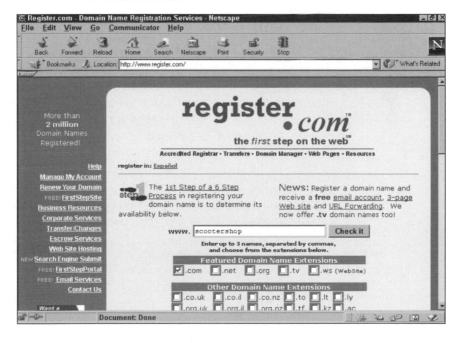

Once you press the "Check it" button, you will be notified whether the domain name you have asked for (in this case, scootershop.com) is available. As you can see in the screen below, we are told that scootershop.com is taken (i.e., the domain name has been registered by someone else). We're also told that scootershop.net and scootershop.org are taken as well:

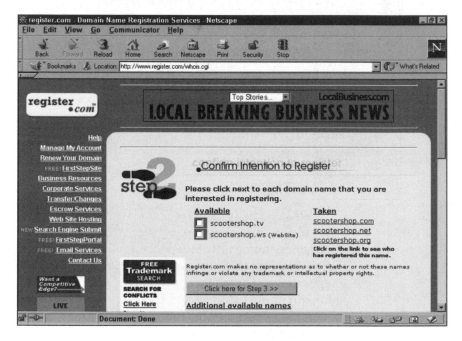

If you want to see who owns any of the "taken" domain names, simply click on them and you'll be able to get the name, address, and phone number of the current owner. For example, by clicking on scootershop.com, you see that scootershop.com is owned by a business in California:

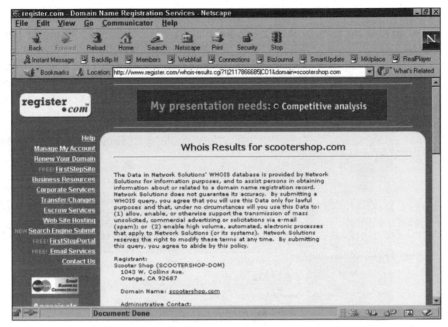

This is exactly the type of problem that a lot of businesses run up against. They have registered or incorporated a business name only to find out later that they can't get the domain name they want because someone else has already registered it. That's why it's usually a good idea to secure a domain name before you choose your business name. By doing this, you avoid having a domain name that doesn't match your business name.

If you find yourself in a situation similar to the one we've described above with scootershop.com, you have a couple of options. The simplest option may be to find an available domain name and change the name of your business to match the domain name you've found. Alternatively, you could continue searching for a domain name that is similar to your company name, but that won't cause too much confusion with your customers. For example, you could see if a domain name like thescootershop.com or thescootershop.net is available. However, as you can see below, both domain names have been taken:

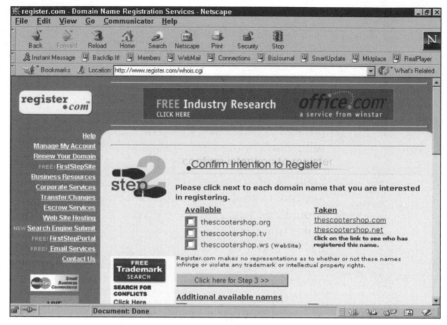

But even if thescootershop.com were available, you might not want to choose this domain name. Why not? It's too similar to scootershop.com, which, as noted earlier, is already owned by another scooter shop in California. In fact, the company has set up its Web site at www. scootershop.com:

This is problematic because your customers may inadvertently leave the "the" off when typing your address in their Web browsers, and they would end up at the above site instead of yours. In essence, you'd be giving business to a competitor!

As this example illustrates, it's important that both your brand name and your Web site address be as distinctive as possible to avoid confusion with other similar companies selling on the Internet. There are tens of thousands of merchants on the Internet all vying for attention, making it difficult for online merchants with similar names to get noticed. Even if the domain name you want is available, you should find out if similar names currently used by online stores might compete with yours. Many online merchants have found it necessary to change their names because their names were being confused with other similar names on the Internet.

When trying to come up with a name for your online store, consider getting a group of friends or colleagues together to brainstorm with you. Alternatively, you could hire a market research firm to hold focus groups with consumers.

Issues to Consider When Choosing a Name for Your Online Store

- Can you get a Web site address (i.e., domain name) for that name?

- Is the name too long?

- Is the name easy to pronounce?

- Are there other Web sites or online stores with similar-sounding or similar-looking brand names or domain names?

- Is your name unique or distinctive enough?

- Is your name memorable and does it make an impression?

- Is the name consistent with the image you want to project?

If you really want to have a domain name that someone else has already registered, such as scootershop.com, you could approach the owner and see if he or she is interested in selling the domain name to you. Many companies register domain names but never activate them. Even a company that is using a domain name may consider selling it to you for the right price.

Finally, if you believe that someone else has registered a domain name that infringes on a trademark that you own, you can pursue legal action against the owner of the domain name in question.

Alternatively, an appeal process has begun with domain names, and it might be possible for you to launch an appeal to see if the other party can be forced to give up the name, if you can prove that they had registered the domain name merely to prevent you from obtaining it, i.e., they were operating in bad faith. To learn about this option, visit a domain registrar, and read about the international domain name appeals process. You can also visit the WIPO Internet Domain Name Processes site at wipo2.wipo.int for more information.

Which raises an important point – it might be a good defensive maneuver for you to register as many domain names as possible early on, related to your store name, your product names, or other words and phrases that, when used as a domain name, might help to drive traffic to your store.

How to Get a Domain Name

To get a domain name, you can go to any one of the accredited domain name registrars on the Internet, including Register.com (www.register.com). You can get a complete list of accredited domain name registrars on the InterNIC Web site at www.internic.com. The list can be viewed alphabetically or by geographic location.

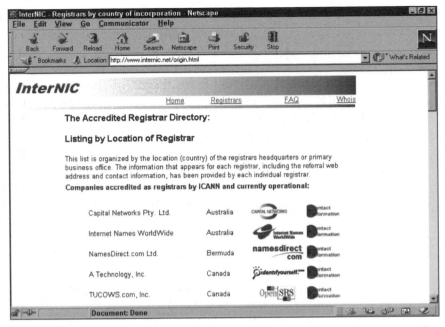

The cost to register a domain name is typically around $35 a year, although you may find slight differences in pricing from one registrar to the next. You don't need to have a Web site in order to register a domain name and most registrars will hold your domain name for you until you are ready to activate it on your online store. Many of the browser-based storefront solutions that we discussed in Chapter 2 allow you to set up a domain name for your online store when you are setting up your account. This removes the need for you to go directly to a domain name registrar. For example, when you purchase an e-commerce package from EarthLink, you are required to choose your domain name during the registration process:

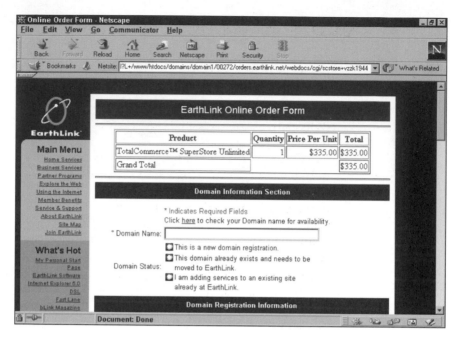

If you have previously registered a domain name and you wish to use it for your online store, you can easily transfer it at this point to EarthLink by typing the existing domain name in the box above, and by selecting "This domain already exists and needs to be moved to EarthLink." Most online stores make it easy for you to do this.

Once you have registered a domain name, you want to make sure that no one is registering similar names, or taking out a trademark similar to your name. To automatically track your name, consider using a service such as NameGuard, offered by NameProtect (www.nameprotect.com). NameGuard is free and it will constantly monitor new U.S. trademark applications and domain name registrations for you and flag any applications/registrations that are identical or very similar to your domain name. It's a great way to keep informed of any potential threats to your brand name. This service will also help you identify companies that may be trying to register your domain name as a trademark. This is a potentially serious situation as you could lose your domain name if a trademark similar to your brand name is granted to someone else.

OFFLINE MARKETING

Perhaps the most important piece of advice we can give you in this chapter is this: don't restrict your advertising and promotional efforts to the Web. Online stores often rely too heavily on online advertising at the expense of more traditional advertising vehicles that may actually produce better results.

Throughout this chapter, we'll review a number of different ways for you to promote your online store on the Web. But it's important not to get too dependent on online marketing for your success. Think about the types of customers you are trying to attract and what the best methods would be to reach those customers. Rather than spending your money advertising on the Web, you may find that a more effective strategy would be to place advertisements in a couple of well-targeted magazines. For example, Noggintops (www.noggintops.com), an online hat retailer, has spent very little on Internet advertising. Instead, the company did some marketing research and identified a number of magazines that appealed to the company's target market: outdoorsmen. Ads featuring the company's Web site address were then placed in those magazines. In fact, the bulk of Noggintops' marketing budget has been spent on offline ads. Our point is that you shouldn't ignore traditional advertising vehicles. Think about how you can use both print (e.g., newspapers, magazines, journals) and broadcast media (radio and television stations) to reach your target audience. Be realistic with your expectations. In years past, many Internet companies invested millions in television ads, often with disappointing results. Many companies learned that brands can't be built overnight. It can take years to build a successful and recognized brand name.

That being said, if you develop any print or broadcast advertising, make sure that your Web address is featured prominently in your ads. You may want to even consider purchasing advertising for the sole purpose of promoting your Web site.

It is important to use your imagination when looking for ways to raise awareness of your Web site. Don't limit yourself to radio, television, and print media. Why not advertise your Web address in buses or subways? How about on newspaper polybags (the plastic bags that newspapers are wrapped in when they are delivered to your front door)? Or in movie theatres? Some organizations have even gone so far as to include their Internet addresses on bananas! The possibilities are endless.

In many respects, marketing a Web site is no different than marketing any product or service. The challenge is to find innovative ways to get the word out.

YOUR RETAIL STORE

If your business has a brick-and-mortar retail presence, use it to promote your online store aggressively. Include your Web address on your receipts, invoices, and shopping bags, and print it on your catalogs and sales literature. Make sure that your Web address is advertised prominently both within your store and outside if you can. Many retailers, unfortunately, don't leverage their retail presence in this way.

GIFT CERTIFICATES

Brick-and-mortar stores give out gift certificates, so why not online stores too? Consider offering an online gift certificate that your customers can give to a family member or a friend. Gift certificates purchased online make great last-minute gifts because they can be sent by e-mail to arrive almost instantly. The recipient can then visit the store's Web site and apply the gift certificate toward the purchase of any products offered by the store. For a good example of an online gift certificate program, visit the online store of Illuminations, a candle retailer (www.illuminations.com):

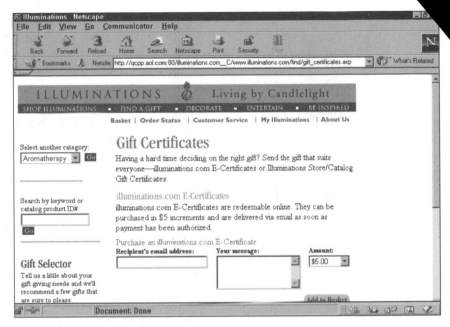

Customers can purchase Illuminations gift certificates in $5 increments. They can pay by credit card and the gift certificate is delivered to the recipient by e-mail as soon as the payment is authorized. The gift certificate is essentially an e-mail message with a number attached to it. The recipient can redeem the certificate on a purchase at Illuminations.com. How does it work? When the recipient checks out of the Illuminations.com store, he or she will be asked to provide the certificate number. You can see this below on the left-hand side of the screen:

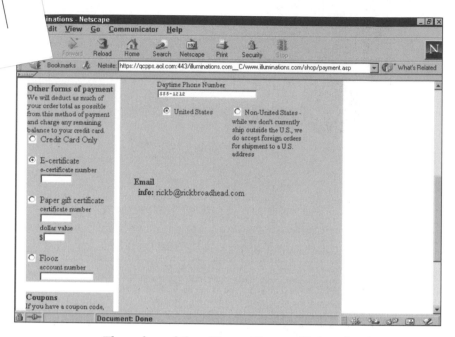

The value of the gift certificate will then be deducted from the total amount of the purchase. Electronic gift certificates not only make great gifts – they're a great way to drive new customers into your online store! Keep in mind that you could increase the attractiveness of gift certificates significantly if you allow customers to specify that they be e-mailed on a particular day – thus becoming the perfect gift for a birthday, anniversary, etc.

CROSS-SELLING

You should get in the habit of cross-selling products in your online store to increase sales. This means that where possible, product pages on your online store should feature accessories or complementary products that your customers may be interested in. For example, consider what Smith & Hawken has done in its online store (www.smithandhawken.com). Whenever a customer views a product, complementary products are displayed on the left-hand side of the page. For example, in the screen below, the product being shown is a Mariposa bench:

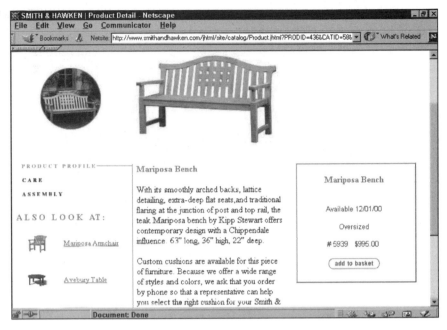

But Smith & Hawken realizes that customers who are interested in purchasing a bench may also be interested in purchasing a matching chair or table. That's why, on the left-hand side of the screen, there is a section called "Also Look At" where these products are displayed.

As you might expect, if you look at the Web page advertising the armchair, the bench is recommended as a complementary product:

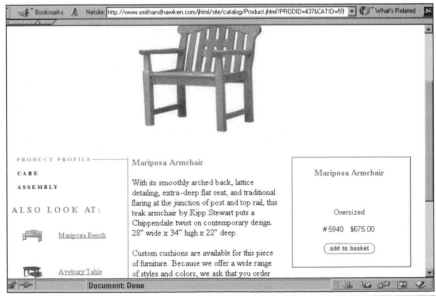

The idea here is to upsell customers. Eddie Bauer employs a similar strategy on its Web site (www.eddiebauer.com). Customers looking at a specific piece of clothing can ask to see coordinating products by clicking on a link in the lower left-hand corner of the screen. In the screen below, for example, a customer viewing a long-sleeve shirt is able to view other products that complement the shirt:

As you can see, cross-selling is an excellent strategy for increasing overall sales in your online store.

PRODUCT REFERRAL SERVICES

Many people find out about Web sites through word of mouth. So make it easy for your customers to tell other shoppers about your online store.

For example, as customers are browsing through your Web site, they may come across products that their friends, co-workers, or family members may be interested in. Or a customer may want to tell a friend or family member about a product he or she would like to receive as a gift. That is why you should make it easy for customers to refer friends and relatives directly to specific product pages on your site. For an excellent example of how this can be done, visit RadioShack's online store (www.radioshack.com). At the bottom of every product page on the site is a link that says, "e-mail this page to a friend." You can see the link in the bottom right-hand corner of the following screen:

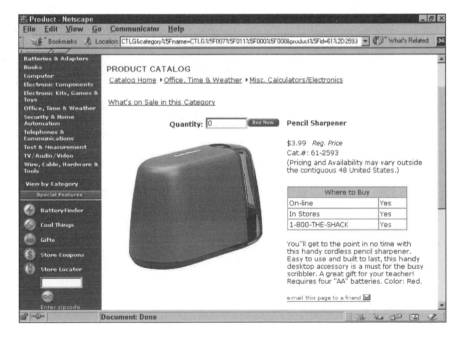

Customers who click on that icon will be taken to another Web page where they are asked to provide the name and e-mail address of a friend:

The recipient will receive an e-mail message like the one below, which invites him or her to visit RadioShack's online store:

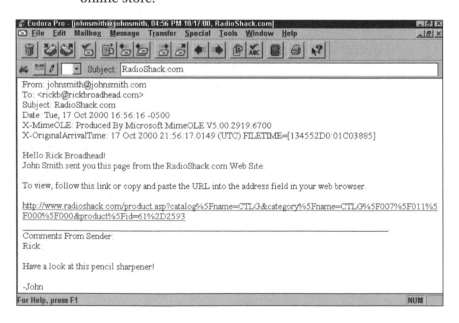

A referral mechanism like this is an effecti\
bring more people into your Web site.

AFFILIATE PROGRAMS

Many online merchants have built successful affiliate programs for their online stores.

An affiliate program involves paying owners of other Web sites a commission for referring customers to your online store. In other words, you reward other Web sites for sending new customers to you. The idea is to find Web sites with visitors who are likely to be interested in your products. To this end, Web site owners usually try to find merchants who sell products or services related to their own Web sites. A Web site with movie reviews may try to affiliate with a merchant who sells movies, and a Web site devoted to golf may align itself with a Web site that sells sporting goods or athletic apparel. It's in a Web site owner's best interests to identify merchants with compatible products because it will increase the likelihood of making lots of sales. For example, suppose you sell travel guidebooks. You could sign up travel agencies to your affiliate program and invite them to create links from their Web sites to yours. You would then pay the travel agencies a commission on any book sales and/or leads you get from their customers.

Affiliate programs are projected to be an increasingly important part of an online retailer's marketing strategy. For example, in a 2000 survey of fifty U.S. online retailers, Forrester Research (www.forrester.com) found that 13 percent of the companies' revenues came from affiliate programs. Forrester estimates that percentage will increase to 20 percent by 2003.

Online retailers with affiliate programs compensate affiliates in different ways. Some merchants pay affiliates strictly for sales (pay-for-sale), while other merchants compensate affiliates if the referred customers turn into a potential lead (pay-per-lead). Other programs may compensate affiliates if a person clicks on an ad on the affiliate's site, regardless of whether that person turns into a lead or ends up purchasing a product. This is called a pay-per-click program.

Affiliate programs can be extremely powerful because they allow you to increase your revenues by having your brand name displayed on dozens if not hundreds of complementary Web sites. There are literally thousands of affiliate programs on the Web. For an example, visit the online store for Staples (www.staples.com) and read about their affiliate program. Web sites that sign up can earn a percentage of every sale for referring customers to Staples.com:

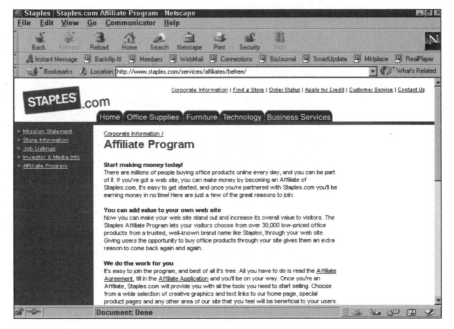

How does it work? There is no cost for affiliates to sign up, but they must first agree to the program's terms and conditions and then complete an online application form that requests information about their Web site.

If a Web site is approved into the program, Staples will provide the owner with a selection of Staples.com graphics that can be placed on the Web site and linked to Staples.com. Every time someone clicks on the link and buys something from Staples.com, the Web site owner will be paid a commission. Staples.com says its affiliate program has been a success, with over thirty thousand Web sites signing up since the program was created.

The commission that you offer your affiliates is up to you. Some firms, like Staples, offer a percentage of sales; other firms offer flat fees. Commission structures can range from less than 1 percent to as high as 50 percent. Flat-fee commissions, on the other hand, can range anywhere from $0.05 to $50.00, or more.

Affiliate programs are popular because they're an inexpensive way of attracting customers to your Web site. In essence, you are getting other Web sites to market your online store for you. Moreover, it doesn't cost a lot to get such a program underway. Best of all, you only have to pay affiliates if they generate sales or leads for you.

Affiliate programs do have a number of drawbacks, however. It can be a burden to keep track of all of your affiliates and process all of the commission checks. Keep in mind that the number of affiliates you have really has no direct bearing on how successful your program will be. For example, even though Staples.com has over thirty thousand affiliates, what really counts is the number of affiliates that are sending significant amounts of business to Staples.com. A lot of online stores have found that many of the Web sites that sign up for their affiliate programs bring in very little business. That is why when you are setting up an affiliate program, your focus should not be on signing up as many Web sites as possible, but on finding those Web sites that can generate the most sales for you. Obviously, it's hard to screen Web sites in advance but eventually you will discover which affiliates are valuable and which are immaterial to your business.

As you might imagine, setting up an affiliate program can take a lot of time and effort, especially once you begin to sign up hundreds of affiliates. You need to screen applicants, track sales from each affiliate, prepare commission checks, and spend time on other administrative functions that take you away from running your online store. For this reason, many online retailers hire organizations called affiliate program providers that specialize in running affiliate programs on behalf of online stores.

We've listed some of the more popular affiliate program providers in the following table.

Affiliate Program Providers

AffiliateShop	www.affiliateshop.com
BeFree	www.befree.com
ClickTrade	www.clicktrade.com
Commission Junction	www.cj.com
EcomWorks	www.ecomworks.com
LinkShare	www.linkshare.com

The cost of using an affiliate program provider varies. For example, BeFree charges a one-time fee of $5,000 plus a monthly commission of either 2 percent of affiliate sales or $3,000, whichever is greater. Commission Junction, on the other hand, charges a one-time setup fee of $795, an annual renewal fee of $595, and then receives 20 percent of your payout – the amount of money you pay your affiliates. Simiarly, ClickTrade receives 30 percent of your payout rate, but there is no setup fee. AffiliateShop charges a setup fee of $199, an annual fee of $50, and a flat monthly fee of about $24.95, but no commission. Which affiliate program provider is best? It all depends on what you are looking for. Services and program features vary from one affiliate program provider to the next, so make sure you carefully consider all your options before making a final decision.

One of the major benefits of using an affiliate program provider is that these organizations will help you find Web sites that can begin linking to your online store immediately. If you're a small business with very little brand name recognition, how is anybody going to find your Web site to learn about your affiliate program? Affiliate program providers maintain a directory of participating online stores so that interested Web sites can quickly find merchants they want to work with.

For an example of how an affiliate program provider operates from an affiliate's point of view, let's look at LinkShare (www.linkshare.com). First you must visit LinkShare's Web site, where you register and provide information about your Web site, including the types of people your Web site tends to attract:

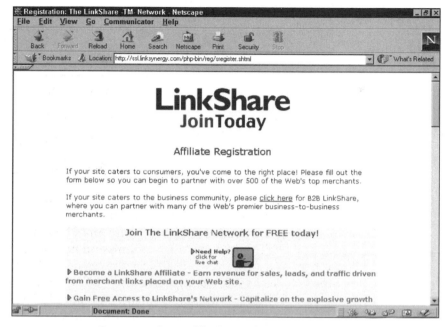

Once you have filled out the registration form, you will see a confirmation screen:

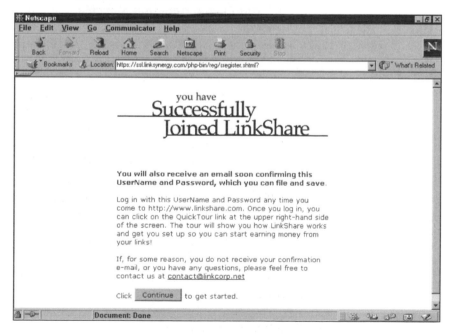

Next, you can browse lists of companies offering affiliate programs through LinkShare and compare the different types of commission structures. There are hundreds of companies to choose from, organized by category:

e-Fact

Search engines account for only a small percentage (6.86%) of traffic to Web sites worldwide.

Source: StatMarket (www.statmarket.com)

You can click on a specific category and browse through a list of available merchants. For example, here are just some of the merchants in the "Clothing & Accessories" category:

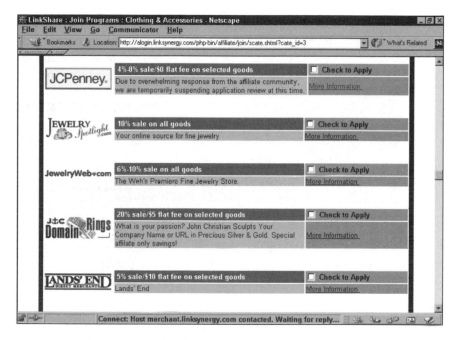

Once you've found a merchant you're interested in, you can view its commission structure:

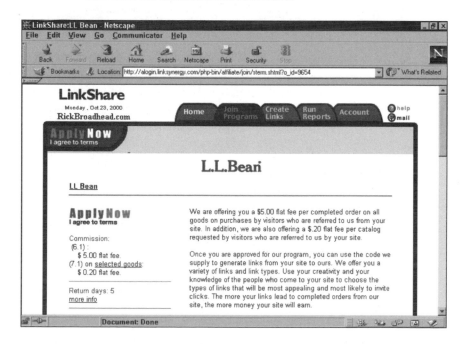

You can immediately apply to become an affiliate by clicking on the "Apply Now" button in the previous screen. You'll receive a message telling you that information about your site has been forwarded to the company for review:

Affiliate program providers give merchants the ability to screen applications and reject those Web sites they don't want to work with. With LinkShare, for example, once an application is submitted by a Web site owner, it is forwarded to the merchant, who reviews it and decides whether to accept the site into its affiliate program. Merchants aren't obligated to accept every application. The merchant must consider factors such as how much traffic the Web site receives and the type of content it contains.

Understandably, merchants are very selective about which Web sites they choose for their affiliate networks because they want to protect their image and not associate themselves with any sites that may not reflect the company's tastes or standards. Merchants usually choose to work with those Web sites that have content and objectives similar or complementary to their own.

Within a few days of applying, the Web site owner will receive an e-mail message from the LinkShare Network, with either a rejection from the merchant that looks similar to this:

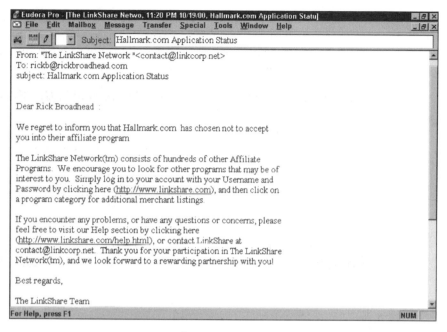

Eudora Pro - [The LinkShare Netwo, 11:20 PM 10/19/00, Hallmark.com Application Statu]

File Edit Mailbox Message Transfer Special Tools Window Help

Subject: Hallmark.com Application Status

From: "The LinkShare Network "<contact@linkcorp.net>
To: rickb@rickbroadhead.com
subject: Hallmark.com Application Status

Dear Rick Broadhead :

We regret to inform you that Hallmark.com has chosen not to accept you into their affiliate program

The LinkShare Network(tm) consists of hundreds of other Affiliate Programs. We encourage you to look for other programs that may be of interest to you. Simply log in to your account with your Username and Password by clicking here (http://www.linkshare.com), and then click on a program category for additional merchant listings.

If you encounter any problems, or have any questions or concerns, please feel free to visit our Help section by clicking here (http://www.linkshare.com/help.html), or contact LinkShare at contact@linkcorp.net. Thank you for your participation in The LinkShare Network(tm), and we look forward to a rewarding partnership with you!

Best regards,

The LinkShare Team

For Help, press F1   NUM

or an approval:

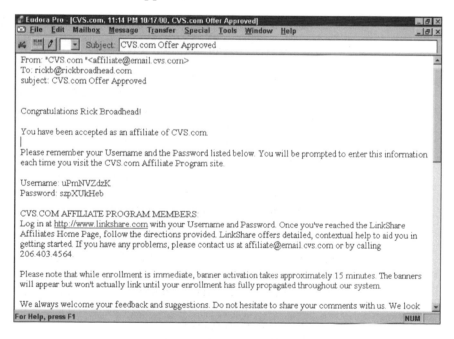

Eudora Pro - [CVS.com, 11:14 PM 10/17/00, CVS.com Offer Approved]

File Edit Mailbox Message Transfer Special Tools Window Help

Subject: CVS.com Offer Approved

From: "CVS.com "<affiliate@email.cvs.com>
To: rickb@rickbroadhead.com
subject: CVS.com Offer Approved

Congratulations Rick Broadhead!

You have been accepted as an affiliate of CVS.com.

Please remember your Username and the Password listed below. You will be prompted to enter this information each time you visit the CVS.com Affiliate Program site.

Username: uPmNVZdzK
Password: szpXUkHeb

CVS.COM AFFILIATE PROGRAM MEMBERS:
Log in at http://www.linkshare.com with your Username and Password. Once you've reached the LinkShare Affiliates Home Page, follow the directions provided. LinkShare offers detailed, contextual help to aid you in getting started. If you have any problems, please contact us at affiliate@email.cvs.com or by calling 206.403.4564.

Please note that while enrollment is immediate, banner activation takes approximately 15 minutes. The banners will appear but won't actually link until your enrollment has fully propagated throughout our system.

We always welcome your feedback and suggestions. Do not hesitate to share your comments with us. We look

For Help, press F1   NUM

If approved, the Web site owner will receive instructions on how to add a banner or link from his or her Web site to the merchant's Web site. In the example above, Rick Broadhead has been approved to be an affiliate of CVS.com (www.cvs.com), the online store for the CVS drugstore chain. On the LinkShare Web site, he can view the links, banners, and buttons that are available to him, and select one for his Web site:

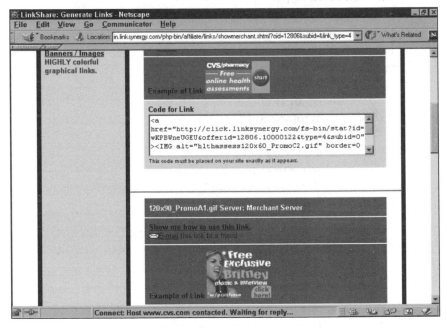

Many affiliate programs make it easy for the Web site owner to link to specific products on the merchant's Web site. For example, CVS.com provides the graphics and code necessary for the Web site owner to create links from his Web site to individual products on CVS.com ranging from disposable bottles to aerosol hair spray:

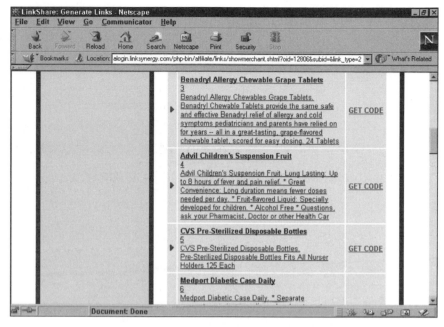

Once Rick has selected a banner and pasted the appropriate code into his Web page, a CVS.com banner appears on his Web site. Here is an example of a basic banner:

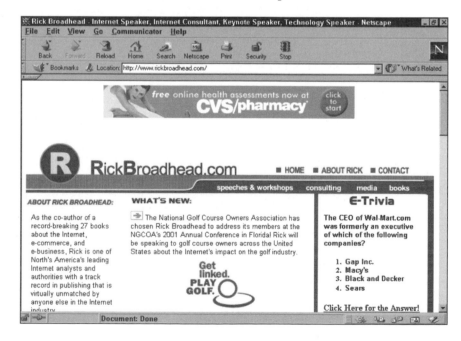

Here is an example of a product-specific banner:

Web site owners are often free to place the banner anywhere on their Web site. However, the idea is to place the banner in a location where a lot of people will click on it. The more people that click on the banner, the more revenue the affiliate can potentially generate.

Once a banner, button, or text link is placed on an affiliate's Web site, LinkShare begins tracking the link immediately. As part of this monitoring process, LinkShare tracks how many people click on the link and subsequently make a purchase at the merchant's Web site. In the example above, LinkShare would begin monitoring how many visitors to Rick Broadhead's Web site click on the CVS.com advertisement (or Benadryl image) and subsequently make a purchase.

Web site owners can log into the LinkShare Web site at any time and run reports to see how their banners are performing and how much commission they've earned:

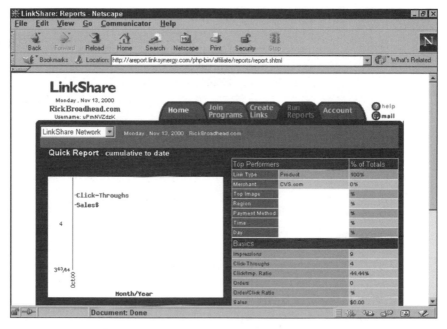

If you're interested in setting up an affiliate program for your online store, start by getting in contact with the various affiliate program providers we listed earlier in the chapter. When comparing affiliate program providers, think about the following questions:

- How much does the affiliate program provider charge you to set up an affiliate program? As explained earlier in the chapter, affiliate program providers have different pricing schemes, so make sure you understand how you will be charged. Also find out if there is a minimum escrow amount that you must give the affiliate program provider (this money is used to pay commissions to your affiliates).

- What types of affiliate programs are offered? As noted earlier, there are three basic types of affiliate programs that you should be familiar with:

1. pay-per-click programs – you pay a Web site for referring a visitor to your online store regardless of whether a sale results or not;

2. pay-per-lead programs – you pay a Web site for referring a visitor to your Web site to fill out a form or perform another action that may lead to an online or offline sale; and

3. pay-per-sale – you pay a Web site for referring a visitor to your Web site who immediately buys a product or service.

- What type of performance tracking is provided? How sophisticated is the performance tracking? What information do the performance reports contain? How frequently are the reports updated? Are the reports delivered by e-mail in addition to being available on the Web?

- How user-friendly is the affiliate management software? What account management features does the software offer? How easy is it for you to update or replace the ads being served by your affiliates?

- What tools exist for communicating with your affiliates, both through the affiliate program provider's Web site and by e-mail? Can you target certain affiliates with special offers?

- Who issues the commission payments to your affiliates? Do you have to, or will the affiliate program provider do that for you?

- How does the affiliate program provider guard against fraud? For example, what happens if the same person clicks on a link to your Web site fifty times – do you have to pay for that?

- Is there any flexibility with regard to payout rates? Can you customize payout rates for different affiliates or do you have to give the same commission structure to everyone?

- Does the affiliate program provider offer any client services to assist you with the implementation of your affiliate program, or are you expected to do it on your own? What technical support is available for both affiliates and merchants? Are any consulting services offered?

- How easy is it for Web site owners to join an affiliate program and create links from their Web sites to yours? To get the answer to this question, we recommend you visit some of the leading affiliate program providers on the Web and try signing up with some of their merchants. By doing this, you'll get a first-hand look at how the process works from an affiliate's point of view.

- What types of link options are available for your affiliates?

- Does the affiliate program provide support for e-mail-based affiliate programs? For example, how easy is it for an affiliate to include links to your Web site in their e-mail messages to customers?

- How many affiliates are part of the company's network? What is the company doing to recruit new affiliates into their network?

If you decide to work with an affiliate program provider, don't rely solely on its Web site to promote your program. You should also promote it on your own Web site and get other Web sites excited about the possibility of joining your affiliate program. For a good example of how this can be done, visit the Shari's Berries Web site (www.berries.com) and read the section on its affiliate program:

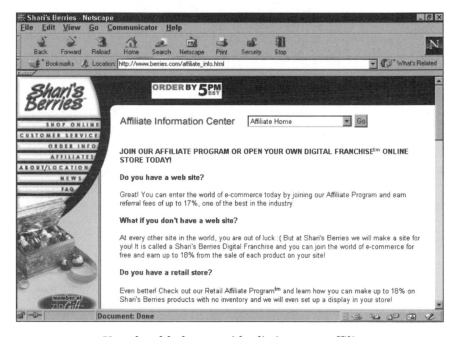

You should also consider listing your affiliate program on the Refer-It.com Web site (www.refer-it.com):

This Web site lists more than three thousand different affiliate programs that Web site owners can join, making it one of the most popular spots for locating affiliate programs. Because there is no cost to have your affiliate program listed on the Refer-It.com Web site, it can be an excellent way to promote your affiliate program and find qualified affiliates. Merchants who list with Refer-It.com have access to real-time reports where they can track the number of clickthroughs to their Web sites.

One final note about affiliate programs: many merchants, in addition to running their own affiliate programs, have become affiliates of other Web sites in order to generate some extra cash. If you are thinking about becoming an affiliate of another Web site, we recommend that you proceed carefully. Having an advertisement for another company on your Web site can compromise your image and credibility. Sometimes, the mere presence of an advertisement on your site can make you look unprofessional to potential and existing clients, especially if it promotes products or services unrelated to your current line of business. Accepting advertising for another company is an implied endorsement for that organization and its product or services. Make sure that you are prepared to make that type of public statement. Keep all of these factors in mind when

considering whether to accept advertisements fo
merchants on your Web site.

This advice may seem contradictory since the whole
purpose of an affiliate program is to get other Web sites to
display advertisements for your company. Won't they look
unprofessional by displaying advertisements for you?
Maybe. When you create an affiliate program, you have to
keep in mind that you're inviting other companies to display your brand name on their Web sites and it's never a
good idea to let another company take control of your
brand name. Sometimes it's hard to control how your affiliates display your advertisements, and in what context.
When launching an affiliate program, make sure you carefully screen your affiliates. In addition, you may want to
build some rules into your affiliate program so that you
have some recourse in the event that an advertisement for
your company is being presented in a way that you find
objectionable.

SYNDICATED E-COMMERCE

From an affiliate's standpoint, one of the problems with
affiliate programs is that once a customer clicks on an
advertisement for a merchant, the person leaves the affiliate's Web site and may never come back. Another drawback
of affiliate programs, as noted above, is that it is hard for
retailers to control how their brand appears on an affiliate's
Web site.

e-Fact

*54% of Web surfers
say the Internet is
the most informa-
tive medium for
advertising, com-
pared to magazines,
newspapers, TV, and
radio.*
Source: Responsys.com
(www.responsys.com)/
IntelliQuest
(www.intelliquest.com)
survey

One solution involves hosting a "mini Web
site" within an affiliate's Web site for the purpose of selling products and services from one
or more participating online retailers. One of
the major attractions of these mini online
stores for affiliates is that online shoppers are
able to complete their transactions on the
affiliate's Web site without having to go to the
merchant's Web site. Mini online stores also give
online retailers better control of their brands
and how they appear on affiliate Web sites.

In essence, syndicated e-commerce allows
online retailers to embed or "syndicate"
scaled-down versions of their online stores in
other Web sites, thus increasing the number of
online storefronts the retailer has.

Companies that specialize in creating mini online stores for retailers include ePod (www.epod.com) and Nexchange (www.nexchange.com).

Here is an example of a mini storefront that Nexchange created on CNN's Web site:

Other companies, like ePod, specialize in creating mini storefronts for merchants (ePod calls them "showcases") that feature only one merchant at a time, in contrast to the Nexchange online store shown above that features multiple merchants:

The cost of creating this type of mini storefront for your business varies depending on the syndication company you decide to work with. Some companies charge flat fees while others take a commission based on your sales.

If you're interested in experimenting with new ways to increase your online sales, miniature storefronts are definitely an opportunity worth investigating. Because they are a relatively new concept, you should ensure that you take the time to learn all about them, particularly any limitations in the "fine print" that might make them a less desirable option.

ELECTRONIC GREETING CARDS

Another way to drive traffic through your online store is to implement an electronic greeting card service. This allows your customers to send an electronic greeting to a family member, friend, or colleague from your online store. For example, the online store of Illuminations (www.illuminations.com) provides a virtual postcard service for its customers. They can select from a variety of images available on the site and then add a personalized greeting:

Customers can preview their virtual postcard and then send it:

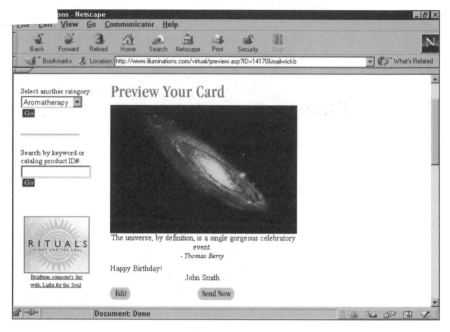

The recipient will receive an e-mail message with a link to the online store where the postcard can be viewed:

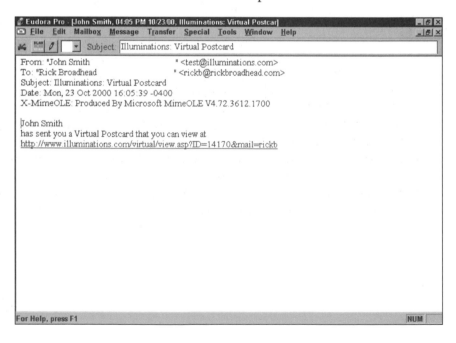

The catch is that in order for the recipient to view the postcard (and the accompanying message), the recipient has to click on the link in the e-mail message and visit the online store. This is a great way to introduce new customers to your online business while at the same time providing your existing customers with a fun yet practical service.

PERMISSION MARKETING

You may have heard the term *permission marketing* before. It refers to a method of online marketing where the merchant asks permission from online shoppers to market to them directly by e-mail. Permission marketing is also known as *opt-in e-mail.*

Permission marketing follows two main principles. First, you only market to those customers who have specifically told you that they are interested in receiving e-mail messages from you. Second, you must give away something in order to get a customer's e-mail address. In other words, shoppers are more likely to give you their e-mail address if you give them an incentive or reward for doing so. This incentive could be a discount on a future purchase, entry in a sweepstakes or contest, or just the promise of relevant advice by e-mail.

e-Fact

Online consumers typically wait for discount promotions to appear before making a repeat purchase at a particular online retailer.
Source: Jupiter Research (www.jup.com)

The easiest way to undertake permission marketing is by establishing a mailing list that customers can join. You can then use the mailing list to send out promotional messages to your customers. The trick is to give your customers an incentive to join your mailing list.

For an example of how a permission-based e-mail marketing program can be implemented, take a look at the following screen from the online store of Payless ShoeSource (www.payless.com). On the front page is a promotion for a "dream trip to Tahiti." Customers are invited to enter their e-mail address into the box on the screen and then press the "Go" button:

A new Web page then appears inviting the customer to join Payless ShoeSource's mailing list:

As you can see, the contest is the "hook" to get customers to spend a few minutes filling out the form that is required to join the mailing list. When customers join the Payless mailing list, they are automatically entered in the contest.

Keep in mind that if you are going to set up a mailing list for your customers, you should clearly tell your potential customers how they can leave the list, and about any other conditions that might apply to the list.

Electronic mailing lists are an excellent marketing tool and one we'll talk more about in the next chapter on customer loyalty. You might also think about using mailing lists for online newsletters – they are another useful way to keep your name in front of your customers.

Don't restrict yourself to your Web site when collecting e-mail addresses from customers. If you have a retail store, have your salespeople at the checkout counter ask customers for their e-mail addresses. Similarly, if you have a call center, collect e-mail addresses from customers when they call in. But regardless of how you collect the information, make sure you let customers know how you intend to use it. For example, if you have a retail store, have your salespeople say something like this to your customers: "We frequently send out notices of sales and other promotions by e-mail. If you have an e-mail address, Mr. Smith, I'd be happy to add it to our database so that you'll receive advance notice of our special events." By asking customers for their e-mail addresses in this fashion, you're clearly stating why you're asking for the information and giving the customer an incentive to provide his or her e-mail address to you.

e-Fact

75% of online consumers who participate in loyalty programs say they are not what motivates them to make an online purchase.
Source: Jupiter Research (www.jup.com)

Renting E-mail Addresses

In the previous section, we introduced you to the concept of permission marketing, which is a technique used to market to people by e-mail. The key challenge in permission marketing is getting people to give you their e-mail addresses. Most Web sites do this by inviting customers to join e-mail lists or online newsletters. Web site owners can then send targeted marketing messages to subscribers who have signed up to their mailing list. But setting up a mailing list on your Web site isn't the only way to use e-mail as a powerful marketing tool.

In addition to setting up your own mailing list, you may want to consider using the services of an advertising network to help you develop and implement an e-mail marketing campaign. E-mail messages typically have higher response rates than banner advertisements, so this type of marketing is gaining more and more popularity. Two of the largest advertising agencies, DoubleClick and Engage, have databases of millions of e-mail addresses from customers who have consented to receive promotional information by e-mail. Web site owners can use these lists to send targeted e-mail advertisements.

e-Fact

Adding the phrase "click here" or "click now!" to a banner ad increases the response rate between 10% and 40%.

Source: Beyond Interactive (www.gobeyond.com)

You should also consider using one of the many permission marketing firms on the Internet that will allow you to use their database of e-mail addresses for a fee. One such example is YesMail.com (www.yesmail.com), a permission marketing firm that has a database of over *fourteen million* e-mail addresses (yes, 14,000,000!). Many businesses feel awkward about sending marketing messages by e-mail because junk e-mail is disliked by almost everyone on the Internet. But as we noted earlier in the chapter, the very essence of permission marketing is that you have an Internet user's permission to market to them by e-mail. Every person in the YesMail database, for example, has consented to having their e-mail address added to the database, so you shouldn't worry about offending anyone.

For small businesses, YesMail has a service called YesConnect whereby small businesses can create their own e-mail marketing campaigns entirely online using their Web browsers. You'll be guided through a series of screens where you can create your e-mail advertisement and select the types of people you want to reach using an advanced set of targeting criteria. YesConnect allows you to choose your target audience based on over two dozen different interest groups ranging from automotive to travel and leisure. In the following example, we're targeting people who have told YesMail they are interested in gardening and/or landscaping:

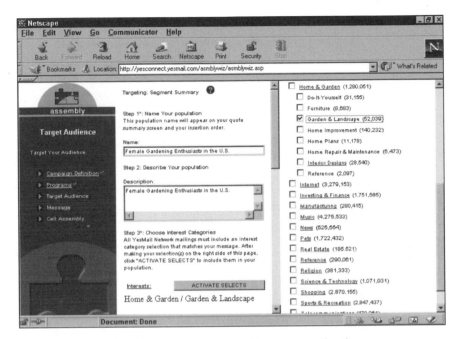

To refine your target audience even further, you can specify what gender, age range, educational background, income, and marital status you are targeting. If you want, you can even restrict your mailing to people who live in a specific zip code! In the example below, we are seeking married women between the ages of eighteen and fifty with an income of $30,000 to $100,000:

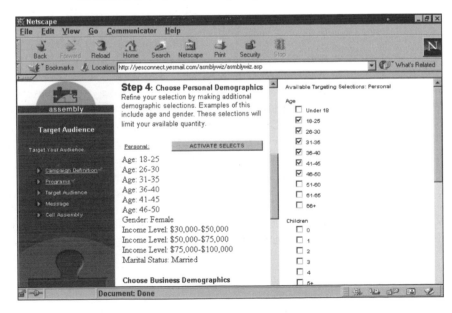

Once you're done selecting your target audience, you'll be told how many people in the YesMail database match the criteria you've selected. In our example, 473 people meet our targeting criteria:

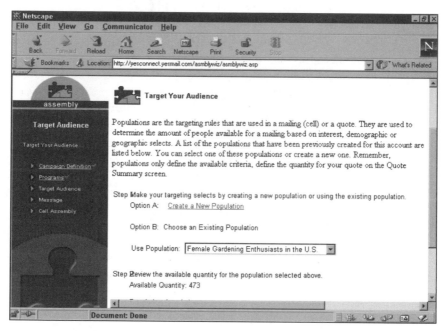

Remember that YesMail's database is not a database of everyone on the Internet. It is only a database of people who have voluntarily added their profiles to YesMail's database because they are interested in receiving offers from advertisers. If the quantity of people that YesMail can target ends up being a small number, you can always go back and make your target audience a bit broader.

Once your target audience has been defined and you're happy with the number of recipients your message will reach, you can begin composing the message you will send out. This process involves several steps, including creating the subject line and text of your message, selecting which format you want your message to be in (i.e., text only or HTML), and choosing the Web address that you want Internet users to click on when they receive

e-Fact

More than 40% of all online transactions by 2003 will stem from Internet partnerships.
Source: Gartner Group
(www.gartner.com)

your promotional e-mail message. At the end of the entire process, you'll be given a cost estimate for your campaign and you'll be able to schedule the start date.

Once the campaign is launched, you can log into the YesConnect Web site to see how many people have responded to your e-mail message. With the advanced tracking features available through YesConnect, you can even analyze the paths that respondents took through your Web site and identify the total number of purchases that resulted from your e-mail campaign. This information will help you understand customer behavior so that you can better plan future e-mail marketing campaigns.

In addition to YesMail, there are a growing number of firms on the Internet that use the concept of opt-in or permission marketing to help online businesses attract targeted visitors to their Web sites. For example, companies like BulletMail (www.bulletmail.com) and PostMasterDirect.com (www.postmasterdirect.com) have accumulated e-mail addresses from thousands of Internet users who have signed up to receive advertising messages that are targeted to their personal interests. You can "rent" these lists and use them to advertise your online store.

Explore the use of such services, but make sure that any service you hire has obtained permission to use the e-mail addresses in its database. Otherwise, you risk annoying hundreds, if not thousands, of Internet users with your advertising.

SEARCH ENGINES AND WEB DIRECTORIES

Many online shoppers use a search engine or a Web directory when they are trying to find something on the Internet. A search engine is a Web site that indexes the contents of millions of Web pages. A Web directory, on the other hand, organizes Web sites by category so that Internet users can easily browse them.

In the following table, we've listed the names and addresses of the most popular search engines and Web directories. Making sure that your Web site is registered with all of these sites is one of the most important things you can do to draw traffic to your store. Why all of them? Your customers (and potential customers) won't all be using the same search engine or Web directory. Some people use Excite, some use AltaVista, some use Lycos, etc. By registering with all the major search engines and Web directories, you have the best chance of being found by online shoppers regardless of what search engine or Web directory they are using.

Popular Search Engines

AltaVista	www.altavista.com
AOL.COM Search	search.aol.com
Ask Jeeves	www.askjeeves.com
Excite	www.excite.com
FAST	www.alltheweb.com
Google	www.google.com
GoTo.com	www.goto.com
HotBot	www.hotbot.com
Lycos	www.lycos.com
MSN Search	search.msn.com
Northern Light	www.nlsearch.com

Popular Web Directories

LookSmart	www.looksmart.com
Open Directory Project	www.dmoz.org
Yahoo!	www.yahoo.com

Having said that, as we will see, it is not necessarily easy to get listed in these search engines and directories. In fact, many of them are moving to a method that requires you to pay to just be considered for inclusion in their listings.

When you submit a Web site to a search engine, your Web site is added to the search engine's full text database, but it does not necessarily get your Web site included in the directory portion of the search engine. Many search engines use a different source for the directory listings, so if you want to get your Web site included in the directory portion of the search engine, you often have to go through a separate submission process. The same is true with Web directories (i.e., you usually have to go through a separate submission process to get your Web site listed in the search engine portion of the Web directory).

Search Engine and Directory Databases

Before you submit your site to any search engine or Web directory, you need to understand how their databases are developed. A search engine database is significantly different from a directory database. Automated computer programs called spiders develop search engine databases. These programs scour the Internet indexing the full contents (i.e., all of the words on a page) of the millions of Web pages they find. These databases are intended to help you find instances of words or phrases on Web sites, similar to a dictionary or book index.

Web directory databases, on the other hand, list Web sites that have been selected by human beings and organized into distinct categories. These databases are similar to the yellow pages, which organizes businesses by topic, and are more useful when you are interested in a specific topic.

The confusion comes from the fact that all the major search engine Web sites now have not only a search engine database, but also a directory database. Often when you do a search on such a Web site, the results that are returned include information from *both* databases. This is also true of Web directory sites, most of which have a search engine database in addition to the directory database. For example, let's do a search on the Yahoo! Web site for "gardens."

At the top of the search results page you will see "Categories, Web Sites, Web Pages, Related News, Events." By default, you will see the search results from the directory database of Yahoo!

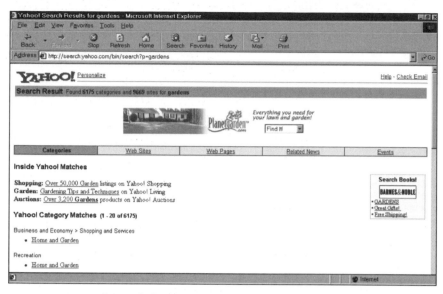

If you click on "Web Pages," you will see the search results from the search engine database of Yahoo!, which is run by the Google search engine.

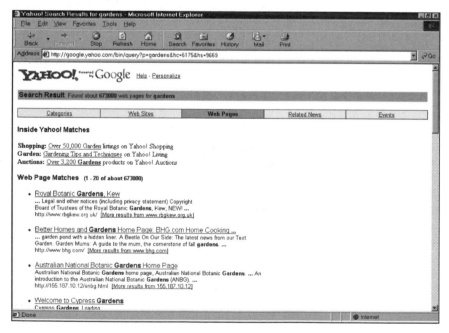

As an Internet merchant, the ideal situation is to have your Web site included in both databases of any search engine or directory Web site.

Submitting Your Web Site to a Search Engine Database

When you launch a Web site, you want to make sure that it is included in the search engine databases of both search engine Web sites and directory Web sites. There is a good possibility that the spider programs that these Web sites use will find your Web site, index it, and add it to their search engine database. However, it could take months for these spiders to discover your site, if they ever do. For these reasons, it's generally a good idea to visit each search engine and directory Web site and manually submit your Web site for inclusion in their search engine databases.

Getting Added to a Search Engine's Database

To add your Web site to a search engine, go to the particular search engine site and look for a link or button somewhere on the main page that says "Add Your Web Site," "Add a Page," or "Add URL" (URL stands for *uniform resource locator* – it means the same thing as "Web address.") Click on the button or link, and you'll usually be directed to a Web page where you can fill out a form and submit your Web site.

Getting Added to a Web Directory's Search Engine Database

Web directory sites may have their own search engine spiders that develop their search engine database, but quite often the Web directory partners with an existing search engine. For example, the Yahoo! Directory has partnered with the Google search engine. When you do a search in Yahoo!, it looks for matches with category names and Web site titles and comments as they appear in the Yahoo! directory, and then looks for matches in the content from individual Web pages found by the Google search engine. In this instance, if you are listed in Google, you will also appear on the search engine portion of Yahoo!, i.e., it's a two-for-one deal. These alliances are very common, so it is worth the time to find out who is partnered with whom and submit your Web site to all the relevant search engines. This will maximize the number of search engine databases you appear in. Here is the Google Web page that describes how to submit your site:

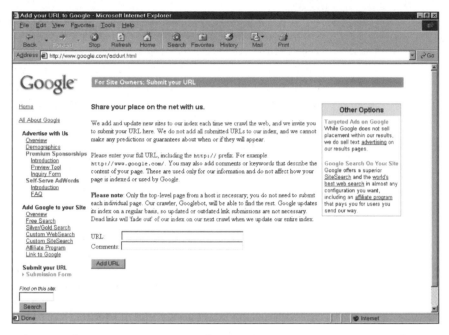

Submitting Your Web Site to a Directory Database

First and foremost, make sure you register your Web site with the major directories that we listed earlier in the chapter, as well as with any other Web directories that pertain to your industry. Look for information on their home pages explaining how you can submit your Web site to their database. You generally have to decide what category and sub-category would best represent your site. In some cases you do not have a choice. For example, if you are an online store wanting to be listed in Yahoo! you must list your site in the "Business and Economy" section. Look through each Web directory's help section to make sure you understand what is required and how to go about properly registering your site.

Second, visit the Web site of each of the major search engines, and determine who provides their Web directory listings. Then visit each of those Web directories and submit your Web site, if you haven't already done so.

Is There a Charge to Submit Your Web Site to a Search Engine or Web Directory?

The answer is that it depends.

If the submission is free, it can take anywhere from a few weeks to a few months for your Web site to be added to the database, assuming that it is accepted for inclusion. Excite's submission page spells this out quite clearly: "Please note that we do not automatically include all submitted sites in our index, and we cannot predict or guarantee when or whether a submitted site might appear in our search results." But don't let this discourage you! Submit your Web site anyway – you have nothing to lose. And don't hesitate to keep submitting it again over time.

The problem is that the Internet is growing so rapidly that many of the search engine and Web directory sites can barely keep up with the massive increase in the number of pages and sites. Not only that, but they complain that many Web sites, particularly adult-oriented ones, continually submit requests for them to check new sites. Hence, they have been falling behind in indexing new sites and pages.

The result is that many search engines and Web directories now charge you a fee to submit your Web site for inclusion in their respective databases. However, payment of these fees does not guarantee that your Web site will be included in the search engine or Web directory database. In some cases the fee may only guarantee that your Web site will be considered for inclusion. Check each search engine's and Web directory's help files for specific information.

Should You Pay to Have Your Web Site Included?

You may be wondering whether it's a good idea to pay to have your Web site included in a search engine and/or Web directory. If a paid submission service is available, we recommend that you use it. In some cases, *it's the only way to get your Web site added to a search engine or Web directory*.

On those Web sites where both free and paid submission services are offered, we still recommend that you opt for the paid submission. Why? As noted earlier in the chapter, with free submission, there is no guarantee that your Web site will ever make it into the search engine or Web directory. By paying, you guarantee that your Web site will at least be considered for the search engine or Web directory in a timely manner. If you use the free submission option, you could be waiting around forever!

One search engine service that you should definitely consider paying for is Inktomi (www.inktomi.com). Inktomi doesn't provide a search engine on its own Web site, but it provides the technology that powers popular search engines like AOL Search (search.aol.com) and MSN Search (search.msn.com). Inktomi allows you to pay to have a Web page, series of Web pages or even your entire site added to the Inktomi database. Once your Web site is included in Inktomi's database, your site will automatically be included in all the search engines that use Inktomi's search engine, including Microsoft, America Online, and dozens of other sites. We suggest that you visit Inktomi's Web site for the latest available pricing information.

Using Automated Submission Programs

It doesn't take a lot of time to register your Web site yourself with each of the major search engines and Web directories. However, some online store owners prefer to use a commercial service such as Submit It! (www.submitit.com) or PositionPro (www.positionpro.com) that automatically registers your Web site with all of the large search engines and directories. If you want to use a commercial search engine submission service, stick to services such as Submit It! or PositionPro that are run by well-known, reputable companies. We strongly recommend that you steer clear of companies that send you unsolicited advertisements by e-mail, promising to list your business in hundreds of search engines for only a couple of hundred dollars. There are countless search engine submission scams out there, and most of them will get you nowhere.

However, a few words of caution. Before using any automated submission service, find out which search engines and Web directories it will submit your site to. In addition, you should recognize that some of these services may not be able to submit your site to the search engines and Web directories that require payment for listings. Therefore, before you sign up with any of these services, make sure you fully understand what you are getting.

Increasing Your Likelihood of Success

Throughout this section, we have talked about the process of submitting your site to search engines and Web directories, and we indicated that you might or might not manage to get listed. Particularly if you are paying a search engine or Web directory to be considered for inclusion in their site, you might want to know if there are ways to design your site so that it is more acceptable for inclusion. Look through the help files of search engines and Web directories to see if they provide any hints, tips, and other guidance for your site. Some, such as LookSmart (www.looksmart.com), have submission criteria you should make sure you follow.

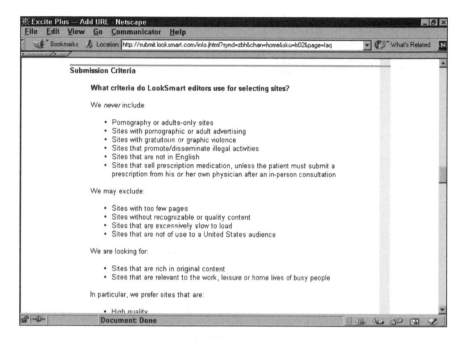

There are no hard and fast rules – it can be a very subjective process. Suffice it to say you can be judged on content, appearance, relevance of your site, and other factors. All we can suggest is that you make your site and/or store as comprehensive and professional as possible, which will undoubtedly increase the likelihood of being listed.

Are Search Engines and Web Directories Effective Marketing Tools?

Working with search engines and Web directories can easily consume a lot of time, and many Web site owners wonder whether the effort is really justified. Internet users rely heavily on search engines and Web directories when they are looking for information on the Web, so it's definitely worth your time to ensure that your Web site is included in all the major search engine and Web directory sites. At the same time, we caution you against going overboard and relying too much on search engines and Web directories to drive traffic to your Web site. Search engines and Web directories are just one part of the marketing mix. Your marketing activities should include using offline media such as radio, television, and print, as well as the other techniques that we discuss in this chapter.

Later in the chapter, we discuss the use of Web site analysis tools such as WebTrends that can help you analyze what search engines and Web directories your customers are using to find you. These types of tools can help you understand how much traffic on your Web site originates from search engines and Web directories. Furthermore, using these tools, you'll be able to quantify the importance of being listed on various search engine and Web directory sites. One of the authors of this book, for example, has discovered that Yahoo! is responsible for a lot of the visits his Web site receives.

SEARCH ENGINE OPTIMIZATION

As we noted at the beginning of this chapter, there are billions of Web pages on the Internet and thousands upon thousands of online stores, all clamoring for attention. When you submit your Web site to a search engine, you typically don't have any control over where your Web site will show up in the site's results list when someone searches for your company name or a keyword related to your business. For example, suppose you open an online store selling pasta products. If someone goes to a search engine, and types in "pasta," you're not going to be very happy if your Web site shows up on the seventh page of results. Most people won't bother looking past the second or third page of results when they are doing a search on the Internet. In fact, many won't even bother looking beyond the first page of results. This means that if your Web site doesn't show up in the top ten or so results for a specific search such as "pasta," the chances of your Web site being seen by Internet users diminish considerably.

Hence, an important part of online marketing involves a process known as search engine optimization – ensuring that your Web site receives prominent placement on all the major search engines. Ideally, you want your Web site to show up on the first page of results when a potential customer searches for a keyword related to your business. Since Web directories are typically compiled and organized by human beings, you really can't optimize your position on a Web directory. That's why the practice of optimization is typically limited to search engines, which use complex algorithms to rank Web pages according to a user's search criteria.

Before we go any further, you need to understand three things. First, there is no simple method or magical formula for achieving good rankings on search engines. Second, every search engine uses different ranking criteria. This is why the same search performed on different search engines will yield different results. It is also why your Web site may be ranked number one on one search engine but appear in the twentieth position on another. Third, search engines are constantly changing the algorithms they use to index Web sites, so your site's ranking on any given search engine may be in a continual state of flux. Most search engines provide some information on their Web sites to help you understand how they rank Web pages. Visit each search engine, read the help files, and try to accommodate as many of the suggestions as possible. For example, the Lycos search engine (www.lycos.com) has a page of information on its Web site with several tips and pointers to help you optimize your Web site's ranking in its index:

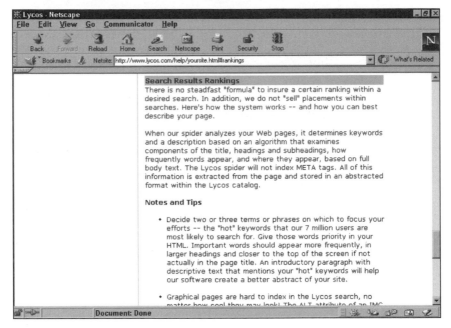

Reading help files like this will help you to understand what you need to do to get a good ranking for your Web site.

That being said, there are some general tips we can offer to help you improve your Web site's ranking on various search engines:

1. *Don't use graphics at the expense of text.* When you create the front page of your Web site, make sure you include lots of text that accurately describes your business. When search engines index your Web site, they can't read images. If your home page consists of a bunch of graphics and very little text, it's difficult for the search engine to properly index your Web site. This means it will be hard for Internet users to find it when they are using a search engine to find products and services. We're not suggesting that you not use graphics on your home page. However, if you use graphics, make sure they are accompanied by lots of text.

2. *Integrate important keywords into your text.* Choose important keywords related to your business and make sure those keywords are strategically positioned on your Web site. For example, this is the advice that Lycos provides to Web site owners: "Decide two or three terms or phrases on which to focus your efforts – the 'hot' keywords that our seven million users are most likely to search for. Give those words priority in your HTML. Important words should

appear more frequently, in larger headings and closer to the top of the screen if not actually in the page title. An introductory paragraph with descriptive text that mentions your 'hot' keywords will help our software create a better abstract of your site."

This doesn't mean that you should blatantly repeat the same words over and over again on your Web site. Rather, when building your Web site, think carefully about the words you are choosing to use on your home page. Make sure you integrate words and phrases into your Web site that you think Internet users will be searching for.

3. *Use meta tags.* Meta tags are pieces of HTML code that you include in your Web site to influence the description that search engines give your Web site (this is called a *description meta tag*) and to influence the words that search engines associate with your site (this is called a *keywords meta tag*).

If a Web site is using meta tags, you can see them by looking at the site's HTML code (the *hypertext markup language* is the computer code used to build pages on the World Wide Web). If you are using the Netscape Web browser, you can look at a Web site's HTML code by choosing "View" from the list of options at the top of your browser, then selecting "Page Source" or "Document Source." If you are using Microsoft's Internet Explorer browser, select "View" from the menu bar, then "Source." For example, here is the HTML code for the Illuminations Web site (www.illuminations.com):

```
Source of: http://www.illuminations.com/ - Netscape              _ 8 X
<!-- saved from url=(0022)http://internet.e-mail -->


<!DOCTYPE HTML PUBLIC "-//W3C//DTD HTML 4.0 Transitional//EN">
<script LANGUAGE="JavaScript1.1">

<!--

    var ua = window.navigator.userAgent
    var msie = ua.indexOf ( "MSIE " )
        document.cookie='c=1;';
        if (document.cookie) {
            if ((parseFloat(navigator.appVersion) < 4.06 ) && (navigator.appName.indexOf("Wel
                then = new Date();then.setTime(then.getTime() + 604800000);
                document.cookie = 'VeriSign=Warned; expires=' + then.toGMTString() + '; (
                win=window.open("browsers.htm",'tCw','width=355,height=225');
            ) else if  ((parseFloat (ua.substring (msie+5, ua.indexOf (";", msie ))) < 4.6) (
                then = new Date();then.setTime(then.getTime() + 604800000);
                document.cookie = 'VeriSign=Warned; expires=' + then.toGMTString() + '; (
                win=window.open("browsers.htm",'tCw','width=355,height=225');
            }
        )

    function Rcertify() {
            popupWin = window.open
            ('http://www.bbbonline.org/cks.asp?id=100103114105612825', 'Participant'
```

If you scroll down a bit, you will be able to see the meta tags that Illuminations is using:

```
Source of: http://www.illuminations.com/ - Netscape

</script>
<html>
<head><title>Candles and candle accessories by Illuminations</title>

<META NAME= "description" CONTENT= "For candles and candle accessories, c
<META NAME="keywords" CONTENT="candles, candle holders, aromatherapy cand
</head>

<!-- candles, candle holders, aromatherapy candles, floating candles, sce
handcrafted candles, beeswax candles, bayberry candles -->

<BODY BGCOLOR="#FFFFFF" LINK="#333366" ALINK="#666699" VLINK="#666666">
<!-- Header Image -->
<!-- hard coded on new homepage, unique to this page only -->
<table WIDTH="632" BORDER="0" CELLPADDING="0" CELLSPACING="0">
<tr>
<td VALIGN="TOP">
<table WIDTH="632" BORDER="0" CELLPADDING="0" CELLSPACING="0">
<tr>
<!-- <td VALIGN="TOP" ALIGN="CENTER">
        <table BORDER="0" CELLPADDING="0" CELLSPACING="0">
        <tr> -->
        <td COLSPAN="9">
                <table BORDER="0" CELLPADDING="0" CELLSPACING="0" WIDTH="
                <tr>
                <td VALIGN="TOP" ALIGN="LEFT"><img SRC="/spring/assets/in
                <td VALIGN="TOP" ALIGN="LEFT"><img SRC="/spring/assets/in
                </tr>
                </table>
        </td>
        </tr>
```

The fourth line on the screen above is the description meta tag. It looks like this: <META NAME= "description" CONTENT= "For candles and candle accessories, come to Illuminations.com, call 1-800-CANDLES, or visit an Illuminations candle store near you.">

The information in a description meta tag is used by the search engine to create a summary description of your Web site. When an Internet user is browsing through a list of search results on a search engine, the summary description from the meta tag is sometimes used to create the abstract that appears under the title of each Web page. Many Internet users rely on these abstracts to help them decide which Web sites to visit. It is therefore important that you create a site summary for your Web site that accurately and concisely reflects its purpose.

The fifth line down on the previous screen looks like this: <META NAME="keywords" CONTENT="candles, candle holders, aromatherapy candles, floating candles, scented candles, illume, illuminate, candle lanterns, candle lamps, illuminations candles, essential oils, holders for candles, candle pillars, tapers, votive candles, tealight candles, candlesticks, sconces, candlescapes, online stores, incense, handmade candles, handcrafted candles, beeswax candles, gel candles">

This is a keywords meta tag, essentially just a list of keywords related to your business. Notice that each keyword in the list is separated by a comma. A keywords meta tag increases the likelihood that your Web site will appear higher on the results list whenever someone docs a search using any of the words or phrases that appear in your tag.

When creating your keywords meta tag, we recommend that you don't repeat the same keyword multiple times in order to try to increase your Web site's ranking. Some search engines have been known to lower a Web site's ranking in their index or remove the site altogether if they discover this type of abuse.

We mention meta tags in this book because so many Web sites use them and because they are often cited as an important online marketing technique. However, the main problem with meta tags is that only some of the large search engines recognize them – many ignore them altogether. Furthermore, on search engines that do pay attention to meta tags, they are only one of several factors used to rank your Web site for users' searches. Therefore, meta tags are not a panacea for getting your site to the top of search engine results list – they are just one of many ways to improve your site's chances of being found on the Web. If you want to find out whether a particular search engine recognizes meta tags, visit its Web site and read the online help files.

Depending on what type of storefront software you used to build your online store, you may or may not be allowed to modify the HTML code that makes up your Web site. In order to create and modify your meta tags, you will need to be able to access the HTML code behind your Web site. Check with the company you are using to host build your online store to see if this is possible. If you are not technically inclined or you're not familiar with HTML code, you may want to hire someone to create your meta tags for you.

4. *Give your Web site a descriptive title.* Make sure that the title of your Web page *describes* your business rather than simply mentioning the name of your business. The title of your Web site is what appears at the very top of the Web browser's window – it is not what appears on the front page of your Web site. For example, take a look at the front page of Foot Locker's online store (www.foolocker.com), shown below:

The title of this Web site is "Foot Locker: The Source for Athletic Footwear and Apparel." Many search engines pay special attention to the words in your Web site's title when they index your Web site. In other words, you *may* increase the likelihood of appearing higher up on a search engine's results list if the words in your title closely match what an Internet user is looking for. By using the terms "athletic footwear" and "apparel" in its title, Foot Locker may improve its ranking in a search engine when someone is searching for those terms. What you shouldn't do is create a title like "Welcome to my Web site" or "Welcome to Foot Locker's Home Page." Titles like this are much too generic. You should try to create a title for your site that is as descriptive as possible.

Your Web site title is also important for another reason: it often appears in a search engine's list of results. Creating a good descriptive title for your Web site is one way to make it stand out from the rest. Internet users are most likely to click on Web sites that have clear, descriptive titles. The title of your Web site is controlled by a line of HTML code in your Web site called the title tag. For example, Foot Locker's title tag looks like this: <TITLE>Foot Locker: The Source for Athletic Footwear and Apparel</TITLE>

You may need to have access to your online store's HTML code in order to change or modify your Web site's title.

5. *Get other Web sites to link to you.* Contrary to popular belief, many search engines look at factors other than what's on your Web site in order to figure out where to rank your site. For example, if a lot of other Web sites link to you, this can help you to get a good ranking on some search engines, such as Google (www.google.com). Generally speaking, the more Web pages that link to your Web site, the more "popular" your Web site is, and the higher your Web site ranks in the Google database. We'll discuss the issue of Web site linking in a little more detail later in the chapter.

Using a Search Engine Optimization Company

Many Web site owners, sometimes in sheer desperation or frustration, have enlisted professional help to try and improve their rankings on search engines. The reason that search engine optimization (SEO) firms are in such demand is explained well by Aaxis (www.aaxis.com), one of many companies that specializes in search optimization: "Over the years the search engines and directories have gotten smarter and keep changing to the point where we have to work very hard to keep up to date on what techniques work best (or at all). Search engine optimization has become a very complex, sophisticated practice that requires constant research, practice, and reevaluation to be effective."

In other words, understanding how search engines work is a complicated business and most Web site owners don't have the time, inclination, or skill to try to manage their own Web site rankings.

Search engine optimization has become a popular business in recent years. Players in this industry include such firms as Aaxis (www.aaxis.com), iProspect.com (www.iprospect.com), Outrider (www.outrider.com), and

Web Ignite Corporation (www.web-ignite.com). There are also many small organizations that offer search engine optimization services. Many Web design and online advertising firms have also entered this market.

Search engine optimization (SEO) firms use a variety of practices to improve Web site rankings for their clients, practices that are beyond the scope of this book. If you're thinking of hiring a SEO firm, evaluate your options carefully. While many search engine optimization companies do honest, legitimate work, there are just as many companies that use unethical techniques and are looking for a way to earn a fast buck. We know of one company, for example, that was duped out of over $2,000 after hiring a company that promised to get it listed in the top ten rankings of all the major search engines. The rankings never materialized, and the company never saw its money again. If the company you hire uses unacceptable techniques to boost your search engine ratings, you could wind up having your Web site banned from a search engine forever.

Search engine optimization is such a complicated business that it's hard to know what techniques a company is using. Even if they're explained to you, you might not understand, and this of course makes it difficult for you to figure out whether a certain practice is ethical or unethical. Before choosing a SEO company to work with, check references and ask to see the company's client list. This will help you to ensure that you are only dealing with legitimate companies that use industry-accepted practices.

If you are interested in learning more about search engine optimization techniques, we highly recommend the I-Search mailing list – a free electronic discussion group devoted to understanding search engine technology. You can access the archives and subscribe by visiting www.audettemedia.com/i-search.

For further information about search engines and Web directories, including lots of links to helpful resources on search optimization, visit the About.com Guide to Web Search (websearch.about.com) as well as Search Engine Watch (www.searchenginewatch.com), a newsletter covering the search engine industry. Search Engine Watch isn't free, but a subscription is well worth the price if you're interested in keeping abreast of the fast-moving search engine industry.

ONLINE SHOPPING DIRECTORIES

Most of the major search engines and Web directories have shopping areas on their Web sites that showcase selected merchants and list hundreds of merchants by product category. For example, here's the shopping section on Excite.com (shopping.excite.com):

Yahoo! (www.yahoo.com) also has a shopping area on its Web site that features thousands of online stores:

as does America Online (www.aol.com):

Many Internet users use one of these shopping directories when looking for online merchants, so it's a good way to get exposure for your online store. However, to get included in a search engine or Web directory's shopping directory, or to become one of its "featured stores" or "premier merchants," you usually need to be an advertising partner or use the site's online storefront software. For example, online stores that are using Yahoo's storefront service, Yahoo! Store, can opt to be included in the Yahoo! Shopping directory. To become an advertiser, you will need to get in contact with the search engine or Web directory's advertising department for details about pricing. America Online, for example, has advertising agreements with a number of large retailers that give these retailers prominent positioning on AOL's shopping directory.

It is important to point out that these types of advertising opportunities often target larger, established retailers as opposed to small businesses, so depending on your advertising budget and the size/profile of your business, you may find that this type of advertising opportunity is not practical or affordable.

ONLINE ADVERTISING AND SPONSORSHIPS

One of the most popular online marketing strategies is to advertise on or sponsor other Web sites that attract the types of people who may be interested in buying your products and services. Suppose, for example, you sell luggage products. Why not advertise your online store on Web sites that attract travelers? For example, you might want to approach a travel Web site, such as one of the popular travel-booking services like Travelocity.com (www.travelocity.com), about sponsoring a section of their site. In addition, many of the popular travel magazines, such as *Condé Nast Traveler* (condenet.com/mags/trav/), have their own Web sites, and accept advertising.

Most Web sites that accept advertising have a section somewhere on the site that provides contact information for advertising inquiries as well as a general overview of advertising and sponsorship opportunities. For example, Travelocity has just such a page on its Web site:

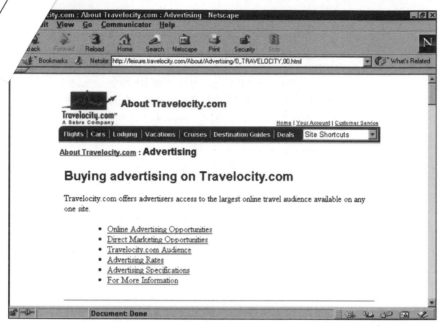

Before choosing to advertise on or sponsor any Web site, make sure that the site is reputable. You don't want to advertise on any Web site with a doubtful reputation or credibility. You should also obtain audited statistics that tell you how many visitors the site receives on a daily, weekly, and monthly basis. Also try to obtain as much demographic information as you can – data on what types of people the site attracts, including average age, income, and spending habits. You want to ensure that the Web site is attracting the same types of people who buy your products, otherwise your advertising dollars are being wasted. You should also find out what types of advertising or sponsorship packages are available and how much they cost. Will the Web site let you track how well your ad is performing? How frequently can you access usage statistics?

Banner Advertisements

Online advertisements come in all different sizes and shapes, just like newspaper ads. However, online advertising often appears in the form of a banner ad. A banner ad is a small rectangular graphic that can either be animated or static. You can design it yourself, or have someone design it on your behalf – it's basically a small Web page or graphic. People can click on a banner ad to be immediately connected to the advertiser's Web site. A banner ad may look like this:

Banner advertisements are usually sold on the basis of page views (every time a person accesses the Web page, that is considered a page view), and page views are usually purchased on a cost per thousand (CPM) basis. For example, if you are told by a Web site that the cost of banner advertising is $60 per CPM, this means that you pay $60 for every thousand page views. This might represent a thousand people looking at that page – or it might mean five hundred people looking at that page two times each. There are hundreds of thousands of Web sites on the Internet that accept banner advertising, including all of the major search engines and Web directories. The key is to find Web sites that attract the types of customers you are interested in reaching. There is no sense buying banner advertising on a Web site if its visitors aren't in your target market.

The average price for a banner is around $30 per CPM, although rates can be much higher or lower depending on the Web site. The cost of a banner ad may also be influenced by the length of the contract you sign, and where on the Web site the banner ad will appear. For example, a banner ad placed in the health section of a Web site may cost more than an advertisement in the gardening section if the health section attracts more visitors. As you might expect, banner advertising on high-traffic sites like Yahoo! is typically more expensive than the industry average.

The cost could also be affected by the way that the site charges for advertisements. It could be based upon the number of "impressions" (i.e., the number of times your ad is actually shown on a Web page) or instead, it might be based upon the number of "click-throughs" (i.e., the number of times people actually click on the ad).

When purchasing banner advertising, you may come across terms like *run of category, run of site, run of network,* and *fixed category,* especially if you are inquiring about advertising on a search engine or Web directory. *Run of category* means that your banner advertisement will be rotated throughout a specific category area on the site (e.g., gardening, travel, etc.), *run of site* means that your banner ad will be rotated throughout the entire Web site, and *run of network* means that your banner ad will be rotated throughout a network of other Web sites that are somehow related to the site you are advertising on. *Fixed category* advertising allows you to display your banner ad on the same page within a category all the time.

Creating Your Own Banner Ad Campaign

Larger Web sites like Yahoo! often require a minimum advertising buy of several thousand dollars. For a small business, this can be prohibitive. An alternative to purchasing banner ads through one of the big search engines and directories is to use a service like Microsoft's AdStore (store.bcentral.com) where small businesses can create their own banner advertising campaigns and place them on select Web sites for a smaller up-front investment:

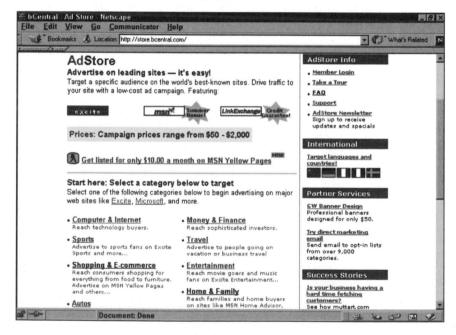

Advertising Networks

If you want professional help with a banner advertising campaign, you may want to consider using an advertising network to help you develop an online advertising campaign and aim it at the right audience. An advertising network typically represents hundreds or thousands of Web sites and works with a merchant to develop targeted campaigns that will run on relevant sites in the network. For example, Engage (www.engage.com), one of the leading U.S. advertising networks, can place banner ads on its network of over four thousand different Web sites. DoubleClick (www.doubleclick.com), another leading U.S. online advertising network, has hundreds of Web sites in its network and can reach more than 45 percent of the U.S. Internet audience. Advertising networks typically use sophisticated "profiling" technology to target your ads at Internet users who would be most interested in the types of products or services you are selling. Engage, for example, maintains a database containing seventy million anonymous behavioral profiles of Internet users. This means that if you are trying to reach, say, women between the ages of eighteen and thirty-five, Engage can use its database to target your banner ads at this audience. In the table below, we've listed some of the leading U.S. advertising networks. We encourage you to contact them if you're interested in learning more about how you can attract shoppers to your online store using banner ads and other online marketing tools.

Leading Advertising Networks in the United States

DoubleClick	www.doubleclick.com
Engage Media	www.engage.com
24/7 Media	www.247media.com

How Effective Are Banner Ads?

We won't kid you – companies have had mixed success with banner ads. Many online shoppers say that they ignore them. Indeed, only 3.2 percent of online advertisers surveyed by Forrester Research said that banner ads were effective in driving traffic to their Web sites.

The problem is that most Web users who see banner advertisements don't click on them. In fact, the average clickthrough rate for banner ads is less than 1 percent. In other words, no more than 1 percent of all the Web users who see banner ads on the Internet actually click on them. That's an even lower response rate than direct mail! But such a dismal clickthrough rate doesn't mean that banner ads are ineffective. Some companies run banner advertising campaigns with the goal of increasing brand awareness. If this is the goal of your online advertising campaign, the number of clickthroughs isn't as important as the number of people who see your banner ad. However, if you are trying to drive traffic to your Web site, you may find that banner advertising is not a good investment.

Given the disappointing performance of banner ads for many businesses, if you're thinking of purchasing banner ads to drive visitors to your online store, make sure you keep your expectations in check.

BANNER EXCHANGE NETWORKS

An alternative to paying for placement of banner ads on Web sites is to participate in one of the advertising barter systems that are available on the Web. These are called banner exchange networks and they're easy to use. Before signing up with a banner exchange network, check with your storefront service to make sure that you are allowed to accept advertising on your online store.

In exchange for your displaying banner advertisements on your Web site for other companies, other companies agree to display your banner ads on their Web sites. The beauty of a system like this is that it costs you nothing. You carry ads for other companies and they carry ads for you. One of the most popular banner exchange networks on the Internet is Microsoft's LinkExchange (www.linkexchange.com) network.

Registering your online store for a banner exchange network is simple. We'll use LinkExchange as an example. First, visit the LinkExchange Web site and click on the "Join Now" or "Sign Up" link. You'll be asked to provide information about your Web site:

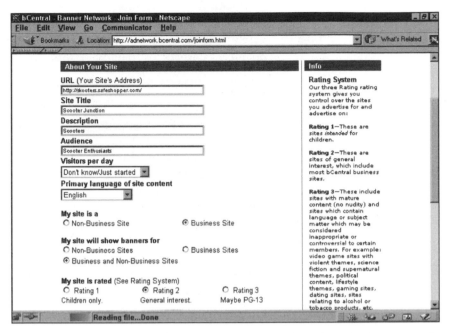

As part of this process, you need to identify the types of Web sites you would like your advertising banner to appear on. You also identify the types of Web sites you are willing to accept banner ads from:

After a few more steps, you select the category that most accurately reflects the subject matter of your Web site. There are dozens of categories to choose from:

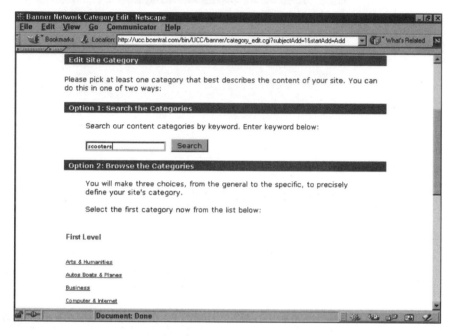

Next, you'll need to insert several lines of computer code into your Web page. (Note that you might not be able to do this if you are using a storefront solution that doesn't allow you to modify the HTML code for your site.) This code is necessary so that you can display banner ads from other Web sites participating in the LinkExchange Banner Network. First, LinkExchange asks you where on your Web site you want to display banner ads from other sites:

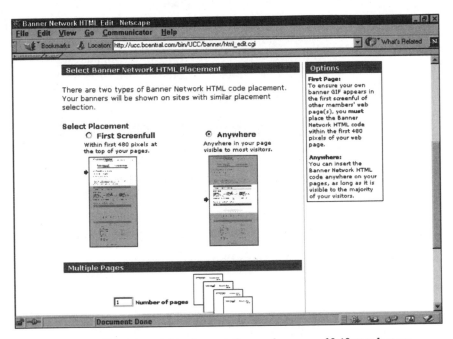

You can either insert the code yourself, if you know how, or LinkExchange will walk you through the process.

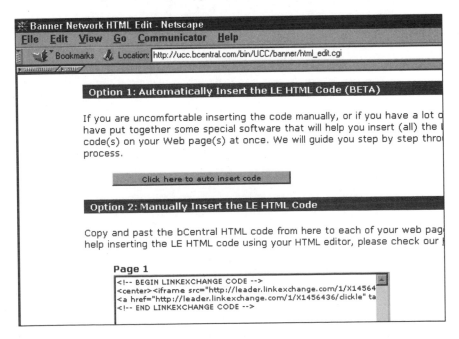

Once you have added the code to your Web site, you upload your banner ad to the LinkExchange Web site from your hard drive or copy it from a Web site. If you don't have a banner ad, you can choose to use the standard banner that LinkExchange creates for you:

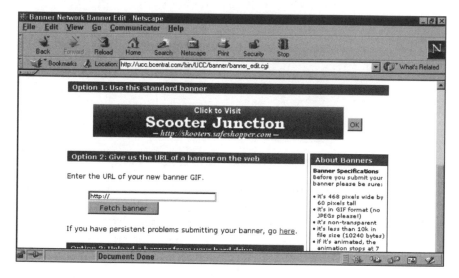

Once you've submitted your banner, it will be submitted to LinkExchange for approval and you'll receive an e-mail message when it's been approved:

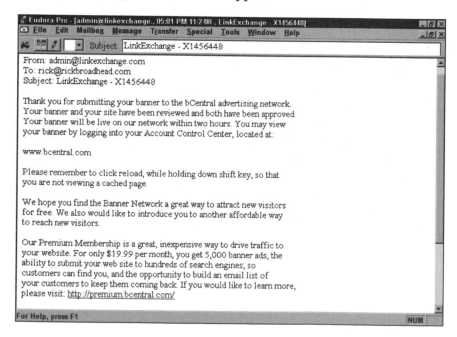

Shortly after you receive your approval, your advertising banner will begin appearing on other sites within the LinkExchange Banner Network and banners from other LinkExchange members will begin appearing on your Web site. Using the LinkExchange Web site, you will be able to monitor how many times your ad has appeared on other sites on the network, and how many clickthroughs your ad has received.

While banner exchange networks are definitely worth exploring, the same warning we gave earlier in the chapter regarding affiliate programs is worth repeating here. Before you start to accept advertising on your Web site, think carefully about the consequences. When banner advertisements for other companies appear on your Web site, it might make your business look unprofessional. When using banner exchange networks, you have very little control over the specific organizations whose banners appear on your Web site. If the products or services they're advertising aren't similar to yours, the banner ads will look out of place. You could also wind up running advertisements for an organization with a questionable reputation.

KEYWORD-BASED ADVERTISING

Many Web sites, including all of the major search engines and directories, offer keyword-based advertising. Here's how it works. You purchase one or more words and/or phrases related to your business. When a customer searches for any of those words, an advertisement for your Web site will appear. The advertisement may be a banner ad or another type of online advertisement that you create. For example, suppose you own a business that sells pools and spas. You could purchase the word "pools" on Yahoo! so that whenever someone searches for this word a banner ad for your company will appear on the search results screen:

> **e-Fact**
>
> *35% of companies say that they would not pay for complete performance monitoring of their Web presence from a third party.*
> Source: Zona Research
> (www.zona.com)

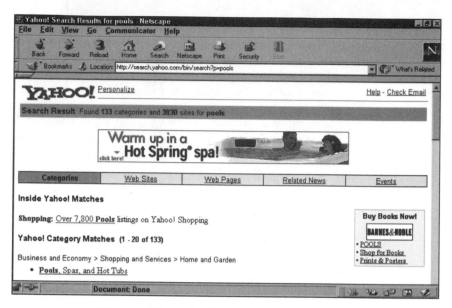

Keyword-based advertising doesn't necessarily involve banner ads. For example, Google (www.google.com), one of the Internet's most popular search engines, allows you to create text ads for your company that will be displayed whenever an Internet user searches for a keyword that you've selected. Google's program, called AdWords (adwords.google.com), is affordable for small businesses because the minimum advertising buy is only $50.

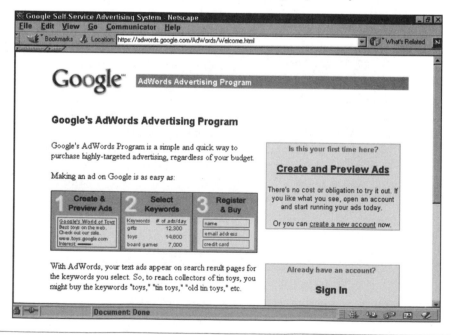

The first step is to create your ad. The ads created by AdWords are small, text-only boxes. You should include the name of your online store, one or two lines to grab the user's attention, and your Web address. In the example below, we're creating an ad for an online store called Rick's Comic Books that sells new and used comic books:

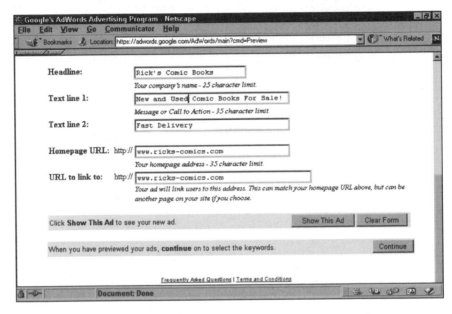

When you're done, a preview of your ad will show up on the right-hand side of the screen:

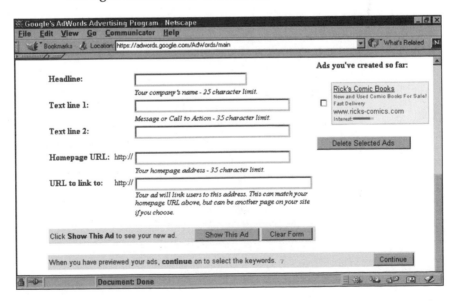

Next, you need to select the keywords you want to purchase. The idea is to come up with words or phrases that
potential customers might be searching for. Whenever an
Internet user searches for a word or phrase that you've purchased, your text ad will show up on the results page. To
find customers who are interested in purchasing comic
books, for example, you could buy a phrase such as "comic
books." If you have a lot of Superman comic books, you
might also want to purchase the word "Superman" to catch
Internet users who might be looking for Superman para-
phernalia:

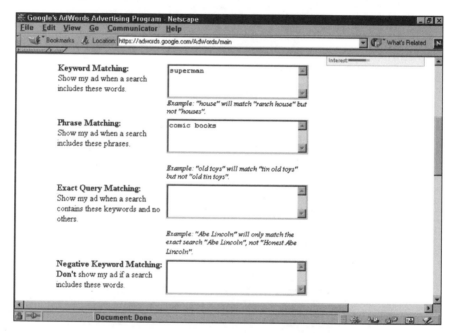

Once your keywords are selected, you'll be shown an
estimate of how many times your keywords are likely to be
used by people on Google. These estimates are based on the
number of times these keywords have been used in the
past. The estimates will also give you an idea of how much
you will have to pay on a monthly basis in order to purchase the keywords you have selected. In our comic book
example, Google estimates that the word "Superman" is
searched for approximately twelve hundred times per day,
and the phrase "comic books" is searched for approximately
three hundred times per day:

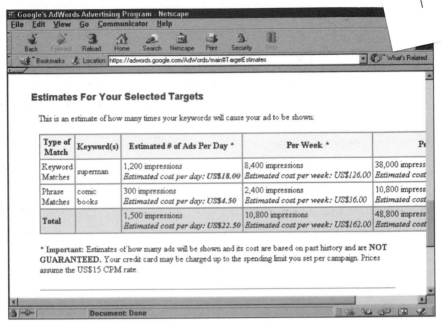

Visit the Google Web site for an explanation of how its advertising rates and fees are calculated. The important thing to remember is that you can cap your advertising spending on Google at any amount you want. For example, you can tell Google that you only want to spend $100 on advertising. Once that level is reached, your ads will automatically stop appearing.

Keep in mind that these statistics do not mean that fifteen hundred people will come to your Web site every day. There is no guarantee that users who see your ad will click on it. Many of the people searching for "Superman" or "comic books" may not be interested in purchasing anything at all. They may be doing research or looking for another Web site. But don't let these limitations stop you from experimenting with online advertising. It is through trial and error that you will figure out what works and what doesn't.

If you're happy with the keywords you selected and you want to proceed with your Google keywords and advertisement, you can sign up for an AdWords account:

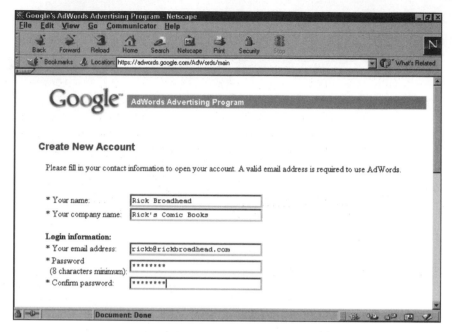

Once your account is created, you'll be able to enter your credit card information and your ad will start running immediately. If you want to add new keywords or create a new advertisement, you can manage all of these activities through the AdWords Web site:

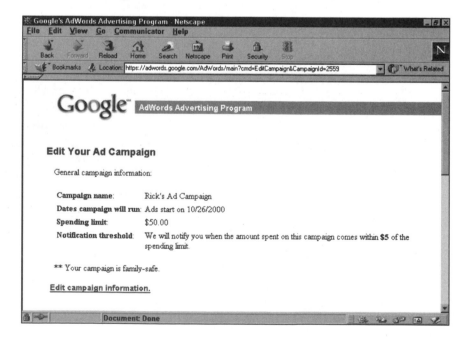

Keyword Research

Part of the challenge in using keyword-based mark the Internet is to pick the keywords that your custome most likely to be using when they are doing searches on search engines and Web directories. This will likely require a bit of brainstorming on the part of you and your staff. Once you've come up with a keyword that you think you want to use, services like Google's AdWords will show you how popular it is. What Google doesn't do, however, is help you come up with the right keywords. That's your job. To help you brainstorm, you might want to check out a few of the search engines that reveal what Internet users are searching for.

For example, Lycos has a service called "The Lycos 50 Daily Report" (50.lycos.com) that shows you what people are searching for on the Lycos search engine. Every week, Lycos publishes the fifty most popular searches from the past week:

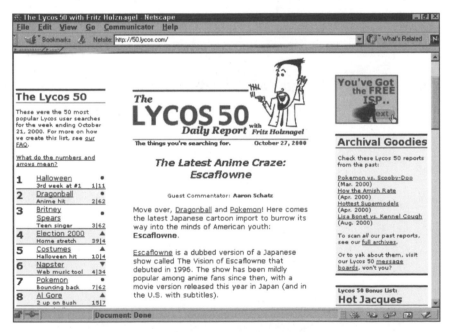

You may also want to check out MetaSpy (www.metaspy.com), a service operated by MetaCrawler, one of the popular search engines on the Internet. MetaSpy will show you what Internet users are searching for right now:

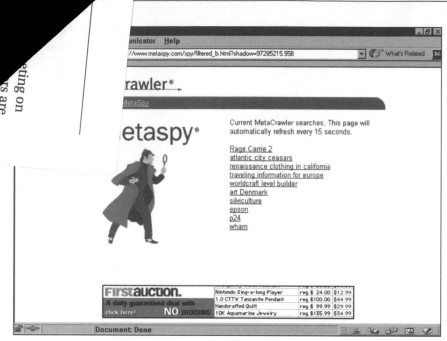

You'll certainly find these services to be entertaining, if not inspirational as well!

BIDDING ON SEARCH TERMS

Some search engines make it possible for merchants to "bid" on keywords so that their Web sites will show up near the top of the results list whenever someone searches for those words. These are called *pay-for-performance* or *pay-per-click* search engines. The price you pay depends on how much you are willing to spend every time someone sees your listing and subsequently connects to your Web site. For example, if you bid $0.25 per clickthrough, you would pay $0.25 for every visitor the search engine sends you.

GoTo.com (www.goto.com) was one of the first search engines to offer this type of advertising opportunity to Web site owners. To understand how the bidding process works, let's look at an example. Suppose you've set up a Web site to sell pasta sauces and pasta products. If an Internet user goes to the GoTo.com Web site and searches for the word "pasta" the person would see a page of results similar to the following:

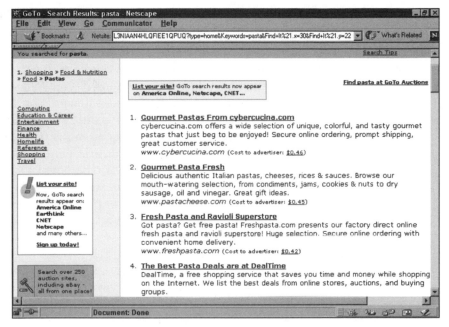

The price that appears in brackets after the description of the Web site is the price the merchant is paying for every clickthrough to his or her Web site. Merchants are listed according to the prices they are willing to pay to attract visitors to their Web sites, from highest to lowest. As you can see, the first merchant on the list, "Gourmet Pastas From cybercucina.com," is paying $0.46 for every clickthrough. The second merchant, with the Web site called "Gourmet Pasta Fresh," is paying $0.45 for every clickthrough. The higher the merchant's bid, the higher its Web site will appear on the results list.

GoTo.com also indexes pages on the Web like the other search engines do, but the listings from its full-text index of Web pages always appear after the paid links. If there is no price in brackets after the description of a Web site, it means that the Web page has come from GoTo.com's full-text index.

Merchants can bid against one another, which means that your ranking on the site is never guaranteed as long as there is another merchant willing to bid more than you. For example, if the "Gourmet Pasta Fresh" Web site were to bid $0.47 for every clickthrough, it would be listed first, and "Gourmet Pastas From cybercucina.com" would fall to second position.

Under this type of a bidding system, you only pay for the visitors who come to your Web site. However, this introduces a problem – the more customers that come to your Web site from GoTo.com, the more you have to pay. This type of spending could get out of hand if your Web site starts to receive a lot of traffic from GoTo.com. For this reason, GoTo.com allows you to set a maximum spending cap if you're concerned about spending too much. There is, however, a minimum advertising commitment of $25.

You can sign up online with your credit card. Once your bids have been accepted (GoTo.com screens all bids to ensure that you bid only on words or phrases that relate to your business), your Web site will appear on GoTo.com under the words or phrases you've selected. At any time, you can log into the GoTo.com Web site (using the password and username that were assigned to you during the signup process) to see how your keywords are performing and add, delete, or modify your keywords:

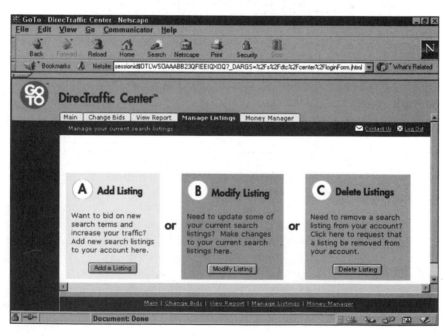

When using a site like GoTo.com, the key is to pick words or phrases that potential customers would be using to find Web sites like yours. The more keywords you bid on, the more traffic your Web site can potentially receive. Don't restrict yourself to only one keyword. For example, if you sell pasta sauces, don't just bid on the word "pasta" – bid on terms like "pasta sauce" or "gourmet pasta" as well.

One word of caution – when using a service like GoTo.com, there is no guarantee that your Web site will receive lots of traffic. It all depends on how many people are using GoTo.com to search for the keywords that you select. In some cases, you may find that your investment results in a minimal amount of traffic to your site.

To learn more about pay-per-click search engines, a useful resource is PayPerClickSearchEngines.com (www.payperclicksearchengines.com).

LINKS FROM OTHER WEB SITES

One of the least expensive online marketing techniques, but perhaps one of the most effective, is getting links from other Web sites. Contact suppliers and manufacturers you work with to see if they will link from their Web sites to yours. Why is this important? Customers often visit the Web sites of manufacturers or suppliers when they are researching a purchase. If the manufacturer provides a link from its Web site to yours, the customer may end up making the purchase online from you. This manufacturer benefits from the sale as well, given that you are selling more product, so it's in the manufacturer's best interest to link to you. You should also contact any industry associations you belong to and ask if they will link to you. The idea is to try to get as many Web sites to link to you as possible. As noted earlier, this can even help you with your placement on search engines, since many search engines take a site's links into account when they decide where to rank it.

If you want to see how many other Web sites are linking to your site, a really useful resource is a Web site called LinkPopularity.com (www.linkpopularity.com):

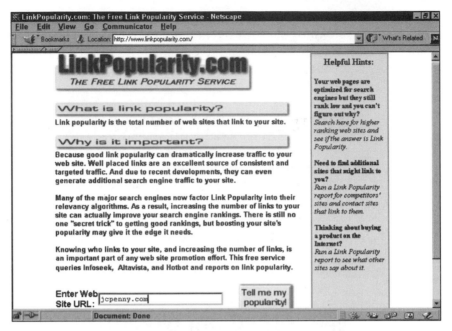

Just enter your Web site address into the box on the LinkPopularity.com Web site. The site will generate a free report listing all of the Web sites linked to yours. In the example below, we've run a report to see how many Web sites are linking to the JCPenney Web site (www.jcpenney.com):

You can also use the LinkPopularity.com site to monitor how many Web sites are linking to your competitors' Web sites. If appropriate, you can contact these Web sites directly and ask that they link to your online store, too!

MONITOR ACTIVITY ON YOUR WEB SITE

Once you invest in an online store, you owe it to yourself to monitor how well your investment is paying off. The number of sales you receive is only part of the picture.

You also want to be able to track the number of people who visit your online store, where they come from, and which search engines and directories they use to find you. This information is vital to your business because it will help you assess whether your marketing activities – both online and offline – are succeeding or failing.

If you don't already receive daily traffic statistics from your Internet service provider, Web hosting service, or online store service, or if the reports you receive don't provide enough detail, consider signing up for one of the many third-party Web site analysis services. In the box below, we've listed some of the more popular programs that will allow you to monitor how your customers are using your Web site.

Popular Web Site Analysis Programs

HitBox	www.hitbox.com
SuperStats	www.superstats.com
WebTrends	www.webtrends.com

One of the most comprehensive programs we've seen is SuperStats (www.superstats.com). For about $30 a month, SuperStats will provide you with a wide variety of reports that help you analyze customer activity on your Web site. For example, SuperStats will prepare reports like this one, which shows you how many visitors your site is receiving every day:

You can also access valuable marketing reports that will show you which Web sites your customers are coming from:

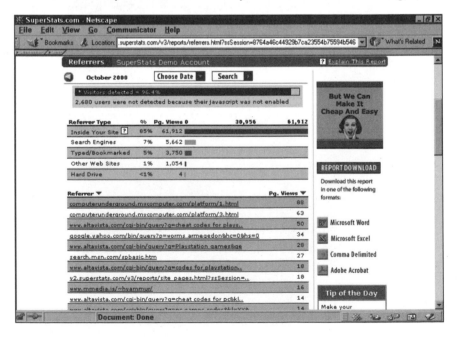

Or how much time customers are spending on your Web site:

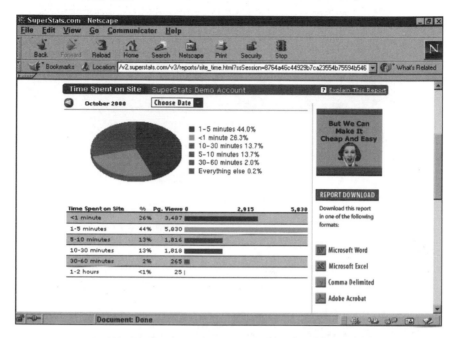

And which Web pages on your site are the most popular:

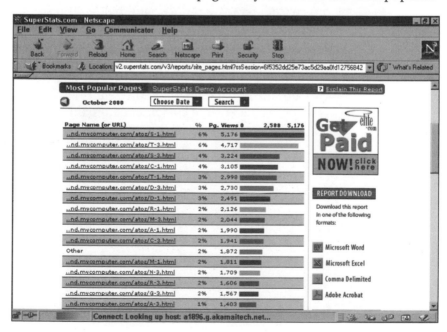

There are also a variety of technical reports that show you everything from which operating systems your customers have to which browsers they are using:

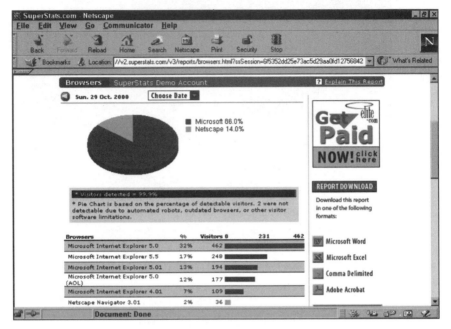

In Chapter 3, we pointed out that two-thirds of all online shoppers abandon their shopping carts before making a purchase. A software program like SuperStats can help you analyze what path customers are taking through your site and what the most popular "exit pages" are so that you can minimize customer abandonment (the *exit page* is the last page visited by the customer before the customer leaves your site):

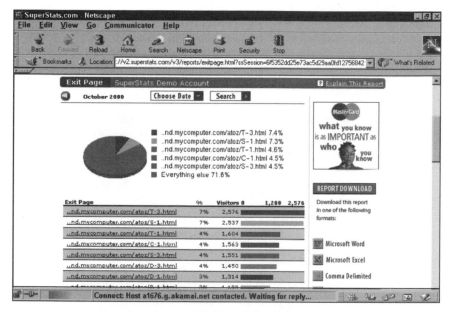

Another powerful Web site tracking program is WebTrends (www.webtrends.com). WebTrends has a number of different versions of its program, ranging from a free "Personal Edition" to an "eCommerce Edition" that will allow you to track sales activity on your Web site. WebTrends is capable of generating very detailed sales reports for your Web site. For example, the following report shows you how much revenue your Web site is generating from repeat customers:

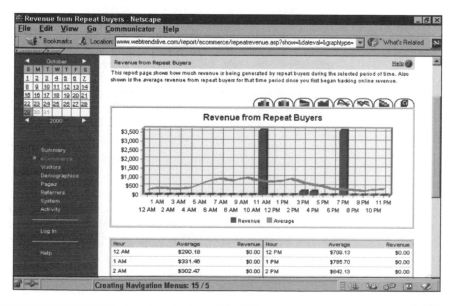

Monthly pricing for WebTrends starts at approximately $38 for the eCommerce Edition and goes as high as $6,000 depending on how many page views your Web site receives a month. We suggest that you visit the WebTrends site for the latest available pricing information.

Most Web site analysis programs work over the Web so you don't need to install or configure any software. You simply cut and paste some code into your Web site, and the service will start to track your Web site immediately. You'll be given a password and username, and you can log into the vendor's Web site at any time to access your reports. In some cases, you may have the option of purchasing Web site analysis software and installing it on your computer. Users of WebTrends, for example, can choose between browser-based versions that provide real-time statistics over the Web and software versions that can be installed on your computer and integrated with internal databases. Several versions of WebTrends software are available depending on your reporting needs and the complexity of your Web site. If you decide to go with a software solution, you will need to have access to the Web servers of the company that hosts your online store. Check with the company hosting your online store to find out if you can use WebTrends. Free fourteen-day trial versions of several of the WebTrends software programs can be downloaded at www.webtrends.com.

When evaluating a Web site analysis program, don't buy strictly on the basis of price. Examine the types of reports you are getting (many services will give you a free trial period or access to sample reports on their Web site) from two perspectives. First, how easy are the reports to read and understand? Second, what type of reports are available and how much detail is provided? In particular, find out if the program will allow you to do any type of advanced e-commerce tracking, such as tracking sales or the performance of your advertising campaigns. While WebTrends, for example, has an e-commerce edition that can track sales information from an online store, we want to point out that most of the entry-level Web site analysis programs do not provide this type of e-commerce tracking. If you are interesting in tracking orders on your Web site and monitoring sales activity for all the products in your online store, you should be prepared to spend significantly more for a product that has these capabilities. However, you may not need these types of tracking options if the storefront solution you are using already provides them.

A final note – many of the Web site analysis services we've mentioned provide free versions of their programs that you can install on your Web site and use immediately. In addition, from time to time, you may come across companies offering free Web site counters that provide very basic visitor tracking on your Web site. Although these services are free, we suggest you think carefully before using them. Why? Many of these free services require you to place an advertisement on your Web site. For example, the free version of the WebTrends service requires that you place a small advertising button on the Web pages you are tracking. Although your Web site visitors can't see your reports, the button is essentially an advertisement on your Web site, and you have to decide whether this is acceptable to you. Some of the free services require you to place a counter on your Web site that displays the number of visits your Web site has received. Do you really want to disclose this information publicly? For example, a customer may visit your Web site and decide not to place an order with you because your counter shows that your Web site has only received twenty visitors in the last six months!

Chapter 7

BUILDING CUSTOMER LOYALTY IN YOUR ONLINE STORE

When it comes to building customer relationships, sometimes it's the little things that count.

"Customer Service – Customers Reign in the New Economy,"
Stephanie Stahl, *Information Week*, 12/11/2000

One of the best indications of success in online retailing is how many repeat customers you have. This is a much more important measurement than how many customers you have, because repeat customers tend to be more loyal and spend more than first-time customers. In addition, it costs more to acquire a new customer than it does to keep the customers you already have. Hence, when creating your online strategy, you should focus not only on acquiring new customers but on keeping them so that they return to your online store again and again.

In this chapter, we review twelve techniques that can help you keep customers coming back to your store and spending more. They are:

- Customer service
- Site registration/personal accounts
- Contests and promotions
- Limited time offers
- Gift reminder services
- Reorder reminder services

- Online communities
- Interactive events
- Compelling content
- Loyalty programs
- Opt-in e-mail
- Personalization

CUSTOMER SERVICE

Perhaps it goes without saying, but we would be remiss if we didn't mention it here. The most important thing you can do to build customer loyalty on your online store is provide excellent customer service.

That, more than anything else we suggest in this chapter, will bring customers back to your store again and again.

e-Fact

21 million U.S. households are interested in home networking.

Source: The Yankee Group (www.yankeegroup.com)

What does excellent customer service entail? Many things, including selling high-quality, reliable products, delivering your products on time, answering e-mail messages promptly, giving customers a broad range of delivery options, making the checkout process as fast as possible, and following all the advice that we offered in Chapter 3, *Tips for Building an Effective Online Store*.

We'll repeat what we said at the beginning of Chapter 3: selling on the Internet is all about exceeding customer expectations.

In an effort to increase customer loyalty and make online shopping more convenient, many online retailers allow customers to register for their own personal shopping accounts.

When customers register for a personal account on an online store, they usually receive special benefits such as faster checkout times, special discounts and promotions, online wish lists, and other features that aren't made available to shoppers who don't register on the site.

Giving customers personal accounts is really no different from getting customers to store their billing information and address books on your Web site for faster checkout, features that we discussed in Chapter 3. One of the benefits of getting customers to register with you is that you can collect their e-mail addresses, and with their permission, send them information about special offers and promotions by e-mail.

Recognizing the potential of site registration as a way to increase customer loyalty, some online retailers have cleverly marketed their site registration features as a preferred customer program.

For an example of this strategy, visit the online store for FTD (www.ftd.com). FTD encourages customers to register on its Web site as "members." Customers are told that, as members, they'll be "eligible for discounts and promotions only enjoyed by our preferred customers":

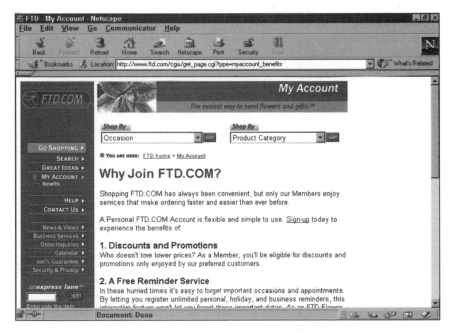

Customers who join FTD.com as a member receive numerous benefits, including:

- lower prices on products and services;

- an e-mail reminder service so they can keep track of birthdays and other special events;

- an online address book where names and addresses of family members and friends can be permanently stored for future orders;

- a monthly newsletter from FTD.com;

- an ongoing record of previous purchases; and

- automatic entry of billing and delivery information so that the same name and address never needs to be entered more than once.

Registration is completely free. To register, customers simply need to fill out an online form like the one below:

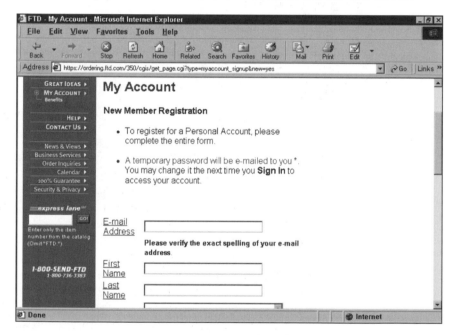

A temporary password is sent to the customer by e-mail. Once received, the customer can access his or her personal account on the FTD.com Web site and begin taking advantage of the special features offered to members:

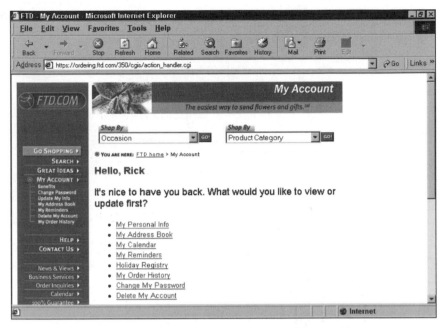

By offering these enhanced services to its customers, FTD benefits from increased customer loyalty. After all, wouldn't you be more inclined to use an online retailer that sends you special offers by e-mail and that stores your preferences on their Web site so that you can make your purchases faster? The key is to make online shoppers feel like they are getting something special when they set up an account with you. In essence, FTD.com is marketing its site registration in a way that's more appealing to customers. Rather than simply encouraging customers to register, it encourages them to register as "preferred customers." FTD.com calls its registered customers "members" and plays up the special benefits that customers get by registering on the site. There's an important lesson to be learned here. The way you package services on your Web site can make a big difference in how they are perceived by your customers.

For another example of a preferred customer club, visit Avon's online store (www.avon.com). Avon has a program called the "A-List" where customers receive "VIP advantages" in exchange for registering on its Web site:

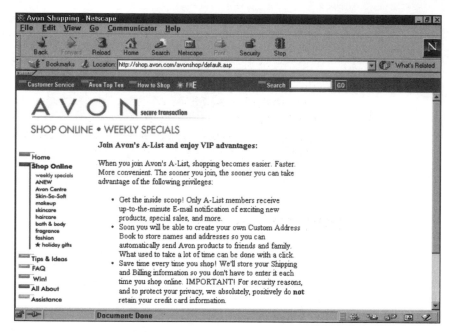

For example, customers who join the A-List receive
e-mail notification of new products and special sales at the
Avon online store. In addition, they can store their shipping
and billing information on the site so that they don't have to
enter it each time they order. Joining is free only requires
that customers fill out a registration form:

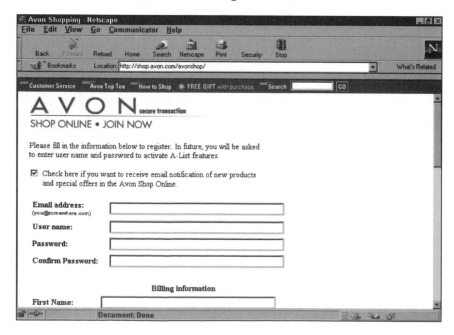

Preferred customer programs like the two we've shown are a great way for online merchants to build long-term relationships with their customers. The more special features and benefits you can offer your customers, the more convenient it will be for them to shop with you. Naturally, if you make it easy for customers to do business with you, they'll return again and again. If you decide to implement a preferred customer program, make sure you display your privacy policy and respect your customers' privacy when collecting information for your program.

CONTESTS AND PROMOTIONS

Promotions can be a great way to grab the attention of a customer who has entered your online store and to build interest in your products. You could give away one of the products that you sell, a service related to your business, or even a gift certificate for your online store. Consider asking one of your suppliers to give you a couple of products that you can give away as part of a contest on your Web site. In return, the supplier gets exposure for its products on your Web site.

Contests are a great way to get customers to register on your Web site. People are busy, so it can be difficult to get customers to take a few minutes out of their hectic schedules to register with you. But a contest can be a great hook.

Consider how the Museum Company (www. museumcompany.com) persuaded customers to register on its online store. Customers who registered on the Web site were given 10 percent off their first purchase:

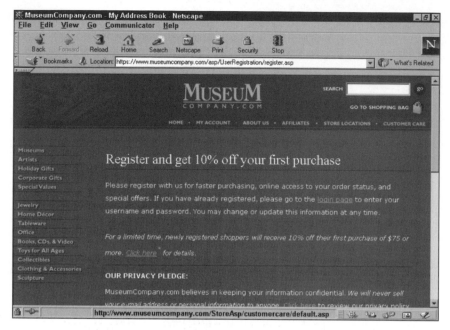

RadioShack (www.radioshack.com) employed a somewhat similar strategy on its online store. The company
entered shoppers in a sweepstakes (with prizes including
personal computers and digital cameras) if they took two
minutes to register on the Web site:

Of course, contests don't need to be linked to site registration. For example, CVS Pharmacy's online store (www.cvs.com) regularly has contests on its Web site to encourage repeat visits:

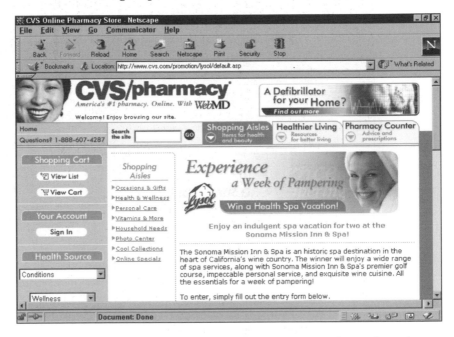

Whenever you run a contest on your Web site, keep in mind the privacy issues we discussed in Chapter 3. When asking shoppers for any personal information, remember to state that any information collected will be used in accordance with your privacy policy.

LIMITED TIME OFFERS

In many respects, an online store is no different from a retail store. For example, customers are likely to respond to product sales and special offers. For this reason, you may want to consider offering product specials and limited time deals from time to time to encourage customers to buy from you. For example, Staples' online store (www.staples.com) regularly offers special deals to its customers:

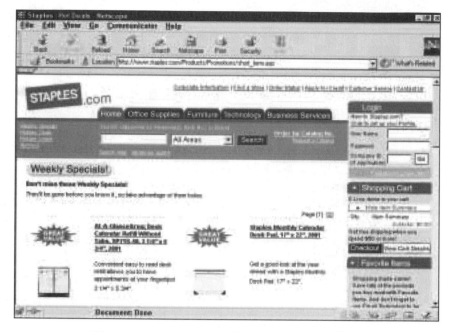

It's important that you don't go overboard with promotions that will dramatically reduce your profit margins or cause you to lose money on every sale. Be smart about the promotions you offer, and make sure they aren't harming you financially. If you decide to make a limited time offer available to your customers, make sure you display the offer prominently on your home page.

GIFT REMINDER SERVICES

Several online stores have implemented gift reminder services that allow customers to store personalized lists of important dates such as birthdays and anniversaries.

Customers who register with a gift reminder service will be notified by e-mail when an important date approaches. The reminder notice is usually accompanied by an advertisement or subtle promotional message from the company operating the service. Since reminder services are usually provided free to customers, they don't generate any direct revenue. However, they are an excellent opportunity for online retailers to promote their brands, drive traffic to their Web sites, and provide a valuable service to their customers at the same time.

For an example of this strategy, visit the online store for The Franklin Mint (www.franklinmint.com). Registered users of The Franklin Mint Web site can store dates for important birthdays, anniversaries, and other special occasions on the site:

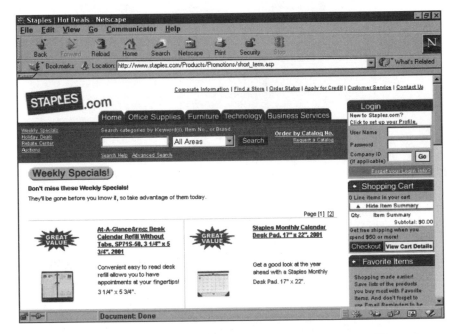

Three weeks before each date, the customer will receive a reminder message from the Franklin Mint. It's a great way to encourage repeat purchases!

REORDER REMINDER SERVICES

If you sell the types of products that customers need to reorder regularly, why not offer customers an online reminder service?

For example, customers of Walgreens' online store (www.walgreens.com) can schedule e-mail reminders so they know when it's time to refill a prescription or reorder a product:

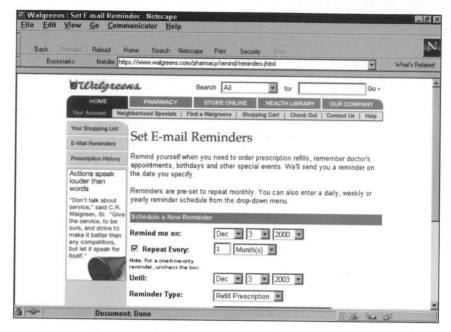

These reminders are optional, of course, but they're a
good way to keep those customers who do opt to receive
them coming back to your store for more.

Online Communities

Some online merchants have found that a great way to
build customer loyalty is to provide discussion groups on
their Web sites where online shoppers can gather, make
new friends, and chat about topics that interest them.

Of course, one of the keys to using this strategy effectively
is building a community that is relevant to the products you
are selling. In other words, don't set up a discussion area and
let your customers chat about anything. Provide discussion
groups that will draw targeted customers to your site – and
bring them back again and again. An excellent example
of this strategy can be found on PETsMART online store
(www.petsmart.com). PETsMART has created an online
community for pet lovers (acmepet.petsmart.com) including
discussion groups, live chat events – even a directory of dog
parks across the United States! Customers can also add photos
of their pets to the site's picture gallery:

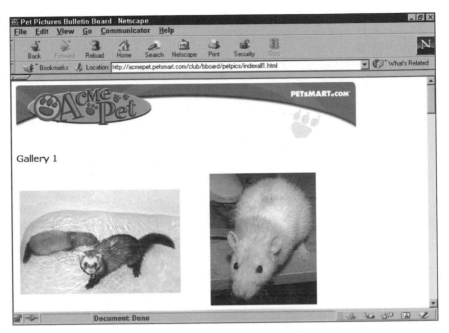

The discussion groups cover almost every pet topic imaginable. There are discussion groups for dogs, cats, birds, horses, frogs, gerbils, ferrets, rabbits, and over two dozen dog breeds:

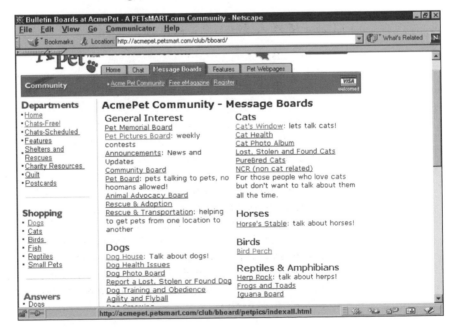

While online communities can be an excellent loyalty-building tool, there are several risks you should be aware of.

First, you need to set some ground rules for your customers and make sure that they observe them. Otherwise, you will end up with customers who use vulgar language in your discussion forums, or who use them solely as a vehicle to advertise penny stocks and other products and services. Forum participants could also end up getting into heated discussions and launching personal attacks on one another.

To avoid these types of problems, PETsMART has established some rules for its discussion groups that customers must follow or be banned from participating:

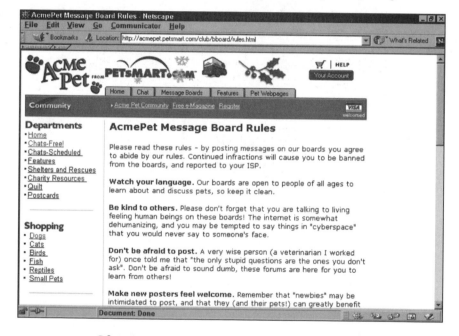

Of course, not everyone will obey the rules, so you've got to monitor your discussion groups closely to make sure no problems arise. This can be very time-consuming, and it will distract you from your main job as an online merchant – selling products. The other risk is that some of your customers will use the message boards as a way to vent their frustrations with your company and its products. Needless to say, this can be a potentially embarrassing situation to find yourself in, and you'll quickly find yourself in "damage control" mode.

Before creating discussion groups on your Web site, think carefully about the benefits and drawbacks of offering this type of interaction to your customers.

INTERACTIVE EVENTS

More and more online stores are holding interactive events on their Web sites to attract customers and build long-term loyal relationships with online shoppers. Hallmark's online store (www.hallmark.com) is a good example of this strategy. Using a service called TalkCity (www.talkcity.com), Hallmark has hosted a series of live chats with ornament artists on its Web site:

It's a great way to turn your static Web site into a two-way conversational and interactive medium that your customers can truly benefit from!

COMPELLING CONTENT

Customers will visit your online store more – and will stick around longer – if you offer valuable information or reference tools on your Web site that relate to the product area that you specialize in. This lets your customers know that you're interested in more than just a quick sale. It also gives shoppers a reason to come back to your store again and again.

You probably have much of this information readily available at your disposal – all you have to do is convert it into a format that can be displayed on the Web. If the information isn't your own, make sure that you obtain any necessary copyright and trademark clearances. Alternatively, you can hire a local expert to contribute articles, commentary, or tips to your Web site, or you can contract with an industry publication to feature its articles on your Web site. You might find that industry experts and industry publications are willing to contribute free content to your online store in exchange for the publicity that your Web site would generate.

Consider what The Sports Authority (www. thesportsauthority.com) has done on its online store. The site's main purpose is, of course, to sell sporting goods. But the site also includes valuable consumer information, including product tips, articles from sports pros, sizing charts, and buyers' guides for over two dozen sports. For example, customers who are interested in purchasing a bicycle helmet can consult an online guide called "How to Buy a Cycling Helmet" so that they can make a more informed buying decision:

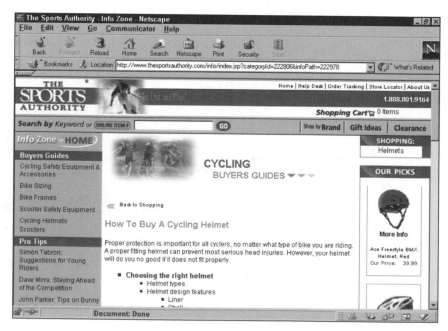

Starbucks provides another excellent example of how to supplement your online store with valuable educational content. Starbucks' Web site (www.starbucks.com), besides selling coffee to consumers, offers an entire section devoted to coffee education, including information on the history of coffee, tasting tips, and advice on how to brew a great cup:

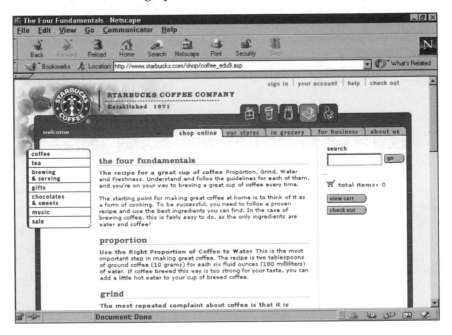

Think about how you might add similar content to your Web site. Remember to keep the content fresh by regularly adding new features and information. If your content becomes stale, customers may lose interest in regularly visiting your Web site.

LOYALTY PROGRAMS

Loyalty programs work well in traditional marketing, so it's not surprising that many online stores have implemented loyalty programs in their online stores. Rather than develop their own loyalty programs, however, most online stores have opted to join a third-party loyalty program such as ClickRewards (www.clickrewards.com):

ClickRewards gives shoppers points called "ClickMiles" every time they shop at a participating online merchant. There is no cost for a shopper to join, and online shoppers can redeem their points for free airline tickets, hotel stays, car rentals, and other prizes (you can see a complete list of rewards at www.clickrewards.com/rewards). For merchants, the ClickRewards program is designed to keep customers coming back to your online store by rewarding them for every purchase they make. But it's not inexpensive to join – the starting cost for merchants who want to participate in the ClickRewards network is approximately $15,000, so you'll need a substantial marketing budget to get involved.

> **e-Fact**
>
> *The more often a customer visits a particular online retailer, the more likely a customer is going to spend an increasing amount of money at that site.*
> Source: Bain & Co. (www.rec.bain.com) and Mainspring (www.mainspring.com)

The problem with online loyalty programs like ClickRewards is that they don't seem to be motivating consumers to purchase more products online. In a survey of twelve hundred online shoppers by Jupiter Research (www.jup.com), only 22 percent of respondents said that online loyalty programs had any effect on their purchasing behavior. And this isn't because consumers aren't joining online loyalty programs. In fact, 75 percent of respondents to the survey said they belonged to an online loyalty program. This isn't surprising since most online loyalty programs are free. Why wouldn't customers join?

The problem is that when it comes to purchasing online, consumers are much more interested in issues such as product selection, customer service, and easy returns. Jupiter's survey found that these issues drive loyalty much more than online loyalty programs do. Customers couldn't care less about earning reward points from your online store if the customer service is terrible and it's a hassle to return unwanted items. If you want your customers to give you repeat business, make sure that you address critical issues such as customer service before you launch an online loyalty program.

e-Fact

A survey of 50 leading online retail Web sites did not find a single one that rated "good" or "excellent" for online customer service.

Source: Gartner Group (www.gartner.com)

With this in mind, a preferred customer loyalty program that requires customers to register on your Web site is probably a better way to improve customer loyalty. For example, the FTD.com preferred customer program that we described earlier in the chapter offers immediate benefits, including faster checkout times and online address books – services that address the all-important customer service issue raised by the Jupiter Research survey. *Customers are more likely to reward you with more frequent purchases if you reward them with services that really matter to them.* Airlines points are nice, but improved customer service is even better!

We don't want to discourage you from investigating and perhaps implementing your own online loyalty program or a program operated by a third-party organization such as ClickRewards. But investigate the costs and merits of these programs carefully, and think about where your marketing dollars are best spent. Especially if you're a small business, you'll probably find that you're better off investing your money in improved customer service and a site registration process (as FTD.com has done) rather than in a points program that may have little impact on customer loyalty.

OPT-IN E-MAIL

In the last chapter, we introduced you to the concept of permission marketing. Permission marketing, also known as *opt-in e-mail*, means getting permission from customers before you market to them by e-mail.

Many online stores have discovered that permission marketing also works as an excellent loyalty-building technique and therefore have built permission marketing strategies into their own Web sites. The idea is to encourage customers to give you their e-mail addresses so that you can send them news and information by e-mail. Regular e-mail communication not only keeps your name in front of your customers, it can strengthen customer relationships and increase repeat visits to your online store.

There are two types of general e-mail communications you may want to have with your customers:

- e-mail alerts or updates that keep your customers informed about special promotions in your online store, new products, and new content on your Web site; and

- an online newsletter providing articles, product tips, or other value-added information of interest to your customers.

An online newsletter is a bigger commitment, since it requires more content and should be sent out on a regular basis. In contrast, e-mail alerts can be sent out as required, can be brief, and don't need to adhere to any type of release schedule. It's up to you whether you want to offer one or both of these types of e-mail to your customers. Some customers, for example, don't want to be bothered receiving sales information from your online store, but would gladly sign up for an online newsletter if it offered valuable information. For an example of a company that offers both a newsletter and e-mail updates, visit the Crutchfield Electronics Web site (www.crutchfield.com). When customers sign up to receive e-mail from Crutchfield, they can choose which type of communication they want to receive:

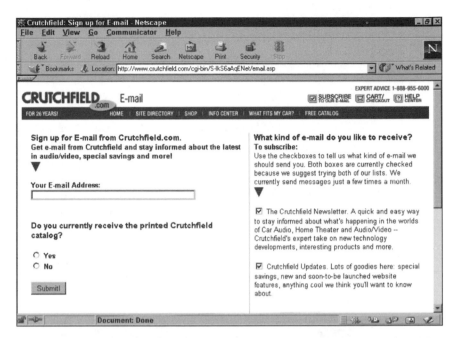

When customers sign up to your e-mail list, you should send them an acknowledgement by e-mail, as Crutchfield does, including information on how to unsubscribe:

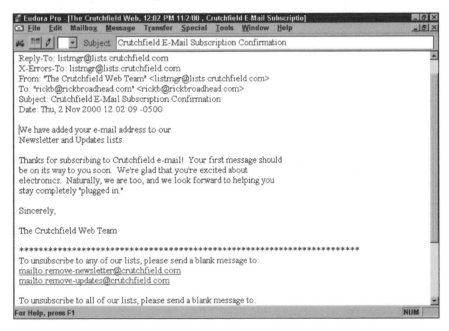

There is a fine line between an e-mail update
and a newsletter, and many stores have rolled
both into a single e-mail list with both functions.
Not only is it less confusing to customers when
they only have one e-mail list to sign up for,
you don't have to worry about maintaining two
separate e-mail lists. For example, PETsMART
(www.petsmart.com) has a weekly electronic
newsletter called PawsPectives. The newsletter
includes helpful information about pet care, Web
site news, and information on product specials:

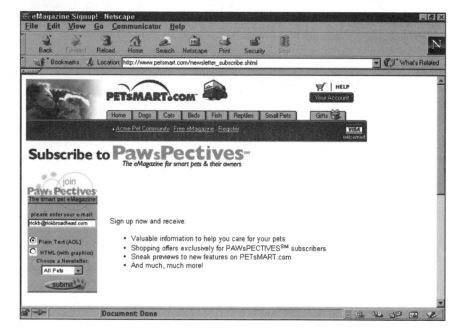

Other organizations have taken a simple approach
to their e-mail lists. The online store for Guess? Jeans
(www.guess.com), for example, invites customers to sign
up for news of upcoming sales and special events by clicking a button on its Web site. The following pop-up window
then appears on the shopper's screen:

As you can see, opt-in e-mail is a powerful way to keep in touch with shoppers and keep them coming back to your online store on a regular basis. Here are ten tips to help you start your opt-in e-mail strategy on the right track:

1. Provide Value

Customers will be turned off an online newsletter if it is nothing more than a sales pitch. Focus on providing relevant, useful information to your customers.

2. Let Customers Know What They Are Getting

When customers sign up for your e-mail list, tell them what they're signing up for. What will they receive? Information on changes to your Web site? The latest store specials? Feature articles? Don't mislead your customers and then surprise them with information they're not expecting.

3. Communicate the Benefits

One of the problems with e-mail is that we receive too much of it. Many customers will hesitate to sign up for a service that will potentially generate even more clutter in their e-mail box. For this reason, make sure you tell your customers what's in it for them. What are the benefits of signing up for your e-mail list?

4. Get Permission First

Remember that permission marketing is based on the customer's agreement to receive information from you by e-mail. Only send your newsletter to customers who choose to subscribe. Don't send it to customers who haven't asked for it, and don't assume that because a customer has bought a product from you, it's permissible to add that customer's e-mail address to your distribution list.

In addition to promoting your newsletter on the front page of your Web site, as many merchants do, you can also promote it during the registration process (if you have one) and when customers are checking out of your online store. Always give the customer the option of saying "yes" or "no" to your newsletter. For example, when customers fill out the registration form on the Foot Locker online store (www.footlocker.com), one of the questions they are asked is "Would you like to receive e-mail updates on future promotions?":

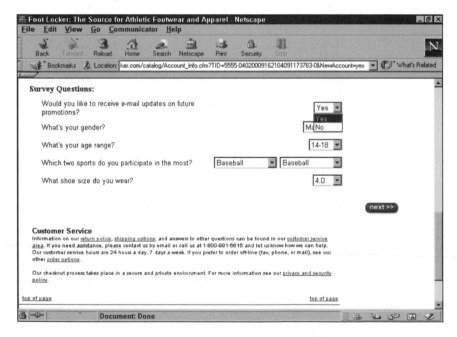

5. Make It Easy for Customers to Subscribe

Make it easy for shoppers to subscribe to your e-mail list. Shoppers may be less inclined to subscribe if it takes more than a couple of seconds to join. If you make customers

In 2000, the average online user received about 40 permission-based marketing messages per year. By 2005, that number will increase 4000% to 1,612.

Source: Jupiter Research (www.jup.com)

answer a long list of questions, they may decide that it isn't worth the hassle. As a result, many online stores allow shoppers to add themselves to their electronic mailing lists with little more than an e-mail address.

A good example can be found on Nordstrom's online store (www.nordstrom.com). Customers who want to receive e-mail updates from Nordstrom only need to enter their e-mail address and specify what types of products they want to receive information about. No other personal information is required:

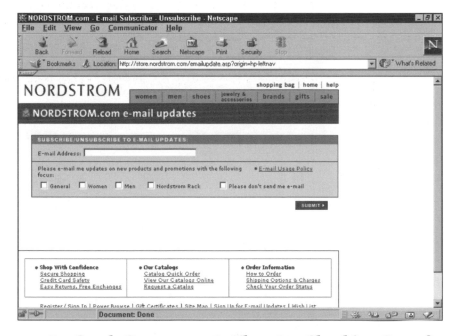

6. Catch Customers As They Are Checking Out of Your Online Store

A good time to collect e-mail addresses from customers is when they are making a purchase from your online store. A good example of this strategy can be found on the Crate and Barrel Web site (www.crateandbarrel.com). The first screen of Crate and Barrel's checkout area looks like this:

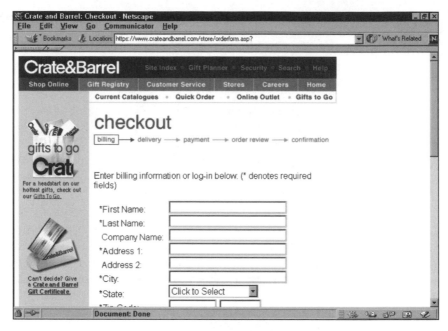

Toward the bottom of the screen, customers can check a box if they are interested in receiving e-mail messages of "news and happenings" at Crateandbarrel.com:

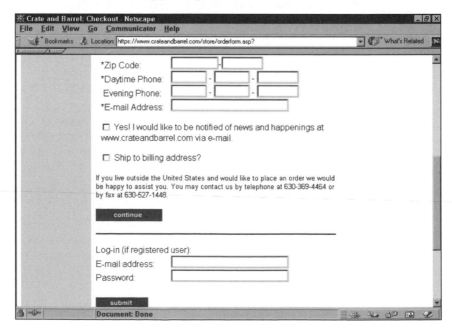

7. Make It Easy for Customers to Unsubscribe

Customers may want to remove themselves from your
e-mail list for various reasons. For example, they may not
like it, they may be going away for an extended period of time,
or they may be changing their e-mail address. Regardless of
the reason, ensure that customers are provided with clear,
easy-to-follow instructions on how to unsubscribe from
your e-mail list. Many online stores send subscribers an
initial welcome message with instructions on unsubscribing.
However, our experience has been that most customers
end up deleting this information or misplacing it, so a better
strategy is to include removal instructions at the end of
every message that you send out. Your customers will
appreciate this and you will, too – it will save you from
having to respond to dozens of angry e-mail messages
from customers who want to get off your e-mail list but
don't know how.

8. Don't Overdo It

Online shoppers hate spam, the Internet term for junk mail.
Don't subject your customers to too much information.
For example, sending out an e-mail message several times
a week is overkill. Gap's online store (www.gap.com) actually
asks customers how frequently they want to receive e-mail
messages from the company. Customers can select "never,"
"major events," or "weekly":

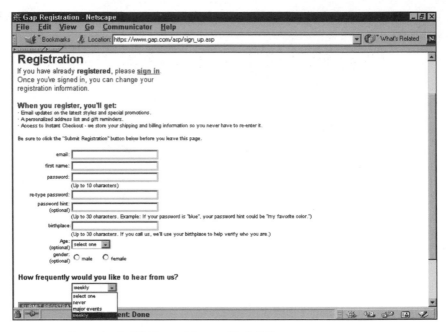

9. Don't Sell Your E-mail Addresses

In Chapter 3, *Tips for Building an Effective Online Store*, we discussed the importance of having a privacy policy on your Web site. Make sure that your privacy policy (or a link to it) is clearly displayed when customers sign up for your e-mail list. Let them know that you're not going to sell their e-mail addresses or any other personal information they give to you. If you abuse the information that customers give you, you'll lose their trust – and their business. When customers of Patagonia's online store (www.patagonia.com) sign up to the company's e-mail list, they are told: "We respect your privacy. Email addresses are not released to third parties":

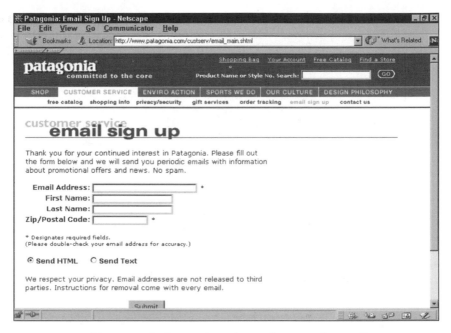

For more information about the use of e-mail as a marketing tool, you may want to visit the Web site of the Responsible Electronic Communications Alliance (www.responsibleemail.org). Formed by a group of organizations involved in e-mail marketing, the Alliance is helping develop industry-wide standards to protect consumer privacy on the Internet:

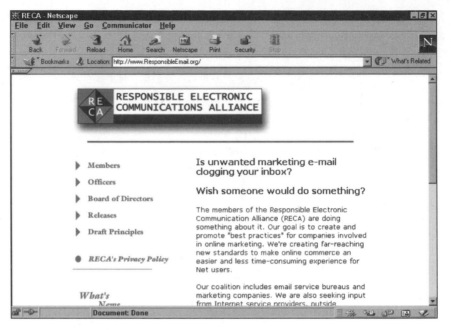

10. Use a Mailing List Program or Permission Marketing Firm

Some businesses attempt to maintain their e-mail lists manually without the aid of any special software, but this can become extremely time-consuming, especially as the number of subscribers to your e-mail list grows. You'll have to deal with e-mail addresses that stop working as well as with people who want to be added and removed from your list. In addition, if you want to target your e-mail messages based on customer tastes and preferences, demographic information, or purchase history, and then track customer response to your e-mail campaigns, you'll need e-mail management software that can handle these tasks.

> **e-Fact**
>
> *The number of youth wireless subscribers (aged 10-24) in the United States will reach 43 million by 2004.*
>
> Source: Cahners In-Stat Group (www.instat.com)

If you want to set up a mailing list for your online store, there are a variety of options available to you. First, check with the storefront solution you are using to see if it includes any sort of mailing list capability.

Alternatively, you may want to use a third-party e-mail management service such as List Builder (lb.bcentral.com), which is part of a group of small business services offered by Microsoft's bCentral service (www.bcentral.com) Builder, shown below, allows you to set up a mailing list on your Web site in just a couple of minutes, without the need for any technical knowledge:

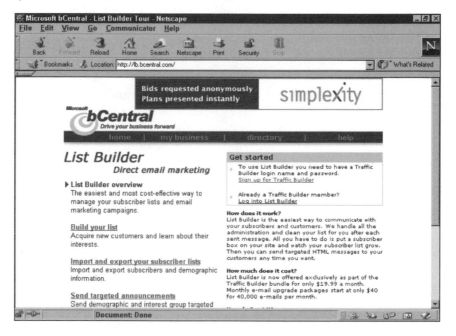

List Builder costs $19.95 a month, which includes access to a variety of other tools to help you grow your online business. You're limited to five thousand messages a month, although additional upgrade packages are available if you need to send more messages.

If you're operating on a really tight budget and can't afford $19.95 a month, Microsoft also offers a free e-mail management service called ListBot (www.listbot.com). However, List Builder has a number of advantages over the free version of ListBot. Most importantly, List Builder is advertising-free. In contrast, the free version of ListBot is supported by advertising messages that will appear in the messages you send to your subscribers. This could be a big turn-off to your customers, who may not appreciate receiving advertisements for other services in your e-mail announcements, especially when they've signed up to receive information from your online store. In addition to being advertising-free, List Builder allows you to create customized survey questions, import and export subscriber lists, and send targeted messages to your customers based on their profile information – features that aren't available in the free version of ListBot.

In the pages that follow, we'll show you what's involved in creating a mailing list for your online store using List Builder.

Once you've signed up for List Builder, you'll be given the opportunity to design the questions that you want to ask customers when they join your e-mail list. This information can be placed in a customizable signup page on your Web site. You can collect a variety of information from your customers, including demographic information (e.g., age, sex, income, occupation, zip code, etc.), information about Internet usage, and information about a customer's interests (the latter will allow you to target e-mail messages based on their product preferences). Once you've created your questions, you can designate each question as optional or mandatory:

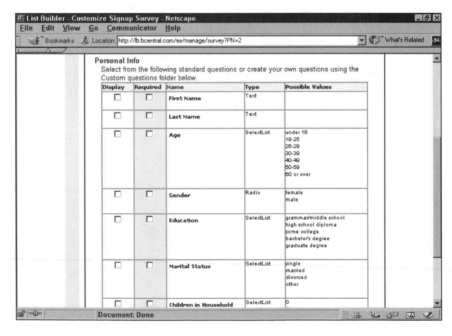

List Builder also gives you the ability to add your own custom questions:

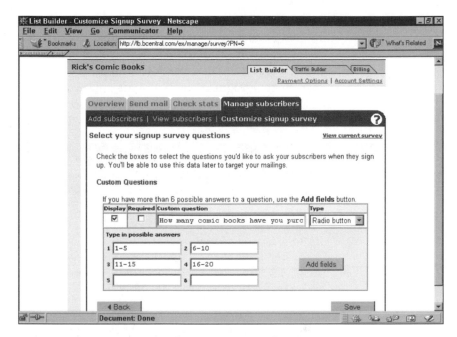

Once you're done preparing the signup survey, you can see a preview:

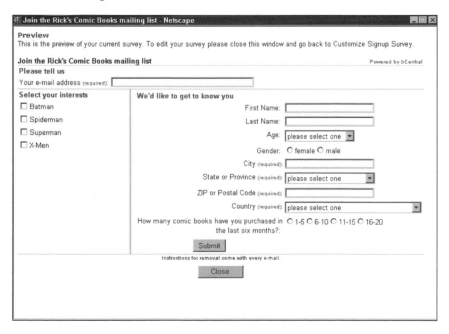

There are three ways to add customers to your mailing list. They can join from a customizable signup page on your Web site, you can manually add e-mail addresses, or you can import e-mail addresses from a database. To place a customizable signup page on your online store, List Builder will give you some HTML code that you should add to your Web site:

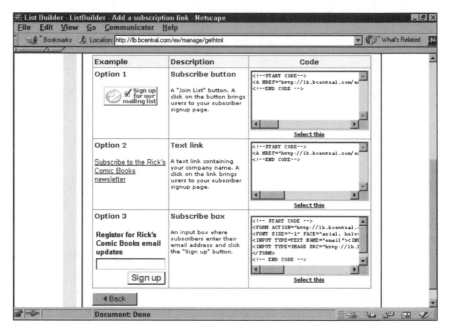

For example, you can place a button like this on your Web site:

Once this code is in place, customers can join your mailing list by clicking on the button and filling out your questionnaire. When you are ready to send a message to your subscribers, you can log into the List Builder site (using the username and password you selected during signup) and compose your message:

As noted earlier, List Builder allows you to target your messages based on the demographic information you have collected from your customers. Simply select what types of customers you want to target, and List Builder will send your message to all of the subscribers that match your criteria:

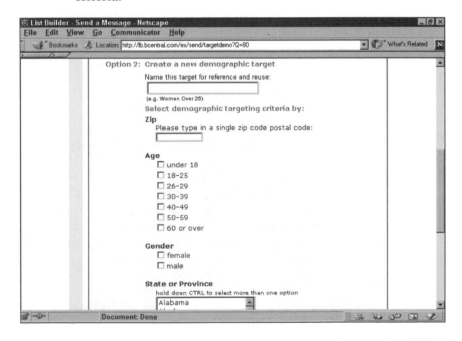

For example, you could send out a message to all the subscribers in Texas or all the subscribers who are male and under the age of thirty. It's quite a powerful capability if you want to target a message to specific types of customers.

At any time, you can log into your List Builder account to modify the demographic questions you ask new subscribers, manage your subscribers, send messages out to the list, and check statistics:

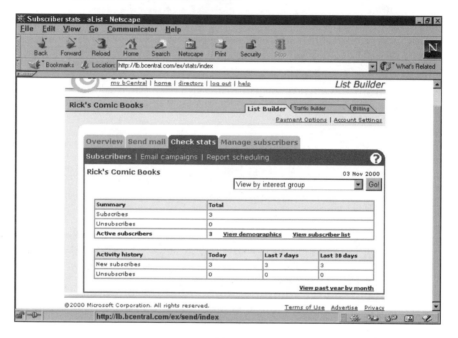

Permission Marketing Firms

More advanced solutions for setting up an e-mail list on your Web site are provided by permission marketing specialists such as ClickAction (www.clickaction.com) and Responsys.com (www.responsys.com).

Lands' End (www.landsend.com), for example, uses software from Responsys to manage its e-mail marketing campaigns. Customers who visit Lands' End's Web site can sign up for the company's "What's New" newsletter:

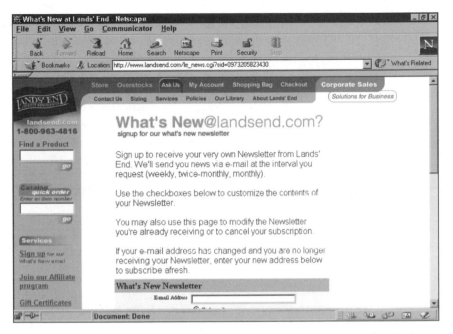

As part of the signup process, customers are asked what type of information they want to receive from Lands' End, and how frequently they want to be contacted:

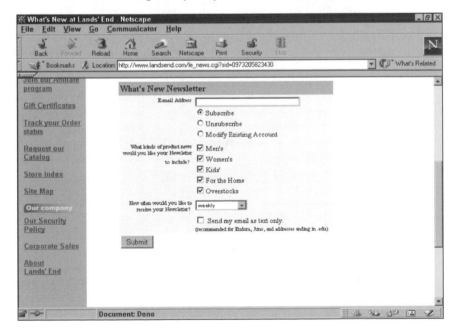

Using a Responsys software package called Interact, Lands' End can create targeted e-mail messages based on the profile information supplied by customers. The Responsys software also enables Lands' End to build profiles of its customers and send personalized e-mail messages to customers based on their buying patterns, Web site behavior, and response to previous e-mail campaigns. The software is easy to use, and online store owners can schedule their own e-mail campaigns through their Web browsers.

Similarly, ClickAction's (www.clickaction.com) e-mail campaign software, called ClickAction ERM (Email Relationship Management), is used by a wide range of online retailers, including Talbots (www.talbots.com), Dean & Deluca (www.deandeluca.com), and Patagonia (www.patagonia.com). ClickAction ERM enables online retailers to collect e-mail addresses and profile information from customers. For example, on the Dean & Deluca Web site, customers can choose what types of special offers they are interested in, and they will receive e-mail updates tailored to their personal interests:

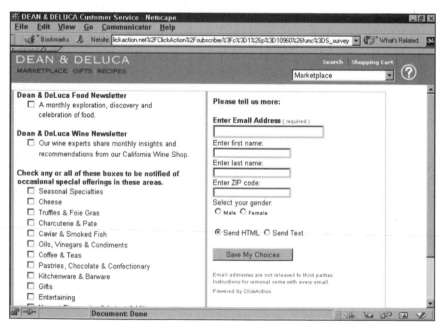

This Web page is actually powered by ClickAction software, which is invisible to the customer. When Dean & Deluca wants an e-mail campaign, it uses special Web-based software provided by ClickAction to send personalized e-mail messages to customers. Campaigns can be prepared based on a variety of different criteria including customer demographics, customer-supplied preference information, Web site behavior, and more.

The benefit of using permission marketing solutions provided by companies such as Responsys and ClickAction is that they enable you to develop highly targeted e-mail campaigns so that you can build better relationships with your customers and increase sales as a result.

The cost of some of these services, however, can be prohibitive for a small business. For example, the minimum investment for setting up an e-mail campaign using Responsys' Interact software is around $10,000 plus a per-message cost. Fortunately, some permission marketing firms are beginning to put together electronic mailing list products aimed at small businesses.

PERSONALIZATION

Many merchants believe some form of personalization is an effective way to increase sales and customer retention. In fact, online personalization strategies have gained so much momentum that an advocacy group called the Personalization Consortium (www.personalization.org) was formed to promote the use of personalization technology:

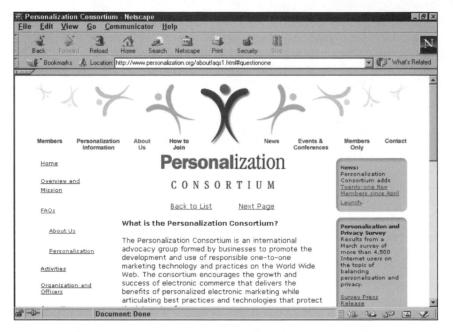

There are many ways to personalize the content and services that customers receive in your online store, including:

- Site registration
- Personalized mailings
- Data analysis tools

Site Registration

First and foremost, as noted earlier in the chapter, if you can get customers to register on your Web site and set up a personal account, you can offer express checkout services, online wish lists, access to previous orders, gift reminders, address books, and other "personalized" services that make customers feel special. We've already shown you how FTD.com has implemented site registration as a way of increasing customer loyalty and personalizing the services for online shoppers. For another example of how site regis-tration can be used to personalize a customer's online shopping experience, visit the Illuminations online store (www.illuminations.com) and look at the "My Illuminations" service:

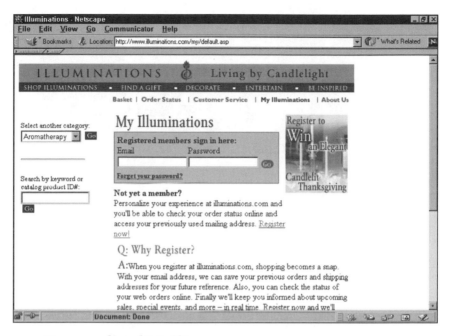

Personalized Mailings

We discussed electronic mailing lists earlier in the chapter and pointed out that they can be an effective marketing tool because they can draw customers to your online store. But most online newsletters send out the same information to everyone.

One alternative to a generic mailing list (where the same newsletter goes out to all your online shoppers) is to have your customers select what types of information they want to receive from you by e-mail. Although it can be more expensive to implement technology that sends out person-alized e-mail messages, you're able to target customers in a way that's not possible with a regular mailing list.

Consider what Bloomingdale's has done on its online store (www.bloomingdales.com). Customers who register on the Web site are asked to select what types of products they are interested in, and Bloomingdale's promises to notify them by e-mail when their favorite items go on sale:

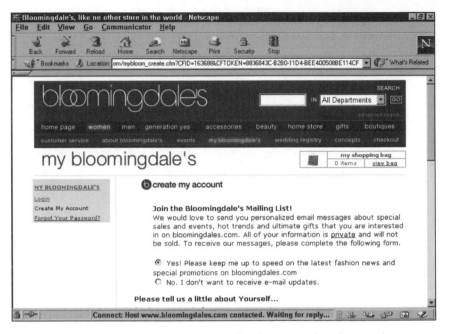

A more extensive example of personalized e-mail can be found on Amazon.com's Web site. Using Amazon.com's "Personal Notification Service," customers specify what types of books, music, and videos they are interested in, and Amazon.com will send out an e-mail alert whenever a new product is released that matches a customer's interests. For example, type in a name like "Britney Spears," and Amazon.com will alert you when she releases a new CD:

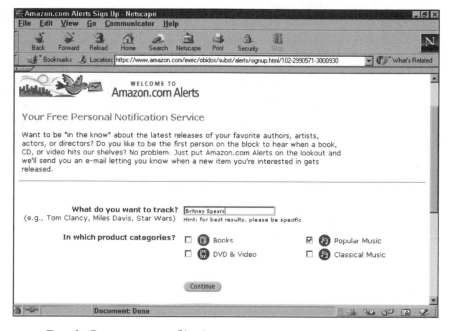

Don't Overpersonalize!

We would be remiss if we didn't point out that there is a danger in getting too personalized. For example, if you start inviting customers to select specific topics they want to receive information about, such as Britney Spears, customers will expect to receive information about Britney Spears and nothing else. Thus, if you want to send out an e-mail message about a special contest you're having in your online store, you really shouldn't be sending it out to the customers who have said they only want to receive information about Britney Spears – even though a lot of those customers would probably be interested in that contest. That's why it's generally a good idea to have a generic e-mail list that customers can join in addition to inviting customers to receive special mailings on topics of interest to them.

Data Analysis Tools

Many online retailers use data analysis tools (sometimes referred to as *data mining tools* or *customer intelligence tools*) to monitor customer behavior in their online stores. Some retailers use custom-developed software programs while others use analytic programs from such companies as Net Perceptions (www.netperceptions.com), NetGenesis (www.netgenesis.com), Personify (www.personify.com), Coremetrics (www.coremetrics.com), and Accrue (www.accrue.com) that specialize in helping online businesses to analyze how customers are using their Web sites. These programs collect information about what Web pages customers are clicking on, what paths customers take through your site, what online advertisements customers have seen, what products they are buying, how customers found out about your site, what online promotions are working or failing, and more. This data is then analyzed and can be used to calculate retention rates, customer acquisition costs, and other useful statistics. The data can also be used to create promotions for shoppers as well as to personalize the content or messages that an online shopper sees. For example, data analysis software could help you to identify all the customers who purchased from you at least three times in the past but who haven't made a purchase in the last six months.

Using all of this data, online retailers can set up *rules-based personalization* strategies that target messages to clients based on their behavior on the site. For example, suppose you are selling designer jeans on your Web site. You could set up a rule that says any customer who has returned more than twice to your designer jeans page should be shown a coupon for $15 off a designer belt. This type of personalization is attractive because it allows retailers to offer real-time promotions to their customers without knowing the identity of the customer. The customer remains anonymous because the personalization is based on the user's clicking behavior and activity on the Web site.

Higher levels of personalization are possible when retailers combine their rules or clickthrough data with information that customers voluntarily provide on the site. For example, many retailers encourage customers to register on their site and provide information about their interests, geographic location, and lifestyle. This customer-provided information can be combined with data about how the customer is using the Web site so that promotions and special product offers can be generated on the fly.

e-Fact

By 2004, marketers in the U.S. will send more than 200 billion e-mail messages annually.

Source: Forrester Research (www.forrester.com)

Collaborative Filtering

In addition to the basic rules-based personalization techniques mentioned previously, many online retailers are implementing advanced personalization strategies they hope will increase both customer loyalty and customer spending in their online stores.

Jeff Bezos, the CEO of online bookseller Amazon.com, once said, "If we have 4.5 million customers, we shouldn't have one store, we should have 4.5 million stores." The idea is that customers are more likely to return to your online store, and buy products from you again and again, if you personalize your online services and tailor them to each customer's needs and interests. As an example of this approach to online selling, Amazon.com (www.amazon.com) has built a service called "New for You" on its Web site that customizes product recommendations for its customers:

When repeat customers visit Amazon.com, they will receive personalized product recommendations based on their purchase history. For example, a person who previously purchased a cookbook on Amazon.com might be shown a new cookbook, whereas someone who previously purchased a Stephen King novel may be shown a similar type of book by another author.

Many Web sites, including Amazon.com, use a process called *collaborative filtering* to make product recommendations to customers. Collaborative filtering can determine what a given customer may be interested in based on what other customers with similar tastes and interests have purchased. For example, a Web site using collaborative filtering technology would gradually build profiles of all the customers visiting its online store, by analyzing what links customers are clicking on and what products they are buying. This information can also be obtained from questionnaires that customers are asked to fill out. Eventually, the site would be able to identify customers who have similar interests and buying patterns. This data is then used to make product recommendations to customers based on what other customers in the group are purchasing. For example, a store may notice that you are interested in buying Anne Rice and Stephen King novels. It will find other people in its database who are also fans of Anne Rice and Stephen King to see what other books they are purchasing, assuming that these books may also be of interest to you.

Other Approaches to Personalization

For another innovative approach to personalization, visit the Lands' End online store (www.landsend.com). Using a service called "My Virtual Model," customers can create virtual models that resemble their body measurements and then try on clothes to see how they look. This service is available for both men and women:

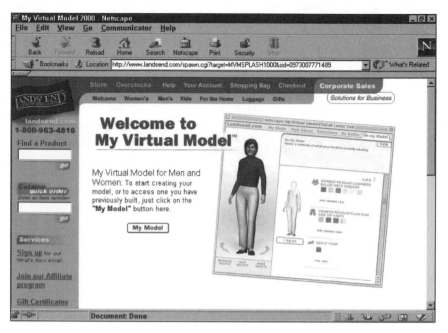

The process takes only a couple of minutes and requires that customers pick a username and password. This will allow shoppers to access their virtual model every time they return to the Lands' End site:

My Virtual Model(TM) - Account - Netscape

My Virtual Model™ at LANDS'END

Please, complete the following fields before continuing. By filling in this Profile, you will be able to use your Virtual Model without having to answer the questionnaire each time. You will also be able to shop with your model on all affiliated sites of the MyVirtualModel.com community.

Username		Example: johndoe
Password		Minimum: 4 characters
Re-type Password		For confirmation

If you forget your password, we will ask you to answer the hint question below.

Hint Question

Hint Answers

We'll send your password to the Email address indicated here.

Email

To create their virtual model, customers need to provide information about their hair color and hair style, eyes, face shape, skin tone, and body measurements:

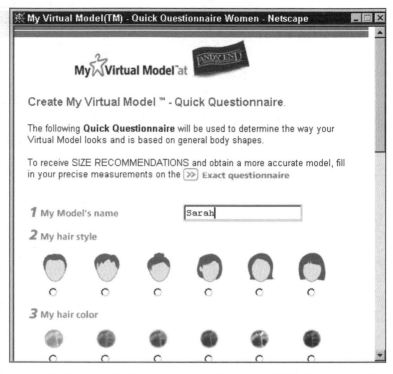

Using this information, Lands' End will build a virtual model resembling the customer:

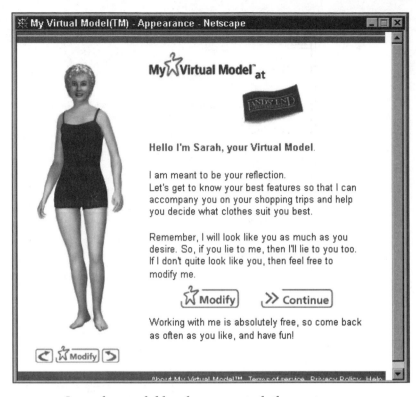

Once the model has been created, the customer receives fashion advice customized to his or her body measurements and features:

The customer also receives wardrobe suggestions and can try outfits on the virtual model to see how they look:

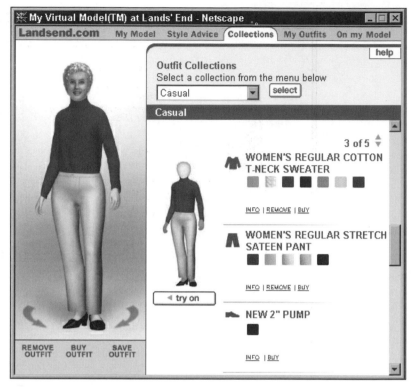

If the customer wants a different view of the outfit, the model can be rotated:

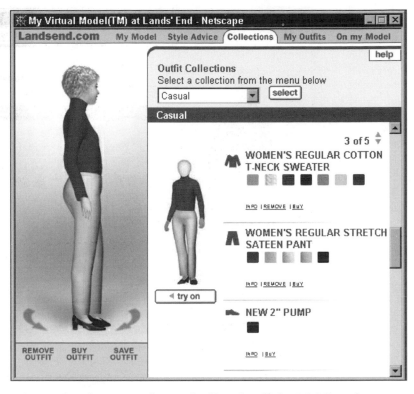

Purchases can be made directly off the My Virtual Model screen. Individual items can be purchased by clicking on the "buy" link that appears underneath each item, or the entire outfit can be purchased by clicking on the "buy outfit" link that appears underneath the model. For customers who need time to mull over their purchase, Lands' End allows shoppers to save their favorite outfits on the site:

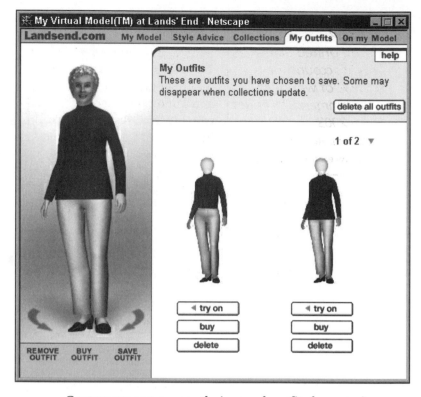

Customers can access their saved outfits by entering their username and password next time they return to the Lands' End site.

As you can see, My Virtual Model not only recommends products to customers, it also allows shoppers to fit clothes to their own body shape so that they can make more informed buying decisions. Lands' End hopes that this increased personalization will increase its online revenues. Since the virtual model feature was introduced, over one million customers have used the service!

Drawbacks of Personalization

Many organizations have found that they have to strike a delicate balance between collecting information from users and relying on data gleaned from online behavior. Depending on your business, you may find that customers don't want to offer a lot of information about themselves because of privacy concerns, forcing you to personalize offers based more on their online behavior. On the other hand, online behavior analysis isn't always appropriate.

e-Fact

The United States will account for 59% of worldwide e-commerce revenues by 2003.

Source: eMarketer
(www.emarketer.com)

For example, if you are selling to businesses, you can't personalize offers based on how the purchasing manager is using your Web site! The offers you make to a business need to be based on the needs of the whole company and not on the needs of individual employees who are browsing through your online store. In these situations, you need to focus on customizing content for the entire organization.

Another drawback with personalization is that it isn't always accurate, or even appreciated. For example, many customers find it annoying when a Web site is continually trying to cross-sell products. It's like being in a retail store with a salesperson that won't leave you alone! In addition, the technology behind personalization software is still rudimentary in many cases, causing shoppers to receive inappropriate product recommendations. Not to mention that it's easy for a Web site to give recommendations to the wrong person. For example, in families where multiple people use a single computer, a family member visiting a Web site such as Amazon.com may receive personalized information that is actually intended for another person in the household who was previously on the site.

Finally, as noted earlier, you also have to be careful about overpersonalizing your Web site. If you give your customers too much personalized content, you limit your sales opportunities because you are offering customers a narrow rather than broad selection of products.

What Does It Cost?

Personalization schemes can be inexpensive or they can be costly (as much as millions of dollars), depending on what you are trying to accomplish. Many of the collaborative filtering technologies that we discussed earlier can cost you well into six figures, although there are some organizations, such as Yo! Networks (www.yo.com) that are designing personalization with smaller businesses in mind:

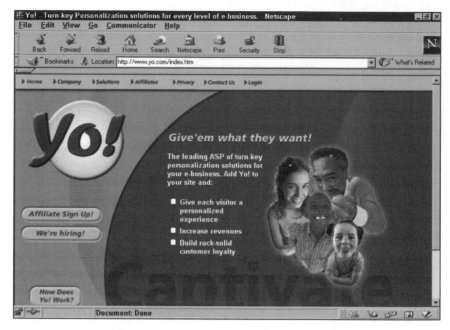

In the table below, we've listed some of the leading vendors of personalization software. You should also investigate the companies we listed earlier in the chapter in our discussion of data analysis software as many of these companies also sell personalization solutions. As noted above, the cost of personalization software can be prohibitive for a small business. If you can't afford the services offered by these companies (and most small businesses can't), speak with the company that is developing your online store to see if there are features that you can implement to personalize the online shopping experience for your customers. At a very minimum, consider implementing one or more mailing lists or online newsletters so that customers can sign up to receive information from you by e-mail.

Examples of Companies Selling Personalization Software

Blaze Software	www.blazesoft.com
Broadbase	www.broadbase.com
BroadVision	www.broadvision.com
E.piphany	www.epiphany.com
Likeminds by Macromedia	www.macromedia.com

NetPerceptions	www.netperceptions.com
Personify	www.personify.com
Yo! Networks	www.yo.com

Chapter 8

101 TIPS FROM ONLINE MERCHANTS IN THE UNITED STATES

...e-commerce isn't really a new way of doing business, it is simply a new medium for conducting business.

Doug Young, Noggintops.com

Although electronic commerce only represents a tiny percentage of total retail sales in the United States, it's growing fast. According to Forrester Research (www.forrester.com), U.S. consumers are expected to buy $143 billion worth of goods and services on the Internet in 2003, up from an estimated $20.3 billion in 1999. In spite of this impressive growth, the last couple of years have been anything but a smooth ride for companies selling online. Many online retailers have failed, pushed into bankruptcy by unrealistic expectations and poor business models. Other companies have been experimenting with different approaches to selling online in an effort to find the right formula for success. To help you benefit from the experiences of other online retailers in the United States, we convened a panel of twenty companies that are selling online and asked them what they've learned so far and what advice they would have for other organizations thinking of opening their own online stores in the coming months and years. Our merchants range from small mom-and-pop businesses like One of a Kind Kid.com, a business operated by a mother out of her home, to larger retail operations like Payless ShoeSource, a chain of over four thousand retail stores in the United States.

OUR PANEL

Tane Chan
Owner, The Wok Shop
Location: San Francisco, California
Industry: Woks and cooking products/accessories
Web Site: www.wokshop.com

Bonnie Clewans
Owner, The Bead Gallery
Location: Buffalo, New York
Industry: Beads
Web Site: www.beadgallery.com

Michelle Donahue-Arpas
Owner, Genius Babies!
Location: Charlotte, North Carolina
Industry: Baby gifts and toys
Web Site: www.geniusbabies.com

Richard Flynn
President, Red Trumpet, Ltd.
Location: York, Pennsylvania
Industry: Collectible CDs, LPs, DVDs, and pre-owned vinyl records
Web Site: www.redtrumpet.com

Jason Friedman
Director of Internet Commerce, J&R Music and Computer World
Location: New York, New York
Industry: Home entertainment and computers
Web Site: www.jandr.com

Kevin Gorman
Owner, WebCyclery, LLC
Location: Bend, Oregon
Industry: Cycling products
Web Site: www.webcyclery.com

Chris Harrower
Chief Information Officer/Director of Sales & Marketing,
Choo Choo Barn
Location: Strasburg, Pennsylvania
Industry: Train-related merchandise
Web Site: www.choochoobarn.com

Bodega Bob Homme
Chief Engineering Officer, The Submarine Store
Location: Gaithersburg, Maryland
Industry: Submarine-related merchandise
Web Site: www.submarinestore.com

Kim Michaux
Owner, One of a Kind Kid.com
Location: Roanoke, Virginia
Industry: Baby and children's clothing and gifts
Web Site: www.oneofakindkid.com

Shell Miller
Owner, Picture Sticks
Location: Bensalem, Pennsylvania
Industry: Heart and balloon-shaped picture frames
Web Site: www.picturesticks.com

Ron Mis
President, Galeton Gloves
Location: Raynham, Massachusetts
Industry: Work gloves
Web Site: www.gloves.net

Christopher M. Mott
President, Mott's Miniatures Inc.
Location: Buena Park, California
Industry: Miniatures and dollhouses
Web Site: www.mottsminis.com

Diane Morgan
Sole Proprietor, Morgan Mailboxes & More
Location: Tewksbury, Massachusetts
Industry: Hand-painted mailboxes
Web Site: www.dianemorgan.com

Sherry Peterson
Vice-President, Main St. Toys
Location: Lindsborg, Kansas
Industry: Toys
Web Site: www.mainsttoys.com

Ray Ritchey
Founder, Childbook.com
Location: Rowland Heights, California
Industry: Chinese children's books/videos/music/software
Web Site: www.childbook.com

Sue Schwartz
Owner, YarnXpress.com
Location: West Milford, New Jersey
Industry: Yarns
Web Site: www.yarnxpress.com

Rob Snell
President, ystore.com
Location: Starkville, Massachusetts
Industry: Web site development for Yahoo! Stores
Web Site: www.ystore.com

Deb Steinberg
President, Nickers & Neighs, Inc.
Location: Whitesboro, Texas
Industry: Horse-related merchandise
Web Site: www.nickers.com

Rhonda Wells
Director of E-commerce, Payless ShoeSource
Location: Topeka, Kansas
Industry: Shoes
Web Site: www.payless.com

Doug Young
President and Founder, Noggintops.com, Ltd.
Location: Congerville, Illinois
Industry: Outdoor hats
Web Site: www.noggintops.com

We asked each panel member to address the following six questions:

1. What are the keys to success when operating an online store?

2. What was the most difficult obstacle or challenge that you faced when you created your online store?

3. What lessons have you learned as a result of setting up your Internet business?

4. What key piece(s) of advice would you offer someone who is thinking of setting up an online store?

5. What is the best feature you've built into your online store?

6. Has your venture into online retailing met your expectations?

In the pages that follow, we present a selection of their responses, organized in a way that highlights important themes and lessons learned. Whether you're already selling online or just beginning the process of setting up an online storefront, the over one hundred tips and pearls of wisdom presented in this chapter will help you build a more successful online business.

QUESTION 1: IN YOUR OPINION, WHAT ARE THE KEYS TO SUCCESS WHEN OPERATING AN ONLINE STORE?

Treat Your Home Page Like Your Front Yard

Diane Morgan, Morgan Mailboxes & More

The most important element of an online store is the Web site itself. This is the first impression that a customer gets when they come to your store. I think of my home page as my front yard. I want it to appear welcoming to the people riding by... I don't want flashing banners, jumping frogs, advertising, music, etc. to clutter up my front yard. The home page should be quick to load, neat, clean, and easy to navigate so the person will open your door and come in to visit.

Hire an Expert

Sherry Peterson, Main St. Toys

Unless you are very knowledgeable about computers and the technical aspects of Web sites and their design, hire someone who is. We feel that it is a necessity to work with someone who is excited about our store and the merchandise we sell, and who is easy to work with. Our technical consultant designed our Web site for us and did all the technical aspects of getting our site up and running. We also receive a lot of e-mails from companies wanting us to subscribe to various services which they provide for a fee. We forward all of those to our consultant and he tells us which ones we should consider, based on his knowledge and expertise. When we were first getting our Web site set up, there were things that we thought we would like to do but we had no idea how to do. That's where a good technical person is a must. He is gradually teaching us how to do changes and additions to our catalog ourselves so that we will eventually become more proficient, but we could never had made it happen in the first place without him.

Give Your Customers As Much Information As Possible

Christopher Mott, Mott's Miniatures

The more information you can put on your site, the better off you will be. This includes product information, as well as information about your policies and shipping information. If it takes you two weeks to ship out an order after you get the order, put that on the Web site. Get it out in the open right up front.

Recognize That the Old Rules of Business Still Apply

Doug Young, Noggintops.com

From the beginning, I had a strong belief that e-commerce isn't really a new way of doing business, it is simply a new *medium* for conducting business. In other words, all the old rules for building a successful business still apply. The hype and the technological glitter of the Internet make it tempting to disbelieve that, to instead believe the size and power of the Internet will carry you... but it's a fatal mistake. The Internet is powerful, but it is not magic.

Be Flexible with Your Web Design

Chris Harrower, Choo Choo Barn

Be flexible... if one design doesn't work, try another (and another... we are on our third version of the Web site right now, and I'm working on some changes once again). Ask questions of your customers. What do they like (or, more importantly, what didn't they like about your site)? What would they like to see? What would make their shopping experience better (easier, quicker)? And ask questions of other business associates, both locally and across the Net. There is even a mailing list called I-Help/Webreview that allows others to comment on your design, and offer their insights into prospective improvements... join it and use it!

[You can join the mailing list by visiting www. audettemedia.com/subscribe.html and selecting I-HelpDesk.]

Have a "Professional" Web Site Design

Bodega Bob Homme, The Submarine Store

If a business is going to be a serious player on the Web, the site must be professionally done. The days of cutesy, schlocky, or homespun Web sites are long gone, at least in the business arena. We invested about $16,000 in the initial site development and, believe me, it was worth every nickel! A professionally done site engenders trust and security among its visitors. We've added about $3,000 or $4,000 of improvements and additional development since its launch. Hey, the Web site is our workhorse! We have never, and will never, sacrifice quality for cost in its development nor will we complain about the money we put into it.

The visitors to an online store cannot touch the products, can't speak directly with a retail representative, and in many cases can only verify a business's credibility or validate its performance after a purchase has been made. Our investment in a site design that not only stimulates purchase (note that it's an all-American red, white, and blue – our market tends to be very patriotic as you might guess) but incorporates elements that engender trust in our visitors – posted privacy statement, security and data handling information, satisfaction/return policy, detailed contact information, testimonials from customers – all elements that help a site visitor get a better feel for the company behind the Web site. The result is a greater sense, on the part of the visitor, that we are a company that they would be secure doing business with, would want to do business with, and that we would meet their expectations of performance.

e-Fact

80% of Internet users agree that their purchasing decisions are strongly influenced by the ability to buy from known, trusted retailers and to buy known, trusted brand names.

Source:
PricewaterhouseCoopers
(www.pwc.global.com)

Deb Steinberg, Nickers & Neighs

Build a clear, easy-to-navigate Web site design that lets visitors know up front what your business is all about. Include links to inform them about the ownership of your business, your privacy policy, and shipping rates, but don't clutter up your front page with that... not everyone cares about the details.

Shell Miller, Picture Sticks

It is imperative that an online shop being built for your business look professional, but also be friendly and easy to navigate. The fact is, over the Internet, your potential market does not have the opportunity to meet you personally, therefore their first impression of your online store is the only chance you have of presenting yourself and your product(s). If your store is not presented in a professional, yet friendly, manner, those shoppers will move on to the next available online store.

Find Good Employees

Jason Friedman, J&R Music and Computer World

Hire the appropriate staff to support your technical, creative, and marketing visions. The applicant who demands the highest salary isn't necessarily the right fit for your type of business.

Remember That Customers Come First

Rhonda Wells, Payless ShoeSource

The real key to success is to always keep your customers' satisfaction as the first and last question of every decision. This is the only test to setting strategies that will be successful. Internet technology is changing so fast that it is easy to get caught up in the excitement of what is new and to spend lots of money and resources putting together a strategy that your customer might not expect or value.

Doug Young, Noggintops.com

"It's the customer, stupid." The long-term survival of your business is directly tied to your ability to completely satisfy your customers. No amount of marketing genius, financial savvy, or technical wizardry will save you from the growing Dot-Com Hall of Flame if you can't keep customers coming back... and bringing their friends.

Think about it, people who are shopping on the Web are some of the most communication-savvy, interconnected people in history. They fire off dozens of e-mails daily to coworkers and friends. They may receive twice as many. They visit chat rooms. They put comments on news group bulletin boards, which are in turn read by hundreds, maybe thousands, of people around the world. An inability to deliver excellence in goods and services will not be hidden for long. Please note this doesn't just refer to quality products delivered with a cheery "Thank You!" on the invoice. It extends to your ability to ship in a timely manner, your treatment of customer complaints, the quality of assistance you give when asked, and your respect for a customer's privacy.

And – unlike the bricks-and-mortar place that may get away with lapses in service because it's the only one of its kind on the block – your online store will be painfully easy to ignore, even easier to forget. Worse yet, your competitors will be literally just a mouse click away.

Deb Steinberg, Nickers & Neighs

Offer extraordinary customer service – answer e-mail immediately, ship within hours, not days of order. I believe that one of the main keys to success in any business is not to meet your customer's expectations, but to exceed them.

Every customer is special, and should feel that their business is important to you. If an item is out of stock, e-mail or phone the customer immediately, and let them make the decision to ship and back order, hold and ship complete, or cancel the item completely.

Sherry Peterson, Main St. Toys

We offer exceptional customer service. We feel that just because a person is shopping over the Internet, it doesn't mean that they don't want prompt, friendly, personal service. We offer free gift-wrapping, personalize enclosure cards to include if the purchase is for a gift, and do everything we can to make sure their shopping experience with us is a good one.

> **e-Fact**
>
> *By making customer service a priority, e-tailers can salvage at least 7.8% of abandoned online orders.*
>
> Source: Datamonitor
> (www.datamonitor.com)

Last Christmas we had a customer call from New York City (we are in a small town in central Kansas), and she wanted to order some toys for her niece's children. Her niece lives in a small town about fifteen miles from us and had given her aunt our toll-free phone number, along with a list of some toys that her children would like for Christmas. After discussing the toys and picking out about three toys for each of four children, the customer said, "Now, how much will it cost me to have them shipped to my niece?" I told her that my husband just happened to be going to that town that same afternoon, and he could gift wrap them and deliver them to her niece's home, at no charge. She was delighted and I will bet that she will call us again this Christmas. That's shopping on the Internet but with the addition of personal service. Good customer service is not that hard to do. It is offering your merchandise at a fair price, treating the customer like you would want to be treated, and giving them better service than they ever expected.

We also think it is important also to make sure that all of us in the store know what is going on with customers who might be calling back about an order or a question, so that if the same person who helped them the first time isn't available, they don't have to start explaining from square one again. That is frustrating to me as a customer and I'm sure it is to others as well. We are a small store so we don't have so many employees to keep informed as larger companies do.

Kevin Gorman, WebCyclery

In order to succeed with an online store, there has to be a reason for people to buy from you rather than your competition. There has to be some sort of value added to the product. In most cases, that "value-add" is going to be customer service. Online customer service is different from in brick-and-mortar stores, in that you rarely get any face-to-face contact. People like to know that their order is being taken care of by a real person. Responding quickly to e-mails and phone calls is an easy way of gaining trust, which helps convert visitors into customers. Confirmation e-mails and updates on back orders also helps. Great customer service also helps with word-of-mouth advertising, while poor customer service can destroy you.

Chris Harrower, Choo Choo Barn

It's not that much different from running a physical store... the customer is the reason you are in business. Customer service is primary. The site must be designed so they can find what they are looking for quickly and easily, but also designed so the casual browser can locate something of interest quickly and easily.

Richard Flynn, Red Trumpet

Remember that your site is a customer-service addition, not a substitute. Make it easy for people to get in touch with you, and help them in every way you can. Why? Because customers who are frustrated still want to hear a human voice that is both knowledgeable and reassuring, and the best Web site in the world can't accomplish that. We've had customers return merchandise for reasons we consider absolutely ludicrous, or ask questions that could earn them warm bunks at the nearest state facilities. But they're our customers, and after we've pulled our hair out in the privacy of the office, we'll almost always call them – yes, by telephone – and do anything reasonable to satisfy them.

Allow Real-Time Credit Card Transactions

Bodega Bob Homme, The Submarine Store

Our ability to execute instant transactions has been instrumental to our commercial success. If a business believes that it can survive on phone and "print this form and fax it" orders from the Web, it is sadly mistaken. We realized, when we did our initial market research, that our two primary competitors were thriving in spite of no online transactional ability. I believe that as soon as we went live with our Web site, many of our competitors' *shoppers* became our *customers* simply because we made it comfortable, easy, and secure for them to purchase *at the moment their purchase decision was made!* Clearly, I can't quantify that but the anecdotal evidence gleaned from the customer feedback we received immediately after taking the store live, and to some degree even still, identifies the ability to execute online transactions from our site as a significant reason for purchasing from The Submarine Store.

Kevin Gorman, WebCyclery

To be taken seriously, an online store also needs to accept credit cards. Making people send a check to a post office box is a big mistake.

Provide Answers to Frequently Asked Questions

Christopher Mott, Mott's Miniatures

Product knowledge is king. We sell product because we know the product. We can answer questions about it and keep the answers to the questions on our site. Every time someone asks us a question about a particular product, we take the answer and put it on the Web site in the hopes of keeping someone from calling in with that question again.

Know When to Apologize

Deb Steinberg, Nickers & Neighs

Know when to say, "I'm sorry, we screwed up. What can we do to make it up to you?" And if an apology is in order, it is much better to do it by phone, if possible. Keep some small items on hand to send as free gifts when you have not met your customers' expectations of service.

Stick to a Business You Know

Christopher Mott, Mott's Miniatures

Don't jump into an e-business because it sounds fun or sounds profitable. It should be something that you understand, are familiar with, or have some experience or expertise in. If you could not see yourself getting a job as a manager in a similar "real" business, don't go in to that "e-business."

Effective Marketing

Doug Young, Noggintops.com

Don't wait to be found... Get found! Some people have the impression that the mere possession of an online store means that their products will be exposed to millions of consumers. In truth, your products will be accessible to millions of consumers, but that in itself has very little bearing on the number of consumers who actually see your product. I have heard the old "needle in a haystack" cliché applied here, but "needle in a needle stack" would be more accurate. Make that a needle in a mountain-sized needle stack. Your online store will just be one invisible electronic blip among millions of other electronic blips. Waiting for people to somehow stumble across your quaint little "back-street" e-shop will leave you dismally disappointed... and broke. You should have a plan for how you are going to market your e-store before you take it online.

Diane Morgan, Morgan Mailboxes & More

Once you have a site up and running, you need to promote, promote, and promote again. This should become part of your normal business tasks. I have joined thirty-five online craft malls that list my products or link back to my site. Not only does this increase my sales potential but it broadens my visibility. The more I put my name and my URL out there the more chances I have that new eyes will see it. Many sites have a links page – take the time to go to those links and post your information on them. Join digest groups, network groups, and organizations that are related to your business. Create a signature for your e-mail messages that includes your name and links to your Web site so every time you e-mail anyone, you've given yourself a free plug by including your Web address. All these steps are developing and building your network.

Bodega Bob Homme, The Submarine Store

Effective marketing has, perhaps, been the single most significant contributor to our success. And, in fact, it can be argued that the application of The Submarine Store's 100%

Satisfaction Guarantee is as much a marketing strategy as it is a customer service strategy. We employ aggressive marketing strategies in a combination of venues, both electronic and traditional. Our electronic newsletter is an excellent advertising and promotional tool and clearly the one with the most immediate and significant effect. Our affiliate program is also quite significant. This program has been very successful in generating business from a variety of different types of Web sites but primarily those associated in some way or another with the submarine community. We have several affiliates who aggressively promote their association with us. This results in an identifiable impact on our revenue as well as significant commission payouts to our affiliates. A significant portion of our visitor traffic is generated from the various search engines. We continuously monitor our placement among the big eight, adjusting our pages and resubmitting as necessary to ensure good placements. In addition, we closely monitor our server logs to detect any significant changes in search engine–generated traffic, either by source (which engine) or the keywords that are bringing visitors to our site.

On the traditional side, we are active in the submarine community with donations of money and merchandise for resale or auction to charities, associations, restoration projects, and museums. (Hey, even the Smithsonian has some of our products on display!) We place print ads in a variety of publications including reunion programs and veteran association directories. We currently have on the planning table for next year billboards at targeted naval bases, an expansion of our presence in targeted glossy magazines and periodicals, and our first incursion into the realm of broadcast media.

Ron Mis, Galeton Gloves

I believe a key driver of success in operating an online store is driving qualified traffic to the site. If the company has an established customer base, and is offering them online purchasing as a new channel, the customers are known and an analysis can be completed of the cost and benefit of driving existing customers to the Web site. But what about new customers? Hoping that high search engine rankings can be achieved and maintained, and that potential new customers will search for and find the company's products is not a great strategy. Traditional and electronic media will most likely be needed to promote the online store and drive qualified leads to view the company's online offering. The economics of using these promotional tools will vary dramatically for startup and established companies. Established businesses already using print and other media to promote their products will likely find the incremental cost of driving sales leads to their Web site to be small and easily justified. Startups will face a much greater challenge, having to allocate the entire cost of their promotion to their initially low online order rates.

Kevin Gorman, WebCyclery

Anyone can have a great site, but the idea of "build it and they will come" no longer holds true. Finding potential customers is a time-consuming and costly process. This includes online marketing, such as getting links from related sites and manufacturers, search engine optimization, and participating in newsgroups, as well as traditional types of marketing, such as print advertising, sending out press releases, and word of mouth. Having and implementing a well-thought-out marketing strategy is a very big part of running an online store.

Listen to Your Customers

Rhonda Wells, Payless ShoeSource

Online, you can ask for your customers' feedback and they are more than willing to give you their point of view. Learning to ask, listen, and respond to your customers' feedback is critical.

Treat Customers As You Would Want to Be Treated

Richard Flynn, Red Trumpet

This does not mean that you have to give in to every whim or suggestion, but responding to concerns in a fair and professional way helps to maintain their respect and loyalty.

Regularly Update Your Web Site

Deb Steinberg, Nickers & Neighs

Change your front page often (at least monthly) to keep it fresh. Some customers will visit your site several times before they ever purchase anything.

Sell Something People Want

Doug Young, Noggintops.com

Yeah, I know. You're thinking: "Duh!" But that obvious principle seems to be continually overlooked by people who just have faith that the Internet will bring droves of people willing to plunk down a credit card for a squirrel-powered blender. Now, granted, the Internet may be the greatest medium around for selling those hard-to-find or niche items (hats, in some ways, being among them), but "hard-to-find" does imply that someone is already looking for it, and "niche" implies that there is a sizable segment of people who will be interested in it. If you don't have firm (and reasonably objective) reasons for believing you will be able to find enough people who will buy your product *in enough quantity to sustain your business*, you shouldn't do it.

Don't Get Carried Away with Bells and Whistles

Rhonda Wells, Payless ShoeSource

When we first brought the site up, other online retailers that were a few years ahead of us were putting together new technologies and gimmicks like "dress-up dolls" and "instant chat," among others. Originally, I was very concerned that our site would launch without all the bells and whistles customers would expect, based on our benchmarking research of other significant retail sites. Regardless of this concern, payless.com launched as a very simple site with navigation that resembled our shopping experience in our stores (shop by gender and size, only show the customer what we have available to sell and ship that day, etc.). As we began planning for future enhancements and modifications to the site, we performed our benchmark analysis of other leading retail sites again. We quickly discovered that what was important on these sites just a few months earlier was no longer important enough to be called out on their home page. We found that content like "dress-up dolls" was now buried several layers down in their sites.

It is clear that new technology is exciting, but it may not be required on your site until after it has proved itself as a useful shopping tool for the customer and a profitable way to drive sales. The only way to know if the new technology is important to your customer is to first be intimate with your customer, versus intimate with technology and your site.

Christopher Mott, Mott's Miniatures

I hate going to a Web site only to be bombarded with banners and buttons for advertisers. Resist the temptation to "junk up" your Web site with this stuff. Keep your graphics and your colors simple. Some sites are really loaded down with high-resolution pictures, moving banners and other images just because more people now have higher-speed modems, DSL and cable connections. Just because you can do something does not mean that you should.

Chris Harrower, Choo Choo Barn

Don't be snowed by all the bells and whistles... if that Flash animation slows things down for your prospective customer, or that panoramic image of your store takes fifteen minutes to download, they won't wait, and they won't be back! Want a bulletin board, chat room, guest book, video clips, etc? Great... but they are secondary (if not tertiary) in importance to service for the customer.

Don't Try to Be Everything to Everybody

Rob Snell, ystore.com

One thing I learned very early on is that what works in my retail stores does not work the same on the Web. In my retail stores we carry a little bit of everything. We're in rural Mississippi. People expect us to be more like the general store of pet supplies, or pop culture, or role-playing games. On the Web, we've done better by focusing on doing a whole lot of one thing rather than being something for everyone.

Build Credibility

Kevin Gorman, WebCyclery

Once you have people coming to your site, you have to be able to convert them into customers. In order to increase your conversion rate, you need to have a site that instills confidence and trust. People are afraid of being cheated, especially since the transaction isn't face to face. Creating a feeling of trust can be difficult. It might be as simple as having your name and business address listed on your site, or it might be as complex as showing credentials, certifications, and awards from entities such as the Better Business Bureau, Gomez.com, or BizRate.com. An "About Us" page seems to help too. People like to feel that they are dealing with a real person, and not just a number on an order.

Have Clear Product Images and Descriptions

Deb Steinberg, Nickers & Neighs

Products should be photographed clearly, and thorough descriptions written including measurements or size equivalents so customers can order your merchandise with confidence. Use a graphic compression service like GIF Wizard (www.gifwizard.com) to shrink graphics to a quick-loading size.

Bonnie Clewans, The Bead Gallery

Make sure the colors don't detract from the product. Some sites are so busy or dark that it is difficult to see the products they are selling.

Answer E-mail Messages Promptly

Sherry Peterson, Main St. Toys

Answer e-mail questions from customers immediately upon receipt. As a customer, I would want to buy from someone who got back with me in a timely manner, and I know that our customers feel the same way. Many times we get two or three e-mails from a customer with various questions before they finally decide on an item and make a purchase. We continually get e-mail responses that say "thanks for your prompt reply." We have decided that some Internet shoppers probably e-mail several businesses with a question, but only hear back from a few. We e-mail the customer back, even if it is to say, "no, we don't have that item, but you might try..." and we give them phone numbers or Web sites of other businesses that might be able to help them. We feel that if we help them find what they are wanting, even if it is another store, they might remember us and try us next time they are shopping for a toy.

Building Customer Loyalty

Sue Schwartz, YarnXpress.com

One of the contributors to YarnXpress's success is the interactive components of the site. It is important to build a site that brings the customers back. All things being equal, one needs to create an environment that piques the customers' curiosity and invites frequent visits. How one does this is as unique as the online shop.

Spend Your Advertising Dollars Wisely

Doug Young, Noggintops.com

The majority of the world's population does not care about your product. Ouch. That's a painful one, but you will be better off if you can come to terms with the truth of it. You are going to have to spend considerable resources – whether time or money – promoting your online store. No matter what you are selling, there are going to be people – a lot of them – who just are not going to buy. Good business sense dictates that every dollar you spend on advertising should bring a return in sales. Therefore, do not waste your money advertising to people who will not buy. Focus in on a segment of people who are likely to buy, then zoom in even further on the segment that is most likely to buy... and buy, and buy. If you have an online sewing supply store, for example, you will get far more advertising bang for your buck by spending a few thousand dollars putting ads in a dozen sewing magazines than you would spending millions on a TV commercial during the Super Bowl.

Focus Your Product Line

Doug Young, Noggintops.com

This is important both at startup and when you begin to grow. As an example, let's say you want to sell books online. You're all revved up and ready to show Amazon.com and Barnes & Noble what's what, so you begin assembling an inventory of titles from *Aardvarks for Fun and Profit* to *Zen Buddhism for Dummies*. Very quickly you discover that there are an awful lot of book categories, so you decide to spend your inventory budget to stock four or five titles in each category. Predictably, your first prospective customer is disgusted to find you have only five mystery novels to choose from. Your second prospective customer is disappointed to find such a poor selection of self-help books. You get the picture. A far better strategy would be to focus on one specific type of book – preferably a type the well-established heavy hitters have been neglecting – and make yourself the best at that.

There are two very significant advantages to this. First, it enables you to gain an essential toehold in the market by setting you apart from competitors who already have the advantage of name recognition, market share, huge inventories, etc. You've got a fighting chance if you can get people thinking and saying, "Yep, they're small, but they've got the best selection of classic mystery novels anywhere, by golly." Second, it allows you to focus your advertising dollars on a narrower market. Look around and you can find a magazine, newsletter, and organization for most any area of interest. And if those exist, you can bet there are dozens of Web sites devoted to it, too. Put your advertising dollars in those places and you will have a more cost-effective ad campaign than the "do-it-all" stores who have to advertise everywhere. This also makes it easier for you to develop advertising content because you'll need to speak to only one area of interest, rather than many. An often overlooked bonus of this niche marketing approach is that people with similar interests tend to hang out together and communicate a lot. Your potential for free word-of-mouth advertising is maximized... and nothing, but nothing, beats good old word of mouth.

Don't Accept Orders for Items You Don't Have in Stock

Sherry Peterson, Main St. Toys

We don't take an order on our Web site unless the item is in stock. We just feel that it is too risky to accept an order when the merchandise isn't sitting in our warehouse. On our Web site it says, "Oops, this item is temporarily out of stock. Please call us at our store for availability," and then lists our toll-free number. When they call us we can tell them when the item is expected in and we take their name and phone number or e-mail address and notify them when the item is back in stock. That is the simplest way for us to handle the situation at this time. It's easier than taking the order and charging their credit card for the item, and then having to issue a credit, in case the manufacturer can't get the merchandise to us for some reason.

Provide Useful Information on Your Web Site

Doug Young, Noggintops.com

These days, the launching of a new Web site will be greeted with roughly the same amount of fanfare as an announcement that your business has acquired a new electric pencil sharpener. The fact that you have a Web site isn't going to impress anyone (except maybe your mother). By now the average Internet shopper has seen and forgotten hundreds of Web sites. With that in mind, be very aware that people will be very unforgiving of Web sites that are uninformative. Many people like Internet shopping because it is easier to comparison shop. Web shoppers tend to be more information-oriented, they want to know the details. They're not just looking for the lowest prices, they're looking for value, and decisions about value demand information. A Web site that is nothing more than an electronic brochure replete with teaser lines and vague product descriptions will not be taken seriously. Server space is cheap, and there's no excuse for not providing all the information a customer could possibly want. Now, that doesn't mean you have to cram the full ingredients list of your vegetarian puppy snacks right on the home page. The beauty of a Web site is that you can structure information in an almost infinite number of layers, allowing the customer to dig as deeply he or she wants. Every time you get a question from a customer, you ought to think about how you can put that information on the Web site. This is very important. I may be a neophyte e-merchant, but I am a veteran Web shopper. If I spend twenty minutes on a search engine looking for a product only to arrive at an anemic Web site that doesn't tell me what I need to know, I'm moving on.

Have a Toll-Free Number

Sherry Peterson, Main St. Toys

I think having a toll-free number helps our business. I know if I had a choice of calling two businesses who might have the same item, if one had a toll-free number and the other one didn't, I'd call the toll-free number first! Several of our suppliers give our toll-free numbers to people who call them asking for retailers also, which is a big help to us. Some of our suppliers also have Web sites where they will have a list of retailers' Web sites and phone numbers, so our toll-free number is listed there too.

Find a Good Web Developer/Designer

Ray Ritchey, Childbook.com

It was important to get the software done for my custom Web site at a fair price. It was a tradeoff between quality, price, and time. It's so easy to get a Web site that does not accomplish what you want it to do. Lots of designers love graphics, which gets out of control. Or technical people who ignore the customer needs. It required a lot of interviewing to find somebody I trusted both to do a good job on the Web site, as well as the credit card processing.

QUESTION 2: WHAT WAS THE MOST DIFFICULT OBSTACLE OR CHALLENGE THAT YOU FACED WHEN YOU CREATED YOUR ONLINE STORE?

Building Credibility

Doug Young, Noggintops.com

I think the single greatest challenge that a new online store faces is building credibility. This has always been the case, but it is perhaps even more true given the recent media storm of dot-com failures and Internet scams. Suppliers will be hesitant to extend lines of credit, and sometimes reluctant to supply you at all. It's a hassle and a risk to get involved with a business that's going to go down in flames in six months. Customers will be cautious (if not outright suspicious) at first, especially if you are a new name. They're wondering if you'll deliver the product in a reasonable time, if it will be what you say it is, and if they'll be treated fairly if there's a problem with the product. If it's a product that the customer is unfamiliar with, they'll be wondering if you really know anything about it yourself. The only solution for that is time or, I should say, time filled with your doing a bang-up job. Show that you can move the supplier's product and pay your bills and you will have all the credibility you need. Customers are a little harder to convince, and you should work harder at convincing them. Before you take your store online, make sure your business is ready to deliver products and customer service that will leave them saying "Wow!" or, if they're not the effusive type, "Yes, that was a most satisfying shopping experience and I would not hesitate to repeat it."

Managing Growth

Bodega Bob Homme, The Submarine Store

Our few-thousand-dollar initial investment for startup was commensurate with our expectations for the size of business we thought we would be operating. Then suddenly, BANG, we're getting overwhelmed by sales volume, opportunities to bring new products to market, expectations from the submarine community for our participation in charitable events, and a hundred other money-burning situations. I mean hey, the success was our own fault and, in hindsight, we should have anticipated it. We did the right things, good site, good products, good rollout marketing, good business processes, and frankly we expected to be successful. However, not as quickly as we were. The *rate* of growth was way beyond anything we could have projected. It came right out of the sun and we had to adapt and overcome quickly before it buried us.

Finally, our capacity and cash flow have caught up with the demands of the business volume. If I had it to do over again, though, I'd come in with a bigger cash reserve and possibly some pipeline to additional capital. Sometimes in the first few months Harry and I felt like that plate-spinning guy who used to appear on the Ed Sullivan show and keep about three dozen plates spinning all at once!

Integrating the Web Site with the Retail Store

Chris Harrower, Choo Choo Barn

Our most difficult challenge remains the same today as it was last year, when the site went online: it's trying to interface our online store presence with our retail point-of-sale software. Due to an incredibly steep learning curve for our employees, we have been utilizing an older, DOS-based POS system (only now being upgraded to Windows). It required that everything on the site be created by hand, and there is no connection between physical inventory and online stock status, except for a manual system on a daily basis. It remains our number-one obstacle, and requires, during busy seasons, several employees working on a daily basis to keep the site current.

Choosing a Web Designer

Deb Steinberg, Nickers & Neighs

It was hard wading through the presentations of Web designers, with quotes of $8,000 to $55,000, and separating the wheat from the chaff. We knew up front what features we wanted on our site, but at that time, there wasn't the plethora of e-commerce solution companies available [as there are today], and costs were higher.

Building the Web Site

Shell Miller, Picture Sticks

Building the site to my specifications was the most complicated challenge I faced. I found many hosts out there that provide Web site services. Almost all of them provide templates you can use to simply throw a Web site together. Unless you want to have a site that looks thrown together, some knowledge of the Internet languages is required. The difficult part was learning how to create the desired look. You need to put a lot of time, energy, and thought into how you want your site to look, and then focus on getting those desired results. I learned a little more than what was provided by the templates to fine-tune my site and give it the look that I wanted. I don't think you will need a masters in the Internet languages – for me it was more like a crash course. This research and knowledge is definitely required to build a site that will be viewed as a professional place to shop.

e-Fact

Approximately 5% of the world's adult population (14 and older) are active Internet users.

Source: eMarketer
(www.emarketer.com)

Becoming Computer Literate

Tane Chan, The Wok Shop

I didn't know anything about computers (and I still don't) – I was intimidated by them. I didn't even know how to turn one on. Since I am computer illiterate and work full-time in my own brick-and-mortar store, an online store seemed impossible and very remote. I had absolutely no knowledge of computers, didn't even own one, didn't even want to learn to e-mail my children away at college because I was intimidated. My son, Mark, is the reason my business went online. He started the whole online business from registering our name, www.wokshop.com, to being the Webmaster and doing all the technical aspects of the Web site. He hired a graphic designer who, with Mark, photographed all the items with a digital camera. I hired a recent college graduate that knew nothing about my products and instructed her to write the text according to how she would like to read it... and would best describe the product to a customer that is interested in it but does not really know how to use it, or to describe the product in such a way that they should buy it because it is practical, different, necessary, and unusual. In other words, the text should answer her curiosity. My job, emphatically emphasized by my son, was to become computer knowledgeable, otherwise the world would pass me by. He bought me the simplest user-friendly computer, an iMac, and encouraged me to learn on my own... hands-on.

Technical Execution

Ron Mis, Galeton Gloves

I've created more than one store at this point, so the obstacles or challenges have changed. But in the beginning I think it was just comprehending how B2B e-commerce would work. It wasn't really happening yet, and everybody was theorizing all kinds of cool and powerful marketing methods, but the basic methods of how it would work weren't clear to me. What wasn't an obstacle was putting up a site. So I did that, and then accumulated data (from the site and from talking to others involved in e-commerce) to begin putting my own theories together. By the time I got to the second and third sites, I had a better grasp of how I thought B2B e-commerce can function, but the technical issues of creating the site became more challenging. So I guess it's kind of shifted. Today I have a much clearer idea of what I want, and probably a harder time getting it technically executed.

Managing Inventory

Sherry Peterson, Main St. Toys

Our biggest obstacle was not knowing what our volume of business would be. It was hard to know how much inventory to have on hand when we first went online. It's still a challenge, but we are learning how to gauge our ordering process better.

Kim Michaux, One of a Kind Kid.com

After getting started, my biggest challenge has been where to store all the inventory – it has taken over my house! I'm not quite to the point where I feel comfortable renting warehouse space.

Building a Market Presence

Sue Schwartz, YarnXpress.com

It was and still is building a presence in my particular market. I, like the many hundreds of thousands of small businesses, am looking for ways to stand apart from the other similar online vendors. At this point in YarnXpress's evolution, I am beginning the process of creative destruction – taking apart things that could be done better, looking for ways to convey our vision in a more unique mode, and expanding the customer base and inventory. I think, in retrospect, the most important challenge was defining what we were not. Keeping the financial plan firm in the first year was a pivotal key to our growth.

Meeting an Aggressive Timeframe

Rhonda Wells, Payless ShoeSource

Our most difficult challenge was our aggressive timeframe. We had been challenged by our senior management staff to put together a team of partners in late February of 1999 and have our site launched by May 28, 1999. This date was important as it was the date of our Board of Directors' meeting and we wanted the Board of Directors to be our first customers. This gave us only three months to put together a team composed of effectively four sub-teams representing all areas of the business: (1) a business team (marketing, merchandising, fulfillment, customer service, financial planning, legal, etc.); (2) an internal information systems team to build all the interfaces to the legacy systems and ensure we launched fully integrated; (3) a technology team (IBM Global Services) to install and develop the site on the IBM Net.Commerce engine; and (4) a design team (Organic) to design the look and feel of the site along with the navigation and functional design.

Realizing That Success Won't Come Overnight

Deb Steinberg, Nickers & Neighs

We built our online store in 1997 and went "live" in early 1998. At that time, dot-com ads were still a rarity, and the Web wasn't yet a part of everyday life. I certainly didn't realize that the old adage "it takes three to five years to build a business" would apply to my new nifty-swifty Web business!

Finding the Right Software Package

Jason Friedman, J&R Music and Computer World

The most difficult obstacle is finding the right software package, that can really do what the salespeople say it can do. Everything looks great in a demo. It takes weeks, if not months, to first research who all the players are in your market niche (this was an even harder challenge four years ago when the Web was less categorized than it is today), then call them all in for demos, then take it upon yourself to write out apples to apples comparisons of how each vendor hit the core topics that concern you. The fun isn't over there. Then there's price and negotiating mutually profitable partnerships. This whole process is tedious and frustrating, and before you think you have it nailed, your top-choice vendor goes out of business or is bought by one of your competitors.

Constantly Outgrowing Our Online Store Technology

Christopher Mott, Mott's Miniatures

I have gone through about five different programs to build and design my site and the online catalog. The current application, number five, is not even a year old and I have been looking to replace it for two months. I realized that it would not meet our needs for longer than eighteen months about seven months after I bought it.... The small startup company will probably have to design, and redesign, and redesign their site several times. These are growing pains. The pain subsides but the time and money they consume are real. There are a lot of inexpensive ways to get started with online selling. You can rent stores from Yahoo!, Amazon and others. That is fine for small operations. But keep your eye on the future. As you start to grow, a small portal that limits you to a few hundred items can eventually hurt you. You outgrow it one day but now you have a large following of customers going to that other portal and no way to bring them forward. You could be stuck running two sites or risk losing part of your customer base.

Working with the Technology

Rhonda Wells, Payless ShoeSource

A significant hurdle for the business team and the internal information systems team was the technology. To ensure that our focus was on the Payless customer, our business team was pulled from the internal core business teams and effectively had no experience with online selling. Our information systems team had the challenge of understanding how our existing legacy systems could merge with the latest e-commerce technologies to develop an online site. I remember having a conversation with our lead information systems partner and she told me that her team had learned ten new [computer] languages in three months (I've lost count of how many new languages they have learned over the last eighteen months). In light of our aggressive plan and our steep learning curve, we are all very proud that [our teams] were able to work together, take ownership and accountability for what had to be done, become a student of the business, and execute.

Marketing

Kevin Gorman, WebCyclery

Marketing was and still is the greatest obstacle. Expending time and money into marketing can be a scary thing. It's hard to quantify results, but without it, there aren't many results at all.

Finding Customers

Diane Morgan, Morgan Mailboxes & More

By far, the most difficult challenge is to find your customer base. You have the Web site, you've done the promotion, but you still need more traffic. I sat down, really analyzed my product, and asked myself some very important questions. Who is my customer, where is my customer, and how do I reach that customer? This holds true for offline marketing strategies, as well. For an example, I thought a whole new customer base for my hand-painted mailboxes might be the real estate industry. I spent two weeks hoofing to real estates agencies in my local area and also contacted online brokers, and I carved another new niche for my product. The brokers give a mailbox to their clients as a housewarming gift and this has proved to be quite successful. The worst thing that can happen is they might say no, but you'll never know if you don't attempt it.

Achieving Synergy between the Web Site and Our Brick-and-Mortar Stores

Rhonda Wells, Payless ShoeSource

I had only been given two rules when I was assigned the job of putting together an Internet presence for Payless ShoeSource: (1) build on our core competencies, don't build a site that is uniquely different from our business today; and (2) do not jeopardize the core business. Our teams have stayed very focused on both of these goals throughout the continued development of the site. Our initiative, immediately after launch, was to build synergy with our 26,000 store associates. I went on the road for six weeks and met with our store operations partners across the United States to share the site with them, answer any questions about the site or the Internet they had, and train them on the site functionality. Today, our store associates will tell you that the online store is the biggest customer satisfaction tool Payless ShoeSource has given them in the last several years. The online store carries all current product in all available sizes. Our inventory position allows the store associate to meet out-of-stock or out-of-season customer requests online. Achieving the goal of customer satisfaction and associate satisfaction was a significant challenge and one Payless.com and Payless ShoeSource did extraordinarily well. Our customer is never asked to choose between the online store and the brick-and-mortar store. We sell our site in our stores and our stores on our site.

Time Management

Kim Michaux, One of a Kind Kid.com

This is truly a full-time business – the advantage to being online is that your hours are flexible. The disadvantage is that you feel like you're always working and just squeezing in your family sometimes!

QUESTION 3: WHAT LESSONS HAVE YOU LEARNED AS A RESULT OF SETTING UP YOUR INTERNET BUSINESS?

The Old Rules of Marketing Still Apply

Ron Mis, Galeton Gloves

E-commerce is still governed by the same rules of marketing that apply in offline channels. So don't think that you can get away from all of the marketing issues (e.g., who is your target market, what are their purchasing criteria, how do you identify and contact them, how does your offer compare to competing offers, etc.) just because you're selling online.

Customers Often Have Unrealistic Expectations

Christopher Mott, Mott's Miniatures

Big companies like Amazon.com are changing the face of mail order. It used to be that when you ordered a product from a mail order catalog, you sent your order in and six to eight weeks later it would arrive. Now giants like Amazon.com have spoiled people. My wife can place an order for a book on Tuesday morning and the damned thing will arrive in the mail on Wednesday or Thursday. And now everyone thinks that all Internet companies have huge warehouses, with twenty-four-hour staffs, and get orders whipped out within seconds of placing their order. I have had people call me on Monday morning telling me that they placed an order at 10 p.m. on Saturday and requested next-day air, and their package was not delivered on Sunday. What do you say to someone like that? How do you answer them without laughing? I think some folks watched too many Road Runner cartoons where the Coyote would drop an order in the mailbox and two seconds later an Acme delivery truck would pull up alongside the road. People really have some misguided expectations of e-commerce. Be aware of it and be prepared to deal with it.

It Costs More and Takes Longer Than You Think It Will

Kim Michaux, One of a Kind Kid.com

There are so many expenses I didn't expect. Like warehouse expense, a faster Internet connection (when you are on most of the day, speed is essential!), and part-time help. Be prepared for unexpected expenses. Like warehousing, software to track inventory, etc., camera to photograph merchandise, shelving or racks for your inventory. It also takes more time than you think it will. There is far more to operating a business than simply photographing items and putting them online. Promoting your site takes days and it is never-ending. People won't even know you exist if you don't promote.

Have a Business Plan

Kevin Gorman, WebCyclery

One of the lessons that I learned is, as with any type of business, that having a business plan is crucial. Without having a business plan, going down a wrong path becomes very easy. As wrong as projections and assumptions may be, having a plan keeps you on track at the very least.

Senior Management Support Is Crucial

Rhonda Wells, Payless ShoeSource

Senior management support is absolutely critical. There is no way to really understand the hurdles in an environment that is new and unknown. We had strong, educated points of view, but no means to provide statistical data to support these. If you try to develop a site with "Monday morning quarterbacks," it will not work. The teams will not be dedicated because the company is not dedicated. It is truly an example of "the shadow of the leader" theory. I've heard many horror stories about lack of senior management support. In the case of Payless ShoeSource, this was never a problem.

Keep Total Control of Your Web Site Development

Jason Friedman, J&R Music and Computer World

Outsourcing is frustrating and expensive. The programmers translating your business into computer code on the other side of town, or sometimes the other part of the world, are usually not more talented than someone you can (and should) hire yourself. Plus, they inevitably (somewhere around 98 percent of the time) code the processes incorrectly, but close enough to the spec so that you still have to pay them twice to fix it.

Invest in Building Business Capacity *Before* You Need It

Bodega Bob Homme, The Submarine Store

The data management, transactional infrastructure, product acquisition, order fulfillment, and customer service modules for online businesses must be robust and effective, and ours are. Maybe I'd better explain that. What I mean is that each of these components must be well-defined, functional, and scaled correctly for the business. I can't stress enough the value of testing each of these before taking the Web business live! These should be developed with one's initial projections in mind but also, as we learned somewhat painfully at the start, with a margin for growth. We critically analyze the market and the existing capacities of our business. This must be an ongoing process. In our case, we expected to be successful but the magnitude of our success way outstripped even our most optimistic projections. That sent us to battle stations for awhile in a frantic effort to upgrade our business infrastructure to keep up with the rate of growth.

Now, however, we're a little saltier. Before we introduce new products or site features, we take the time to build the capacity of our business first. To be perfectly honest, and many of your readers will be able to identify with this, the enthusiasm of bringing a new product or idea to market tends to generate a momentum of enthusiasm and energy all its own. The tendency is to launch and then address the additional burdens placed on the delivery or administrative infrastructure at some later time. But you have to resist the sense of urgency. Thankfully, we learned this lesson early on with minimal damage!

> **e-Fact**
>
> *33% of online customers expect an e-mail response regarding delivery times within five hours, with the majority expecting it within four.*
>
> Source: Jupiter Research (www.jup.com) and the NPD Group (www.npd.com)

Smaller Is Better

Rob Snell, ystore.com

Not only is it okay for people to know that you're a little guy, it's actually an advantage. People like dealing with the owner of a business, especially when you run a professional operation. If you order from Amazon.com, what are the odds that you'll get a personal note from Jeff Bezos? If you order from our company, you deal with the owners.

Keep It Simple!

Chris Harrower, Choo Choo Barn

We've all heard the "KISS" principle, and it applies in e-commerce more than anywhere else. People don't want to wade through page after page of how great you are, how you are the only, the best, the finest, the fastest, and other superlatives. They want to buy what they came for, and move along! By all means, add your information, but don't be hurt if very few people actually read about how wonderful you are.

You Have to Work Hard to Drive Traffic to Your Web Site

Diane Morgan, Morgan Mailboxes & More

> Just because you built it, doesn't mean that they will come. You have to constantly promote your Web address. Advertise the Web site address everywhere: return address labels, your checking account address, business cards, fliers, ads, product tags, letterhead, e-mail signature, etc. Always carry business cards for distribution.

Make Backups of Your Web Site and Databases

Christopher Mott, Mott's Miniatures

> In June of 1999 the server that my Web site resides on, which was being co-located by my ISP at a national data center, experienced "thermal damage" (it caught on fire). And the wet-behind-the-ears tech at the data center destroyed their only backup of my database. Fortunately I had a copy that was only a few days old. It took a full seven days to get back up and running. The only other backup we had was from several months prior. I shudder at the thought of having to reenter months of inventory updates and site changes.

Ease of Use Is Paramount

Shell Miller, Picture Sticks

> I cannot stress enough that the "ease of use" is the most important factor in the online business. No one will shop in your store if they cannot navigate your site, and the easier you make it to purchase your products determines the success of your online store. We all love the convenience of Internet shopping; the whole "Click here to buy" theory is why online shopping has come as far as it has. I know I will never buy from a site that I cannot navigate, and I never purchase anything online without using my credit card. I can only expect that my potential customers share the same type of opinion.

Success Requires Careful Integration of New Business Models with Old Ones

Rhonda Wells, Payless ShoeSource

To launch a site is really the easy part. The tough part is understanding how the new business model will survive and be cohesive with your current business model. For example, when we started, we had a world-class distribution center. However, it was a distribution center, not a warehouse. We had to learn how to warehouse product to be able to guarantee fulfillment of orders and we had to learn how to pick individual orders versus fill orders that would flow to our over 4,600 stores on a routine basis. It required building new core competencies while leveraging the existing ones. When you're operating within areas like fulfillment and merchandising, where we are considered experts, it is most difficult to remember to challenge "how we've always done it" with "how should it be done for the online store." Building partners across the entire organization is what made us successful in building new processes and core competencies.

Web Site Design Is an Evolving Process

Richard Flynn, Red Trumpet

Be ready and willing to throw away everything you've done and start from scratch. Graphic designers inevitably get tired of looking at work they did months ago; programmers learn and change, and eventually notice that there's a better, faster, and cleaner way of coding everything they coded last year. Just like any software project, your site will have a Release 2.0. Besides keeping your staff happy, a fresh look and new features will keep your customers interested too.

Don't Underestimate the Importance of Word of Mouth

Diane Morgan, Morgan Mailboxes & More

Always remember your customer is the top priority. You have spent a lot of time, money and energy to get that customer to come through your front door. Repeat customers and word of mouth are extremely important to a small business. I want a happy customer who has a pleasant shopping experience with me so they will come back, and tell their friends about my site.

Sherry Peterson, Main St. Toys

Word of mouth is still a good way to increase your volume of business. We got a phone order from a lady in a Colorado. After she placed her order, she asked me where we were located and when I told her Kansas she said, "You're kidding! The person who told me you had this toy and gave me your phone number was in Italy!" She had been in a chat room discussing a certain toy and someone in Italy who had ordered one recommended us.

Michelle Donahue-Arpas, Genius Babies!

We've watched a number of the "big boys" go under. They spent on average hundreds of dollars in marketing for *each* customer who visited their site. They offered products with deep discounts, free shipping, coupons, discounts, etc. We offer fair prices, with *great* customer service – personalized free gift wrapping and handwritten cards... the little things. Our best marketing has all been free... by word of mouth, from our happy customers.

Protect Yourself against Fraud

Bonnie Clewans, The Bead Gallery

Make sure you have a system for verifying addresses and preventing credit card fraud. I was a victim and I learned so much from this one incident. The banks and credit card processors have a lot of small print and basically the merchant winds up footing the bill for the fraud.

Christopher Mott, Mott's Miniatures

Protect yourself by establishing a set of policies for the handling of online transactions, post them on your site, and make sure to link to them from every page of your site and from the checkout pages of your shopping basket. Most of your transactions are going to be credit cards, and credit card companies take care of their cardholders first. So you are in the position of being found guilty and having to prove your innocence when a customer submits a chargeback request to their bank. If you don't know what a chargeback is, just open an online business and you soon will. It is when a credit card customer disputes the charge on their card. And it can be a lot of paperwork. The merchant is at a disadvantage under current laws because the agreement you sign with the bank says that you have to get a signature on the draft. Without that signature you have to prove that you did not charge the customer's card without their authorization. Keep printed records of everything, and get tracking numbers on packages and signatures on deliveries. Have orders called in on an 800 number so you get a record of their call. In some cases your order policies will have to build as you go, learning by circumstances when your policies don't cover a specific instance and then updating your policies to cover it in the future. And establish "Terms of Use" for your site that include the acceptance by your customer of your ordering policies, even if they place their order by means other than the shopping basket.

Complete Technology Solutions Are Few and Far Between

Rhonda Wells, Payless ShoeSource

The infrastructure can make or break your business model. There are no "end-to-end" solutions in this technology. What this means is that you have one piece of software as an engine, another for back-end tracking, another for personalization, another for... We brought up the site on the Net.Commerce engine, which allowed us to bring up a very basic selling site, but we had very limited ability to know and understand the activity on our site. To make this happen, we now have thirteen packages that hang off of this engine. Each one of these packages will upgrade yearly and the integration to the other packages will all create significant jeopardy in the success of the upgrade. This dynamic could mean you would spend your entire information systems resource time upgrading packages versus improving the site to meet customer expectations. Infrastructure and marketing costs are keeping many online initiatives from being able to reach profitability. Today, there are few answers in this area. It is such a widespread and known problem that many vendors are working toward more end-to-end solutions.

E-commerce Requires a Lot of Commitment and Hard Work

Doug Young, Noggintops.com

I am often approached by people wanting to start a little e-store "on the side" for extra income, or as a career that would allow a lot of free time and flexibility. First off, there is no such thing as a Web site that maintains itself, improves itself, and promotes itself. All of those things are an ongoing necessity and require a tremendous amount of time. I can count on one finger the number of weeks I worked less than sixty hours in the past year. A seventy-hour week is common, eighty to ninety not unheard of. Now, I'm not saying that's a good thing or that's how it should be... in fact I'm rather hoping that will change in the near future. The point is starting an online store and nurturing it to self-sufficiency, then profitability, is no walk in the park. Second, a half-hearted online store is usually seen as such by customers, either immediately due to second-rate Web site qualities, or after two or three visits in which nothing on the Web site ever changes, leaving them wondering if there really is anyone "in there."

Deb Steinberg, Nickers & Neighs

The most important lesson I learned is that the Internet is not like the Kevin Costner movie *Field of Dreams* and the quote "If you build it, they will come." Putting a store on the Web is no different from putting it on a street corner! It requires the same amount of nurturing, marketing, advertising, and *time* to grow and succeed.

Sue Schwartz, YarnXpress.com

Owning and operating a business is a very time-consuming task. A company is only as good as the service it provides. There is no such thing as "fast money" and the hours are ridiculously long. One must be prepared to sacrifice much to build a successful online business, or any business for that fact!

Plan Ahead on Everything

Chris Harrower, Choo Choo Barn

Take the time to walk through your entire process, and see where it might break down (because those "might"s will become "will"s once you go live). Have a plan for any eventuality... The Boy Scouts are right: Be Prepared.

Marketing and Technical Staff Need to Respect Each Other's Roles

Jason Friedman, J&R Music and Computer World

Let the technical people do their jobs and the marketing/business development people do theirs. You can't be in worse shape than when you put too much faith in your technical lead, and next thing you know he is negotiating contracts with your vendors. Or vice versa when a business development person starts taking on deals that are technically unfeasible.

Implement a Flexible Search Tool

Richard Flynn, Red Trumpet

One of the best features of any site is a flexible search tool. Go beyond simple word searches to provide searches by field, price range, selection, and anything else you can think of – all while maintaining some order of simplicity. We revamped our search tools after learning that more than 80 percent of our users find their purchases by searching rather than browsing. You need to be flexible enough to listen to people, and then implement changes based on feedback.

Don't Overinvest

Ron Mis, Galeton Gloves

Look at all of the business-to-consumer businesses that have flamed out, many after burning through hundreds of millions of dollars. Incredible! How many companies do that when selling through traditional channels? A smarter course can be to take it slow, do some tests, figure out what works and then increase your spending. Let the other guy go out of business from charging ahead too fast. Use your cash wisely because it's valuable stuff.

Assume Your Customers Are Internet Novices

Doug Young, Noggintops.com

Never assume people entering your online store will be Web-proficient. The Internet is such a fascinating phenomenon, has so many uses, and has caused such a stir that many people who have previously had no need of or interest in computers are wading into it. Your Web site must be excruciatingly easy to navigate. All relevant information must be "hit-you-in-the-face" easy to find. Using my store as an example, one of the most important pieces of information a hat store needs to make available is a size chart. So we put a big old button marked "Sizing Info" on every single page of the Web site. Good enough, right? Nope. Just about every day someone e-mailed to ask for sizing instructions. It got to be so routine that I made up a form e-mail to send in response to the question. Then it finally soaked in. If people have to ask that regularly, it ain't obvious enough. We added a text link that said "Click here to find your size!" in bright red letters directly under each hat. E-mail inquiries about size dropped off immediately. I shudder to think about the number of people who didn't bother to e-mail for instructions and just left in frustration. Find the most novice Internet users — you can to test your Web design... and learn from them.

Ask Your Family and Friends for Feedback

Shell Miller, Picture Sticks

Constructive criticism is crucial. It's better to hear harsh words from friends and family who are out to help you, than it is to have a badly built site that is losing customers and not know why.

Read the Fine Print

Diane Morgan, Morgan Mailboxes & More

Learn to read the small print in any contractual agreement that you encounter on the Internet. If it seems too good to be true, you know it is. I print out all contracts, thoroughly read them, highlight items I'm unsure of, ask questions and more questions until I'm satisfied. I have no clue who the person on the other end of this computer is, you can't make personal judgements by sight, so investigate for your own safety.

Try It Yourself before Outsourcing

Kevin Gorman, WebCyclery

> When WebCyclery first went online, we hired an advertising agency to help us. We wanted help with usability, but at that time we didn't really know it. After spending thousands and thousands of dollars, all that we ended up with was business cards and a disdain for advertising agencies. After that we brought everything in-house. I learned how to use graphics programs, I read books on usability and design, I joined related discussion groups. I became an expert on usability, design and graphics, and advertising. Now, I make sure to familiarize myself with anything before I outsource it.

Choose Your Web Developer/Web Designer Carefully

Doug Young, Noggintops.com

> The Internet is absolutely filled with well-meaning Web designers and ambitious sales representatives who will try to sell you services that you don't need. Would-be e-merchants are easily misled because they are more naive (I was, still am in some cases) and they are usually desperate to "get it going" either in terms of getting the store online or increasing sales. There are a lot of self-proclaimed "Web developers" out there offering their services. I recently spoke to an entrepreneur who was ready to plunk down several thousand dollars for some Web developer to build him an "online store." Examination of the design revealed that the Web site was going to be little more than a glorified electronic brochure with poorly designed navigation and no order management functions. Ordering was to take place via a primitive form page where the customer would *manually type in the order and e-mail it.*
>
> After bursting his bubble by telling him his store would be approximately five years out of date, I happily informed him that for less than $1,000 he could buy a number of storefront software packages that would allow him to build a store with minimal Web design skills and that would already have integrated into it features like a shopping cart, online ordering and credit card verification capability, shipping and tax calculation, automatic e-mail order confirmation, customer database, product database with inventory

tracking, search feature, and a host of other online store basics. He walked away looking as though he had been snatched from the jaws of a lion. I'm sure the Web developer was very disappointed (I'm smiling even now to think of it). To my knowledge, there are no laws requiring Web developers to practice within their range of competence, so it's going to be up to you to make sure you don't fall victim to "e-malpractice." If you're going to use the services of other professionals, make sure you check them out very carefully. Demand references and follow up on them. Make the developer prove they've built online stores that work. Building a Web site is something that a lot of thirteen-year-olds can do these days. Building an e-commerce-enabled Web site is something else altogether and requires that the developer be intimately familiar with customer behavior, customer service, and retail business functions.

Not Everyone Is Comfortable Ordering Online

Sherry Peterson, Main St. Toys

Even though we have a secure shopping cart system, we still have customers call and give us the order over the phone. Sometimes they don't feel comfortable giving their credit card number over the Internet, or sometimes they don't understand the ordering process because they are new users, so they would rather call us. That's fine with us, we are happy to help them either way. That's where that personal customer service comes into play again!

Stick to the Products You Know

Christopher Mott, Mott's Miniatures

In a virtual store, there is no limit to the number of products you can display, unlike in a real store where you are limited by shelf space. And with manufacturers and distributors offering drop-shipping services it can be very tempting to try to set up your own Amazon.com and try to sell everything to everyone. But, just as with a "real" store, you need to establish in your business plan exactly what it is you want to accomplish with the business – what the focus of its products and services is going to be – and then stay focused. Resist the temptation to display products on your site just because you can. If it is not something that you would put on the shelves of your real store, don't put it on your Web site. I have been tempted more than once to expand my selection into trains. I have wanted to sell trains for fifteen years, and every so often I get a little itch and order some catalogs from distributors and go through them. But, after the blood returns to my brain, I realize that I don't know anything about trains. I haven't touched a model train since I was a boy. And I couldn't answer even the most rudimentary question about trains if my life depended on it. I have put some gift items on my site but they don't sell, because they are not what people are coming to my site to buy.

Don't Go Live During the Busiest Time of the Year

Chris Harrower, Choo Choo Barn

Our store went online during the month of October, and we spent the Christmas holidays being very thankful that we had had the intervening month to work on system processes that we had missed in our planning.

Know Who You're Competing Against

Deb Steinberg, Nickers & Neighs

Know your competition, and answer for yourself why your customer should buy from you instead of them. Ask yourself how you are different from your competitors, and what you do better. When I wrote my business plan, I researched all the online and catalog competitors, even making purchases to determine service levels and shipping times. Before I could really believe that my business could be successful, I had to know what I could do better than my competitors, and how my business would be different. Over the last few years, the number of Web stores competing for my customers has increased tremendously, and with each new competitor, I do enough research to determine that we still do it "best." However, "best" doesn't mean cheapest, it means the entire shopping experience, including shipping costs, quality of merchandise, pricing, shipping time, etc.

Treat Customer Feedback Seriously

Jason Friedman, J&R Music and Computer World

Have someone at the top closely monitor customer feedback. At JandR.com this is me. When you send mail to "Webmaster," it goes directly into my mailbox. I read every single piece of feedback our customers have about our site. I use this to judge when a feature on our site needs fixing and send it off to quality control appropriately, and generally gauge demand for more features to keep customers happy and coming back. The reason I say it should be read by someone on top is because it is all too easy to delete feedback e-mail from customers, and I don't trust anyone else for making sure that every single concern gets addressed, no matter how tedious it is to follow up to make sure it gets done.

Be Wary of Search Engine Optimization Companies

Doug Young, Noggintops.com

There are a fair number of ill-meaning scam artists seeking to blatantly rip you off and, again, we highly enthusiastic and hungry entrepreneurs are easy targets. One of the biggest scams right now is in the area of so-called search engine optimization. Within twenty-four hours of going online you will receive a host of offers to register you with all the major search engines and a thousand minor search engines for just $19.95 or some such bargain price (been there, done that). Some make more extravagant claims about actually boosting your position in search engine results... for more money, of course (been there, done that, too). Most of these services use automated submission software that is greatly despised by search engines companies because it clogs up their system. Most search engines make a concerted effort to negate these services, successfully I might add, judging by the huge number of people who have found these services to be utterly worthless. Use of these services can even delay your search engine registration because the search engine may respond to your automated submission attempt by purposely excluding your Web site for a time.

While there are a limited number of firms who have demonstrated they can optimize search engine placement, they do their work on a case-by-case basis and thus are very expensive. You must be certain that search engine placement is important in reaching your market before investing in their services. Though a little tedious, search engine registration is quite simple and is better done manually. Unfortunately, this lesson cost me a bit of money and two or three precious months of search engine invisibility.

You Can Sell Online from Anywhere!

Sherry Peterson, Main St. Toys

The customer usually doesn't care where we are located as long as they can get the item they want by the time they need it. As I said before, we are located in the Midwest, but most of our orders come from larger cities all over the country. I've decided that there are more people who don't want to fight the traffic and fight the crowds to do their shopping. They can also search on the Net to find hard-to-find items and have them shipped much easier than running all over town and still not finding what they want.

Be Careful with Banner Advertising

Doug Young, Noggintops.com

Another form of scam is the peddling of overpriced banner ads on Web sites with trumped-up traffic claims. Even if the Web site *appears* to be reaching your desired target market, be very cautious. Demand references and, when checking them, get very specific about results they have received. If you do decide to proceed with paid advertising on a Web site, try to get a one- or two-month cancelable contract, rather than a whole year's worth. That way you can pull out and cut your losses if it isn't doing anything for you.

Know Your Customer

Deb Steinberg, Nickers & Neighs

Know your customer, what they want, and provide it. Do your homework regarding your target market, know the demographics, and continuously refine your product offerings until they can't resist making a purchase. Know when to "bite the bullet" and mark things down – blow items out, and learn from the experience.

Be Prepared to Sell Small-Ticket Items

Sherry Peterson, Main St. Toys

> We ship lots of small items and I guess I assumed that most people would only purchase larger items over the Internet. One of our first Internet sales was a $5.99 Koosh ball. The customer was in New York City and she knew exactly what she wanted. It was easier for her to do a search on the Internet and find us, call on our toll-free number, and have it shipped than to get in her car and drive around looking for the ball.

Put Customers' Needs First

Chris Harrower, Choo Choo Barn

> Be flexible, and give the customers what they want, not what you want, or what you think *they* want. When we first went live, I had spent a month or so creating this wonderful JavaScript that would pop up a picture of any item in a small window on people's computers, allowing them to click to see any item, but removing the necessity of having pictures on each catalog page, thereby slowing the load time of that page considerably. Well, that JavaScript was wonderful, and powerful, and didn't work on the computers of about 15 percent of our customers! While 15 percent may not seem like a big problem, even one unhappy customer can hurt your business. In the end, the JavaScript was thrown away, and a simpler solution was put in place, to meet our customers' needs.

QUESTION 4: WHAT KEY PIECE(S) OF ADVICE WOULD YOU OFFER SOMEONE WHO IS THINKING OF SETTING UP AN ONLINE STORE?

Find a Knowledgeable Web Developer/Web Designer

Sherry Peterson, Main St. Toys

> Find that key person who is knowledgeable about the Web and Web site design. It will cost you to hire someone with the expertise you need, but in the long run I think it is

essential to having a successful Internet business. I know there are computer programs out there that let you design your own Web site, but if you want a professional-looking site that is functional, it takes a lot of knowledge that the average person doesn't have. We are a small company, but that doesn't mean that we can't be professional in how we do business. Most businesses start small and if they do things in a professional manner they grow into larger companies.

Don't Let Your Web Designer Control You

Chris Harrower, Choo Choo Barn

Do the necessary research and find a good local company if you don't have the time to learn how to make your own Web pages. If you do hire an outside company to do your work, make sure you are happy with it! Make your Web site reflect your company, not the design company! There are a lot of designers out there (not all designers, but there are a lot) who want to make themselves look good, not make you look good (I know... I used to be one of those. I was more interested in making sure people knew what I could do than in what worked for the company I was supposed to be representing).

Don't Be Afraid of Failure

Bodega Bob Homme, The Submarine Store

Every successful entrepreneur has some (usually very entertaining) story of a venture that failed. We submariners who served during the Cold War used to have a saying when we played tag with the Soviet boats. "Sometimes you get the Bear, sometimes the Bear gets you!" When the bear gets you, get the damage under control, return to port, put everything back in order, and get the heck back out there and do it again! You will never be able to hit a home run unless you step up to the plate and swing at a pitch. And the more times you are at bat, the greater your number of chances to knock one out of the park!

Research Your Online Business Carefully

Sue Schwartz, YarnXpress.com

I would suggest that anyone who is considering an online store carefully research the demand prior to building the business. An online shop needs to offer something different than the retail bricks-and-mortars do. I would never advise someone to build an online store just to build one. The expectation that you build it and the dollars roll in is just not true. Marketing strategies need to be explored and implemented. You need to understand your target audience.

Some people believe that an online business is easier than a bricks-and-mortar establishment. I would encourage anyone who subscribes to this belief to revisit the research.

Make Customer Satisfaction Your Number-One Priority

Rhonda Wells, Payless ShoeSource

I would have to reiterate that the key advice is to know your customer and set realistic strategies to meet the customers' needs. Keep your customers' satisfaction as the first and last question of every decision. You can have a great site that is "overbuilt," but you won't have a chance at profitability.

You Have to Be Responsive to Your Customers

Tane Chan, The Wok Shop

Be prepared to spend hours (if you are a small business) on the computer answering inquiries with a personal touch and acknowledging orders immediately; then shipping out orders same day or next day. Online customers are ordering online because they want prompt service – you must acknowledge their order immediately and status of shipping.

Previous Retail or Catalog Experience Gives You an Advantage

Rob Snell, ystore.com

If you already have a "real store" or a mail order company, you're already 50 percent of the way to being e-commerce ready. If you have a credit card processing account, access to UPS or FedEx shipping, and you sell a product that has ever been sold by catalog, you have the seeds of what it takes to grow a successful e-commerce operation. Most of the people I talk to are new entrepreneurs who know that they want to sell their stuff online, but they don't know how to set up an account with a distributor, or get a line of credit at the bank. If you already have the "business" stuff down, the e-commerce part isn't as hard as you think. Successful catalog and mail order companies can transition to the Web because they already have the fulfillment and customer service parts down, and this is a killer for fast-growing mom-and-pops. I see so *many* of the new Yahoo! Stores I work with hit a choke point around $10,000 a month in sales. They have too many orders for one person to handle, but not enough profit to hire a staff. And there's another choke point around $50,000–$60,000 a month where they need a computer person, and a phone system, and all of this infrastructure, and they're not sure if they want to out-lay the capital to grow the company to another profitable level. Having a good-looking, fast-loading, e-commerce-enabled Web site is the first leg of a very long journey. I cringe when I see an Internet service provider say, "Build a complete e-store in thirteen minutes!" I understand the marketing, but the last thing we need are 500,000 more bad e-commerce sites. It's the commerce part of e-commerce [that's important]. It's almost like saying, get your MBA in minutes by buying *these* eighty-five textbooks. Just because someone has the tools, doesn't mean they know how to use them.

Be Realistic with Your Expectations

Deb Steinberg, Nickers & Neighs

Examine your motives and expectations, and determine that they are honest and realistic.

Richard Flynn, Red Trumpet

If you are hoping to make a quick buck, forget it. We are very fortunate that our team consists of music lovers first, which helps us relate better to our customers. To make a million overnight, you have to be both good and lucky. Best to focus on being good – the part you can actually control.

Bonnie Clewans, The Bead Gallery

E-commerce takes time to develop. Don't expect to go online and start getting thousands of orders. It takes hard work to market your business on a budget.

Your Web Site Is a Tool

Christopher Mott, Mott's Miniatures

Your Web site is *not a business, it is a tool.* Do not think that you can open a Web site and make money. You still have to run a business. Back in 1995 I built Web sites for other companies as a way of supplementing my income. I even tried opening my own Web design company. What I soon discovered was that there were a lot of people out there who thought that owning an Internet business was like some kind of magic. That a Web site could just make money all day and all night and the owner of a Web site could sit on an island in the Bahamas and sip drinks with little paper umbrellas in them. These were people who had no clue what it is to actually own or run a business. I think this has best been represented by the number of virtual companies who close, or sell off.

Make Sure You Really Want to Do This

Diane Morgan, Morgan Mailboxes & More

Make sure this is really what you want to do. You have to be completely dedicated and have drive, ambition, motivation, and perserverance to get your business running successfully and to maintain it. The e-commerce world is no longer a nine-to-five job. It's really twenty-four hours, seven days a week.

Kim Michaux, One of a Kind Kid.com

Make sure you have the passion for what you're doing – you're going to spend a lot of hours doing it! You need the passion to keep you going on the bad days.

Make Sure That You Have Products in Inventory

Bonnie Clewans, The Bead Gallery

Turnaround time is extremely important for online shoppers. I have had people ask about setting up a Web site where they would take orders and only then would they try to obtain the merchandise. I strongly advise against this, as my biggest concern for all of us doing e-business is reputation and honesty. I have many repeat customers who gladly accept my suggestion for a substitution if a specific item is out of stock. Almost all my orders go out within forty-eight hours and they are shipped complete.

Don't Go Overboard with Technology

Doug Young, Noggintops.com

Technology is a tool, it is not itself the solution. Technology will not sell your product. Your ability to communicate *meaningful* content to the consumer is what will sell your product. That fact should be the guiding force as you design and build your online store. Web site construction is a technical thing, Web site *design* is not. The person responsible for the layout of your store, the part that the customer sees and interacts with, should be someone who is extremely customer-oriented. He or she should also be intimately familiar with how your particular product is best presented to the customer. If you're hiring a professional Web developer, don't count on them to know how to sell your product and service your customer.

e-Fact

41% of online consumers have wanted to return a product purchased from an online shopping site, but decided it was just too much hassle to do so.

Source: PricewaterhouseCoopers (www.pwcglobal.com)

New technologies and Web site enhancements appear every day. Before you hastily add them to your online store, you should give some thought as to whether it will really add to the customer's shopping experience on *your* Web site. For example, I recently visited an online store that had one of those chat windows you could use to talk to a live sales representative. I clicked on it and received a friendly message saying someone would be available to assist me in a moment. So I waited… and waited… and waited. Out of curiosity, I quickly fired off an e-mail of the question while dialing the customer service phone number. After just a few seconds on hold, I spoke with someone who answered my question. Less than an hour later, I received an e-mail response answering my question. Not too bad. The online chat window? I finally got bored waiting and terminated the session. Maybe it was just an off day. Maybe they were having some technical difficulties (the bane of online existence). In any case, my immediate perception was that they had employed a technology that they were not able to use effectively. To their credit, they had effective alternative avenues for customer assistance, but the risk of turning people off by showcasing an ineffective one is not worth it, in my opinion, no matter how cool it seems to be. I want to make it clear that I'm not bashing live chat windows. If you have the personnel to employ them effectively I have no doubt that they can be a great asset. The same can be said for 3-D graphics, video, audio, and animations. They may have their place, but you need to make sure that it genuinely adds to the quality of the shopping experience before you add it to your Web site. An online store should not be just a collection of whiz-bang technologies. It should be a cohesive unit that guides the customer to the product and to the sale.

An Online Business Must Be Run Like Any Successful Brick-and-Mortar Business

Jason Friedman, J&R Music and Computer World

J&R's philosophy is to always keep the customer happy, concentrate on customer satisfaction, smooth fulfillment, competitive pricing, and constant inventory replenishment. These are principles that must be followed whether you are talking about setting up a brick-and-mortar or online storefront.

Business Skills Are Essential

Bodega Bob Homme, The Submarine Store

Too often Web entrepreneurs focus on the "e" in e-business. Focus on the business! Knowing about the Web or how to build a Web site or any of the myriad processes and functions of the Web is not going to make your business successful. This knowledge may be a component of your potential success but business is about business, not the venue in which it is conducted, not the supporting processes. Business! If you have only a passing understanding of good business practices, team up with or hire someone who does. Conversely, if you know your business but are unfamiliar with its execution on the Web, team up with or hire someone who does. In short, critically analyze your strengths, compare them to those required by your venture, be humble enough to identify the areas that are insufficient in your skill or knowledge inventory, and be smart enough to team up with or hire others with the skill set necessary to ensure your success.

Choose Your Technical Platform Carefully

Richard Flynn, Red Trumpet

Build your Web site on a stable and secure technical platform. Downtime, slow response time, and security failures devastate the credibility of an e-commerce presence. Customers appreciate sites that run crisply and are always available. Factors contributing to the reliability of your site include the server hardware, operating system, Internet connection, Web server software, and programming environment.

Create a Business Plan

Kevin Gorman, WebCyclery

Create a business plan. It's one of the hardest things you will do, but it is also the most important. Going through the process of creating a business plan makes you really think about what you want, and how you are going to get it. It is an extremely useful tool, something that you will be able to use to help you find your way when things don't go the way you expected.

Ray Ritchey, Childbook.com

Do a business plan and figure out your customers' needs and what you can do to satisfy them better than your competition. Is this a sustainable advantage? What can be done to make it so? Do a worst-case cash flow projection.

QUESTION 5: WHAT IS THE BEST FEATURE YOU'VE BUILT INTO YOUR ONLINE STORE?

Synergies with Our Retail Stores

Rhonda Wells, Payless ShoeSource

The simplistic, yet synergistic, shopping experience that mirrors our customers' shopping experience in our stores. This feature has engaged 26,000 store associates in selling our site in our stores and has drawn countless positive e-mails from our customers. The customer really appreciates not having to figure out how to work our site, they simply want to buy our great value, fashion, and quality footwear.

A Monthly Contest

Deb Steinberg, Nickers & Neighs

We have a horse trivia game that is challenging and fun. We select a winner each month and give away a nice prize. Many people visit our site every month just to get their name on the list for the prize!

Kevin Gorman, WebCyclery

The best feature that we have on our site is our contest/newsletter. We let people sign up to win a monthly giveaway. In doing so they can sign up for our newsletter, which allows us to continue to market to them and keep them as a customer.

Myself

Sue Schwartz, YarnXpress.com

YarnXpress.com is a reflection of my love of knitting and yarn. It is a creative place that people can visit and become part of an active and creative community.

Personal Service

Tane Chan, The Wok Shop

E-mailing each and every customer thanking them for their business and asking them about the particular product(s) they bought. This is so personal and each customer takes it very personally and even acknowledges this gesture with much appreciation. This is what I mean when I said to be prepared to spend hours on the computer... whether your message is brief or long, it makes a difference.

My approach to a successful online business may not apply to other businesses. My line of products are "ethnic" or special and not available in most regions of the United States (my main business), so I really have to describe the product very clearly and briefly and the photo has to be very clear. Prospective customers cannot just walk into a department store or specialty store in their area and see the item. My customers are really depending on my text, copy, description, and photo to sell them and then my own input as if I am conversing with them in the physical store. Many of my customers are purchasing my products without ever seeing them or touching them, and they really don't know what to expect. They have put their trust in me to deliver exactly as described and satisfaction guaranteed; and I do. After ten months of a Web site and five months of online ordering, I have yet to have a disappointed or dissatisfied customer. In fact, all the customers that have taken the time to comment on our Web site, products, service, prices, etc. have given us an "excellent" rating and I have met many new "friends" through cyberspace.

My online small business is run like my brick-and-mortar business... good, knowledgeable, prompt, honest, friendly service... I do through e-mail and cyberspace what I normally do in the store. I e-mail my customers as if I am talking to them in the store. I even recommend items and advise them on use, etc. I correct or suggest online orders because from experience I know what goes with what and they appreciate and thank me so much. I either call them or e-mail my suggestions or corrections. Since their orders are being shipped, I save them time, hassle, returns and money. About 25 percent of my customers do not order online, but they visit the site, do their homework and call in their order because they don't feel comfortable releasing their credit card number online; and some customers call in their orders because they have questions. So, as I mentioned earlier, I do sell a different type of product which requires a different approach and selling technique and I have found that this very personalized approach is what works for me. I would consider our online business a success and I look forward to improving it and adding more items. I listen to my customers and know that if one customer is asking about an item not featured, other customers will too.

Our Submarine Community Center

Bodega Bob Homme, The Submarine Store

There we provide our shipmates and their families with discussion forums, a newsletter, electronic postcards, reunion announcements, shipmate locators, a news clipping service, original articles, a calendar of events in the submarine community, a Web directory, as well as topical chat rooms – all of these are submarine-oriented, of course. Granted, they all serve to drive traffic to our site but their development and maintenance are a marketing expense, we derive no direct revenue from their existence and, according to the feedback we receive, this area of our site is extremely well received and greatly appreciated by the community we serve.

Real-Time Inventory

Richard Flynn, Red Trumpet

In a business like ours, when items go out of stock, they can be gone forever, so accurate inventory is vitally important. Having to tell customers who placed an order that items are unavailable is embarrassing and diminishes credibility. We've employed complex inventory tracking that combines ordering, shipping, receiving, and the shopping cart system on our site to produce a constantly up-to-date count of units on hand for any item. Once an item is no longer available, it vanishes from the site immediately. This has proven to be one of our greatest assets. (As an aside, this was also a lesson we learned, since we had to take a complete inventory about a dozen times before the site was up and running! Needless to say, it convinced us of the value of real-time inventory tracking.)

Our Product Knowledge

Christopher Mott, Mott's Miniatures

I think the best feature the site has is the knowledge of the owners of the business. In my case, it is our knowledge of the products we sell, fifty years' worth in three generations.

The Internet is the most effective tool we have for communicating that knowledge to customers. An example is the amount of product description we give our products. We sell dollhouses which come in either a do-it-yourself kit or finished, or anywhere in between. The product I sell is not the kind of product that is sold in every store in America, or is something that everyone understands. It is not like a vacuum cleaner that you can get anywhere. There are all kinds of houses. We sell kits that start at $40 and finished mansions that can reach $20,000. If you arc going to sell one of the more expensive houses, say a kit that costs $500 or $1,000, you have to explain to people how that kit is different from a kit that costs $40. And how what we sell is different from a $20 plastic dollhouse you get at Toys-R-Us. It is especially important when they are buying it over the Internet and can't walk into a local showroom and touch it like a vacuum cleaner. This is a pretty obscure product. Some products have one- or two-page descriptions. We describe in as much detail as possible what a customer gets, what they don't get, and what they will end up with. We have fifty years' experience running a retail store and helping people find the product they arc looking for. We have managed to take that experience and translate it into a tool that sells products twenty-four hours a day, in every country on the planet.

The "About Us" Section

Sherry Peterson, Main St. Toys

A feature that I like about our catalog is a section that's titled "About Us" and shows a photo of the four people who own the store. It also tells about where we are located and what our mission statement is, so if people don't want to do business with a machine, it makes it feel a little more personal. I wondered if people really went to that section of the catalog, but I just had a customer last week ask me what my name was again, and she said, "I'm in your catalog and I'm looking at your picture."

User-Friendliness

Doug Young, Noggintops.com

We worked hard to make navigation around the Web site easy, both in terms of finding something and getting back to where you were. We provide multiple avenues for getting questions answered: a Frequently Asked Questions (FAQ) button, links to our e-mail on every page, and easy-to-find telephone numbers. You want people wondering about how many of your products they should buy, not about what your shipping rates are, what your return policy is, how to contact you, etc. We excluded features and "window trappings" that don't add to the functionality of the Web site.

Elaborate backgrounds may be pretty and animated juggling monkeys may be cute, but they also slow down the speed of the Web site. Many people still have relatively slow Internet connections, and many people shop online in a hurry (i.e., over their lunch break). In any case, nobody likes to navigate around a slow Web site.

We organized our products into categories and put the information and pictures in layers. We provide small (fast-loading) "thumbnail" pictures of each hat along with a brief description so that customers can quickly decide which hats they might want to look at in more detail. When they see something that piques their interest, they can click on the thumbnail and see a large picture with a detailed product description. If they want more detail, they can click on that picture to see a really big picture with multiple angles, color choices, etc. Some Web sites just cram a bunch of product descriptions and large pictures all on one page, which makes a slow-loading page and requires the customer to waste time looking at things they might not be interested in, which increases the risk that they will leave before finding what they want. When leaving your store is as easy as one finger movement, you don't want to make your customers impatient. The arrogant belief that your products are "worth waiting for" will be a costly one.

Educational Resources

Jason Friedman, J&R Music and Computer World

From day one, back in 1996, we had a JavaScript-based online technical glossary. In other words, in the description of a computer, the term "100BaseTX" will be hyperlinked, and when clicked on will pop up a small window explaining the term. When an average user wants to buy his first computer, knows how much he wants to spend, and sees that features like this can make a computer more expensive, he wants to know what it means. Most sites take it for granted that customers understand the jargon as well as the people writing the copy. This is obviously not true: just ask a customer in any computer store who you see hiding in the corner scared to ask what he thinks might be an obvious question. This initial feature is indicative of the hundreds of other features we have put in place in the following four years.

Our site is geared towards being the computers, electronics, and music site for everybody. Most of the items we sell are highly technical. People know they want them, but have a hard time distinguishing one Greek-sounding feature from the next. We have an entire team dedicated to distilling this information for the customer, in the form of Buyer's Guides, in-depth product reviews, carefully plain-English written product descriptions, and standardized product specification sheets so customers can compare most of our catalog of 400,000 products side-by-side, apples to apples. We also offer unique exclusive multimedia content so the customer can actually watch a home-grown infomercial on a product and never feel that they are missing anything by not coming down to the store. The only thing our site is missing at this point is the ability for the customer to physically pick up and touch the product via virtual reality. Rest assured, we're working on it.

> **e-Fact**
>
> *Only one in four Web sites meets minimum standards for Internet users with disabilities.*
> Source: Forrester Research
> (www.forrester.com)

Online Credit Card Processing

Diane Morgan, Morgan Mailboxes & More

The best feature I added to my site was merchant account and shopping cart features. I spent about six months researching different merchant account services that would be best for my business needs. My sales increased dramatically when I offered credit card services. I think this served two purposes. This provided legitimacy, credibility, and professionalism to my business from the customer's point of view. The convenience of online payment increases the chances of the customer purchasing your product. A chance of a completed sale decreases dramatically once the customer leaves your "store," so you have to make it as easy and convenient as you can. When I first started the Web site, I didn't have a real order form system or a merchant account. The customer had to either e-mail, fax, or phone in an order and then send a check for payment. I've found that if the customer doesn't order at that first initial sit-down at the computer and has to do "more work" on their end, there's a good possibility you've lost that sale.

QUESTION 6: HAS YOUR VENTURE INTO ONLINE RETAILING MET YOUR EXPECTATIONS?

Sherry Peterson, Main St. Toys

Yes and no. When we first went online I think we all thought we were going to be flooded with orders immediately and we were sort of disappointed that we weren't. Then after we talked and sort of reevaluated things, we decided that it's not good to grow too fast and that it would have probably been too much for a small company like us to handle. (I might say at this point our corporation is made up of my husband and me and our daughter and her husband. She and I own the majority of the stock, do the buying, and manage the store and the catalog.) Now that our catalog has been online for about three years and has grown steadily, it has allowed us to learn more about e-tailing as we have grown and made changes along the way. Maybe sure and steady does win the race after all! Our online catalog has been a scary but exciting venture. I'm in my early fifties, so a few years ago if someone had told me I was going to have a catalog on the Net I would have said they were crazy, but it's just been a wonderful experience. I am by no means a computer whiz and have learned so much in the last four years it's incredible. Every day I'm amazed by something that happens in a day's work and I can't wait to go to work to see what the day will bring.

Kevin Gorman, WebCyclery

Yes and no. From a financial standpoint, it has not. When I started I thought that I would be making millions of dollars, and would have trouble keeping up with demand. Of course, that didn't happen, but we do continue to grow and that's exciting. What I've learned has far surpassed my expectations. I started this business because I like bikes and took an HTML class in college. What I've learned in the past two years is more than I learned in college, and would make me an extremely valuable asset to any company.

Richard Flynn, Red Trumpet

As relative newcomers in the field of online retailing, we weren't entirely sure what to expect when we launched our site. We've experienced a strong but inconsistent rise in sales that surprises us on some days and disappoints on others. This is partially due to our minimalist approach to marketing: we've actually publicized our site more slowly than we could have. We want to be certain before we entice people to spend all of their money at our store that our fulfillment process is solid and there are no delays under high load. In some ways, achieving terrific customer satisfaction (which we had even before launching our site) is a bar we've raised very high for ourselves: it means that everything we do must meet the same high standards people have come to expect from our company. I have found this venture into e-commerce very fulfilling from a professional standpoint. After fifteen years of inconsistent challenges in the corporate world, I was becoming too complacent and taking too few risks. In fact, the risks are vitally important to me as a business owner, since I have learned much more from failures than successes. Red Trumpet has provided an opportunity to put together a team of players that share my enthusiasm, dedication, and willingness to take risks – careful, thoughtful, researched risks – that are essential in the new business climate. And though we enjoy the challenges and risks of our business model, we also remember that our business is based on turning a profit, which we have done every quarter since inception.

Ray Ritchey, Childbook.com

It's been a lot slower than I thought on the growth. Cash flow is a headache, as is importing items from overseas. Having a business with inventory is a headache. You try to guess what the customer will buy, and if you guess too high, you have a lot of money sitting there on a shelf doing nothing. If you guess too low, you have unhappy customers with items on back-order.

Bonnie Clewans, The Bead Gallery

When I started online five years ago, I would get an order about once a week. After I started marketing my site, orders started arriving almost daily and now I get several order per day. The online orders are larger than my walk-in business and I am competing with large mail-order businesses. I have received orders from all over the world and developed relationships with customers from practically all fifty states. Customers enjoy our online help as well as personalized service. I looked at my competitors and decided to offer whatever service they did not.

Deb Steinberg, Nickers & Neighs

My initial expectations were naive and unrealistic. However, as reality set in, I was able to temper and adjust my expectations. At this point I can say that my business is growing very nicely, and we have a large number of repeat customers. We are beginning to experience some name and brand recognition within our target market, and have achieved a 100 percent increase in sales over 1999.

Chris Harrower, Choo Choo Barn

Oh, yeah! The leadership of the company had met early on in the process, and said that, if we reached a certain dollar amount in the first year of this process, we would be happy, but that we understand that it may take several years to reach that lofty goal (like any new startup). Well, in the first year online, we hit a sales volume that was *seven times* the initial projection and there seems to be no limit where it will go from here!

Kim Michaux, One of a Kind Kid.com

It has been great! I love it. I am able to stay home with my children, work flexible hours. The downside is that I feel like I'm always working. It's hard to get away for weekends and I've yet to figure out how to go away for a week. But that isn't any different from a non-Web-based business. I think opening an online store is the best of everything. The flexible hours are wonderful for moms – just have to give up some sleep! If you're thinking about starting an online business, go for it! If I can do this, anyone can. It *is* a lot of hard work, but in exchange, you get a flexible schedule and your own business.

Rhonda Wells, Payless ShoeSource

Absolutely. Our expectations were pretty simple: (1) build on our core competencies, while building synergy with our stores; (2) do not jeopardize the core business, let the customer shop and buy our great product anywhere, anytime.

Diane Morgan, Morgan Mailboxes & More

My online experience has more than met my expectations. It took me two years to get where I am today but I have a full-time, successful online business and I have hired my first part-time employee to help keep up with the demand in orders. Not only do I have steady growth in sales, I now have businesses contacting me who are interested in my products.

Shell Miller, Picture Sticks

At first I was under the impression that a Web site selling my products was all that I needed to be a successful online business. I was mistaken. I needed to put as much energy into finding my customers as I did into building my Web site. Once the rose-colored glasses were removed I hit the market with advertising and promotional ads, and the business has since benefited more than I expected. The key is to build the site, find the customers and then keep them coming back.

Bodega Bob Homme, The Submarine Store

The only thing I can compare it to is the time when I was a little boy, about five, and my twelve-year-old neighbor got a go-cart for his birthday. One day, he, some of his older friends, and his dad were out in the pasture field riding it and they offered to let me take it for a spin. I can't imagine what they were thinking but, man, was I excited as they strapped me into that baby! I hit the gas, took off, and was so freaked by the ride (my first), and the speed (seemed like about Mach 2), and the noise (the engine sits right behind your head when you're only about four feet tall) that all I could do was hang on breathlessly and try to avoid the creek, the large rocks, the cows, and the people, while trying not to tip over or drive over the rather steep bordering hillside. I was too petrified to take my foot off the gas, so there I was, a five-year-old strapped to an out-of-control cruise missile, zipping around at full speed, scaring the hell out of the livestock, the observers, and myself! I couldn't get the situation under enough control to realize that I had to take my foot off the accelerator. All I could concentrate on was doing my best not to hit anything. Well, thankfully, the thing finally ran out of gas and I coasted to a stop, pale, shaking, breathless, wide-eyed, and with my foot still rigid against the accelerator.

The Submarine Store has certainly not run out of gas! In fact we're still growing at a rate far beyond our projections, but we've finally managed to get this baby under control.

Tane Chan, The Wok Shop

Yes... but it has consumed my evenings and nights because I am a mom-and-pop business with no pop (I'm a widow). Since I started e-mailing each and every customer, whether the message is long or short, I spend a minimum of four hours every night on my computer. The results are so incredible. The responses from customers are so gratifying, it's all worthwhile.

Christopher Mott, Mott's Miniatures

It has actually surpassed my expectations. When I took over the company in the mid-80s I noticed that a lot of customers we had were out-of-town or foreign visitors who did not have shops like mine near them and asked if we would ship to them. It was something that was done only on a limited basis before I took over. But my feeling was, what the heck. If I've got it, I'll put it in a box and send it to you. I built up the mail order as time went on but then we lost our tourist location, a spot we had been at for thirty-four years. We had to move and we lost that constant flow of tourists. Now we had to pay to advertise to find customers. By 1994, I was on the verge of shutting down our mail order operations because it was too expensive to advertise, print catalogs, and own an 800 number for the dwindling orders we were receiving.

I had been looking for a way to reach out to people electronically through these new "online" services, AOL and CompuServe, but they were terribly expensive. I considered a CD catalog or even trying to create my own "bulletin board" (remember those!) where people could download price lists and small pictures. To make a long story short, I found the "My Space" on AOL and put up a page. In 1995, we had our worst mail order year, every month was down from the prior year. But I decided to give the Internet one more year. The requests for catalogs and products continued to grow and more and more people were calling about product they had seen on our Web pages. By 1996, we had our own www and a secure order form. By 1998, we had our first shopping cart. Internet sales have been growing at the average rate of 96 percent per year over the last four years and are expected to remain at this level for the next three to five years. I kick myself every day when I think of the domain names I could have owned back then. Who knew! Now my company is bursting at the seams. Last November I was thinking about advertising on Yahoo! and my wife said absolutely not, we can barely keep up with the orders we have. She was right.

Doug Young, Noggintops.com

I would say that on the whole my online store experience is meeting my expectations. Perhaps that is due to the fact that I tried to keep my expectations on a realistic level to begin with. I envisioned that sales would follow a slow, steady growth curve, and so they have, for the most part. There have been some sudden large spurts as a result of some fortuitous publicity, but mostly it has been a lot of hard work and constantly, constantly, prospecting for customers. Anyone thinking an online store is going to be an easy way to get rich quickly is going to be very disappointed. I can tell you it has not been a case of simply sitting back and watching the orders magically roll in. We feel like we earn every single order. Apparently our customers feel we are earning them, too, as they are showing a level of customer loyalty and repeat purchases that has – happily – gone beyond our expectations. As I keep telling myself, "It's the customer, stupid!" I would have to say we're right where we want to be and looking forward to more of that slow, steady growth.

Jason Friedman, J&R Music and Computer World

Yes and no. I have done many things with the site that I have wanted to, but by the same token, there have been many things that I have wanted to do since 1996, and because of time, resources, and technological limitations, have still been unable to do.

Sue Schwartz, YarnXpress.com

YarnXpress.com has surpassed my expectations and fulfilled some of my dreams. I did not expect the revenue that a fully automated shopping cart offers. Going from the inefficient mode of accepting checks to the real-time processing of credit cards gave us access to a cash flow that enabled us to grow within the first couple of months online.

We have now grown to a point that our orders will be filled by a fulfillment center in another state. A new member of the YarnXpress.com staff will maintain the Regional Events information portion of the site. Our sample knitters and crocheters have increased threefold. And we have had the unsurpassed pleasure of assisting some very talented knit and crochet designers enter the market. I am thrilled with our growth and sometimes overwhelmed with the future!!!

Chapter 9

CAN YOU DO IT?

Far from thinking that the Internet has been overhyped, most analysts believe we are underestimating the effect it will have on our lives. Online shopping has tripled in the last year.

"New Media: From start-up to dot woe: Are dot.coms an endangered species? Following a recent wave of closures, as backers pull the financial plug, Imogen O'Rorke looks at the future of the industry."

Imogen O'Rorke, *The Guardian*, 11/27/2000

Just as we were finishing off this book, the retail dot-com collapse was in full swing. All around us, day by day, came word of yet another online retailer shutting down. Pet supply stores. Online furniture stores. Bookstores. Hockey supply stores. Camera stores.

You name it – they tried to sell it. And they failed – miserably. The fact is, they didn't sell, and they went out of business.

A sense of gloom invaded the Internet towards the end of 2000. Web site after Web site appeared with a notice that indicated that it had gone out of business:

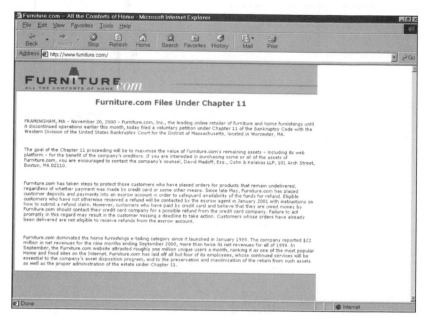

Sites such as www.dotcomgraveyard.com became a handy source of information to track the ongoing devolution of the Internet online selling marketplace.

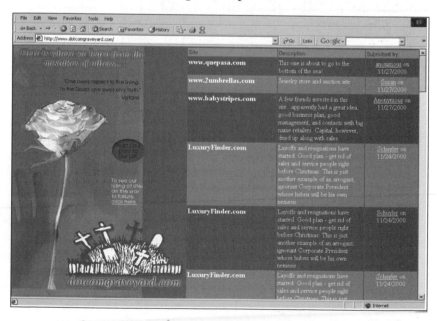

Some sites, such as BeautyJungle, tried to put a humorous spin on their demise:

Internet publications and news Web sites, always eager to keep up with the latest trends, reported on the ongoing collapse with breathless consternation. Reports abounded on which sites had designed the nicest "death notice."

The entire affair seemed to be, for many, actually a bit of fun.

Yet the smell of death that surrounded the world of Internet retail at the end of 2000 should not have come as any surprise – and does not mean that the entire concept of selling online is invalidated.

IS E-BUSINESS DEAD?

Was it all but a dream?

Well, if your impression of e-commerce comes from the stock market and the dot-com hysteria of the last few years, you might think so. The dot-com collapse might convince you that there is no future for retail on the Internet.

There is another way to think about this state of affairs though: we should all be delighted that so many of the early Internet retailers and dot-com startups quickly met the great liquidator in the sky. After all, everyone now knows that plenty of these early pioneers were built on shaky foundations: business plans that didn't make sense, inadequate financing, unrealistic expectations, poor management, or a lack of understanding of markets.

Then there was the fact that the hysteria simply led to a situation in which greed took over, and all common sense was thrown out the window. Quite simply, a dot-com start-up became a way for lots of people to make lots of money without any real substance to the deals at hand.

They ended up where they deserved to be, and plenty of people were happy to see them go.

After all, the collapse helps to return the world of the Internet and e-commerce to sanity – and allows folks like you to get on with the job of figuring out how you might be able to sell things online.

E-BIZ IS NOT DEAD!

Our attitude is that far from being dead, e-business is thriving.

Get beyond the dot-com hype, and you can find countless people (as we did in Chapter 8) who have been successful at selling online.

Building successful businesses.

Winning customers.

Making a profit.

Quite evidently, as more and more people use the Internet in every aspect of their lives, it has come to play a huge role in our consumer behavior. It has become a sales channel. Not one that replaces traditional sales channels, but one that augments them.

And the fact is, those individuals who learn to work with it, understand it, experiment with it, and who integrate it into their existing lines of businesses, will share to a greater degree in whatever the Internet might offer us in the future.

e-Fact

The average U.S. Internet user is 41 years old.
Source: Gartner Group
(www.gartnergroup.com)

That's why perhaps the best thing you can do when it comes to selling online is this: try it, work with it, and learn from it, while all the time being realistic in what you are doing.

Which leads to the final question. Can you do it? Can you sell online?

We think so! And when you do, we'd love to hear from you!

Jim and Rick

jcarroll@jimcarroll.com / rickb@rickbroadhead.com

INDEX